# Schooling in

# Capitalist America

Ch 1 & 6

# SCHOOLING
## *in* CAPITALIST
# AMERICA

*Educational Reform and the*
*Contradictions of Economic Life*

•

**SAMUEL BOWLES**
*and*
**HERBERT GINTIS**

Haymarket Books
Chicago, Illinois

First published in 1976 by Basic Books in New York
© Samuel Bowles and Herbert Gintis

This edition published in 2011 by
Haymarket Books
PO Box 180165
Chicago, Illinois 60618
773-583-7884
info@haymarketbooks.org
www.haymarketbooks.org

Trade distribution in the United States by Consortium Book Sales and Distribution,
www.cbsd.com

ISBN: 978-1-60846-131-8

Cover design by Eric Ruder.

Published with the generous support of Lannan Foundation and the Wallace Global Fund.

**Printed in the United States** on recycled paper containing 100 percent postconsumer waste in accordance with the Green Press Initiative, www.greenpressinitiative.org.

Library of Congress Cataloging in Publication Data is available.

10 9 8 7 6 5 4 3 2 1

# CONTENTS

•

*Preface to the 2011 Edition:* Schooling in Capitalist America *Revisited*    *ix*

*Preface*    *xiii*

## Part I

### THE CONTRADICTIONS OF
### LIBERAL EDUCATION REFORM

1. *Beyond the Educational Frontier: The Great American Dream Freeze*    *3*

2. *Broken Promises: School Reform in Retrospect*    *18*

## Part II

### EDUCATION AND THE STRUCTURE OF ECONOMIC LIFE

3. *At the Root of the Problem: The Capitalist Economy*    *53*

4. *Education, Inequality, and the Meritocracy*    *102*

5. *Education and Personal Development: The Long Shadow of Work*    *125*

## Part III

### THE DYNAMICS OF EDUCATIONAL CHANGE

6. *The Origins of Mass Public Education*    *151*

7. *Corporate Capital and Progressive Education*    *180*

8. *The Transformation of Higher Education
   and the Emerging White-Collar Proletariat*    *201*

9. *Capital Accumulation, Class Conflict, and Educational Change*    *224*

# Part IV

**GETTING THERE**

10. *Educational Alternatives*      245
11. *Education, Socialism, and Revolution*      264


*Appendices*      289
*Notes*      304
*Index*      333

*To Huck, Corinna, and Eve*

# PREFACE TO THE 2011 EDITION

•

# Schooling in Capitalist America *Revisited*

The project that eventually resulted in *Schooling in Capitalist America* (1976) began in 1968, stimulated by the then raging academic debates and social conflicts about the structure and purposes of education. Our first collaboration resulted from a request by Reverend Martin Luther King, Jr. for a series of background papers in preparation for the Poor People's March just prior to his death. At the same time one of us drafted a memo on educational policy at the request of Senator Robert Kennedy, then a candidate for the Democratic Party's nomination to run for president. Jonathan Kozol's explosive *Death at an Early Age*, a teacher's front-line report on the failure of city schools, had been published a year earlier. The ideas that eight years later appeared in *Schooling* did not originate in the library or the seminar room, they came from our encounters with the reality of U.S. education in the church basement classrooms of school boycotts and in conversations with teachers and educational policy makers.

Like many others, we were then, and remain, hopeful that education can contribute not only to a more productive economy but to a flourishing life for all people and to the more equal sharing of its benefits. Our distress at how woefully the U.S. educational system was then failing these enlightened objectives sparked our initial collaboration; its continuing failure has prompted our recent return to the subject.

The three basic propositions of the book concern human development, inequality, and the process of social change.

Concerning human development we showed that while cognitive skills are important in the economy, the most important contribution of schooling to individual's economic success lay elsewhere. We advanced the position that schools prepare people for adult work roles, by socializing people to function well (and without complaint) in the hierarchical structure of the modern corporation or public office.

Schools accomplish this by what we called the correspondence principle, namely by structuring social interactions and individual rewards to replicate the environment of the workplace. We thus focused attention not on the explicit curriculum but on the socialization implied by the structure of schooling. Our econometric investigations demonstrated that little of the contribution of schooling to later economic success is not explained by the cognitive skills learned in school.

Second, we showed that parental class and other aspects of economic status are passed on to children in part by means of unequal educational opportunity, but that the economic advantages of the descendants of the well-to-do go considerably beyond the superior education they receive. We used the then available statistical data to demonstrate that the United States fell far short of the goal of equal economic opportunity and that genetic inheritance of cognitive skill—as measured on standard tests—explains at most a very small part of the high degree of intergenerational persistence of affluence and poverty within families.

Finally, our historical studies of the origins of primary schooling and the development of the high school suggested that the evolution of the modern school system is accounted for not by the gradual perfection of a democratic or pedagogical ideal but by a series of class and other conflicts arising through the transformation of the social organization of work and its rewards. In this process the interests of the owners of the leading businesses tended to predominate but were rarely uncontested. We later (in *Democracy and Capitalism*\*) developed the idea that schools and the public sector generally are loci of conflicts stemming from the contradictory rules of the marketplace and the democratic polity.

How do we now view this work? For most of the intervening third of a century we have researched and taught subjects quite removed from the questions we addressed in *Schooling*. In recent years, however, we have returned to writing about school reform, how economic institutions shape the process of human development, and the importance of schooling, cognitive skill, and personality as determinants of economic success and their role in the intergenerational perpetuation of inequality.

In light of the outpouring of quantitative research on schooling and inequality in the intervening years, the statistical claims of the book have held up remarkably well. In particular, recent research by us and others taking advantage of advances in econometrics and using far better data than was available in the early seventies has entirely vindicated our major results. Among these are our estimates of high levels of intergenerational persistence of economic status, the unimportance of the heritability of IQ in this process, and the fact that the contribution of schooling to cognitive development plays but a modest part in explaining why those

---

\* Bowles and Gintis (1986).

with more schooling have higher earnings. Indeed most recent estimates of the intergenerational transmission of economic inequality indicate that we probably underestimated its extent, rather than the opposite, as some of our critics contended.[*] Our view that in explaining economic inequality differences in cognitive and other skills are less important than differences in personality and affective aspects of behavior has been strongly affirmed by the recent work of the University of Chicago Nobel Laureate James Heckman and others.[†]

Recent research—our own and others' reported in our recent *A Cooperative Species: Human Reciprocity and Its Evolution*—has also affirmed an aspect of our work that some considered to be utopian at the time of its publication. This is our conviction that many, probably most people are deeply committed to treating others fairly—now documented by the new field of behavioral economics in literally hundreds of experiments in over fifty different cultures[‡]—and that partly for this reason inequality, far from greasing the wheels of economic progress is more often sand in the gears.[§]

On current reflection, the main shortcomings of the book reflect the times in which we wrote. The long 1960s economic boom and the antimaterialist countercultural currents that it fostered perhaps led us to underemphasize the value of schooling in contributing to productive employment. But the more important shortcoming, we think is programmatic. We avoided for the most part the question of what schools *should be*, focusing instead on what schools actually *are* and *do*. Nor did we devote much attention to how economic systems other than capitalism might better facilitate achieving the enlightened objectives of schooling. We took it as obvious that a system of democratically run and employee-owned enterprises coordinated by both competitive markets and governmental policies was both politically and economically viable as an alternative to capitalism. We remain convinced of the attractiveness of such a system, but are less sanguine about its feasibility, and more convinced that reforms of capitalism may be the most likely way to pursue the objectives that we embraced at the outset. While the book endorses the idea that radicals—even revolutionaries—must also be reformers, we provided little guidance to either policy makers, teachers, or students seeking practical positive steps to bring about long-term improvements in edu-

---

[*] The evidence is surveyed in Bowles and Gintis (2002) and Bowles, Gintis, and Groves (2005).

[†] See Bowles, Gintis, and Osborne (2001) and Heckman, et al. (2010) and the empirical studies cited there.

[‡] Bowles and Gintis (2011) and Gintis, et al. (2005) are introductions to this new literature.

[§] Bowles (2012); Bowles and Jayadev (2007); and Bowles and Gintis (1998).

cational structure and practice.

Partly because we are now reasonably certain that we had the facts right, we remain committed to our overall approach to schooling—embedding the analysis of education in the evolving structure of the economy and the polity, and giving attention to the noncognitive as well as conventional effects of education. Today, no less than during the stormy days when *Schooling* was written, schools express the conflicts and limitations as well as the hopes of a divided and unequal society; and they continue to be both testing grounds and battlegrounds for building a more just and freer life for all.

Santa Fe, New Mexico
and Budapest
July 2011

---

Bowles, Samuel. 2012. *The New Economics of Inequality and Redistribution.* Cambridge: Cambridge University Press.

Bowles, Samuel and Herbert Gintis. 1986. *Democracy and Capitalism: Property, Community, and the Contradictions of Modern Social Thought.* New York: Basic Books.

———. 1998. *Recasting Egalitarianism: New Rules for Markets, States, and Communities.* London: Verso.

———. 2002. "The Inheritance of Inequality." *Journal of Economic Perspectives* 16, no. 3, 3–30.

———. 2011. *A Cooperative Species: Human Reciprocity and Its Evolution.* Princeton, NJ: Princeton University Press.

Bowles, Samuel, Herbert Gintis, and Melissa Osborne Groves, eds. 2005. *Unequal Chances: Family Background and Economic Success.* Princeton, NJ: Princeton University Press and Russell Sage Foundation.

Bowles, Samuel, Herbert Gintis, and Melissa Osborne. 2001. "The Determinants of Earnings: A Behavioral Approach." *Journal of Economic Literature,* XXXIX (December): 1137–76.

Bowles, Samuel and Arjun Jayadev. 2007. "Garrison America." *The Economists' Voice* 4, no. 2, Article 3.

Gintis, Herbert, Samuel Bowles, Robert Boyd, and Ernst Fehr, eds. 2005. *Moral Sentiments and Material Interests: The Foundations of Cooperation in Economic Life.* Cambridge, MA: MIT Press.

Heckman, James, J. E. Humphries, P. LaFontaine, and N. Mader. 2010. *Hard Evidence on Soft Skills.* Chicago: University of Chicago Press.

# PREFACE

•

In writing this book over a period of seven years, we have had the help of a large number of friends and other critics. We have borrowed ideas and advice freely and extensively, as our footnotes amply reveal. Among those who have contributed to this book, we would particularly like to thank: Mike Albert, Chris Argyris, Rod Aya, Bill Behn, F. Bohnsack, Harry Braverman, Amy Bridges, Jim Campen, Martin Carnoy, Mike Carter, Steve Cohen-Cole, Joel Denker, Peter Doerringer, Rick Edwards, Sarah Elbert, Jay Featherstone, Ann Ferguson, Alex Field, David Gordon, David Gold, Marilyn Goldberg, Andre Gorz, Allen Graubard, Zvi Griliches, Virginia Held, David Hogan, Steve Hymer, Christopher Jencks, John Judis, Carl Kaestle, Jerry Karabel, Clarence Karier, Michael Katz, Patti Lanich, Bill Lazonick, Margaret Levi, Henry Levin, Steve Marglin, Peter Meyer, Stephan Michelson, Val Nelson, Pattylee Parmalee, David Plotke, Paddy Quick, Michael Reich, Barbara Roemer, Paul Smith, Paul Sweezy, Bill Torbert, David Tyack, Jim Weaver, Bill Weber, Janice Weiss, Tom Weisskopf, and Eli Zaretsky. But the list of names, extensive as it is, fails to capture our debt to others. Our work is indebted to and an expression of the new wave of political consciousness of the past decade and a half. We have learned from our mistakes, our successes, and from our comrades in the struggle to make a better world. We owe a particularly great debt to radical economists around the United States and to our organization, the Union for Radical Political Economics. Finally, we are indebted to the Ford Foundation for a three-year grant, without which the statistical and historical studies that underlie this book could not have been undertaken.

A word of apology to our Latin American and Canadian friends. It will perhaps not surprise you to learn that the word "America" gracing the title of our book refers not to the entire Western Hemisphere, as a correct interpretation of the word would imply, but to the United States. This tribute to current usage in this country is a reminder that cultural imperialism affects even the most fundamental aspects of our consciousness—the way we communicate.

# Part I

# THE CONTRADICTIONS OF LIBERAL EDUCATIONAL REFORM

# CHAPTER 1

# Beyond the Educational Frontier:

# The Great American Dream Freeze

> Those who take the meat from the table
> Preach contentment. . . .
> Those who eat their fill speak to the hungry
> Of wonderful times to come . . . .
> Those who lead the country into the abyss
> Call ruling too difficult
> For the ordinary.
> BERTOLT BRECHT, 1937

"Go West, young man!" advised Horace Greeley in 1851. A century later, he might have said: "Go to college!"

The Western frontier was the nineteenth-century land of opportunity. In open competition with nature, venturesome white settlers found their own levels, unfettered by birth or creed. The frontier was a way out—out of poverty, out of dismal factories, out of the crowded Eastern cities. The frontier was the Great Escape.

Few escaped. Railroad companies, mine owners, and, before long, an elite of successful farmers and ranchers soon captured both land and opportunity. The rest were left with the adventure of making ends meet. But throughout the nineteenth century, the image of the frontier sustained the vision of economic opportunity and unfettered personal freedom in an emerging industrial system offering little of either.

With the closing of the Western frontier in the latter part of the nineteenth century and with the growing conflicts accompanying the spread of the now established "factory system," a new ideology of opportunity became the order of the day. The folklore of capitalism was revitalized: Education became the new frontier. Rapidly expanding educational opportunity in the twentieth century has met many of the functions served earlier

3

by the Western frontier. Physical escape? Out of the question. But in school, an objective competition—as the story goes—provides an arena for discovering the limits of one's talents and, thence, the boundaries of one's life pursuit. Educational reformers have proposed an end run on economic strife by offering all children an equal opportunity to make it. Those who have failed to measure up have only themselves to blame.

For half a century or more, the educational system provided an admirable safety valve for the economic pressure cooker. Larger numbers of children completed high school and continued on to college every year. Most thought they were getting ahead, and many were. But by the late 1950s, the educational frontier was pressing its limits. Already a third of the age group was entering college; over the next decade, the fraction would rise to almost half. College graduates were driving cabs; others were collecting unemployment checks. Some were on welfare. The once relatively homogeneous appearance of the system of higher education was rapidly giving way to a hierarchy of colleges, dominated at the top by the elite Ivy League schools and descending through a fine gradation of private schools, state universities, and community colleges. Not surprisingly, a decade later, the expansion of education was slowed to a crawl. Between 1968 and 1973, the percentage of high-school graduates going on to college fell from 55 percent to 47 percent.[1] Public support for education began to wane. The fraction of all municipal school bond issues voted down in referenda doubled—from about a quarter in the mid-1960s to about a half in the early 1970s.[2] The percentage of national output devoted to educational expenditures, having more than doubled in the thirty years since 1940, fell slightly.[3]

Like the nineteenth-century prairie settler, the late twentieth-century student has come to realize the fancy of flight. The school system has been increasingly unable to support the myth of equal opportunity and full personal development. And the fading of the American Dream, hardly confined to education, has been a persistent theme of recent years.

The decade of the 1960s burst upon a complacent public in successive waves of political and cultural conflict. Their formative years untouched by depression, mobilization, and total world war, youth of the emerging generation were afforded more than a glimpse of the future of the American Dream. Large numbers were less than enthusiastic. Discontent often took the form of sporadic, but intense, political assaults against economic inequality in the United States. Minorities, women, welfare recipients, students, and working people have periodically brought the issue of inequality into the streets, forced it onto the front pages, and thrown it into the legislature and the courts. The dominant response of the privileged has been concern, tempered by a hardy optimism that social programs can be devised to alleviate social distress and restore a modicum of social harmony. Not exempt from this optimism has been modern academic economics and sociology. At the core of this conventional wisdom has rested the conviction that, within the "free enterprise" system of the United States, significant social progress can be achieved through a combination of enlightened persuasion and governmental initiative, particularly in the spheres of education and vocational training.

The social movements of the sixties and seventies did not limit their attack to inequality. The period witnessed a growing reaction against authoritarian and repressive social relationships. Wildcat strikes, worker insubordination, and especially, absenteeism became a serious problem for union bosses and for employers. Black people in open revolt against centuries of discrimination demanded control of their communities. Armed students seized administration buildings, general strikes swept the colleges, and police patrolled high-school study halls. What appeared to many as the cornerstone of social stability—the family itself—was rocked by a women's movement which challenged the sexual division of labor and the monopolization of personal and social power by males.

While the "law-and-order" forces gathered guns and adherents, the liberal community sought a more flexible answer. The "soft" human relations school of labor management enjoyed a boom. Civil rights legislation was passed. Some of the more oppressive laws defining women's place were repealed. But the key response to the movement against repressive social relations appeared in education. A free-school movement, reflecting the highest ideals of progressive students and parents, was welcomed by major foundations and supported by the U.S. Office of Education. The "open classroom" was quickly perceived by liberal educators as a means of accommodating and circumscribing the growing antiauthoritarianism of young people and keeping things from getting out of hand. Free schools proliferated.

The educational system, perhaps more than any other contemporary social institution, has become the laboratory in which competing solutions to the problems of personal liberation and social equality are tested and the arena in which social struggles are fought out. The school system is a monument to the capacity of the advanced corporate economy to accommodate and deflect thrusts away from its foundations. Yet at the same time, the educational system mirrors the growing contradictions of the larger society, most dramatically in the disappointing results of reform efforts.

By now, it is clear to many that the liberal school-reform balloon has burst. The social scientists and reformers who provided the intellectual impetus and rationale for compensatory education, for school integration, for the open classroom, for Project Headstart and Title I, are in retreat. In political as much as in intellectual circles, the current mood is one of retrenchment. In less than a decade, liberal preeminence in the field of educational theory and policy has been shattered. How did it happen?

The disappointing results of the War on Poverty and, in a larger sense, the persistence of poverty and discrimination in the United States have decisively discredited liberal social policy. The record of educational reform in the War on Poverty has been just short of catastrophic. A major Rand Corporation study, assessing the efficacy of educational programs, concluded that ". . . virtually without exception all of the large surveys of the large national compensatory educational programs have shown no beneficial results on the average."[4] The dissemination of the results of the Office of Education's Survey of Educational Opportunity—the Coleman Report—did nothing to bolster the fading optimism of the school reformers.[5] Coleman's massive 1966 study of 600,000 students in over 4,000 schools had been mandated by the Civil Rights Act of 1964; ostensibly, it was designed to provide statistical support for a policy of financial redistribution that would correct educational inequality. But while Coleman and his associates did identify positive effects of a few aspects of the school—such as teacher quality—the weight of the evidence seemed to point to the virtual irrelevance of educational resources or quality as a determinant of educational outcomes. Studies by economists in the latter 1960s revealed an unexpectedly tenuous relationship of schooling to economic success for blacks.[6] By the early 1970s, a broad spectrum of social-science opinion was ready to accept the view put forward by Jencks et al. in their highly publicized study, *Inequality*: that a more egalitarian school system would do little to create a more equal distribution of income or opportunity.[7]

The barrage of statistical studies in the late 1960s and early 1970s—the Coleman Report, Jencks' study, the evaluations of compensatory education, and others—cleared the ground for a conservative counterattack. Most notably, there has been a revival of the genetic interpretation of IQ. Thus Arthur Jensen—sensing the opportunity afforded by the liberal debacle—began his celebrated article on the heritability of IQ with: "Compensatory education has been tried and apparently it has failed."[8] In the ensuing debate, an interpretation of the role of IQ in the structure of inequality has been elaborated: The poor are poor because they are intellectually incompetent; their incompetence is particularly intractable because it is inherited from their poor, and also intellectually deficient, parents.[9] An explanation of the failure of egalitarian reform is thus found in the immutability of genetic structure. (This idea is not new: An earlier wave of genetic interpretations of economic inequality among ethnic groups followed the avowedly egalitarian, but largely unsuccessful, educational reforms of the Progressive Era.[10]) Others—Edward C. Banfield and Daniel P. Moynihan prominent among them—have found a ready audience for their view that the failure of liberal reform is to be located not in the genes, but in the attitudes, time perspectives, family patterns, and values of the poor.[11]

Free schools have fared better than egalitarian school reform. But not much—the boom peaked in the early 1970s. Today, much of the free-school rhetoric has been absorbed into the mainstream of educational thinking as a new wrinkle on how to get kids to work harder. Surviving free schools have not developed as their originators had hoped. The do-your-own-thing perspective found little favor with the majority of parents. Financial support has become harder to locate. Critics of the free-school movement increasingly raise the time-honored question: Are the majority of youth—or their elders—capable of making good use of freedom? Minus some of the more petty regulations and anachronistic dress codes, perhaps the schools are about all that can be expected—human nature being what it is, the complexity of modern life, and so forth.

These times, then, project a mood of inertial pessimism. Not a healthy conservatism founded on the affirmation of traditional values, but a rheumy loss of nerve, a product of the dashed hopes of the past decades. Even the new widespread search for individual solutions to social ills is not rooted in any celebration of individuality. Rather, to many people—viewing the failure of progressive social movements—the private pursuit of pleasure through consumption, drugs, and sexual experimentation is seen as the only show in town. Liberal social reform has been reduced to a program of Band-Aid remedies whose most eloquent vision is making do with the inevitable. In the camp of the optimists, there remain only two groups: One, those who mouth old truths and trot out tired formulas for social betterment in the vain hope that the past decade has been a quirk, a perverse and incomprehensible tangle in the history of progress which will —equally incomprehensibly—shake itself out. The other group, like ourselves, have been driven to explore the very foundation of our social order and have found there both a deeper understanding of our common situation and a conviction that our future is indeed a hopeful one.

We began our joint work together in 1968 when, actively involved in

7

campus political movements, and facing the mass of contradictory evidence on educational reform, we became committed to comprehensive intellectual reconstruction of the role of education in economic life. Setting out to bring the total theoretical, empirical, and historical evidence of the social sciences to bear on the problem of rendering education a potent instrument of progressive social reform, we fully expected the results of this analysis to take novel and even radical forms. Moreover, we approached this task with a single overarching preconception: the vision of schools which promote economic equality and positive human development. Beyond this, we have questioned everything; we have found the social changes required to bring about what we would call a good educational system to be—while eminently feasible—quite far-reaching.

Some of the statistical results of this investigation, which will be reported in detail in later chapters, shed light on what are and are not reasons for the faltering of reform efforts. First, liberal strategies for achieving economic equality have been based on a fundamental misconception of the historical evolution of the educational system. Education over the years has never been a potent force for economic equality. Since World War I, there has been a dramatic increase in the general level of education in the United States, as well as considerable equalization of its distribution among individuals. Yet economic mobility—i.e., the degree to which economic success (income or occupational status) is independent of family background of individuals—has not changed measurably. And the total effect of family background on educational attainment (years of schooling) has remained substantially constant. Thus the evidence indicates that, despite the vast increase in college enrollments, the probability of a high-school graduate attending college is just as dependent on parental socioeconomic status as it was thirty years ago. Moreover, despite the important contribution of education to an individual's economic chances, the substantial equalization of educational attainments over the years has not led measurably to an equalization in income among individuals.

Second, the failure of reform efforts as well as the feeble contribution of education to economic equality cannot be attributed to inequalities among individuals in IQ or other measured cognitive capacities, whether of genetic or environmental origin. Thus while one's race and the socioeconomic status of one's family have substantial effect on the amount of schooling one receives, these racial and family background effects are practically unrelated to socioeconomic or racial differences in measured IQ. Similarly, while family background has an important effect on an individual's chances of economic success, this effect is not attributable to the genetic or environmental transmission of measured IQ. Thus the bitter debate of recent years over the "heritability of intelligence" would seem to be quite misplaced. Indeed, the salience of these issues in educational circles appears to be part of a widespread overestimation of the importance of mental performance in understanding education in the United States and its relationship to economic life. The intensive effort to investigate the effect of educational resources on the cognitive attainments of different races and social classes loses much of its rationale given the wide variety of statistical sources which indicate that the association of income and occupational status with an individual's educational attainment is not due to measured mental skills. More surprising, perhaps, for the bulk of the population, the dollar payoff to increased education—while strongly dependent on race and sex—is related to IQ only tenuously, if at all. Thus the standard educational practice of using IQ and test scores as a criterion for access to higher educational levels has little merit in terms of economic (not to mention educational) rationality and efficiency, except perhaps for the extremes of the IQ-distribution curve.

These results suggest that it is a mistake to think of the educational system in relation to the economy simply in "technical" terms of the mental skills it supplies students and for which employers pay in the labor market. To capture the economic import of education, we must relate its social structure to the forms of consciousness, interpersonal behavior, and personality it fosters and reinforces in students. This method gives rise to our third comment on the reform process. The free-school movement and related efforts to make education more conducive to full human development have assumed that the present school system is the product of irrationality, mindlessness, and social backwardness on the part of teachers, administrators, school boards, and parents. On the contrary, we believe the available evidence indicates that the pattern of social relationships fostered in schools is hardly irrational or accidental. Rather, the structure of the educational experience is admirably suited to nurturing attitudes and behavior consonant with participation in the labor force. Particularly dramatic is the statistically verifiable congruence between the personality traits conducive to proper work performance on the job and those which are rewarded with high grades in the classroom. Like the egalitarian reformers, the free-school movement seems to have run afoul of social logic rather than reaction, apathy, inertia, or the deficiencies of human nature.

As long as one does not question the structure of the economy itself, the current structure of schools seems eminently rational. Reform efforts must therefore go beyond the application of logical or moral argument to a public

9

who probably understand these social realities far better than most advo-cates of the liberated classroom. Indeed, an impressive statistical study by Melvin Kohn indicates that parents are significantly affected by their job experiences—particularly those of dominance and subordinacy in work—and that these, in turn, are realistically reflected in the attitudes they ex-hibit toward the rearing and training of their children. Moreover, our historical investigations suggest that, for the past century and a half at least, employers have been similarly aware of the function of the schools in preparing youth psychologically for work. They have applied their con-siderable political influence accordingly.

How can we best understand the evidently critical relationship between education and the capitalist economy? Any adequate explanation must begin with the fact that schools produce workers. The traditional theory explains the increased value of an educated worker by treating the worker as a machine.[12] According to this view, workers have certain technical speci-fications (skills and motivational patterns) which in any given production situation determine their economic productivity. Productive traits are en-hanced through schooling. We believe this worker-as-machine analogy is essentially incorrect, and we shall develop an alternative at length in the chapters that follow. At this point a short sketch will suffice.

The motivating force in the capitalist economy is the employer's quest for profit. Profits are made through hiring workers and organizing produc-tion in such a way that the price paid for the worker's time—the wage—is less than the value of the goods produced by labor. The difference between the wage and the value of goods produced is profit, or surplus value. The production of surplus value requires as a precondition the existence of a body of wage workers whose sole source of livelihood is the sale of their capacity to work, their labor power. Opposing these wage workers is the employer, whose control of the tools, structures, and goods required in pro-duction constitutes both the immediate basis of his power over labor and his legal claim on the surplus value generated in production.

Capitalist production, in our view, is not simply a technical process; it is also a social process. Workers are neither machines nor commodities but, rather, active human beings who participate in production with the aim of satisfying their personal and social needs. The central problem of the em-ployer is to erect a set of social relationships and organizational forms, both within the enterprise and, if possible, in society at large, that will channel these aims into the production and expropriation of surplus value.[13] Thus as a social process, capitalist production is inherently an-tagonistic and always potentially explosive. Though class conflicts take many forms, the most basic occurs in this struggle over the creation and expropriation of surplus value.

It is immediately evident that profits will be greater, the lower is the total wage bill paid by the employer and the greater is the productivity and intensity of labor. Education in the United States plays a dual role in the social process whereby surplus value, i.e., profit, is created and expropriated. On the one hand, by imparting technical and social skills and appropriate motivations, education increases the productive capacity of workers. On the other hand, education helps defuse and depoliticize the potentially explosive class relations of the production process, and thus serves to perpetuate the social, political, and economic conditions through which a portion of the product of labor is expropriated in the form of profits.

This simple model, reflecting the undemocratic and class-based character of economic life in the United States, bears a number of central implications which will be elaborated upon and empirically supported in the sequel.

First, we find that prevailing degrees of economic inequality and types of personal development are defined primarily by the market, property, and power relationships which define the capitalist system. Moreover, basic changes in the degree of inequality and in socially directed forms of personal development occur almost exclusively—if sometimes indirectly— through the normal process of capital accumulation and economic growth, and through shifts in the power among groups engaged in economic activity.

Second, the educational system does not add to or subtract from the overall degree of inequality and repressive personal development. Rather, it is best understood as an institution which serves to perpetuate the social relationships of economic life through which these patterns are set, by facilitating a smooth integration of youth into the labor force. This role takes a variety of forms. Schools foster legitimate inequality through the ostensibly meritocratic manner by which they reward and promote students, and allocate them to distinct positions in the occupational hierarchy. They create and reinforce patterns of social class, racial and sexual identification among students which allow them to relate "properly" to their eventual standing in the hierarchy of authority and status in the production process. Schools foster types of personal development compatible with the relationships of dominance and subordinacy in the economic sphere, and finally, schools create surpluses of skilled labor sufficiently extensive to render effective the prime weapon of the employer in disciplining labor— the power to hire and fire.

Third, the educational system operates in this manner not so much through the conscious intentions of teachers and administrators in their day-to-day activities, but through a close correspondence between the social relationships which govern personal interaction in the work place and the social relationships of the educational system. Specifically, the relationships of authority and control between administrators and teachers, teachers and students, students and students, and students and their work replicate the hierarchical division of labor which dominates the work place. Power is organized along vertical lines of authority from administration to faculty to student body; students have a degree of control over their curriculum comparable to that of the worker over the content of his job. The motivational system of the school, involving as it does grades and other external rewards and the threat of failure rather than the intrinsic social benefits of the process of education (learning) or its tangible outcome (knowledge), mirrors closely the role of wages and the specter of unemployment in the motivation of workers. The fragmented nature of jobs is reflected in the institutionalized and rarely constructive competition among students and in the specialization and compartmentalization of academic knowledge. Finally, the relationships of dominance and subordinacy in education differ by level. The rule orientation of the high school reflects the close supervision of low-level workers; the internalization of norms and freedom from continual supervision in elite colleges reflect the social relationships of upper-level white-collar work. Most state universities and community colleges, which fall in between, conform to the behavioral requisites of low-level technical, service, and supervisory personnel.

Fourth, though the school system has effectively served the interests of profit and political stability, it has hardly been a finely tuned instrument of manipulation in the hands of socially dominant groups. Schools and colleges do indeed help to justify inequality, but they also have become arenas in which a highly politicized egalitarian consciousness has developed among some parents, teachers, and students. The authoritarian classroom does produce docile workers, but it also produces misfits and rebels. The university trains the elite in the skills of domination, but it has also given birth to a powerful radical movement and critique of capitalist society. The contradictory nature of U.S. education stems in part from the fact that the imperatives of profit often pull the school system in opposite directions. The types of training required to develop productive workers are often ill suited to the perpetuation of those ideas and institutions which facilitate the profitable employment of labor. Furthermore, contradictory forces external to the school system continually impinge upon its operations. Students, working people, parents, and others have attempted to use education to attain a greater share of the social wealth, to develop genuinely critical capacities, to gain material security, in short to pursue objectives different —and often diametrically opposed—to those of capital. Education in the United States is as contradictory and complex as the larger society; no simplistic or mechanical theory can help us understand it.

Lastly, the organization of education—in particular the correspondence between school structure and job structure—has taken distinct and characteristic forms in different periods of U.S. history, and has evolved in response to political and economic struggles associated with the process of capital accumulation, the extension of the wage-labor system, and the transition from an entrepreneurial to a corporate economy.

We believe that current educational reform movements reflect these dynamics of the larger society. Thus the free-school movement and, more generally, youth culture are diffuse reactions to the reduced status and personal control of white-collar labor and its expression in repressive schooling. The extent to which the educational establishment will embrace free schooling depends to some extent on the political power of the parents and children pressing these objectives. But the long-run survival of the free school as anything but an isolated haven for the overprivileged will depend on the extent to which the interpersonal relationships it fosters can be brought into line with the realities of economic life. The increasing complexity of work, the growing difficulty of supervising labor and the rampant dissatisfaction of workers with their lack of power may foretell a sustained effort by employers to redesign jobs to allow limited worker participation in production decisions. Experiments with job enlargement and team work are manifestations of what may become a trend in the soft human relations school of personnel management. A co-opted free-school movement, shorn of its radical rhetoric, could play an important role in providing employers with young workers with a "built-in" supervisor. In this, it would follow the Progressive Movement of an earlier era. This much, at least, is clear: the possibility of schooling which promotes truly self-initiated and self-conscious personal development will await a change in the work place more fundamental than any proposed by even the softest of the soft human relations experts. For only when work processes are self-initiated and controlled by workers themselves will free schooling be an integral part of the necessary process of growing up and getting a job. Nor, we suggest, are these necessary changes limited to the work place alone; they entail a radical transformation of the very class structure of U.S. society.

The impact of the current movement for equalization of schooling— through resource transfers, open enrollment, and similar programs—likewise hinges on the future of economic institutions. Education plays a major role in hiding or justifying the exploitative nature of the U.S. economy. Equal access to educational credentials, of course, could not arise by accident. But were egalitarian education reformers to win spectacular victories —the social relationships of economic life remaining untouched—we can confidently predict that employers would quickly resort to other means of labeling and segmenting working people so as to fortify the structure of power and privilege within the capitalist enterprise.

In short, our approach to U.S. education suggests that movements for educational reform have faltered through refusing to call into question the basic structure of property and power in economic life. We are optimistic indeed concerning the feasibility of achieving a society fostering economic equality and full personal development. But we understand that the prerequisite is a far-reaching economic transformation. An educational system can be egalitarian and liberating only when it prepares youth for fully democratic participation in social life and an equal claim to the fruits of economic activity. In the United States, democratic forms in the electoral sphere of political life are paralleled by highly dictatorial forms in the economic sphere. Thus we believe that the key to reform is the democratization of economic relationships: social ownership, democratic and participatory control of the production process by workers, equal sharing of socially necessary labor by all, and progressive equalization of incomes and destruction of hierarchical economic relationships. This is, of course, socialism, conceived of as an extension of democracy from the narrowly political to the economic realm.

In this conception, educational strategy is part of a revolutionary transformation of economic life. Under what conditions and by what means such a movement might be successful is discussed toward the end of our investigation. But the broad outlines of such an educational strategy are clear. We must press for an educational environment in which youth can develop the capacity and commitment collectively to control their lives and regulate their social interactions with a sense of equality, reciprocity, and communality. Not that such an environment will of itself alter the quality of social life. Rather, that it will nurture a new generation of workers— white and blue collar, male and female, black, white, brown, and red— unwilling to submit to the fragmented relationships of dominance and subordinacy prevailing in economic life.

It will not have escaped the reader that the economic transformation which we envision, and which is the basis for our optimism, is so far-reaching and total in its impact on social life as to betoken a new stage in the development of U.S. society. Moreover, it requires an historical consciousness on the part of citizens of a type uncommon in our history.

Perhaps only at the time of the American Revolution and the Civil War have any significant numbers of people been aware of the need consciously to remake the institutions which govern their everyday lives and structure the quality of their social development. Yet to attain the social prerequisites for equality and full human development as a natural byproduct of economic life requires no less than this in the contemporary United States. Even the most sympathetic reader will understandably ask what view of the dynamics of historical change leads us to believe such a period might be at hand. In a word, we are impressed by Karl Marx's observation that fundamental social change occurs only when evident possibilities for progress are held in check by a set of anachronistic social arrangements. In such periods, basic social institutions lose their appearance of normality and inevitability; they take on the air of increasing irrationality and dispensibility. In these conditions individuals, and especially those groups and classes most likely to benefit from progress, consciously seek alternative social arrangements. It is for this reason that the history of the human race, despite its tortuous path and periodic retrogression, has been basically progressive.

In short, history in the long run seems to progress through a blending of reason and struggle. We take strong exception to such voguish historical pessimisms as Konrad Lorenz's view that:

The ever-recurrent phenomena of history do not have reasonable causes. . . . Most of us fail to realize how abjectly stupid and undesirable the historical mass behavior of humanity actually is.[14]

United States society offers all the material, technical, and organizational preconditions for a new stage in human liberation, but its economic institutions prevent progress from taking place. While there is nothing inevitable about a democratic socialist movement bursting through the fabric of irrational social relationships, the possibility grows yearly. More and more frequently and in ever-wider spheres of social life—of which education is merely one—the anachronism of our social institutions is impressed upon us.

But is an egalitarian and humanistic socialism even technically possible? Some have suggested that inequality and dehumanized social relationships are imposed upon us by the very nature of modern technology. In the words of Jacques Ellul, a well-known critic of modern life:

Technique has become autonomous; it has fashioned an omnivorous world which obeys its own laws and which has renounced all tradition. . . . Man himself is overpowered by technique and becomes its object.[15]

This common view, we believe, is quite unfounded. Technology, we shall argue, can only increase the set of alternatives open to society toward the satisfaction of its needs. Harmful social outcomes are the product of irrational power relationships in the dynamic of social choice, not the inevitable product of scientific rationality or technological necessity. Even the modern organization of work in the corporate enterprise, we suggest, is not technically rational but, rather, is geared toward the reproduction of contemporary patterns of property and power. Democratic and participatory work is not only more human, it is also more in line with modern technology.

Another common objection to the possibility of an egalitarian society must be squarely faced: the seeming inevitability of bureaucracies controlling our lives. According to this view, aptly expressed by Robert Michels in his classic *Political Parties*:

It is organization which gives birth to the domination of the elected over the electors, of the mandatories over the mandates, of the delegates over the delegators. Who says organization says oligarchy.[16]

Indeed, the ossification of the Russian Revolution and the souring of innumerable reform movements has convinced many that, to use Seymour Martin Lipset's words, ". . . the objective of the mass-based elite is to replace the power of one minority with that of another."[17] The problem with this view is that all of the historical examples on which it is based involve economic systems whose power relations are formally undemocratic. While governmental bureaucracies have not been terribly responsive to the needs of the masses, it is fair to say they have been responsive to groups in proportion to their economic power. Thus economic democracy should be a precondition—though hardly a guarantee—to truly representative government. With its appearance, Michels' "iron law of oligarchy" can be relegated to the proverbial trash bin of history.

Finally, it might be objected that the types of changes we envision are incompatible with basic human nature. The view we expound in this book is that the antagonisms, insecurities, provincialisms, egotisms, competitiveness, greed, and chauvinism which we observe in U.S. society do not derive from innate biological needs or instincts or infirmities. Rather, these are reasonable responses to the exigencies and experiences of daily life. Just as slavery, feudalism, and political autocracies have been viewed in their time as the only systems compatible with the Natural Order, so it is with U.S. capitalism. Yet in the contemporary United States, we perceive a nearly universal striving among people for control over their lives, free space to grow, and social relationships conducive to the satisfaction of group needs. The concept which infuses our vision of educational reform and social transformation is that of an irrepressible need for individuality and community. Most likely, this is a result of an interaction between innate characteristics and concrete historical circumstances. A proper organization of educational and economic life, we believe, can unleash a people's creative powers without recreating the oppressive poles of domination and subordinacy, self-esteem and self-hatred, affluence and deprivation.

A revolutionary transformation of social life will not simply happen through piecemeal change. Rather, we believe it will occur only as the result of a prolonged struggle based on hope and a total vision of a qualitatively new society, waged by those social classes and groups who stand to benefit from the new era. This book is intended to be a step in that long march.

# CHAPTER 2

•

# Broken Promises:

# School Reform in Retrospect

We shall one day learn to supercede politics by education.
RALPH WALDO EMERSON

Educational reform in the past decade has hardly marked a major innovation in social policy. Rather, it has seemed to most, including its most ardent supporters, a natural extension of over a century of progressive thought. Its apparent failure is not only disconcerting in its social consequences, but casts strong doubt on liberal educational theory as a whole, and invites a thorough reassessment of its basic concepts and their historical application.

In this chapter, we begin with a review of liberal educational views in their most cogent and sophisticated forms. We then proceed to assess their validity as revealed in both the historical record and contemporary statistical evidence. The discrepancy between theory and practice, we shall suggest, has been vast not only in recent years, but throughout the years for which evidence is available. The educational system has rarely behaved according to traditional precepts; rarely has it promoted either social equality or full human development. This conclusion bids us to offer a critique of traditional educational notions—one sufficiently detailed to motivate the alternative presented in later chapters in this book.

The use of education as a tool of social policy has a long and eminent history. For instance, the period from 1890–1920, marking the transition of the U.S. capitalist system from its earlier individualistic competitive structure to its contemporary corporate form, presented a picture of acute social dislocation much as our own.[1] Andrew Carnegie, a major protagonist of this drama, responded to the growing breakdown of "law and order" among working people with the National Guard, trainloads of strikebreakers, and the notorious Pinkerton men. But the survival of the new order over the long haul, all agreed, called for a bit more finesse. "Just see," Carnegie pointed out, "wherever we peer into the first tiny springs of the national life, how this true panacea for all the ills of the body politic bubbles forth—education, education, education."[1a] Carnegie proceeded, in the lull between battles, to found the Carnegie Foundation for the Advancement of Teaching. The Carnegie Foundation and its offshoots continue to this day to play a critical role in the evolution of U.S. education.

Carnegie's advocacy of schooling as the solution of the all-too-evident social ills of his day was echoed by other corporate leaders, by university presidents, trade union officials, and politicians; education quickly became the chosen instrument of social reformers.[2] Nor has enthusiasm waned with the passing years. Three-quarters of a century later, President Lyndon B. Johnson could proclaim that ". . . the answer for all our national problems comes down to a single word: education." Why education for this critical role? The focal importance of schooling in U.S. social history and the attention devoted to it by current policy-makers and social critics can be understood only in terms of the way reformers have accommodated themselves to the seemingly inevitable realities of capitalist development.

Whatever the benefits of the capitalist economy, its modern critics and defenders alike have recognized that a system based on free markets in land and labor and the private ownership of the means of production, if left to itself, would produce a host of undesirable outcomes. Among these include the fragmentation of communities, the deterioration of the natural environment, alienated work and inhuman working conditions, insufficient supplies of necessary social services, and an unequal distribution of income. (We will describe the workings of the capitalist economy in some detail in the next chapter.) The classical laissez-faire doctrine has been largely rejected in favor of what we call progressive liberalism. The basic strategy of progressive liberalism is to treat troublesome social problems originating in the economy as aberrations which may be alleviated by means of enlightened social programs. Among these correctives, two stand out: education and governmental intervention in economic life. Figuring prominently in the writings of liberals, both have become essential instruments of economic growth. Both, it is thought, can serve as powerful compensatory and ameliorative forces, rectifying social problems and limiting the human cost of capitalist expansion.

The importance of education and state intervention as complements to the normal operation of the economy cannot be denied. Yet these correctives have not resolved the problems to which they have been directed. Inequality, class stratification, racism, sexism, destruction of community and environment, alienating, bureaucratic, and fragmented jobs persist.

Rising per capita income has, if anything, heightened dissatisfaction over them to the point of unleashing a veritable crisis of values in the advanced capitalist societies in Europe and America.

The thrust of many modern critics of capitalism is not merely to berate the operation of its economic institutions per se, but to argue that education and state policy are relatively powerless to rectify social problems within the framework of a capitalist economy. The liberal position is, of course, that insofar as any reform is possible, it is possible within the present system, and can be achieved through enlightened social policy. The only constraints, it argues, are those dictated by technology and human nature in any materially productive society and, therefore, are common to any advanced economic system.

We take our stand with the critics. In this book, we shall focus our analysis on the educational system, maintaining that the range of effective educational policy in the United States is severely limited by the role of schooling in the production of an adequate labor force in a hierarchically controlled and class-stratified production system. Capitalism, not technology or human nature, is the limiting factor.

### Democracy and Technology in Educational Theory

> The minds . . . of the  great body of the people are in danger of really degenerating, while the other elements of civilization are advancing, unless care is taken, by means of the other instruments of education, to counteract those effects which the simplifications of the manual processes has a tendency to produce.
>
> JAMES MILL, 1824

Scholars abhor the obvious. Perhaps for this reason it is often difficult to find a complete written statement of a viewpoint which is widely accepted. Such is the case with modern liberal educational theory. Discovering its conceptual underpinnings thus requires more than a little careful searching. What exactly is the theory underlying the notion of education as "panacea"? In reviewing the vast literature on this subject, we have isolated two intellectually coherent strands, one represented by John Dewey and his followers—the "democratic school"—and the other represented by functional sociology and neoclassical economics—the "technocratic-meritocratic school." These approaches are best understood by analyzing the way they deal with two major questions concerning the limits of educational policy. The first concerns the compatibility of various functions schools are supposed to perform. The second concerns the power of schooling to perform these functions. We shall treat each in turn.

In the eyes of most liberal reformers, the educational system must fulfill at least three functions. First and foremost, schools must help integrate youth into the various occupational, political, familial, and other adult roles required by an expanding economy and a stable polity. "Education," says John Dewey in *Democracy and Education*, probably the most important presentation of the liberal theory of education, "is the means of [the] social continuity of life." We refer to this process as the "integrative" function of education.

Second, while substantial inequality in economic privilege and social status are believed by most liberals to be inevitable, giving each individual a chance to compete openly for these privileges is both efficient and desirable. Dewey is representative in asserting the role of the school in this process:

It is the office of the school environment . . . to see to it that each individual gets an opportunity to escape from the limitations of the social group in which he was born, and to come into living contact with a broader environment.[3]

Many liberal educational theorists—including Dewey—have gone beyond this rather limited objective to posit a role for schools in equalizing the vast extremes of wealth and poverty. Schooling, some have proposed, cannot only assure fair competition, but can also reduce the economic gap between the winners and the losers. We shall refer to this role of schooling in the pursuit of equality of opportunity, or of equality itself, as the "egalitarian" function of education.

Lastly, education is seen as a major instrument in promoting the psychic and moral development of the individual. Personal fulfillment depends, in large part, on the extent, direction, and vigor of development of our physical, cognitive, emotional, aesthetic, and other potentials. If the educational system has not spoken to these potentialities by taking individual development as an end in itself, it has failed utterly. Again quoting Dewey:

The criterion of the value of school education is the extent in which it creates a desire for continued growth and supplies the means for making the desire effective in fact. . . . The educational process has no end beyond itself; it is its own end.[4]

We refer to this as the "developmental" function of education.

For Dewey, the compatibility of these three functions—the integrative, the egalitarian, and the developmental—derives from basic assumptions concerning the nature of social life. First, he assumed that occupational roles in capitalist society are best filled by individuals who have achieved the highest possible levels of personal development. For Dewey, personal development is economically productive. Second, Dewey assumed that a free and universal school system can render the opportunities for self-development independent of race, ethnic origins, class background, and sex. Hence the integrative, egalitarian, and developmental functions of schooling are not only compatible, they are mutually supportive.

But why may this be so? Dewey locates the compatibility of the three functions of education in the democratic nature of U.S. institutions.[5] For Dewey, the essence of self-development is the acquisition of control over personal and social relationships; and in this process, education plays a central role:

> ... Education is that ... reorganization of experience which adds to the meaning of experience, and which increases ability to direct the course of subsequent experience.[6]

It follows in this framework that integration into adult life and self-development are compatible with equality of opportunity precisely in a democratic setting. In Dewey's own words:

> The intermingling in the school of youth of different races, differing religions, and unlike customs creates for all a new and broader environment. Common subject matter accustoms all to a unity of outlook upon a broader horizon than is visible to the members of any group while it is isolated. ... A society which is mobile and full of channels for the distribution of a change occurring anywhere, must see to it that its members are educated to personal initiative and adaptability.[7]

Dewey argues the necessary association of the integrative, egalitarian, and developmental functions of education in a democracy. A more recent liberal perspective argues only their mutual compatibility. This alternative view is based on a conception of the economy as a technical system, where work performance is based on technical competence. Inequality of income, power, and status, according to this technocratic-meritocratic view, is basically a reflection of an unequal distribution of mental, physical and other skills. The more successful individuals, according to this view, are the more skillful and the more intelligent. Since cognitive and psychomotor development are vital and healthy components of individual psychic development and can be provided equally according to the "abilities" of the students upon their entering schools, the compatibility of the three functions of the educational system in capitalism is assured.

The popularity of the technocratic-meritocratic perspective can be gleaned from the policy-maker's reaction to the "rediscovery" of poverty and inequality in America during the decade of the 1960s. Unequal opportunity in acquiring skills was quickly isolated as the source of the problem.[8] Moreover, in assessing the efficacy of the educational system, both of preschool enrichment and of other school programs, measures of cognitive outcomes—scholastic achievement, for example—have provided the unique criteria of success.[9] Finally, the recent failure of educational policies significantly to improve the position of the poor and minority groups has, among a host of possible reappraisals of liberal theory, raised but one to preeminence: the nature-nurture controversy as to the determination of "intelligence."[10]

This technocratic-meritocratic view of schooling, economic success, and the requisites of job functioning supplies an elegant and logically coherent (if not empirically compelling) explanation of the rise of mass education in the course of industrial development. Because modern industry, according to this view, consists in the application of increasingly complex and intellectually demanding production technologies, the development of the economy requires increasing mental skills on the part of the labor force as a whole. Formal education, by extending to the masses what has been throughout human history the privilege of the few, opens the upper levels in the job hierarchy to all with the ability and willingness to attain such skills. Hence, the increasing economic importance of mental skills enhances the power of a fundamentally egalitarian school system to equalize economic opportunity.

This line of reasoning is hardly new. Well before the Civil War, educational reformers had developed the idea that the newly emerging industrial order would provide the opportunity for a more open society. In 1842, Horace Mann, then secretary of the Massachusetts State Board of Education and the most prominent educational reformer of the nineteenth century, put the case this way:

> The capitalist and his agents are looking for the greatest amount of labor or the largest income in money from their investments, and they do not promote a dunce to a station where he will destroy raw material or slaken industry because of his name or birth or family connections. The obscurest and humblest person has an open and fair field for competition.[11]

Unlike earlier economic systems in which incomes and social status were based on landed property which could easily be passed on from generation to generation, in the modern industrial era, Mann argued, one's station would be determined by one's own abilities and will to work:

*23*

In great establishments, and among large bodies of laboring men, where all services are rated according to their pecuniary value . . . those who have been blessed with a good common school education rise to a higher and a higher point in the kinds of labor performed, and also in the rate of wages paid, while the ignorant sink, like dregs, and are always found at the bottom.[12]

Thus, under the new capitalist order, an educational system which provides to all children the opportunity to develop one's talents can insure progress toward a more open class system and a greater equality of economic opportunity. Horace Mann was unambiguous in asserting that:

. . . Nothing but universal education can counter work this tendency to the domination of capital and the servility of labor. If one class possesses all of the wealth and the education, while the residue of society is ignorant and poor . . . the latter in fact and in truth, will be the servile dependents and subjects of the former.[13]

The modern technocratic-meritocratic perspective avoids Mann's class analysis but retains his basic assertions. According to the modern view, the egalitarianism of schooling is complemented by the meritocratic orientation of industrial society. Since in this view ability is fairly equally distributed across social class, and since actual achievement is the criterion for access to occupational roles, differences of birth tend toward economic irrelevance. Since whatever social-class-based differences exist in an individual's "natural" aspirations to social status are minimized by the competitive orientation of schooling, expanding education represents a potent instrument toward the efficient and equitable distribution of jobs, income, and status. If inequalities remain at the end of this process, they must simply be attributed to inevitable human differences in intellectual capacities or patterns of free choice.

Thus as long as schooling is free and universal, the process of economic expansion will not only be consistent with the use of education as an instrument for personal development and social equality; economic expansion, by requiring educational expansion, will necessarily enhance the power of education to achieve these ends. So the argument goes.

If we accept for the moment the compatibility of various functions of education, we are confronted with a second group of questions concerning the power of education to counteract opposing tendencies in the larger society. If the education system is to be a central social corrective, the issue of its potential efficacy is crucial to the establishment of the liberal outlook. Dewey does not withdraw from this issue:

. . . The school environment . . . establishes a purified medium of action. . . . As a society becomes more enlightened, it realizes that it is responsible not to transmit and conserve the whole of its existing achievements but only such which make for a better future society. The school is its chief agency for the accomplishment of this end.[15]

But such generalizations cannot substitute for direct confrontation with the thorny and somewhat disreputable facts of economic life. In the reality of industrial society, can the school environment promote either human development or social equality? Self-development may be compatible with ideal work roles, but can education change the seamy realities of the workaday world? Equality may be compatible with the other functions of education, but can the significant and pervasive system of racial, class, and sexual stratification be significantly modified by "equal schooling"?

Early liberals viewing the rising industrial capitalist system of the eighteenth and early nineteenth centuries did not ignore the dehumanizing conditions of work. Adam Smith, betraying his celebrated respect for the working person, notes:

In the progress of the division of labor, the employment of the far greater part of those who live by labor . . . comes to be confined to a few very simple operations. . . . But the understandings of the greater part of men are necessarily formed by their ordinary employments. . . . [A man employed] generally becomes as stupid and ignorant as it is possible for a human creature to become.[16]

Yet he did believe that social policy could successfully counter the deleterious effects on the individual worker's development:

His dexterity in his own particular trade seems . . . to be acquired at the expense of his intellectual, social and martial virtues. But in every improved and civilized society this is the state into which the laboring poor . . . must necessarily fall, unless government takes some pains to prevent it.[17]

But modern liberal commentary has been less optimistic about the power of the educational environment to offset the dehumanizing conditions of work. Twentieth-century liberals have preferred to argue that proper education could improve the work environment directly by supplying experts with "well-balanced social interests." According to Dewey:

. . . The tendency to reduce such things as efficiency of activity and scientific management to purely technical externals is evidence of the one-sided stimulation of thought given to those in control of industry—those who supply its aims. Because of their lack of all-around and well-balanced social interests, there is not sufficient stimulus for attention to the human factors in relationships in industry.[18]

This balance would be supplemented by the natural "desire and ability to share in social control" on the part of educated workers:

... A right educational use of [science] would react upon intelligence and interest so as to modify, in connection with legislation and administration, the socially obnoxious features of the present industrial and commercial order. ....
It would give those who engage in industrial callings desire and ability to share in social control, and ability to become masters of their industrial fate.[19]

This approach became a fundamental tenet of educational reformers in the Progressive Era. Education, thought Dewey, could promote the natural movement of industrial society toward more fulfilling work, hence bringing its integrative and developmental functions increasingly into a harmonious union.

To complete our exposition of liberal theory, we must discuss the power of the educational system to promote social equality. For Dewey, of course, this power derives from the necessary association of personal growth and democracy—whose extension to all parts of the citizenry is a requisite of social development itself. In the technocratic version of liberal theory, however, the egalitarian power of the educational system is not automatically fulfilled. Were economic success dependent on race or sex, or upon deeply rooted differences in human character, the ability of schooling to increase social mobility would of course be minimal. But according to the modern liberal view, this is not the case. And where equal access is not sufficient, then enlightened policy may devise special programs for the education of the poor: job training, compensatory education, and the like.

Poverty and inequality, in this view, are the consequences of individual choice or personal inadequacies, not the normal outgrowths of our economic institutions. The problem, clearly, is to fix up the people, not to change the economic structures which regulate their lives. This, indeed, is the meaning of the "social power" of schools to promote equality.

Despite persistent setbacks in practice, the liberal faith in the equalizing power of schooling has dominated both intellectual and policy circles. Education has been considered not only a powerful tool for self-development and social integration; it has been seen, at least since Horace Mann coined the phrase well over a century ago, as the "great equalizer."

## Education and Inequality

Universal education is the power, which is destined to overthrow every species of hierarchy. It is destined to remove all artificial inequality and leave the natural inequalities to find

> their true level. With the artificial inequalities of caste, rank,
> title, blood, birth, race, color, sex, etc., will fall nearly all
> the oppression, abuse, prejudice, enmity, and injustice, that
> humanity is now subject to.
>
> LESTER FRANK WARD, *Education* c. 1872

A review of educational history hardly supports the optimistic pronounce-
ments of liberal educational theory. The politics of education are better
understood in terms of the need for social control in an unequal and
rapidly changing economic order. The founders of the modern U.S. school
system understood that the capitalist economy produces great extremes of
wealth and poverty, of social elevation and degradation. Horace Mann and
other school reformers of the antebellum period knew well the seamy side
of the burgeoning industrial and urban centers. "Here," wrote Henry Barnard, the first state superintendent of education in both Connecticut and
Rhode Island, and later to become the first U.S. Commissioner of Education, "the wealth, enterprise and professional talent of the state are concentrated . . . but here also are poverty, ignorance, profligacy and irreligion,
and a classification of society as broad and deep as ever divided the ple-
beian and patrician of ancient Rome."[20] They lived in a world in which, to
use de Tocqueville's words, ". . . small aristocratic societies . . . are formed
by some manufacturers in the midst of the immense democracy of our age
[in which] . . . some men are opulent and a multitude . . . are wretchedly
poor."[21] The rapid rise of the factory system, particularly in New England, was celebrated by the early school reformers; yet, the alarming
transition from a relatively simple rural society to a highly stratified industrial economy could not be ignored. They shared the fears that de Tocqueville had expressed following his visit to the United States in 1831:

When a work man is unceasingly and exclusively engaged in the fabrication of
one thing, he ultimately does his work with singular dexterity; but at the same
time he loses the general faculty of applying his mind to the direction of the
work. . . . [While] the science of manufacture lowers the class of workmen, it
raises the class of masters. . . . [If] ever a permanent inequality of conditions . . . again penetrates into the world, it may be predicted that this is the
gate by which they will enter.[22]

While deeply committed to the emerging industrial order, the far-sighted
school reformers of the mid-nineteenth century understood the explosive
potential of the glaring inequalities of factory life. Deploring the widening
of social divisions and fearing increasing unrest, Mann, Barnard, and others proposed educational expansion and reform. In his Fifth Report as
Secretary of the Massachusetts Board of Education, Horace Mann wrote:

Education, then beyond all other devices of human origin, is the great equalizer of the conditions of men—the balance wheel of the social machinery. . . . It does better than to disarm the poor of their hostility toward the rich; it prevents being poor.[23]

Mann and his followers appeared to be at least as interested in disarming the poor as in preventing poverty. They saw in the spread of universal and free education a means of alleviating social distress without redistributing wealth and power or altering the broad outlines of the economic system. Education, it seems, had almost magical powers.

The main idea set forth in the creeds of some political reformers, or revolution-izers, is, that some people are poor because others are rich. This idea supposed a fixed amount of property in the community . . . and the problem presented for solution is, how to transfer a portion of this property from those who are supposed to have too much to those who feel and know that they have too little. At this point, both their theory and their expectation of reform stop. But the beneficent power of education would not be exhausted, even though it should peaceably abolish all the miseries that spring from the coexistence, side by side of enormous wealth, and squalid want. It has a higher function. Beyond the power of diffusing old wealth, it has the prerogative of creating new.[24]

The early educators viewed the poor as the foreign element that they were. Mill hands were recruited throughout New England, often disrupting the small towns in which textile and other rapidly growing industries had located. Following the Irish potato famine of the 1840s, thousands of Irish workers settled in the cities and towns of the northeastern United States. Schooling was seen as a means of integrating this "uncouth and dangerous" element into the social fabric of American life. The inferiority of the foreigner was taken for granted. The editors of the influential *Massachusetts Teacher*, a leader in the educational reform movement, writing in 1851, saw ". . . the increasing influx of foreigners . . ." as a moral and social problem:

Will it, like the muddy Missouri, as it pours its waters into the clear Mississippi and contaminates the whole united mass, spread ignorance and vice, crime and disease, through our native population?

If . . . we can by any means purify this foreign people, enlighten their ignorance and bring them up to our level, we shall perform a work of true and perfect charity, blessing the giver and receiver in equal measure. . . .

With the old not much can be done; but with their children, the great remedy is *education*. The rising generation must be taught as our own children are taught. We say *must be* because in many cases this can only be accomplished by coercion.[25]

Since the mid-nineteenth century the dual objectives of educational reformers—equality of opportunity and social control—have been intermingled, the merger of these two threads sometimes so nearly complete that it becomes impossible to distinguish between the two. Schooling has been at once something done for the poor and to the poor.

The basic assumptions which underlay this comingling helps explain the educational reform movement's social legacy. First, educational reformers did not question the fundamental economic institutions of capitalism: Capitalist ownership and control of the means of production and dependent wage labor were taken for granted. In fact, education was to help preserve and extend the capitalist order. The function of the school system was to accommodate workers to its most rapid possible development. Second, it was assumed that people (often classes of people or "races") are differentially equipped by nature or social origins to occupy the varied economic and social levels in the class structure. By providing equal opportunity, the school system was to elevate the masses, guiding them sensibly and fairly to the manifold political, social, and economic roles of adult life.

Jefferson's educational thought strikingly illustrates this perspective. In 1779, he proposed a two-track educational system which would prepare individuals for adulthood in one of the two classes of society: the "laboring and the learned."[26] Even children of the laboring class would qualify for leadership. Scholarships would allow ". . . those persons whom nature hath endowed with genius and virtue . . ." to ". . . be rendered by liberal education worthy to receive and able to guard the sacred deposit of the rights and liberties of their fellow citizens."[27] Such a system, Jefferson asserted, would succeed in ". . . raking a few geniuses from the rubbish."[28] Jefferson's two-tiered educational plan presents in stark relief the outlines and motivation for the stratified structure of U.S. education which has endured up to the present. At the top, there is the highly selective aristocratic tradition, the elite university training future leaders. At the base is mass education for all, dedicated to uplift and control. The two traditions have always coexisted although their meeting point has drifted upward over the years, as mass education has spread upward from elementary school through high school, and now up to the post-high-school level.

Though schooling was consciously molded to reflect the class structure, education was seen as a means of enhancing wealth and morality which would work to the advantage of all. Horace Mann, in his 1842 report to the State Board of Education, reproduced this comment by a Massachusetts industrialist:

The great majority always have been and probably always will be comparatively poor, while a few will possess the greatest share of this world's goods. And it is a wise provision of Providence which connects so intimately, and as I think so indissolubly, the greatest good of the many with the highest interests in the few.[29]

Much of the content of education over the past century and a half can only be construed as an unvarnished attempt to persuade the "many" to make the best of the inevitable.

The unequal contest between social control and social justice is evident in the total functioning of U.S. education. The system as it stands today provides eloquent testimony to the ability of the well-to-do to perpetuate in the name of equality of opportunity an arrangement which consistently yields to themselves disproportional advantages, while thwarting the aspirations and needs of the working people of the United States. However grating this judgment may sound to the ears of the undaunted optimist, it is by no means excessive in light of the massive statistical data on inequality in the United States. Let us look at the contemporary evidence.

We may begin with the basic issue of inequalities in years of schooling. As can be seen in figure 2–1, the number of years of schooling attained by an individual is strongly associated with parental socioeconomic status. This figure presents the estimated distribution of years of schooling attained by individuals of varying socioeconomic backgrounds. If we define socioeconomic background by a weighted sum of income, occupation, and educational level of the parents, a child from the ninetieth percentile may expect, on the average, five more years of schooling than a child in the tenth percentile.[30]

A word about our use of statistics is in order. Most of the statistical calculations which we will present have been published with full documentation in academic journals. We provide some of the relevant technical information in our footnotes and Appendix. However, those interested in gaining a more detailed understanding of our data and methods are urged to consult our more technical articles.

The data, most of which was collected by the U.S. Census Current Population Survey in 1962, refers to "non-Negro" males, aged 25–64 years, from "non-farm" background in the experienced labor force.[31] We have chosen a sample of white males because the most complete statistics are available for this group. Moreover, if inequality for white males can be documented, the proposition is merely strengthened when sexual and racial differences are taken into account.

Additional census data dramatize one aspect of educational inequalities:

FIGURE 2–1.

*Educational Attainments Are Strongly Dependent on Social
Background Even for People of Similar Childhood I.Q.s*

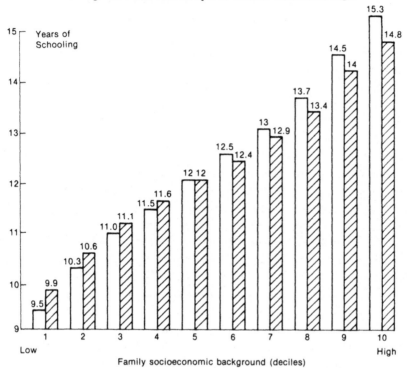

Family socioeconomic background (deciles)

NOTES: For each socioeconomic group, the left-hand bar indicates the estimated average number of years of schooling attained by all men from that group. The right-hand bar indicates the estimated average number of years of schooling attained by men with IQ scores equal to the average for the entire sample. The sample refers to "non-Negro" men of "non-farm" backgrounds, aged 35–44 years in 1962.[36]
SOURCE: Samuel Bowles and Valerie Nelson, "The 'Inheritance of IQ.' and the Intergenerational Transmission of Economic Inequality," *The Review of Economics and Statistics*, Vol. LVI, No. 1, February 1974. Reprinted by permission of the President and Fellows of Harvard College.

the relationship between family income and college attendance. Even among those who had graduated from high school in the early 1960s, children of families earning less than $3,000 per year were over six times as likely *not* to attend college as were the children of families earning over $15,000.[32] Moreover, children from less well-off families are *both* less likely to have graduated from high school and more likely to attend inexpensive, two-year community colleges rather than a four-year B.A. program if they do make it to college.[33]

Not surprisingly, the results of schooling differ greatly for children of different social backgrounds. Most easily measured, but of limited importance, are differences in scholastic achievement. If we measure the output of schooling by scores on nationally standardized achievement tests, children whose parents were themselves highly educated outperform the children of parents with less education by a wide margin. Data collected for the U.S. Office of Education Survey of Educational Opportunity reveal, for example, that among white high school seniors, those whose parents were in the top education decile were, on the average, well over three grade levels in measured scholastic achievement ahead of those whose parents were in the bottom decile.[34]

Given these differences in scholastic achievement, inequalities in years of schooling among individuals of different social backgrounds are to be expected. Thus one might be tempted to argue that the close dependence of years of schooling attained on background displayed in the left-hand bars of Figure 2–1 is simply a reflection of unequal intellectual abilities, or that inequalities in college attendance are the consequences of differing levels of scholastic achievement in high school and do not reflect any additional social class inequalities peculiar to the process of college admission.

This view, so comforting to the admissions personnel in our elite universities, is unsupported by the data, some of which is presented in Figure 2–1. The right-hand bars of Figure 2–1 indicate that even among children with identical IQ test scores at ages six and eight, those with rich, well-educated, high-status parents could expect a much higher level of schooling than those with less-favored origins. Indeed, the closeness of the left-hand and right-hand bars in Figure 2–1 shows that only a small portion of the observed social class differences in educational attainment is related to IQ differences across social classes.[35] The dependence of education attained on background is almost as strong for individuals with the same IQ as for all individuals. Thus, while Figure 2-1 indicates that an individual in the ninetieth percentile in social class background is likely to receive five more years of education than an individual in the tenth percentile; it also indicated that he is likely to receive 4.25 more years schooling than an individual from the tenth percentile with the same IQ. Similar results are obtained when we look specifically at access to college education for students with the same measured IQ. Project Talent data indicates that for "high ability" students (top 25 percent as measured by a composite of tests of "general aptitude"), those of high socioeconomic background (top 25 percent as measured by a composite of family income, parents' education, and occupation) are nearly twice as likely to attend college than students of low socioeconomic background (bottom 25 percent). For "low ability" students (bottom 25 percent), those of high social background are more than four times as likely to attend college as are their low social background counterparts.[37]

Inequality in years of schooling is, of course, only symptomatic of broader inequalities in the educational system. Not only do less well-off children go to school for fewer years, they are treated with less attention (or more precisely, less benevolent attention) when they are there. These broader inequalities are not easily measured. Some show up in statistics on the different levels of expenditure for the education of children of different socioeconomic backgrounds. Taking account of the inequality in financial resources for each year in school and the inequality in years of schooling obtained, Jencks estimated that a child whose parents were in the top fifth of the income distribution receives roughly twice the educational resources in dollar terms as does a child whose parents are in the bottom fifth.[38]

The social class inequalities in our school system, then, are too evident to be denied. Defenders of the educational system are forced back on the assertion that things are getting better; the inequalities of the past were far worse. And, indeed, there can be no doubt that some of the inequalities of the past have been mitigated. Yet new inequalities have apparently developed to take their place, for the available historical evidence lends little support to the idea that our schools are on the road to equality of educational opportunity. For example, data from a recent U.S. Census survey reported in Spady indicate that graduation from college has become no less dependent on one's social background. This is true despite the fact that high-school graduation is becoming increasingly equal across social classes.[39] Additional data confirm this impression. The statistical association (coefficient of correlation) between parents' social status and years of education attained by individuals who completed their schooling three or four decades ago is virtually identical to the same correlation for individuals who terminated their schooling in recent years.[40] On balance, the available data suggest that the number of years of school attained by a child depends upon family background as much in the recent period as it did fifty years ago.

Thus, we have empirical reasons for doubting the egalitarian impact of schooling. But what of those cases when education has been equalized? What has been the effect? We will investigate three cases: the historical decline in the inequality among individuals in years of school attained, the explicitly compensatory educational programs of the War on Poverty, and the narrowing of the black/white gap in average years of schooling attained.

Although family background has lost none of its influence on how far one gets up the educational ladder, the historical rise in the minimum legal school-leaving age has narrowed the distance between the top and bottom rungs. Inequality of educational attainments has fallen steadily and substantially over the past three decades.[41] And has this led to a parallel equalization of the distribution of income? Look at Figure 2–2. The reduc-

FIGURE 2–2.

*Equalization of Education Has Not Been*
*Associated with Equalization of Income.*

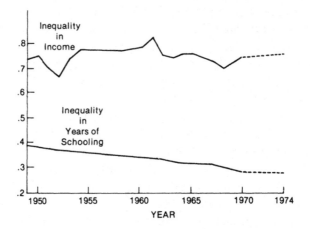

NOTES: The upper line shows the trend over time in the degree of inequality of income, as measured by the standard deviation of the natural logarithm of annual income of males aged twenty-five or older. The lower line shows the trend over time in the degree of inequality of years of schooling, as measured by the coefficient of variation (the standard deviation divided by the mean) of the years of schooling attained by males aged twenty-five and older. Data for 1970 to 1974 are estimates based on U.S. Census data.

SOURCE: Barry Chiswick and Jacob Mincer, "Time Series Changes in Personal Income Inequality in the U.S.," *Journal of Political Economy*, Vol. 80, No. 3, Part II (May-June 1972).

tion in the inequality of years of schooling has not been matched by an equalization of the U.S. income distribution.[42] In fact, a recent U.S. Labor Department study indicates that as far as labor earnings (wages and salaries) are concerned, the trend since World War II has been unmistakenly away from equality. And it is precisely inequality in labor earnings which is the target of the proponents of egalitarian school reforms.[43] But does the absence of an overall trend toward income equality mask an equalizing thrust of schooling that was offset by other disequalizing tendencies? Perhaps, but Jacob Mincer and Barry Chiswick of the National Bureau of Economic Research, in a study of the determinants of inequality in the United States, concluded that the significant reduction in schooling differences among white male adults would have had the effect—even if operating in isolation—of reducing income inequality by a negligible amount.[44]

Next, consider that group of explicitly egalitarian educational programs brought together in the War on Poverty. In a systematic economic survey of these programs, Thomas Ribich concludes that with very few exceptions, the economic payoff to compensatory education is low.[45] So low, in fact, that in a majority of cases studied, direct transfers of income to the poor would have accomplished considerably more equalization than the educational programs in question. The major RAND Corporation study by Averch came to the same conclusion.

Lastly, consider racial inequalities. In 1940, most black male workers (but a minority of whites) earned their livelihoods in the South, by far the poorest region; the education gap between nonwhites and whites was 3.3 years (38 percent of median white education).[46] By 1972, blacks had moved to more affluent parts of the country, and the education gap was reduced to 18 percent (4 percent for young men aged 25–34 years).[47] Richard Freeman has shown that this narrowing of the education gap would have virtually achieved black/white income equality had blacks received the same benefits from education as whites.[48] Yet the income gap has not closed substantially: The income gap for young men is 30 percent, despite an education gap of only 4 percent.[49] Clearly as blacks have moved toward educational (and regional) parity with whites, other mechanisms—such as entrapment in center-city ghettos, the suburbanization of jobs, and perhaps increasing segmentation of labor markets—have intensified to maintain a more-or-less constant degree of racial income inequality. Blacks certainly suffer from educational inequality, but the root of their exploitation lies outside of education, in a system of economic power and privilege in which racial distinctions play an important role.

The same must be concluded of inequality of economic opportunity between men and women. Sexual inequality persists despite the fact that women achieve a level of schooling (measured in years) equivalent to men.

We conclude that U.S. education is highly unequal, the chances of attaining much or little schooling being substantially dependent on one's race and parents' economic level. Moreover, where there is a discernible trend toward a more equal educational system—as in the narrowing of the black education deficit, for example—the impact on the structure of economic opportunity is minimal at best. As we shall presently see, the record of the U.S. school system as a promoter of full human development is no more encouraging.

## Education and Personal Development

> The government of schools . . . should be *arbitrary*. By this mode of education we prepare our youth for the subordination of laws and thereby qualify them for becoming good citizens of the republic. I am satisfied that the most useful citizens have been formed from those youth who have not known or felt their own wills til they were one and twenty years of age.
>
> BENJAMIN RUSH, 1786

School has never been much fun for children. For parents as well, the school has often seemed an alien world, hostile or indifferent to the concerns of its charges. Indeed, the annals of U.S. education exhibit what amounts to an historical constant: the dreary and rigid countenance of the school. With the ground swell of muckraking journalism in the decade of the 1890s, Joseph Mayer Rice could rock the educational establishment with his "exposé" of the schools:

> The unkindly spirit of the teacher is strikingly apparent; the pupils, being completely subjugated to her will, are silent and motionless, the spiritual atmosphere of the classroom is damp and chilly.[50]

Sensationalism? Hardly, at least to anyone with firsthand knowledge of the schools of the time. Yet sixty-eight years and a vigorous reform movement later, Charles Silberman, an editor of *Fortune* magazine and author of a highly touted three-year Carnegie Foundation study of U.S. education, is pained to find:

> . . . The grim joyless places most American schools are, how oppressive and petty are the rules by which they are governed, how intellectually sterile and aesthetically barren the atmosphere, what an appalling lack of civility obtains on the part of the teachers and principals, what contempt they unconsciously display for children as children.[51]

Rice himself was particularly concerned with the regimentation of students, with teachers who ". . . blindly led their innocent charges in singsong drill, rote repetition, and meaningless verbiage."[52] Relic of a previous age? Not quite. How unsettlingly similar is Silberman's description of a typical classroom in the late 1960s. Singsong drill may be out, but retained is the essence of regimentation:

> . . . The slavish adherence to the time-table and lesson-plan, the obsession with routine *qua* routine, the absence of noise and movement, the joylessness and repression, the universality of the formal lecture or teacher-dominated "discussion."[53]

Our argument in this section is simple enough: Since its inception in the United States, the public-school system has been seen as a method of disciplining children in the interest of producing a properly subordinate adult population. Sometimes conscious and explicit, and at other times a natural emanation from the conditions of dominance and subordinacy prevalent in the economic sphere, the theme of social control pervades educational thought and policy. The forms of school discipline, the position of the teacher, and the moral conception of the child have all changed over the years, but the overriding objective has remained.

Unlike our modern educational critics, the intellectual leaders of the New England Puritan communities thought little of children. "You are all naturally in a miserable state and condition," preached the cheery Jonathan Edwards. "In a little while you will be in eternity, some sooner and some later. . . . God is angry with you every day. How dreadful to have God angry with you. . . . Consider how it will be when you come to die and are unconverted." Children, it appeared, were ungodly, altogether too playful, lacking in seriousness, and ill-disposed toward work. Worse still, some parents appeared less than fully committed to countering the natural tendencies of the young.

As early as 1647, the General Court (legislature) in Massachusetts invoked the power of schooling to reinforce the moral training of the family. The preamble of a law allowing local taxation for the support of public schools in that year outlined the evident need for such legislation:

> It being one chiefe project of that ould deluder, Satan, to keepe men from the knowledge of the Scriptures, as in former times by keeping them in an unknowne tongue, so in these latter times by perswading from the uses of tongues, that so at lease the true sence and meaning of the originall might be clouded by false glosses of saint seeming deceivers. . . .[54]

Not much came of the legislation, but the view that children needed some special disciplining to root out their susceptibility to error persisted. On the eve of the "Common School Revival" in 1834, Federalist Judge Joseph Story advised teachers to ". . . repress the inordinate love of innovation of the young, the ignorant, and the restless."[55]

That the school could supplement the beneficial effects of family up-bringing, first voiced by the Puritan educators, became commonplace in the nineteenth century as the influx of immigrant workers threatened to "dilute" Yankee morality. Turn-of-the-century educational theorist Edward A. Ross stated the mission of schools succinctly, namely:

> . . . to collect little plastic lumps of human dough from private households and shape them on the social kneadingboard.[56]

A statement signed by seventy-seven college presidents and city and state school superintendents and published by the U.S. government in 1874 put the case this way:

> In order to compensate for lack of family nurture, the school is obliged to lay more stress upon discipline and to make far more prominent the moral phase of education. It is obliged to train the pupil into habits of prompt obedience to his teachers and the practice of self control in its various forms.[57]

While the educational practice of regimentation of children has persisted, the fundamentalist conception of a child as immoral or savage has given way, through various stages, to a more appreciative view. To modern educators, the child appears as the primitive embodiment of the good and the natural—the noble savage, if you will. Children are spontaneous and joyful, unpredictable and trusting—traits to be cherished but sadly evanescent in the path toward maturity.[58]

At the same time, the educator's view of the family has changed. Once the trusted engine of moral training for youth, to which the school was considered a complement and ballast, the family increasingly appears in the writings of educators as the source of the child's inadequacy. Thus in the thought of the culture of poverty and cultural deprivation advocates, the school has been elevated to the status of family surrogate in the well-engineered Society.[59] The social roots of this transformed concept of the family-school relationship have little to do with any alteration in family structure, and less to do with any heightening of the public morality. The impetus stems rather from the professional educator's profound mistrust of, and even fear of, the families of black and poor children, and in an earlier period, of Irish and other immigrant families.[60] Nor is this mistrust alien to the logic of social control. For all its nobility, the noble savage remains savage, and integration into the world of adults requires regimentation.

The most striking testimonial to the hegemony of the social-control ideology is perhaps its clear primacy even among those who opposed such obvious manifestations of the authoritarian classroom as corporal punishment and teacher-centered discussion. The most progressive of progressive educators have shared the common commitment to maintaining ultimate top-down control over the child's activities. Indeed, much of the educational experimentation of the past century can be viewed as attempting to broaden the discretion and deepen the involvement of the child while maintaining hierarchical control over the ultimate processes and outcomes of the educational encounter. The goal has been to enhance student motivation while withholding effective participation in the setting of priorities.

Hence, like the view of the child, the concept of discipline has itself changed. Two aspects of this change are particularly important. First, the once highly personalized authority of the teacher has become a part of the bureaucratic structure of the modern school. Unlike the teachers in the chaotic early nineteenth-century district schools, modern teachers exercise less personal power and rely more heavily on regulations promulgated by higher authorities. Although frequently prey to arbitrary intervention by parents and other community members, the nineteenth-century teacher was the boss of the classroom. The modern teacher is in a more ambiguous position. The very rules and regulations which add a patina of social authority to his or her commands at the same time rigidly circumscribe the teacher's freedom of action.

Second, the aim of discipline is no longer mere compliance: The aim is now "behavior modification." Prompt and obedient response to bureaucratically sanctioned authority is, of course, a must. But sheer coercion is out of keeping with both the modern educator's view of the child and the larger social needs for a self-controlled—not just controlled—citizenry and work force. Discipline is still the theme, but the variations more often center on the "internalization of behavioral norms," on equipping the child with a built-in supervisor than on mere obedience to external authority and material sanctions.[61]

The repressive nature of the schooling process is nowhere more clearly revealed than in the system of grading, the most basic process of allocating rewards within the school. We will have gone some distance toward comprehending the school as it is—in going behind the educational rhetoric—if we can answer the question: Who gets what and why?

Teachers are likely to reward those who conform to and strengthen the social order of the school with higher grades and approval, and punish violators with lower grades and other forms of disapproval, independent of their respective academic and cognitive accomplishments. This fact allows us to investigate exactly what personality traits, attitudes, and behavioral attributes are facilitated by the educational encounter.

Outside of gross disobedience, one would suspect the student's exhibition of creativity and divergence of thought to be most inimical to the smooth functioning of the hierarchical classroom. For the essence of the modern educational encounter is, to use Paolo Freire's words, that teaching:

> ... becomes an act of depositing, in which the students are the depositories and the teacher is the depositor. Instead of communicating, the teacher issues communiques and makes deposits which the students patiently receive, memorize, and repeat. This is the "banking" concept of education. . . . The teacher teaches and the students are taught. . . . The teacher chooses and enforces his choice and the students comply. . . . The teacher acts and the students have the illusion of acting through the action of the teacher.[62]

Others refer to this conception as the "jug and mug" approach to teaching whereby the jug fills up the mugs.

Thus the hostility of the school system to student behavior even approaching critical consciousness should be evident in the daily lives of students. Getzels and Jackson[63] have shown that high school students perceive this to be the case. They subjected a group of 449 high school students to an IQ test and a battery of exams which purport to measure creativity.[64] They found no appreciable correlation between measured IQ and measured "creativity." The top 20 percent in IQ on the one hand, and in creativity on the other, were singled out and asked to rank certain personality traits (a) on the degree to which they would like to have these traits, and (b) on the degree to which they believed teachers would like the student to have. There was virtually complete agreement by the high IQ and the high creatives on which traits are preferred by teachers; in other words, these students view the demands made upon them in a similar way. However, the two groups disagreed on what traits they themselves would like to have: The correlation between the two groups' ratings of the personality traits "preferred for oneself" was quite low.[65] Most striking of all, however, was the finding that, while the high IQs' "preferred traits" correspond closely to their perception of the teachers' values, the high creatives' ranking of preferred traits was actually inversely related to the perceived teachers' ranking.[66] The high creatives do not fail to conform; rather they do not wish to conform.[67]

Getzel and Jackson's is but one of the many studies which link personality traits to school grades. We have undertaken a review of this literature, the results of which support the following interpretation.[68] Students are rewarded for exhibiting discipline, subordinacy, intellectually as opposed to emotionally oriented behavior, and hard work independent from intrinsic task motivation. Moreover, these traits are rewarded independently of any effect of "proper demeanor" on scholastic achievement.

Rather than plowing through this mass of data, we shall present the results of the most extensive of our sources. In the early 1960s, John L. Holland undertook a study of the determinants of high school success among a group of 639 National Merit Scholarship finalists—males for the most part in the top 10 percent of students in IQ and the top 15 percent in class rank.[69] Holland collected four objective measures of cognitive development from his subjects' College Entrance Examination Board tests.[70] In addition, he collected some sixty-five measures of personality, attitude, self-concept, creativity, and home life through testing the students, their parents, and obtaining various ratings from their teachers.[71]

We have extensively analyzed this massive body of data.[72] Our first conclusion is that, while the group's high academic rank is doubtless related to their above-average IQs, differences in scholastic achievement among them were not significantly related to their grades, despite a good deal of variation in both achievement and grades within the group. More telling, however, is the fact that many of the personality variables were significantly and positively related to grades. Most important were the teachers' ratings of the students' *Citizenship* and the students' self-evaluation of *Drive to Achieve*.[73] Neither of these variables had any significant impact on actual achievement measures!

These results are not in themselves surprising. It is to be expected that students will be rewarded for their conformity to the social order of the school (*Citizenship*) as well as their personal motivation to succeed within the nexus of this social order (*Drive to Achieve*). Only the most naive would expect school grades to depend on scholastic achievement alone.

But what do *Citizenship* and *Drive to Achieve* really reflect? In a liberated educational encounter, we would expect these traits to embody some combination of diligence, social popularity, creativity, and mental flexibility. Yet statistical analysis of the Holland data reveals a strikingly different pattern. Students who are ranked by their teachers as high on *Citizenship* and *Drive to Achieve* are indeed more likely to be diligent (e.g., they are high on such measures as *Deferred Gratification, Perseverance*, and *Control*) and socially popular (e.g., they are high on *Social Leadership* and *Popularity*). But they are, in fact, significantly below average on measures of creativity and mental flexibility (e.g., they are low on such measures as *Cognitive Flexibility, Complexity of Thought, Originality, Creativity*, and *Independence of Judgment*).[74] Moreover, further statistical analysis shows that these same traits of creativity and mental flexibility are directly penalized in terms of school grades, holding constant test scores, *Citizenship*, and *Drive to Achieve*.

The conclusions from this body of data seem inescapable. Conformity to the social order of the school involves submission to a set of authority relationships which are inimical to personal growth. Instead of promoting a healthy balance among the capacity for creative autonomy, diligence, and susceptibility to social regulation, the reward system of the school inhibits those manifestations of personal capacity which threaten hierarchical authority.

We have emphasized elements on the "hidden curriculum" faced in varying degrees by all students. But schools do different things to different children. Boys and girls, blacks and whites, rich and poor are treated differently. Affluent suburban schools, working-class schools, and ghetto schools all exhibit a distinctive pattern of sanctions and rewards. Moreover, most of the discussion here has focused on high-school students. In important ways, colleges are different; and community colleges exhibit social relations of education which differ sharply from those of elite four-year institutions. In short, U.S. education is not monolithic; our analysis will be expanded accordingly in future chapters.

Why do schools reward docility, passivity, and obedience? Why do they penalize creativity and spontaneity? Why the historical constancy of suppression and domination in an institution so central to the elevation of youth? Surely this is a glaring anomaly in terms of traditional liberal educational theory. The naive enthusiasm of the contemporary free-school movement suggests the implicit assumption that no one had ever tried to correct this situation—that the ideal of liberated education is simply a new conception which has never been tried. Even sophisticated critics, such as Charles Silberman, tend to attribute the oppressiveness of schooling to simple oversight and irrationality:

> What is mostly wrong with public schools is not due to venality or indifference or stupidity but to mindlessness. . . . It simply never occurs to more than a handful, to ask why they are doing what they are doing to think seriously or deeply about the purposes or consequences of education.[75]

Yet, the history of the progressive-education movement attests to the intransigence of the educational system to "enlightened change" within the context of corporate capitalism.

Progressivism has been the keynote of modern educational theory embracing such pillars of intellect and influence as John Dewey, Charles W. Elliot, Alfred North Whitehead, William James, and G. Stanley Hall. The birth of the Association for the Advancement of Progressive Education in 1918 was merely the political codification of an already active social movement whose aim, in the words of its founder Stanwood Cobb, ". . . had little of modesty. . . . We aimed at nothing short of changing the entire school system of America."[76] Subscribing to Dewey's dictum that ". . . education is the fundamental method of social reform, . . ." the statement of principles of the Association for the Advancement of Progressive Education held its aim to be ". . . the freest and fullest development of the individual, based upon the scientific study of his mental, physical, spiritual, and social characteristics and needs."[77] However avant-garde today's liberal educationists feel themselves to be, they envision little more than did the Progressives in the dawning years of the century. Schooling was to provide the child with the freedom to develop "naturally" with a teacher as guide, not taskmaster. Intrinsic interest not external authority was to motivate all work. The leitmotif of the day was "taking the lid off kids," and the aim was to sublimate natural creative drives in fruitful directions rather than to repress them. Emotional and intellectual development were to hold equal importance, and activity was to be "real life" and "student-directed."

The mass media dramatically attest to the ideological victory of the Progressives: Professional journals, education textbooks, and even the various publications of the U.S. Office of Education mouthed the rhetoric of Progressivism. As Lawrence A. Cremin, a foremost historian of the Progressive Movement in education, notes:

> There is a "conventional wisdom" . . . in education . . . and by the end of World War II progressivism had come to be that conventional wisdom. Discussions of educational policy were liberally spiced with phrases like "recognized individual differences," "personality development," "the whole child," "the needs of learners," "intrinsic motivation," "persistent life situations," "bridging the gap between home and school," "teaching children, not subjects," "adjusting the school to the child," "real-life experiences," "teacher-pupil relationships," and "staff planning." Such phrases . . . signified that Dewey's forecast of the day when progressive education would eventually be accepted as good education had now finally come to pass.[78]

Yet the schools have changed little in substance.

Thus we must reject mindlessness along with venality, indifference, and stupidity as the source for oppressive education. A more compelling explanation of the failure to combat repression in U.S. schooling is simply that progressive education, though triumphant in educational theory, was never given a chance in practice. Indeed, this argument is often used by those adhering to the liberal perspective. Thus Raymond E. Callahan traces the failure of Progressivism to the growing preoccupation with order and efficiency in educational practice at the same time that progressive education was capturing hearts and minds in educational theory. Callahan argues that:

... Very much of what has happened in American education since 1900 can be explained on the basis of the extreme vulnerability of our schoolmen to public criticism and pressure and that this vulnerability is built into our pattern of local support and control.[79]

The direction the formal educational system took in this situation was dictated by the power of business interests and the triumphant ideology of "efficient management." Again Callahan:

What was unexpected [in my investigation] was the extent not only of the power of the business-industrial groups, but of the strength of the business ideology. ... I had expected more professional autonomy and I was completlye unprepared for that extent and degree of capitulation by administrators to whatever demands were made upon them.[80]

This vulnerability had great implications for student, teacher, and administrator alike. "Business methods" in schools meant that administrators were to be recruited from the ranks of politicians and especially businessmen, rather than professional educators, and their orientation was toward cost-saving and control rather than quality of education. Business methods also meant that the teacher was to be reduced to the status of a simple worker, with little control over curriculum, activities, or discipline, and whose accountability to the administrator again involved classroom authority rather than the quality of classroom experience. Lastly, the student was reduced to an "object" of administration, "busy-work," and standardized tests coming to prevail over play and self-development.

In short, the history of twentieth-century education is the history not of Progressivism but of the imposition upon the schools of "business values" and social relationships reflecting the pyramid of authority and privilege in the burgeoning capitalist system. The evolution of U.S. education during this period was not guided by the sanguine statements of John Dewey and Jane Addams, who saw a reformed educational system eliminating the more brutal and alienating aspects of industrial labor. Rather, the time-motion orientation of Fredrick Taylor and "Scientific Management," with its attendant fragmentation of tasks, and imposition of bureaucratic forms and top-down control held sway.

Thus there are some grounds for the opinion that the modern liberal view of the self-developmental capacities of schooling has not been falsified by recent U.S. experience; rather, it has never been tried. A historian of Progressivism in U.S. education might well echo Gandhi's assessment of Western civilization: "It would be a good idea."

## *A Preface to the Critique of Liberal Educational Reform*

> Ignorance is the mother of industry as well as of superstition. Reflection and fancy are subject to err; but a habit of moving the hand or the foot is independent of either. Manufacture, accordingly, prospers most where the mind is least consulted, and where the workshop may . . . be considered an engine, the parts of which are men.
> ADAM FERGUSON
> *An Essay on the History of Civil Society,* 1767

Decades of broken promises cast strong doubt on modern liberal educational theory. But the anomalies which arise when theory and practice are juxtaposed cannot lay it finally to rest. As Thomas Kuhn has noted, even in the physical sciences, only a recognizably superior alternative seals the fate of faulty but generally accepted dogma.[81]

All the more true is this observation in the social sciences. In the case of liberal educational theory, the failures of educational reform we have presented are by no means decisive. The "necessary connection" among the integrative, egalitarian, and developmental functions of education may appear only in the long run. Capitalism may still be young, and does seem to promote a rhetoric of tolerance and egalitarianism, as well as a supreme emphasis on individualism and human development. That this rhetoric is consistently thwarted in practice may simply represent a perverse institutional inertia. While educational policy has failed in the past, maturity and increased expertise may render it vastly more potent in the future. No one ever claimed reform to be easy—only ultimately possible with proper dedication. Finally, there may be tangible limits—technologically determined— to the degree of social mobility, due to inherent differences in mental ability. The possibility has been asserted forcefully by such writers as Arthur Jensen and Richard Herrnstein.[82]

In short, decent respect for liberal theory demands it be critiqued on theoretical grounds as well as in terms of the social outcomes it predicts, and, preferably, with an alternative in mind. This will be our goal. While detailed presentation of our alternative will await Chapters 4 and 5, our argument may be summarized simply enough here: the failure of progressive educational reforms stems from the contradictory nature of the objectives of its integrative, egalitarian and developmental functions in a society whose economic life is governed by the institutions of corporate capitalism.

Both the democratic and technocratic versions of liberal education theory focus on the relationships into which individuals enter upon adult-hood. In Dewey's democratic version, political life is singled out as central, while for the technocratic version, the technical aspects of production hold the honored position. Both have been blind to—or at least treated in quite unrealistic manner—the social relationships of capitalist production. Dew-ey's overall framework seems emminently correct. His error lies in charac-terizing the social system as democratic, whereas, in fact, the hierarchical division of labor in the capitalist enterprise is politically autocratic. More-over, his central thesis as to the economic value of an educational system devoted to fostering personal growth is untrue in capitalist society. Dewey's view requires that work be a natural extension of intrinsically motivated activity. The alienated work of corporate life is inimical to intrinsic motivation.

In corporate capitalist society, the social relations of production con-form, by and large, to the "hierarchical division of labor," characterized by power and control emanating from the top downward through a finely graded bureaucratic order.[83] The social relationships of the typically bureaucratic corporate enterprise require special attention because they are neither democratic not technical.

For Dewey, democracy is, in essence, ". . . a mode of conjoint com-municative experience . . ." which ". . . repudiates the principle of external authority . . . in favor of voluntary disposition and interest." In this sense, the dominant forms of work for which the educational system prepares youth are profoundly antidemocratic. Under capitalism, work is character-ized not by conjoint, but by hierarchical "communicative experience," and rigid patterns of dominance and subordinacy, where personal interaction is dictated primarily by rules of procedure set by employers: Dewey's "volun-tary disposition" of the worker extends only over the decision to work or starve.

Dewey is of course aware of the undemocratic control of production in capitalist society; indeed, he refers explicitly to ". . . those in control of industry—those who supply its aims." But he avoids the fatal consequence of this admission for his theory by de-emphasizing democratic process and focusing on outcomes: the quality of the decisions made by industrial aristocrats. The dehumanized nature of work—in Dewey's time, exempli-fied by Taylorism and time-motion studies, and today, by the "human relations" school of organizational theory—is attributed to their "one-sided stimulation of thought," and hence responsive to liberal educational ex-posure. Here Dewey exhibits in raw form the liberal proclivity to locate the source of systemic failures in the shortcomings of individuals and to propose "expert" solutions which respect—even reinforce—the top-down control of social life under corporate capitalism.[84] Surely he could not have been unaware of the forces in a market-oriented economy forcing managerial decision continually toward profit maximization to which end secure hierarchical authority and flexible control of the enterprise from the top are prime requisites.[85]

Similarly, the technocratic version of liberal educational theory suffers from an extremely partial characterization of the capitalist system. The major error in the technocratic school is its overemphasis on cognitive skills as the basic requirement of job adequacy. We shall show that cognitive requirements are by no means determinate, and indeed, can account for little of the association of education and economic success. Had the technocratic school looked at the social rather than the technical relations of production, it might have been more circumspect in asserting the compatibility of the integrative, egalitarian, and developmental functions of schooling. Indeed, it might have found that the way in which the school system performs its integrative function—through its production of a stratified labor force for the capitalist enterprise—is inconsistent with its performance of either developmental or egalitarian functions. Focusing on cognitive variables, it cannot even entertain the idea that the correspondence between the social relations of production and the social relations of education—the essential mechanism of the integrative function of schooling—might preclude an egalitarian or truly humanistic education.

Thus the modern economy is a product of a social as well as a technical revolution. In the development of productive organization from precapitalist forms, through the relatively simple entrepreneur-worker relationship of the early factory system based on piecework, immediate supervision, and direct worker assessment to the modern complex, stratified, and bureaucratically ordered corporation or governmental organ, not simply the technical demands of work, but its social organization have changed drastically. Seen from the present, the Industrial Revolution may appear as a simple upgearing of the pace of technological change. From the point of view of those experiencing it, however, it constituted a thoroughgoing social upheaval involving not only radically new institutions in the governance of economic activity, but a radically different pattern of social interactions with demanding and pervasive requirements on the level of individual psychic functioning. Values, beliefs, modes of personal behavior, and patterns of social and economic loyalties were formed, transformed, and reproduced in the process of bringing the individual into line with the needs of capital accumulation and the extension of the wage-labor system.

## Conclusion

> Of manufactures, of commerce, of both individual and national prosperity, nay even of science itself, the extended and abundant increase tends to complete the fatal circle; and, by decay, convulsion, anarchy, and misery, to produce a new and renovated order of things. In an advanced state of society, where the meridian is attained or passed, nothing can prevent or even protract the evil day, except the revivifying influence of education.
>
> THOMAS BERNARD, "Extract from an Account of the Mendip Schools," *Report of the Society for Bettering the Condition of the Poor*, 1799

The record of actual successes and failures of education as reform is not sufficient either to accept or to reject the liberal outlook. But it must be a point of departure in any serious inquiry into its potential contribution to social improvement. The record, as we have shown, is not encouraging. First, despite the concerted efforts of progressive educators of three generations, and despite the widespread assimilation of their vocabulary in the United States, schools, by and large, remain hostile to the individual's needs for personal development. Second, the history of U.S. education provides little support for the view that schools have been vehicles for the equalization of economic status or opportunity. Nor are they today. The proliferation of special programs for the equalization of educational opportunity had precious little impact on the structure of U.S. education, and even less on the structure of income and opportunity in the U.S. economy. It is clear that education in the United States is simply too weak an influence on the distribution of economic status and opportunity to fulfill its promised mission as the Great Equalizer. Schooling remains a meager instrument in promoting full participation of racial minorities in the United States— indeed, even the expensive pilot projects in this direction seem to have failed rather spectacularly.

The educational system serves—through the correspondence of its social relations with those of economic life—to reproduce economic inequality and to distort personal development. Thus under corporate capitalism, the objectives of liberal educational reform are contradictory: It is precisely because of its role as producer of an alienated and stratified labor force that the educational system has developed its repressive and unequal structure. In the history of U.S. education, it is the integrative function which has dominated the purpose of schooling, to the detriment of the other liberal objectives.

More fundamentally, the contradictory nature of liberal educational reform objectives may be directly traced to the dual role imposed on education in the interests of profitability and stability; namely, enhancing workers' productive capacities and perpetuating the social, political, and economic conditions for the transformation of the fruits of labor into capitalist profits. It is these overriding objectives of the capitalist class—not the ideals of liberal reformers—which have shaped the actuality of U.S. education and left little room for the school to facilitate the pursuit of equality or full human development. When education is viewed as an aspect of the reproduction of the capitalist division of labor, the history of school reforms in the United States appears less as a story of an enlightened but sadly unsuccessful corrective and more as an integral part of the process of capitalist growth itself.

We cannot rule out the possibility that a future dramatic and unprecedented shift toward equality of educational opportunity might act as a force for equality. Nor do we exclude the possibility that open classrooms and free schools might make a substantial contribution to a more liberating process of human development. Indeed, we strongly support reforms of this type as part of a general strategy of social and economic transformation. But to consider educational change in isolation from other social forces is altogether too hypothetical. The structure of U.S. education did not evolve in a vaccum; nor will it be changed, holding other things constant. Education has been historically a device for allocating individuals to economic positions, where inequality among the positions themselves is inherent in the hierarchical division of labor, differences in the degree of monopoly power of various sectors of the economy, and the power of different occupational groups to limit the supply or increase the monetary returns to their services. Thus equalization of educational outcomes, rather than reducing inequality, would more likely simply shift the job of allocating individuals to economic positions to some other "institution." Similarly, a less repressive educational system will produce little more than the "job blues" unless it can make an impact upon the nature of work and the control over production.

This much, at least, we can say with some certainty: Repression, individual powerlessness, inequality of incomes, and inequality of opportunity did not originate historically in the educational system, nor do they derive from unequal and repressive schools today. The roots of repression and inequality lie in the structure and functioning of the capitalist economy. Indeed, we shall suggest in the next chapter that they characterize any modern economic system—including the socialist state—which denies people participatory control of economic life.

# Part II

## EDUCATION AND THE STRUCTURE OF ECONOMIC LIFE

# CHAPTER 3

•

# At the Root of the Problem:
# The Capitalist Economy

> [The capitalist market] is in fact a very Eden of the innate rights of man. There alone rule freedom [and] equality. . . . On leaving this sphere of . . . exchange of commodities . . . we think we can perceive a change in the cast of characters. He, who before was the money owner, now strides in front as capitalist; the possessor of labor-power follows as his laborer. The one with an air of importance, smirking, intent on business; the other hesitant, like one who is bringing his own hide to market and has nothing to expect but—a hiding.
>
> KARL MARX, *Capital*, 1867

The halting contribution of U.S. education to equality and full human development appears intimately related to the nature of the economic structures into which the schools must integrate each new generation of youth. We have seen both liberal educational reform and the social theories on which reform is based flounder on an incomplete understanding of the economic system. We do not intend to repeat these mistakes. We must devote enough attention to the nature of U.S. economic institutions to securely base a realistic alternative educational theory. No facile or superficial snapshot of the U.S. economy will do. We do not wish to hide the fact that our analysis of U.S. capitalism will require attention to some difficult problems in economic theory. Indeed this substantive excursion into economics on which we now embark may seem to the reader out of place in a book on education. Yet only through such a study, we believe, can one understand the workings of the U.S. educational system and the means to change it.

The economy produces people. The production of commodities may be considered of quite minor importance except as a necessary input into people production. Our critique of the capitalist economy is simple enough: the people production process—in the workplace and in schools—is

53

dominated by the imperatives of profit and domination rather than by human need. The unavoidable necessity of growing up and getting a job in the United States forces us all to become less than we could be: less free, less secure, in short less happy. The U.S. economy is a formally totalitarian system in which the actions of the vast majority (workers) are controlled by a small minority (owners and managers). Yet this totalitarian system is embedded in a formally democratic political system which promotes the norms—if not the practice—of equality, justice, and reciprocity. The strongly contrasting nature of the economic and political systems can be illustrated by the diametrically opposed problems faced in maintaining their proper functioning. For the political system, the central problems of democracy are: insuring the maximal participation of the majority in decision-making; protecting minorities against the prejudices of the majority; and protecting the majority from any undue influence on the part of an unrepresentative minority. These problems of "making democracy work" are discussed at length in any high school textbook on government.

For the economic system, these central problems are nearly exactly reversed. Making U.S. capitalism work involves: insuring the minimal participation in decision-making by the majority (the workers); protecting a single minority (capitalists and managers) against the wills of a majority; and subjecting the majority to the maximal influence of this single unrepresentative minority. A more dramatic contrast one would be hard pressed to discover. High school textbooks do not dwell on the discrepancy.

The undemocratic structure of economic life in the United States may be traced directly to the moving force in the capitalist system: the quest for profits. Capitalists make profits by eliciting a high level of output from a generally recalcitrant work force. The critical process of exacting from labor as much work as possible in return for the lowest possible wages is marked by antagonistic conflict, in contract bargaining and equally in daily hassles over the intensity and conditions of work. The totalitarian structure of the capitalist enterprise is a mechanism used by employers to control the work force in the interests of profits and stability.[1] In this and succeeding chapters we will describe this economic system in more detail and analyse its substantial implications for educational policy.

Our first step is to analyse the market and property relations of capitalism, for it is here that formal political equality, legal reciprocity, and voluntary free market exchange are translated into economic domination. Of prime importance is the severely unequal ownership of productive and financial resources. Were these more or less equally distributed, economic life might not be undemocratic. The concentration of control of these resources, however, means the majority must exchange their only productive property (their capacity to labor) for a wage or salary, thereby agreeing to give formal jurisdiction over their economic activities to owners and managers. Thus formal equality in the political sphere and equal exchange in competitive markets give rise to relationships of dominance and subordinacy within the confines of the capitalist enterprise.

But these power relationships are still only formal. Once within the *formally* totalitarian factory or office, what prevents workers from wresting control of their activities from their employers? What prevents workers, through the combined power of their potential unity, from altering the terms of their contract with employers toward satisfying their own needs? Part of the answer lies again in market and property relations: the employer has the formal right to hire and fire. This right is effective, however, only when the cost to workers is high; that is, when there is a large pool of labor with the appropriate skills available in the larger society, into which workers are threatened to be pushed. Indeed, we shall suggest that the maintenance of such a "reserve army" of skilled labor has been a major, and not unintended, effect of U.S. education through the years.

Part of the answer to maintaining the dominance of the employer over workers lies in the direct application of force: the passage of antilabor laws and the use of the police power of the state. It is precisely against this "solution" that workers have fought their major battles and won some significant victories over the past century. The direct application of force by no means insures the maintenance of capitalist power relations, however, in part because its unlimited and undisguised use may be counterproductive, and in part because the labor-capital contract cannot stipulate all, or even most, of the requirements to insure the profitability and stability of the enterprise.

We shall argue that a major instrument wielded by owners and managers in stabilizing a totalitarian system of economic power is the organization of the production process itself. The long run success of any totalitarian system requires a widely accepted ideology justifying the social order and a structure of social relationships which both validates this ideology through everyday experience, and fragments the ruled into mutually indifferent or antagonistic subgroups.

The capitalist enterprise is no exception to this pattern. The accepted ideology is the technocratic-meritocratic perspective described in the previous chapter. The chosen structure of social relationships is the hierarchical division of labor and bureaucratic authority of corporate enterprise. The system of stratification is by race, sex, education, and social class, which often succeeds admirably in reducing the creative power and solidarity of workers.

These assertions concerning the reproduction of the power relations of economic life will be supported in this chapter. We shall also discuss their systemic implications as to the nature of economic inequality and personal development in U.S. society. We suggest that the quality of work life is inimical to healthy personal development and indeed, the structure of power in the economy would be threatened by institutions (such as liberated education) which promote full human development. Moreover, we argue that the alienated character of work as a social activity cannot be ascribed to the nature of "modern technology," but is, rather, a product of the class and power relations of economic life. Though the structural changes required are far-reaching, unalienated work can be achieved without sacrificing the material conveniences of modern life. Similarly, we suggest that economic inequality is a structural aspect of the capitalist economy and does not derive from individual differences in skills and competencies. While the extent of inequality is subject to change through changes in the structure of the economy, it is hardly susceptible to amelioration through educational policy.

In the succeeding two chapters we shall discuss how education fits into this picture. We shall suggest that major aspects of the structure of schooling can be understood in terms of the systemic needs for producing reserve armies of skilled labor, legitimating the technocratic-meritocratic perspective, reinforcing the fragmentation of groups of workers into stratified status groups, and accustoming youth to the social relationships of dominance and subordinacy in the economic system.

### Class, Hierarchy, and Uneven Development

> The village blacksmith shop was abandoned, the roadside shoe shop was deserted, the tailor left his bench, and all together these mechanics [workers] turned away from their country homes and wended their way to the cities wherein the large factories had been erected. The gates were unlocked in the morning to allow them to enter, and after their daily task was done the gates were closed after them in the evening.
>
> Silently and thoughtfully, these men went to their homes. They no longer carried the keys of the workshop, for workshop, tools and keys belonged not to them, but to their

> master. Thrown together in this way, in these large hives of industry, men became acquainted with each other, and frequently discussed the question of labor's rights and wrongs.
> TERRANCE POWDERLY,
> Grand Master Workman, Knights of Labor,
> "Thirty Years of Labor," 1889

MARKET AND PROPERTY RELATIONSHIPS

The market and property institutions in the United States define the legal rights and obligations for all individuals involved in economic activity. The most important of these institutions are: (1) private ownership of the means of production (land, resources and capital goods), according to which the owner has full control over their disposition and development; (2) a market in labor, according to which (a) the worker does not own, by and large, the tools of his or her trade, and (b) the worker relinquishes formal control over his or her labor time during the stipulated workday by exchanging it for pay.

It is the interaction of these market and property institutions which leads to the prevailing pattern of dominance and subordinacy in production. By no means does private ownership of capital alone lead to the overarching power of business elites to control economic life. Indeed, ownership is merely an amorphous legality. Thus in state socialist countries such as the Soviet Union, many of the patterns of economic control found in the United States are observed although private ownership of capital is nonexistent. Indeed, the degree to which education is similar in capitalist and state socialist countries can be attributed, we believe, to the similarity in their respective mechanisms of social control in the economic sphere. For markets and private property give economic elites a degree of power in the United States comparable to that enjoyed by a state socialist elite through direct political channels. The decisions of U.S. business leaders become operational only insofar as natural resources and labor can be quickly, effectively, and cheaply drawn into their sphere of control. To this end, flexible and responsive markets are necessary in a private ownership economy, although hardly sufficient in themselves. Finally, the market in labor will not operate when workers have attractive alternatives to wage employment. The fact that workers do not own the tools and equipment they use and the fact that there is an absence of alternative sources of livelihood insure that most individuals must offer their services through the labor market.

These system-defining institutions, of course, did not appear full-blown at a point in time in the United States. Indeed, this form of economic organization is quite unique in the history of civilization. Its sway is an

*57*

episode covering about two centuries and embracing at no time more than a substantial minority of the world's population. Its emergence required centuries of struggle on the European Continent. The very idea that the building blocks of society—human beings (labor) and nature (land, the physical environment and tools)—could be regulated by the forces of supply and demand on a free market would have been inconceivable and repugnant even as late as the seventeenth century. An efficient organizational form for the control of the labor of most by a few which did not involve direct coercion—as under slavery or serfdom—was equally inconceivable.

In the United States, unlike Europe, market and property institutions were developed and strengthened quite rapidly. For preindustrial America already possessed essential elements of a capitalist class structure. United States capitalism sprang from a colonial social structure closely tailored to the needs of British mercantile policy.[2] Whereas, in Europe, the transformation of property relations in land from a system of traditional serfdom and feudal obligation to the capitalist form of private ownership required half a millennium of conflict and piecemeal change, in the United States, private property was firmly established from the outset. Only in seventeenth-century New England did land-use patterns approximate communal property relations of an earlier European era.[3] In areas held by native Americans, communal property relations also predominated. With these exceptions, private property and markets in land and capital were the rule in the United States since the early days of colonization. However, the emergence of a developed market in labor, perhaps the most critical aspect of capitalist growth, involved at least two centuries of protracted and often bitter struggle.

A work force conducive to vigorous capitalist expansion requires a supply of workers large enough to satisfy the needs of capital while maintaining a "reserve army" of potential workers of sufficient size to keep wages and worker demands at a minimum. This requires, as we have seen, that workers have little recourse but to sell their labor power—i.e., that they be separated from their own means of production. These conditions were far from fulfilled in colonial America.

First, colonial America was characterized by an abundance of land and by scarce supplies of labor: The extensive Western frontier and the ease of entry into craft and artisan production thinned the labor supply up to the turn of the twentieth century. Thus free labor was not the basis of early capitalist development in North America. Over half of the white colonists during the first century of settlement were indentured servants. Black slavery added enormously to the labor supply: At the time of the Civil War, over one-third of the Southern population were slaves.

Ensuring the conditions for rapid capital accumulation—an adequate and cheap labor supply—in a land-abundant and labor-scarce continent was no simple task. Slavery and indentured servitude were but one solution. The development of a well-functioning labor market required huge influxes of immigrants: before the Civil War, Northern Europeans of Irish, German, English, Scotch, and Scandanavian stock, and later on, Eastern and Southern Europeans. Since the Civil War, also, the continual erosion of labor-intensive single-family farming in agriculture and the encroachment of the "cash nexus" on the household has added millions of workers —black and white, male and female—to the wage-labor force.

The second aspect of the development of the market in labor involves the separation of workers from their instruments of production. By the time of the American Revolution when private property was the rule, the ownership of the means of production was still quite widespread. About 80 percent of the nonslave adult males in the United States were independent property owners or professionals—farmers, merchants, traders, craftsmen or artisans, businessmen, lawyers, doctors, and so on. By 1880, this figure had fallen to 33 percent and, at present, more than 90 percent of all adults in the labor force are nonmanagerial wage and salary workers.[4] In the course of this transformation to a wage-labor system, the family farm fell to corporate agri-business; craft-organized shops were replaced by the factory system; and the services became bureaucratized.

This process has been far from placid. Rather, it has involved extended struggles with sections of U.S. labor trying to counter and temper the effects of their reduction to the status of wage labor.[5] That these radical thrusts have been deflected, by and large, into manageable wage or status demands bespeaks the power of the economic system to legitimize its changing structure, but in no way suggests that the perpetuation of the capitalist system was ever a foregone conclusion. Indeed, we shall argue in later chapters that the shifting patterns of educational reform throughout U.S. history have been, in part, responses to the threat of social unrest accompanying the integration of new groups into the wage-labor system.

THE SOCIAL RELATIONS OF WORK

In our analysis of U.S. education, we want to compare the social relations of the work process with those of the educational system. But what is the nature of day-to-day work relationships? Understanding market and property institutions alone cannot elucidate the experiences of individuals within factories and offices. Thus we now turn to a direct examination of the social relations of work to comprehend the dominant characteristic of work in contemporary U.S. society: its pervasive autocratic nature.

In 1971 there were 12.5 million businesses in the United States. Well over three-quarters of these were small individual proprietorships—primarily farms, stores, restaurants, auto repair shops, and the like. Less than two million were corporations. Much of the work performed in these small businesses we would label "independent production." This sphere consists of a large number of family or industrial enterprises where one or several workers own and control their tools and facilities, and where they work independently perhaps with the aid of small number of apprentices and temporary employees. Second, there is a large number of entrepreneurial enterprises, owned by one or two small capitalists who are often from the same family and employing a number of hired workers. Firms of the independent production and entrepreneurial type comprise more than 90 percent of all U.S. businesses, although they account for only a little over a quarter of the paid work force. The addition of self-employed individuals brings this up to about 33 percent.

Third, there is the large and growing corporate sector, involving large-scale production and organized along bureaucratic and hierarchical lines. This sector dominates the U.S. economy as a whole and, in turn, is dominated by a small number of economic giants. The largest 200,000 businesses in 1971 (1.6% of all businesses) accounted for three-quarters of all sales. The smallest eight and one half million (the bottom two-thirds of all businesses) accounted for 2.4% of all sales. Compared with Exxon and General Motors, even most corporations are small. In fact, compared with these giants, most countries are small. The largest one tenth of one percent of all corporations owned 60% of all corporate assets; the smallest 94% of all corporations owned less than 8% of all corporate assets. In 1973, the largest one hundred manufacturing corporations (less than one-fifth of 1 percent of this category) owned over 43 percent of manufacturing assets and captured 49 percent of the profits in the manufacturing sector. In that same year, the largest five hundred manufacturing corporations (in all, one-tenth of 1 percent of all manufacturing establishments) employed three-fourths of all workers in manufacturing. The corporate sector as a whole, while comprising less than one-tenth of all firms, employs nearly half of the paid labor force and has been growing rapidly since the 1880s.[6]

These profit-oriented businesses by no means exhaust the social relations of work in the contemporary United States. In addition, there is the state sector which employs teachers, police and fire fighters, social workers, and clerks and white collar office workers. While organized similarly to the private corporate sector, it does not market its products and does not produce for profits. Though related to it, the state sector lies outside capitalist production. The state sector has shown a rapid rate of growth, presently employing about one-sixth of the paid work force.[7]

Finally, there is the important sphere of domestic or household production. It involves child-rearing, food preparation, and housekeeping. Workers in this sphere, although not counted as belonging to the work force in official U.S. publications, comprise about half of all economically active adults. Household workers are predominantly women and operate outside the market in labor, although quite frequently, they are holding paid jobs as well. Household workers ordinarily own their means of production and produce for their own and their family's use rather than for sale. Domestic production is geared primarily not to profits, but rather toward the satisfaction of the needs of the nuclear family. Domestic production, strictly speaking, lies outside capitalist production.

In sum, about two thirds of all paid workers are employed in the corporate and state sectors; the number of workers in these two sectors is growing considerably faster than the labor force as a whole. People increasingly work in large organizations which severely curtail their individual and collective control over decision-making and work activities. These agencies and work places are bureaucratically ordered in the sense that social activities are governed by regulations promulgated by management. Decision-making and accountability are organized according to the hierarchical division of labor, where control over work processes is arranged in vertical layers of increasing authority with ultimate power resting nearly exclusively in the top echelon of owners and managers.[8]

Interestingly, control of the immediate process of production by owners and managers is a new phenomenon in the history of capitalism. In its earliest stages, the role of the capitalist was limited to money lending and commerce. The production process itself remained in the hands of the producers. In a more advanced stage, the capitalist supplied the raw materials and tools, and lay claim to the products. While payment took the form of a wage (usually piece rate), the task itself was under the worker's personal jurisdiction. Thus, in the once standard "putting out system" in textiles, the capitalist would supply a family with raw thread or cloth at the beginning of the week and pick up the finished or partially finished goods on his next "round." Similarly, in share-cropping, the capitalist supplied land, seed, fertilizer, and perhaps animals, then took a fixed share of the agricultural produce at the end of the growing season. Thus capitalism evolved in Europe for centuries and in the United States for decades without the direct intervention of the capitalist into the production process itself.[9] In the United States, only in the Southern slave-plantation sector was hierarchical control the general rule; this was, to some extent, true under the sharecropping and crop-lien systems following the Civil War as well.

The rise of entrepreneurial capital early in the nineteenth century in the United States marked the transition to control of work by nonworkers. In metal work, textiles, shoes, and other basic industries, independent crafts and putting out were replaced by the factory system. Entrepreneurial organization, where an employer controlled the work of a large number of laborers either directly or through a small number of white-collar intermediaries and foremen, offered several advantages over the more traditional methods. Through direct supervision, the pace of work and the length of the work day could be significantly increased. The employer could draw on an inexpensive labor pool of women and children; he could even finance the importation of low-wage immigrant labor.[10] The entrepreneur had financial and marketing resources which allowed the utilization of large-scale technology not open to individual workers, or even groups of workers organized into cooperatives. As a result, with the rise of entrepreneurial capital, groups of formerly independent workers were increasingly drawn into the wage-labor system. Working people's organizations advocated alternatives to this system; land reform, thought to allow all to become an independent producer, was a common demand. Worker cooperatives were a widespread and influential part of the labor movement as early as the 1840s.[11] The strongest workingmen's organization of the 1860s, the National Labor Movement, located the oppression of workers in the "wages system"[12] and promoted cooperative worker enterprises while remaining hostile to strikes. The cooperative movement reached a peak shortly after the Civil War but failed because sufficient capital could not be raised. The cooperative effort of the even more influential Knights of Labor in the 1880s foundered on the same problem, as well as the overt discrimination by capitalist suppliers and transporters. As Grob notes:

> Even when funds were available the desire for profits often became so overwhelming that many cooperatives were turned into joint stock companies. Stockholders then became intent on paying low wages. Not unimportant were the discriminations practiced by competitors who feared the success of cooperative enterprises.[13]

Agricultural cooperatives—in grain storage, dairy farming, and other types of production—encountered similar obstacles.

62

The preconditions for a new stage of more intensive control of the workers through the development of bureaucratic forms were established in the period 1890–1920. This period marked the emergence and consolidation of the large corporate enterprise. Prior to this time, with the exception of textiles, the corporate form was limited to the capital-intensive and quasi-public transportation and finance sectors: banks, canals, and railroads predominating. In the sphere of production itself, the entrepreneurial form reigned supreme. Thus Gardiner Means aptly describes the situation in 1860:

In the major industrial center of Pittsburgh, with 17 foundries, 21 rolling mills, 76 glass factories, and 47 other manufactories, not a single manufacturing enterprise was incorporated.[14]

Indeed, prior to 1880, the possibilities of expansion in transportation and finance provided sufficient outlets for capital accumulation to satisfy even the wealthiest. But beginning in the 1880s, the direct onslaught upon the heart of the growing economy—its manufacturing sector—began in earnest. The first phase of corporate merger saw control of the production of basic commodities—e.g., oil, sugar, rubber, railroads, and wholesale grains—fall into the hands of a few giant corporations. The second, and more dynamic, phase involved one enterprise controlling the whole production process from raw materials to the finished products—e.g., Armour and Swift in meat packing, American Tobacco Co. in tobacco, Carnegie and Morgan in steel, and DuPont in chemicals. In 1897, total capitalization of all corporations individually valued at $1 million or more came to only $170 million. Just three years later, total capitalization stood at $5 billion, and in 1904, at over $20 billion.[15] In the modern era corporate, expansion has continued to usher in a degree of world-wide division of labor unknown to earlier periods through the auspices of the multinational corporation.

The change from an entrepreneurial capitalism to its modern corporate form, we shall argue, was reflected in educational policy and theory. If the birth of the factory system fueled the nineteenth-century common-school movement which molded mass primary education, the rise of the corporate economy fostered the twentieth century Progressive Movement which lent modern secondary education its characteristic stamp.

UNEVEN DEVELOPMENT

Patterns of inequality, the nature of work life, and the demands made on the educational system thus undergo qualitative transformation from decade to decade. Our discussion of market and property relations shows clearly the tendency for the capitalist system to extend horizontally by progressively supplanting craft, household, family farming, and other types of production with wage labor and production for profit. At the same time, our discussion of the social relations of work illustrates the tendency for an evermore sophisticated vertical deepening of hierarchical mechanisms of control. But there is yet a third striking characteristic of the dynamic of capitalist growth: the extent to which the process is neither uniform nor complete. Rather, capitalist development is uneven.

Uneven development—the rapid growth in some economic sectors, regions or spheres of life coupled with the stagnation and exploitation of other areas—is a pervasive phenomenon, some of whose manifestations can only be mentioned in passing. For instance, there is a strong tendency for the economy to generate rapid growth in commodity forms (consumer goods and private services) while other social spheres important for social welfare (the natural environment, community, social justice and quality of work) stagnate or even deteriorate. Similarly, there is a clear tendency toward unbalanced regional development between different parts of the country, and between urban and rural areas. Finally, there occurs highly uneven development between rich and poor nations within the international capitalist sphere.

Of more direct importance to our analysis, however, is the tendency toward uneven development of the various sectors of the economy characterized by radically different social relations of production: rapid growth in the corporate and state sectors with stagnation in the spheres of independent, entrepreneurial and household production.

Uneven development is directly related to the unequally distributed ownership of capital and the associated inequalities in both political power and access to economically relevant information. Economic growth involves dramatic technical and organizational breakthroughs, the opening up of new markets, the development of new products, and the tapping of new sources of raw materials and labor. There is little predictable or gradual about economic development. Those who possess the capital, political power, and information to quickly take advantage of this tumultuous change, reap profits; they place themselves favorably in a position to take advantage of the next opportunity. Those without these resources must merely wait for the results of economic progress to "trickle down."

From the very first, in the United States, capital was quite unequally distributed among individuals. In the mercantile pre-Civil War North, 200 or so families controlled the major trade, credit, and financial institutions.[16] Rich and politically powerful, they provided the basis for industrial development, westward expansion, and the capitalization of agriculture. After the Civil War, the South and the West developed their own indigenous circle of capitalist wealth of considerable, if not comparable, power.

The concentration of capital leads to uneven development in several related ways. Its superiority of resources allows the privileged minority to drive out small-scale opposition through superior market power, more coordinated organization and planning, ability to employ advanced and large-scale technology, and a correspondingly higher rate of capital accumulation. Were this not enough, concentrated capital has consistently supplemented its power by securing a stronghold in government and thereby obtained legislation, judicial opinion, and, where necessary, armed intervention to aid its expansion.[17]

An important consequence of these sharply contrasting patterns of technological advance and capital accumulation, in which the most profitable regions and industries are exploited by the dynamic corporate sector, is the stagnation of backward regions and of low-profit, highly competitive entrepreneurial and independent production sectors of the economy. This counterpoint of growth and stagnation lends a characteristic stamp to economic inequality. Although some of the dynamism of the corporate sector does trickle down to the other parts of the economy, owners of the means of production in less powerful sectors—e.g., the entrepreneurial capitalist, the self-employed worker or professional, the small proprietor, and the household—are effectively denied direct access to the dynamic forces in the economy.

Parallel to, and partially as a result of, uneven development of the corporate sector is the uneven development of the capitalist work force. Uneven development of the labor force, which plays a role in the way education treats racial and ethnic minorities, may be described as follows. Groups with distinctive social class, racial, ethnic, and sexual characteristics have been historically drawn into the U.S. wage-labor system in successive "waves." Each has tended to be, at first, a group which is superexploited and socially branded, but with the passage of time, with political organization and representation, and with the appearance of another wave of new wage laborers to fill the lowest occupational slots, each has secured a foothold in particular spheres and levels of production.[18]

These waves of integration of new groups into capitalist production have occurred at critical stages in the growth of the economy and, hence, their experiences have been qualitatively different, both in terms of occupation and mobility chances. Thus the experience of nineteenth-century native, white craft workers drawn into factory production with the ascendance of entrepreneurial capital cannot be equated with the experience of Northern European immigrants in the first wave of capitalist expansion, when the majority of new jobs were essentially deskilled. Both are distinct from the later wave of Southern and Eastern European immigration associated with a second surge of corporate consolidation in the late nineteenth century when ethnic "underclasses" became stable elements of the urban-class structure. Similarly, the occupational shift of U.S. blacks from Southern agriculture to urban wage labor in the post-World-War-I period differs in a number of important ways from the experiences of their predecessors.[19] This shift permitted an upgrading of white ethnic workers, for which they had struggled for two decades. No less, the historical movement of women in and out of the wage-labor sector, while maintaining their positions in household production, gives the analysis of female oppression a character-istic stamp.[20] In the most recent period, this is marked by their appear-ance on the market as a vast number of highly qualified female workers in a period in which occupational growth is limited to the low-level, white-collar jobs associated with bureaucratized production.

Uneven development of the economy leads rather naturally to the seg-mentation of workers into distinct groups based on their unique historical experiences in the process of integration into the capitalist economy, on the relative power they have attained in various sectors, on their relative social, racial, ethnic, and sexual cohesiveness as well as on their differential treat-ment by employers. Besides the obvious segmentations of white/nonwhite, male/female, "ethnic"/"WASP," and the like, there is a more embracing segmentation between those who operate in the so-called "primary" and "secondary" labor markets. The primary segment is located predominantly in the corporate and state sectors, where jobs are characterized by relatively high wages and a modicum of job security assured through white- and blue-collar unions. In the primary labor market sector, where bureaucratic order and the hierarchical division of labor is the rule, there are clear job ladders, seniority rules, and opportunities for promotion. Credentials of various types here play an important role and workers are predominantly adult, but not aged, white males.

Alongside this primary sector, there is a secondary segment. Here jobs are characterized by low wages, great employment instability and worker turnover, and little unionization. In the secondary labor market, job lad-ders are few and there is little chance for promotion. Educational creden-tials are not important requirements for job entry; jobs leave little room for learning skills, and workers are not paid according to training and skills. Finally, workers are relatively powerless vis-à-vis the employer; threat and coersion are the usual means of enforcing compliance. A large portion of the jobs in the small-scale entrepreneurial capitalist sector may be considered part of this secondary labor market although the lowest-level white- and blue-collar jobs in the corporate sector also take this form.[21] Secondary employment is the expected lot of the most oppressed social groups: blacks, Puerto Ricans, Chicanos, native Americans, women, the elderly, youth, and other minority groups.[22]

In this overall discussion of market and property relations, the social relations of work, and the dynamics of uneven development, the reader should be impressed with the need to place individuals in society into identifiable groups for the purpose of analysis. Rather than viewing the social order as a continuum of social statuses, we speak of classes. A class is a group of individuals who relate to the production process in similar ways. A class structure emerges naturally from the institutions of U.S. capitalism. Property relations are an essential aspect of class; no less important are the relations of control. Considering the class structure in the broadest outline, capitalists own and control the means of production. Workers, conversely, do not own the products of their labor, nor do they own or control the tools, buildings, and facilities of the productive process.

A more detailed and analytically useful picture of the class structure distinguishes different segments within both the capitalist and working class. Capitalists in the dominant corporate sector may be distinguished from owners of small businesses. Workers in different sectors and on different levels in the hierarchical division of labor within a sector likewise form distinct social strata, as do workers in different segments of the labor market.

Understanding the dynamics of class relationships is essential, we believe, to an adequate appreciation of the connection between economics and education. For the institutions of economic life do not work mechanically and mindlessly to produce social outcomes, but rather change and develop through the types of class relationships to which they give rise. The educational system is involved in the reproduction and change of these class relationships and cannot be understood by simply "adding up" the effects of schooling on each individual to arrive at a total social impact.

Classes are important because individuals in U.S. society do not relate to each other as individuals alone, but as groups. That is, class is a social concept, and classes are defined only through how they relate to other classes. Similarly, social strata within classes can be ascertained only by their relationships of potential harmony and conflict with other strata. Class conflict may occur within a sector—for example, between workers and owners in the entrepreneurial sector—or between sectors—such as between corporate capitalists in agri-business and small farmers. The common daily experiences in production and common struggles against opposed classes, or in cooperation with allied classes, give rise to a common—not identical—set of values and perceptions, or a common consciousness, within a class. We will have much more to say about this in later chapters.

We turn now to a detailed consideration of an important consequence of the structure of the capitalist economy: the nature of work. We suggest that work relations both produce and in turn are dramatically affected by, class struggle and division. These struggles spill over to the educational sphere with regularity, where they supply some of the dynamic of educational change.

### Work, Class, and Personal Development

> Who built the seven towers of Thebes?
> The books are filled with the names of kings.
> Was it kings who hauled the craggy blocks of stone? . . .
> In the evening when the Chinese wall was finished
> Where did the masons go? . . .
>
> BERTOLT BRECHT

No sophisticated educational theory has overlooked the fact that schools prepare youth for economic life. Approaches to educational reform have differed, however, in the way they view the demands which this role imposes on the schools. The failure of the technocratic-meritocratic viewpoint, we have argued, lies in stressing the technical rather than the social relationships of production and in presenting the economic role of education largely as the production of job skills. The weakness of John Dewey's otherwise penetrating version, on the other hand, lies in its unrealistic faith in the increasingly democratic nature of work in the course of capitalist development.

In this section, we try to correct these theoretical shortcomings by offering a detailed analysis of the social structure of jobs. We suggest that the nature of work is a fundamental determinant of personal development; a central factor being the degree to which workers have control over planning, decision-making, and execution of production and tasks, as well as sufficient autonomy to express their creative needs and capacities. In capitalist society (due to the operation of the forces outlined in previous sections) work is largely devoid of these qualities for most people. The character of work is not an inevitable consequence of modern technology. This—it is often believed—inherently requires hierarchy, bureaucracy, top-down control, task fragmentation, and wide skill differentials. Rather, the social relationships of work are products of the dominant class and power relationships in the U.S. society. If meaningful educational reform requires a transformation of production relations, as we believe, we must begin by creating a new social structure, not a new technology.

WORK AND PERSONAL DEVELOPMENT

Material satisfaction is only one of the functions of work. Others include the economic security of the worker, social relationships among workers, and—most important—the development of the human potentialities of the worker as a social being, as a creator, and as a master of nature. In the process of production the worker produces not only material products, but himself or herself as well. According to Marx:

[Labor is] a process going on between man and nature, a process in which man, through his own activity, initiates, regulates, and controls the material re-actions between himself and nature. He confronts nature as one of her own forces. . . . By thus acting on the external world and changing it, he at the same time changes his own nature.[23]

The connection between work and social life is a central question in sociology. As the sociologist Elliot Jacques eloquently attests:

. . . working for a living is one of the basic activities in a man's life. By forcing him to come to grips with his environment, with his livelihood at stake, it confronts him with the actuality of his personal capacity—to exercise judgment, to achieve concrete and specific results. It gives him a continuous account of his correspondence between outside reality and the inner perception of that reality, as well as an account of the accuracy of his appraisal of himself. . . . In short, a man's work does not satisfy his material needs alone. In a very deep sense, it gives him a measure of his sanity.[24]

Accordingly, in proportion as work is broad or narrow, stimulating or monotonous, it develops or stunts one's abilities. Moreover, since individuals develop their personalities and consciousness through the way they relate to productive activity, work is a basis for the formation of consciousness along class lines. Insofar as capitalists and workers, farmers and wage laborers, white-collar and blue-collar workers, male wage laborers and housewives are subject to different experiences in production, they tend to develop distinct cultures, life styles, interests and ideologies. Thus social stratification and fragmentation of the working class is itself intimately related to the experience of individuals in production.

The experience of work has a pervasive impact on the overall tenor of life. Doctors, medical researchers, and psychiatrists have noted a direct relationship between work satisfaction and basic physical and mental health. In an impressive fifteen-year study of aging,[25] Palmore found that the best predictor of longevity was job satisfaction! Job satisfaction and general happiness, moreover, predicted longevity better than a rating by an examining physician of physical functioning, or a measure of the use of tobacco, or genetic inheritance—and this despite the notorious inability of questionnaires to measure actual job satisfaction. Moreover, Arthur Kornhauser, in his study of blue-collar workers,[26] found that 40 percent of his sample of 407 auto workers had symptoms of mental instability. The key correlation was between job satisfaction and mental health.

The social relationships of work also affect other areas which, at first glance, would seem to be quite unrelated to work—for instance, the political behavior of individuals. The degree of control over work is a determinant of degree of alienation from, or participation in, the political process. Individuals who have relatively more opportunity to participate in decisions on the job are likely to participate in politics. Thus Verba and Nie, in their admirable statistical analysis *Participation in America*,[27] say ". . . the social status of an individual—his job, education and income—determines to a large extent how much he participates in politics. It does this through the intervening effects of a variety of 'civic attitudes' conducive to participation: attitudes such as a sense of efficacy, of psychological involvement in politics, and a feeling of obligation to participate."

Why? Because there is a tendency for experiences in one sphere of life to generalize to all. Even the analysis of the relationship between work situation and child-rearing values suggests that autocracy in the work place is inimical to the development of a commitment to participation and to democracy in political life.[28]

Work experience is also closely related to leisure activities. This fact has been noted repeatedly in studies of the free-time activities of Americans.[29] In the face of these studies (and common sense as well), it is surprising to find numerous sociologists maintaining that in affluent "post-industrial societies" such as the United States, the quality of work is increasingly unimportant, while the quality of leisure occupies a central place in individual welfare.[30] In fact, the two go hand in hand! Thus, in an intensive and well-controlled study, William R. Torbert exhibited the direct relationship between degree of control in work and the vitality of leisure activity. Torbert studied 209 men, obtaining a job rating reflecting their degree of control over decision-making, control over pace and quantity of work, and the routine versus creative character of their activities. He also obtained a measure of leisure involvement on the basis of the degree of energy, learning, and commitment that characterize their free-time activities.

Torbert obtained a measure of job involvement, reflecting the subjective satisfactions of the worker, his feelings of challenge, variety, and interest on the job. He found that there is a very strong relationship between job rating (degree of control) and job involvement on the one hand, and leisure involvement on the other. Indeed, the two measures of control and involvement on the job explain 81 percent of the variation in leisure involvement. Even among workers with similar occupational status and educational level, the relationship between job control, job involvement, and leisure-time involvement was substantial.[31]

Finally, and perhaps most importantly from the perspective of this book, the nature of work provides a pattern of prerequisites which affect the nature of personal development in families and schools. In short, the quality of work has an impact on the individual extending far beyond immediate satisfaction on the job. The degree of control over processes, outcomes, and interpersonal relationships determines the extent to which work is a creative, socially constructive outlet. The challenge of work, or lack thereof, measurably affects the development of the worker's physical, cognitive, emotional, and other capacities. And finally, the content of work, its prestige and social contribution, are basic elements of the individual's self-esteem.

It is a major indictment of our social system that most people view their jobs as, at best, a painful necessity. While wages, physical working conditions, and job security have improved dramatically over the years for most workers, there is still discontent. Absenteeism, high turnover, wildcat strikes, industrial sabotage, and willful laxity of job performance increased dramatically in the past decade. *Work in America*, a recent Department of Health, Education and Welfare report, documents that only 43 percent of white-collar and 24 percent of blue-collar workers in a large representative sample say they are satisfied with their jobs.[32] Good pay and working conditions are not enough—workers want creative and meaningful jobs. Or, in the words of the HEW report: "What the workers want most, as more than 100 studies in the past 20 years show, is to become masters of their immediate environments and to feel that their work and they themselves are important—the twin ingredients of self-esteem."[33]

The testimony of thousands of workers and dozens of recent studies is starkly reminiscent of Marx's description of alienated labor written 130 years ago:

> What, then constitutes the alienation of labor? First, the fact that labor is *external* to the worker, i.e., it does not belong to his essential being; that in his work, therefore, he does not affirm himself but denies himself, does not feel content but unhappy, does not develop freely his physical and mental energy but mortifies his body and ruins his mind. The worker therefore only feels himself outside his work, and in his work feels himself outside himself. . . . It is therefore not the satisfaction of a need; it is merely a *means* to satisfy needs external to it. . . . External labor, labor in which man alienates himself, is a labor of self-sacrifice, of mortification.[34]

The worker experiences this alienation in the form of powerlessness, meaninglessness, isolation, and self-estrangement. Powerless because work is bureaucratically organized, ruled from the top, through lines of hierarchical authority, treating the worker as just another piece of machinery, more or less delicate and subject to breakdown, to be directed and dominated. Meaningless because it is divided into numberless fragmented tasks, over only one of which the worker has some expertise, and whose contribution to the final product is minimal, impersonal, and standardized. Meaningless, equally, because the worker who produces goods designed for profit rather than human needs realizes only too well how dubious is his or her contribution to social welfare. Producing steel, the factory pollutes the atmosphere and streams. Making automobiles, the product congests, smogs, kills, and finally, after three-score months of "service," dies. Selling insurance, success depends only on the worker's relative cunning and talent in conning the customer.

Moreover, the worker is normally isolated in work. Fragmentation of tasks precludes solidarity and cooperation. Hierarchical authority lines effectively pit workers on different levels against one another, and since workers do not cooperatively determine the important decisions governing production, no true work community develops. Lastly, the powerless, meaningless, and isolated position of the worker leads to the treatment of work merely as an instrument, as a means toward attaining material security, rather than an end in itself. But work is so important to self-definition and self-concept that the individual's self-image crystallizes as a means to some ulterior end. Hence the worker's self-estrangement.

That a person may be self-estranged—alienated from essence and psyche—has been characterized as the kernel of the worker's self-concept, whether blue-collar or white-collar. As Erich Fromm notes in *The Sane Society*:

[A person] does not experience himself as an active agent, as the bearer of human powers. He is alienated from these powers, his aim is to sell himself successfully on the market. His sense of self does not seem from his activity as a loving and thinking individual, but from his socioeconomic role . . . he experiences himself not as a man, with love, fear, convictions, doubts, but as that abstraction, alienated from his real nature, which fulfills a certain function in the social system. . . . His body, his mind, and his soul are his capital, and his task in life is to invest it favorably, to make a profit of himself. Human qualities like friendliness, courtesy, kindness are transformed into commodities, into assets of the "personality package" conducive to a higher price on the personality market.[35]

### WORK, POWER, AND TECHNOLOGY

The market in labor and the separation of workers from control of their joint activities reduce labor-power in essential respects to the status of a commodity: an object bought and sold, moved about in response to supply and demand, and disembodied in culture and consciousness from the worker's personally fulfilling social activities. Nor will the prudent employer consider the creative needs of workers in organizing jobs, unless this happens to contribute, by chance, to the profits. Indeed, the internal social relations of the enterprise, especially the systems of hierarchical control which are the hallmark of alienated labor, strengthen and deepen in the course of economic growth. Finally, uneven economic development and segmentation of the work force contribute to the formation of a reserve army of relatively rootless, powerless, and underemployed social groups. This army is drawn into the labor force in times of peak economic activity and released during downturns. Low-paying, highly insecure, often unsafe and unhealthy, boring and oppressive, these secondary jobs are the archetype of alienated labor.

But the case that alienated labor in the United States is the product of capitalist organization cannot be made quite so simply. Suppose workers could choose their own form of social organization. Would they not be forced to reproduce the same social relations of work as the capitalist, or else be forced to give up the benefits of advanced technology? If so, technology, and not capitalism, would lie at the heart of the problem. The tendency of even the state socialist countries to imitate capitalist production processes certainly gives much weight to this version of technological determinism.

Yet, we believe the argument that alienated labor is the necessary consequence of modern technology to be fundamentally incorrect. First, there is ample evidence (we will review it shortly) that, even within the confines of existing technologies, work could be organized so that to be more productive and more satisfying to workers. That these opportunities exist and are resisted by employers points to the unresponsiveness of job structure and content to the workers' needs. Second, technology itself is not the result of a socially unbiased advance of knowledge. Rather, it reflects the monopolization of control over technical information by captains of industry. Techniques might be rejected simply because they threaten "authority" in the work place. The history of technology represents an accumulation of past choices made, in the most part, by and in the interests of employers. Hence even the limits of present technologies cannot be taken for granted.

Third, that alienated labor is not a technical but an essentially social phenomenon derives precisely from the fact that labor is not a commodity, but rather a living, active agent. What workers "sell" is not work but formal jurisdiction over their capacity to work. The commodity exchanged in the labor market we call (following Marx) labor power. Labor power is the ability of the individual to contribute to the production process in its current technical and organizational form, and includes the worker's physical and mental skills and behavioral characteristics.

The profit of the capitalist, however, is not determined by the labor power of the worker, but the actual labor—the living, concrete productive activity engaged in during work. This actual labor depends on the ability of the employer, through his power relationships with workers, to enforce production norms and minimize the costs thereof. When the capitalist buys a lathe he gets just that—a lathe with given and known specifications and production characteristics for a given price. When he "buys" a worker, however, he gets not work itself, but a problem: how to get work out of the worker. The problem is solved through maintaining and reinforcing his power vis-à-vis the worker. Thus capitalist production is at heart a social and not merely a technical process. And alienation is a class and not a technological phenomenon.

That the hierarchical division of labor is not necessarily efficient contradicts many deeply held, but empirically unsubstantiated, opinions. We shall discuss three of these. The first is that victory of the factory system over traditional work forms during the Industrial Revolution demonstrates the efficiency of the hierarchical division of labor in the context of advanced technology. The second is that the fragmentation and routinization of jobs lends, in itself, to increased productivity despite its deleterious effect on worker satisfaction. The third and most important is that no other known form of work organization is more productive than the hierarchical division of labor. We believe all three to be incorrect.

Rather, we argue that the success of the factory system in the early stages of the Industrial Revolution was due primarily to the tapping of cheap labor supplies, the extension of the hours of work, and the forced increase in the pace of work; that job fragmentation is a means of reducing the solidarity and power of workers; and that increased worker participation in production decisions results nearly uniformly in increased productivity.

Let us begin with the division of labor in the Industrial Revolution.[36] Just as today many attribute the success of the giant corporation to its bureaucratic order, so many attribute the success of the early capitalist entrepreneur to his implementation of a minute division of labor. Adam Smith, the first of the great proponents of capitalism among economists, gave three reasons for the increased technical superiority of job fragmentation.[37] First, said Smith, specialization to a narrow task increases the dexterity and speed of operation of each worker. Second, the minute division of labor saves time otherwise lost in passing from one task to another. Third, job specialization allows the introduction of machinery rigidly engineered to specific operations.

While Smith's reasoning is appealing, we agree with Stephen Marglin's argument that it is probably incorrect. The argument concerning time-saving in passage from task to task is correct, but implies only that the worker must process a large amount of material at each stage. Instead of spinning a few yards of thread, then weaving it, then fulling and dyeing, spinning more yarn, etc., the efficient worker will spin a great deal, thus minimizing time loss. In continuous process industries, where excessive standing time between stages is impossible (e.g., in steel production, where the product must be treated while it is still at the proper temperature), Smith's argument is consistent with a work group of equals—each performing all operations at different times. But this is exactly how a group of guild journeymen operated! This argument cannot explain the ascendance of capitalist production.

For similar reasons, Smith's third argument is not relevant. The use of specialized machinery will increase the number of separate steps in the production process and perhaps require a larger work group in a continuous process industry, but requires neither hierarchy, inequality, nor job specialization. Also, the early putting-out and factory system did not use technologies very different from peasant and guild production. An excellent example of this is the shoe industry in the United States—one of the leading sectors in the transformation of the social relations of production prior to the Civil War—which moved from craft through putting-out to factory production using essentially the same hand-tool technology. Shoe-making machinery was introduced considerably after the organization of shoe factories.

Thus we are left with Smith's first argument: Job fragmentation leads to increased dexterity on the part of each worker. However, Marglin's evidence suggests that all the various skills in early factory and putting-out production were quickly learned—by children as well as adults. For instance, it required only six weeks for an average fourteen-year-old to learn the art of weaving cotton. During the Napoleonic Wars, when all able-bodied English men were enlisted, women quickly learned wool weaving and took their place.[38] Much the same occurred in the United States during World War II when women extensively replaced men in the factories and offices on the home front. No lengthy training periods were required for most jobs; this seems to be a general rule when the level of general skills is sufficiently great in society. Even in the current exceptions to this rule in areas of specialized technical expertise (e.g., computer, chemical, and electronic technologies), egalitarian training and recurrent educational opportunities involving the worker's moving between work and schooling throughout life could reduce job fragmentation, probably with no deleterious effect on efficiency.

Why, then, the historical emergence of factory production? The answer seems to be that it was an effective means of economic and social control. First, if all workers could perform all tasks, their knowledge of the production process would allow them to band together and go into production for themselves. In the guild system, this was prevented by legal restrictions—the guildmasters had control over the number of new masters admitted, and all production had to be under the direction of a legal guild-approved master. In "free enterprise," this form of control was interdicted.

Second, even within the capitalist firm, the employer's control depended on the lack of control of each worker. To allow all workers the capacity to deal knowledgeably and powerfully with all parts of the production process both increases their sense of control and autonomy and undercuts the employer's legitimacy as the coordinator of production. Yet it is this legitimacy which maintains his position of financial control and intermediary between direct producers and consumers. Job enlargement and democratic worker control would soon threaten the political stability of the firm. That this policy of "divide and conquer" through task fragmentation was central in the minds of bosses is amply illustrated in Marglin's cited essay.

But if early factories used apparently similar technologies as the contemporary worker-controlled operations, why were the former able to undersell, and eventually displace, their more traditional competitors? The answer seems to lie in the system of hierarchical control as a direct means of increasing the employer's power over workers. Having all workers under one roof allowed the capitalist to increase drastically the length of the work week. Instead of making his or her own work-leisure choice, the capitalist worker is forced to accept a twelve- or fifteen-hour workday, or have no work at all. Since all workers were paid more or less subsistence wages independent of length of work day, the factory system drastically reduced labor costs. Moreover, the system of direct supervision in the factory allowed the capitalist to increase the pace of work and the exertion of the worker. Lastly, the factory system used pools of pauper, female, and child labor, at lower wages than able-bodied men.

As a result, the capitalist was able to pay generally higher weekly wages to the male labor force, while reducing the cost of output and accruing huge profits. It was their greater capacity to accumulate capital, to reinvest and expand, which tipped the balance in favor of capitalist enterprise. But this was due to increased exertion of labor, not the technical efficiency of the factory system. This situation forced the independent producers to increase their own workday to meet falling prices of their product, but these producers maintained their position alongside the factory for over a quarter of a century. The survival of a substantial sector of the modern U.S. economy, still organized along the lines of craft or household production, attests to the vitality of this precapitalist form of organization.

Eventually, however, the factory system did win out on technical grounds. The reasons are interesting in light of our discussion of technological determinism. First, because only the capitalist producer had the financial resources to invest heavily in new machinery. Inventors sought to meet their needs by gearing their innovations to types compatible with the social relations of factory production. Second, because of the large number of independent producers, it would have been impossible to protect patent rights; whereas, the large size of the capitalist firm provided a stable and conspicuous market for the inventor. Third, many inventors aimed at allying with a capitalist partner and going into production for themselves.

All these factors lent to the pattern of technical innovation a strong bias toward the hierarchical, fragmented production relationships of the capitalist firm. Rather than technology merely dictating the social form of production, the reverse occurred sufficiently widely to cast strong doubt on the usual technological determinism.

The above analysis, while referring to the "First Industrial Revolution" in Great Britain, quite likely has close parallels in the U.S. experience. The historical work remains to be done,[39] but there are examples. In a study of the development of the U.S. steel industry, Katherine Stone concludes that the social organization of work arose not from technological necessity, but from the power relationships of steel production.[40]

In the period from 1890–1910, steel came of age in the United States. Spurred by the merger activities of J. P. Morgan and Andrew Carnegie, U.S. Steel became the world's first billion-dollar firm. By 1901, it controlled 80 percent of the U.S. market. The vigorous growth of this industry, which involved large-scale introduction of new techniques and machine processes in production, relied firmly on the hierarchical division of labor. Yet prior to 1890, steel production was characterized by a great degree of worker control over production. Skilled workers contracted with management, receiving a price per ton of steel based on a sliding scale which reflected the current market price of steel. The skilled workers then hired other workers ("unskilled") whom they paid out of their pockets, and agreed on a division of the receipts among themselves. Through their knowledge, their control over the work process, and the power of their union (the Amalgamated Association of Iron, Steel and Tin Workers), these skilled workers had de facto veto power over any management-proposed changes in the work process—including technological innovation.

This situation posed a crucial dilemma for the early steel magnates: How could technical innovation be introduced without the benefits accruing to the workers themselves? Clearly, only by breaking the power of workers to control the process of production. In 1892, Henry Clay Frick was called on to do the job. Workers were locked out of the Homestead Mill, armed Pinkerton troops were called in, and a "nonunion shop" was declared. After a long and bitter struggle, the Amalgamated Steel Workers Union was destroyed, hierarchical procedures were instituted, innovation proceeded apace, and the future of a high-growth and high-profit steel industry was assured. As David Brody concludes:

> In the two decades after 1890, the furnace worker's productivity tripled in exchange for an income rise of one half; the steel worker's output doubled in exchange for an income rise of one-fifth. . . . The accomplishment was possible only with a labor force powerless to oppose the decisions of the steel men.[41]

Here we have a clear case of profit rather than efficiency determining the social division of labor. And once centralized control is imposed, it does seem to follow that efficiency dictates fragmented and routinized jobs. Indeed, there is a general proposition deduced from many laboratory experiments in organizational theory, which Victor Vroom has concisely expressed in his survey of experimental literature in industrial social psychology:

> ... [the evidence indicates that] decentralized structures have an advantage for tasks which are difficult, complex, or unusual, while centralized structures are more effective for those which are simple and routinized.[42]

Conversely, this proposition asserts that, given that the corporate unit is based on centralized control, the most efficient technologies will be those involving routinized, dull, and repetitive tasks. In a decentralized environment, the exact reverse would be true. The common opinion as to the superior productivity of fragmentation, as based on the observed operation of centralized corporate enterprise, is simply a false inference from the facts.

Finally, the opinion that there is no known organizational technique superior to hierarchical control seems also controverted by the extensive evidence of the efficiency of worker participation in decision-making. Thus Vroom notes that even moderate worker participation in decisions and goal-setting increases productivity. He found that the average quality of decisions made by a group is, moreover, greater than the average quality of individual decisions; the best results are obtained when individuals think up solutions individually, then evaluate, and choose among these solutions as a team.[43]

Let us give an example. The MIT-sponsored Scanlon Plan of "participatory management" has been tried in many U.S. plants. This plan gives workers limited power to organize and improve the work process and the working conditions; it guarantees them a share in the proceeds of cost reduction. In one study of ten plants, the average yearly increase in productivity amounted to 23.1 percent,[44] or roughly seven times the national average rate of productivity growth. Clearly, a stable and long-term dialogue among workers, technicians, and planners would even increase this fertile activity.

These results are replicated in many other individual studies: When workers are given control over decisions and goal setting, productivity rises dramatically.[45] The recent study, *Work in America,* records at least a dozen cases of reorganization of production toward greater worker participation which simultaneously raised productivity and worker satisfaction.[46] As Blumberg states:

> There is scarcely a study in the entire literature which fails to demonstrate that satisfaction in work is enhanced or . . . productivity increases accrue from a genuine increase in worker's decision-making power. Findings of such con-

sistency, I submit, are rare in social research. . . . The participative worker is an involved worker, for his job becomes an extension of himself and by his decisions he is creating his work, modifying and regulating it.[47]

But such instances of even moderate worker control are often instituted in marginal areas or in firms fighting for survival. When the crisis is over, there is often a return to "normal operating procedure." The threat of workers escalating their demand for control is simply too great. The usurpation of the prerogatives of hierarchical authority is quickly quashed. Efficiency in the broader sense is subordinated to the needs of bureaucratic control.

Thus no real workers' control of production is really possible as a general phenomenon under capitalism. With the recent escalation of worker discontent, mindful of the efficiency gains of having "contented workers," capitalists have intensified their search for alternatives to economic democracy which might for a time restore harmony and morale in the enterprise. These include work team production, job enlargement and job rotation, worker representation on managerial boards, and the like, while the capitalist maintains rigid control over the organization as a whole. Even here there have been impressive productivity gains at times, though these schemes hardly represent an alternative to economic democracy.

The inefficiency of the hierarchical division of labor is due to its denying workers room for the employment of their creative powers. In a situation where workers lack control over both the process and the product of their productive activities, their major concerns are to not work themselves out of a job and to protect themselves from the arbitrary dictates of management. Their concern for the efficiency of the operation is at best, perfunctory. Efficiency-mindedness is often opposed as contrary to their interests.[48] Thus, the above studies ignore a potential productivity gain from worker control: that gain which arises from greater worker receptivity to technical change and reorganization of the work place when workers control the process and share in the benefits of change. Significantly, many unions oppose current work reorganization schemes—even those allowing token worker participation—because workers have little defense against being displaced by productivity increases and do not stand to share in whatever profit increases may result. Workers normally harbor a tremendous reserve power of effectiveness and inventiveness, awaiting only the proper conditions to be activated.

The burden of proof has shifted markedly to those content that hierarchical forms of production are the necessary price of ever-increasing affluence. Work is for the most part "meaningless" and repressive, not because of the nature of technology and the division of labor, but because of the nature of class relationships.

Why, then, has a democratic organization of work not emerged in the existing socialist countries? If not a proof that technology requires hierarchical authority, does this fact not at least suggest the inevitable tendency for bureaucracies to come to control people's lives in modern society? We believe not. First, numerous plants in China, Cuba, and Chile (during the Allende period) exhibited a substantial degree of worker control of production with positive results.⁴⁹ Second, the state socialist countries of Eastern Europe were never democratic. Rather, the ruling elites have always maintained their power through top-down control of production, a centralized party structure, and the military. It is, therefore, not surprising that they have instituted a hierarchy in the work place characteristic of corporate capitalist production.

THE ECONOMICS OF CONTROL

We have suggested that the imperatives of control better explain the hierarchical division of labor than does the nature of technology. But we must investigate why control is desired, especially if it conflicts in many cases with technical efficiency. Indeed, we must explain what the implications of control maintenance are for the social relations of work and, hence, what types of demands the economic system makes on the educational system as a whole.

In general, work will be structured by employers to achieve two complementary objectives. The first is to reproduce their positions of privilege in the hierarchy of production. A closely related second objective is to secure adequate long-term profits, without which the enterprise would cease to exist. Thus profits are sought as an instrument in maintaining the class position as the directors of the firm and as their source of income.⁵⁰

In the joint pursuit of profits and the perpetuation of their class standing, employers seek three immediate objectives—sometimes complementary and sometimes in conflict. These are: technical efficiency, control, and legitimacy. Technical efficiency dictates that work be organized to maximize output for a given set of inputs—labor, raw materials, and equipment. Control over the production process requires the retention of decision-making power at the top; its maintenance is always problematical. Wherever possible, workers demand control over the decision-making about working conditions toward the improvement of their condition. Organizing production hierarchically and fragmenting tasks divides workers on different levels against one another and reduces the independent range of control for each. Both of these weaken the solidarity (and hence, limit the group power) of workers and serve to convince them, through their day-to-day activities, of their personal incapacity to control, or even of the technical unfeasibility of such control. Enter the principle of "divide and rule".[51]

Further, work must be organized so as to make the authority relationships in the firm appear at best just, or at least inevitable. That is, relationships among superiors, subordinates, and peers must not violate the norms of the larger society. The right of the superior to direct as well as the duty of the subordinate to submit must draw on general cultural values. It is for this reason that a superior must always have a higher salary than a subordinate, whatever the conditions of relative supply of the two types of labor. It is also for this reason that in the United States, with its characteristic patterns of racial and sexual prejudices, blacks and women cannot, in general, be placed above whites or men in the line of hierarchical authority. Also, employers ordinarily structure work roles so that young people will not boss older people. In terms of personal attributes, self-presentation is important: However well they actually function technically, individuals must act, speak, and dress commensurate with their position and must actively protect their prerogatives and relative authority.[52] Educational credentials enter here as well: employers find it desirable to vest hierarchical authority in well-educated workers, not only because higher levels of schooling may enable an employee to better do the work at hand or because the more-educated seem more fit by their demeanor to hold authority, but also simply because educational achievement—as symbolized by one sort of sheepskin or another—legitimates authority according to prevailing social values. We will consider how these criteria for job placement impose limits on educational policy; we will consider them in more detail presently.

The importance of legitimacy cannot be overemphasized in understanding the social relations of corporate enterprises. If one takes for granted the basic economic organization of society, its members need only be equipped with adequate cognitive and operational skills to fulfill work requirements; they need only to be provided with a reward structure to motivate individuals to acquire and supply these skills. U.S. capitalism accomplishes the first of these requirements through the family, school, and on-the-job training and the second through a wage structure patterned after the job hierarchy.

However, the social relations of production cannot be taken for granted. The bedrock of the capitalist economy is the legally sanctioned power of the directors of an enterprise to organize production, to determine the rules that regulate workers' productive activities, and to hire and fire accordingly; all this is done with only moderate restriction imposed by workers' organizations and government regulations. But this power can be exercised forcefully against united opposition only sporadically. Violence alone is not a stable basis for the exercise of power. Rousseau put it better: "The strongest man is never strong enough to be always master, unless he transforms his power into right and obedience into duty."[53] Where the assent of the less-favored cannot be secured by power alone, it must be part of a total process whereby the existing structure of work roles and their allocation among individuals are seen as ethically acceptable or perhaps technically necessary.

In some social systems, the norms that govern the economic system are quite similar to those governing other major social spheres. Thus in feudal society, the authority of the lord of the manor is not essentially different from that of the political monarch, the church hierarchy, or the family patriarch; the ideology of "natural estates" suffuses all social activity. No special normative order is required for the economic system. But in capitalist society, to make the hierarchical division of labor appear just is no easy task; the autocratic organization of the enterprise clashes sharply with the ideals of equality, democracy, and participation that pervade the political and legal spheres. Thus the economic enterprise as a political dictatorship and social caste system requires a rather elaborate defense. The mechanisms used to place individuals in unequal (and unequally rewarding) positions require special justification.

In a fundamental sense, our "model" of the corporate enterprise views the internal social relationships of production as imposed by employers in their own interests and geared toward mediating the inherent conflict between capital and labor. Employer rationality dictates that workers be treated on a par with machines and raw materials—a means toward the end of profits. Worker rationality dictates that activities conform as closely as possible to personal and social goals. Thus profits are contingent on the ability of employers to elicit proper performance from workers in the face of the latter's lack of concern with the objective of profit, and to reduce the total power of workers by limiting and channeling coalitions among them —divide and conquer. The hierarchical division of labor maximizes the control of management, increases the accountability of workers by fragmenting jobs and responsibility, and thwarts the development of stable coalitions among workers.

This last point assumes special importance in the large corporate enterprise. The fragmentation of worker solidarity is accomplished in large part by maximizing the social distance between workers on different levels in the hierarchy of authority and skills. Not only does this reduce the total power of workers vis-à-vis employers, but it insures that superiors feel sufficiently alienated from their underlings that they act only in the interests of the "organization" and according to the dictates of their own superiors. Thus the smooth transmission of orders from the top to the bottom of the hierarchy is enhanced. Maximizing the social distance between hierarchical levels involves hiring directly on the basis of educational credentials, social class, life style (dress, manner of spech, and other social identifications), as well as race, sex, and age.

Indeed, the employer's thrust toward maintaining and increasing the social distance between groups of workers assumes a particularly dynamic dimension when we look at the frequent confrontations between management and labor in the "organized sector." Employers will resist wage demands wherever possible. However, under pressure, so our model tells us, they are likely to accede to those demands of a coalition of workers that (a) do not threaten their security of control, (b) increase the social distance between groups of workers, and (c) do not undermine the legitimacy of the allocation of roles in the organization. Thus it is not surprising that some workers themselves often demand (and are granted) higher wages or privileges which de facto exclude other groups of workers on the basis of educational credentials, racial and sexual characteristics, and artificially maintained skill differences. Such demands are relatively cheap and help to enforce the internal social order of the enterprise because they reinforce the internal stratification and fragmentation of worker solidarity.

In short, power and technology both enter into the employer's criteria of job organization and hiring. Neither can be well understood unless the class basis of the social relations of production are placed front and center.[54] Alienated labor is the result. And, we shall see, so is repressive education.

## The Structure of Economic Inequality

Q: Why does the foreman get more than the laborer?

A: Because the foreman's work is of more value than the laborer's.

Q: There are differences of character as well as of skill between two workmen. Why do capitalists run after men, and will give them very high wages for skill, and a combination of good qualities?

A:  Capitalists give wages to workmen in proportion to their productiveness.

Q:  If there are two boys starting in life, one of the son of a man who has accumulated capital, and the other of a man who has not, shall I be right in saying that the boy without this advantage can never be a capitalist?

A:  No.

Q:  But what is to make him a capitalist?

A:  Saving.

HENRY BARNARD,
*Papers for the Teacher*, 1866

Our analysis of the sources of economic inequality and social immobility closely parallels that of the work process, in that both stem from the property and market institutions of capitalism, from the social relationships of work and from the dynamics of uneven development. We intend to support the assertion that the roots of inequality in the United States are to be found in the class structure and the system of sexual and racial power relationships. The school system is then but one of several institutions which serve to perpetuate this structure of privilege. But education is relatively powerless to correct economic inequality. Indeed, the class, sex, and race biases in schooling do not produce, but rather reflect, the structure of privilege in society at large. The prima facie case for using education as an instrument for economic equalization is thus weak. If, as we argue here, inequality has its origins in the structure of the capitalist economy, educational reform will be a powerful force for equalization only to the extent that it can alter those aspects of the economic system which provide the institutional bases of inequality. Indeed, we believe that educational reform can become an integral part of an assault on privilege. But we are moving ahead of our story. We will return to these issues in our concluding chapters.

In the immediate post-World-War-II period, U.S. social scientists exhibited an optimism that, in the context of a rapidly advancing economy, inequality would wither away to politically manageable if not ethically justifiable levels. Arthur Burns celebrated what he detected as ". . . democratization of the distribution process . . ." as ". . . one of the greatest social revolutions of history."[55] But by the early 1960s, it was painfully evident that the heralded natural trend toward equality had not fared well. Despite vigorous growth, a vast expansion of education, and the extension of the "progressive" income tax, Social Security, and other welfare programs, inequality in income has remained essentially unchanged. This relative constancy is documented in Figure 3–1. It shows the percentage of total family income accruing to each fifth in the income distribution in 1910, 1947, and 1972.

FIGURE 3–1.
*Income Inequality in the United States
Has Been Constant Since 1910*

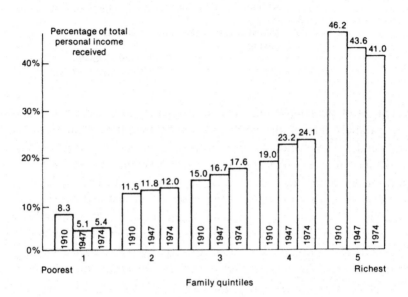

NOTE: Each bar shows the percentage of income received by the indicated quintile in the years 1910, 1947, and 1972. SOURCE: Gabriel Kolko, *Wealth and Power in America* (New York: Praeger, 1962), p. 48, Table IV; council of Economic Advisors, *Economic Report of the President* (Washington, D.C.: U.S. Government Printing Office, 1971), p. 149, Table 38; U.S. Bureau of the Census, *Statistical Abstracts of the U.S.*, Washington, 1974.

Moreover, the introduction of inheritance taxes has done little to alter the distribution of wealth: The wealthiest 1 percent of Americans holds about one-fifth of all wealth, and about one half of all corporate stock.[56] The remaining one-half of corporate stock is owned almost entirely by the wealthiest fifth of the population.[57] The top fifth also accounts for nearly all personal savings in the economy, and hence, tends to maintain its position of wealth from generation to generation.[58] The degree of wealth inequality has remained unchanged since World War II.[59]

Viewing this panorama of persistent inequality, the liberal community of the 1960s grew to emphasize ever more heavily the age-old distinction between inequality of economic opportunity and inequality of economic outcomes. According to this perspective, inequality of economic outcomes (income, status, or job desirability) is necessitated by the very structure of

*86*

industrial society. Its harshest effects can be no more than ameliorated through enlightened social policy. Thus John Gardner, then President of the Carnegie Corporation and later to become Secretary of the U.S. Department of Health, Education and Welfare, could confidently state:

> Most human societies have been beautifully organized to keep good men down. . . . Birth determined occupation and status. . . . Such societies were doomed by the Industrial Revolution. . . . [But] when a society gives up hereditary stratification . . . dramatic differences in ability and performance . . . emerge . . . and may lead to peaks and valleys of status as dramatic as those produced by hereditary stratification.[60]

Progressive social policy, according to this perspective, must recognize the sober necessity of limiting aspirations as to equality of outcomes, while setting its sights on providing all with a fair shot at unequal economic reward. Social equity can then be assessed by the extent to which discrimination based on social background, religion, sex, or race have been eliminated. In this liberal perspective, the capitalist economy, though marred by substantial inequalities of income, can become the true meritocracy when finally shorn of anachronistic prejudices.

Gardner's view reflects two important strands in contemporary liberal social theory, one from economics and the other from sociology. Economists have argued that competition among profit-seeking employers will insure that the best workers are hired regardless of sex, race, or other distinctions of birth. Employers who persist in discriminating will overlook talented prospective employees and adopt an irrational job structure. As a result they will make less profits, expand more slowly than more "enlightened" employers, and eventually go out of business entirely. Milton Friedman's statement of the argument is exemplary:

> The purchaser of bread does not know whether it was made from wheat grown by a white man or a negro, by a Christian or a Jew. In consequence, the producer of wheat is in a position to use resources as effectively as he can, regardless of what the attitudes of the community may be toward the color, the religion, or the other characteristics of the people he hires. Furthermore . . . a businessman or an entrepreneur who expresses preferences in his business activities that are not related to productive efficiency is in effect imposing higher costs on himself than are other individuals who do not have such preferences. Hence, in a free market they will tend to drive him out.[61]

From sociology, Gardner borrowed the ideas of Talcott Parsons, the dean of liberal sociology. He saw the advance of the modern capitalist economy as a trend away from "particularistic" mechanisms for the determination of status and economic success; it is a trend toward the application of more "universalistic" criteria. The result, wrote Parsons, would be the demise of "ascribed status" in favor of "achieved status."[62] Thus, in the eyes of the dominant schools of contemporary U.S. sociology and economics, the "performance orientation" and "organizational rationality" of employers, the impersonality of the labor markets and the "structural differentiation of the economic sub-system" all conspire to eliminate discrimination based on sex, race, and family background.

Yet the facts concerning inequality of economic opportunity do not support this theory. Women's suffrage and a more liberal attitude toward the "woman's place" in the home and on the job has not enhanced the economic situation of women relative to men. The slackening of racial prejudice—attested to in numerous recent surveys—and the dramatic educational gains made by blacks have resulted in little occupational or income gains for blacks relative to whites.[63] Finally, the considerable expansion of education over the years has not increased social mobility. There is no evidence of a lessening of the economic importance of family background on life chances. And family background is important indeed: our data indicate that individuals whose parents were in the top socioeconomic decile earn, on the average, well over twice as much as those from families in the bottom decile.[64]

A fundamental error in the liberal theory of a trend toward equality of economic opportunity, we believe, is the notion that inequality of income and inequality of economic opportunity are fundamentally distinct and analytically separate phenomena. Our approach is to explain both forms of inequality as inseparable manifestations of the underlying structure of economic life. Specifically, we offer evidence that both forms of inequality are directly related to the market and property relationships which define the capitalist system, to the social relationships of work, and to the tendency toward uneven development.

Market and property relationships establish the legal, economic, and political context in which the income distribution process works. The uneven development of the capitalist economy generates not merely "pockets of poverty" but extensive income disparities between the corporate and state sector of the economy on the one hand, and the competitive and household sectors on the other. The political and economic power of the owners and managers of the corporate and state sectors results in the appropriation of the gains of technological advance and new investment opportunities by a small and privileged group. Workers in the state and corporate sector benefit, too, from their protected position. But their bargaining strength is seriously weakened by potential competition or replacement by underpaid and underemployed workers in other sectors of the economy. The segmentation of the labor force weakens the power of labor as a whole and acts as an immediate cause of much of the inequality between men and women, between blacks and whites, between the rural and urban born, and so on.

Inequality is also affected by the social relations of work, the principles which govern the allocation of jobs, authority structures, and wage differentials within the enterprise. Income inequalities based on such characteristics as educational credentials, sex, age, and race are a reflection not only of uneven development, but also the internal power relations of the capitalist enterprise. Differences in the social relationships of work also account for the economic inequality which exists between the unpaid household worker and the "employed" worker. The division of tasks and economic rewards within the household is a reflection of the sexual division of labor and is influenced by the power relationships between men and women, between adults and children. The roots of adult male supremacy in the household are to be found, we believe, in part, in customary sex roles supported by tradition and reinforced by legal discrimination and, in part, by the greater financial independence of adult males stemming from the segmented structure of the labor force in the capitalist economy. Inequality within the household goes beyond the inequality recorded in Figure 3–1 and is a pervasive and central aspect of capitalist (and most other) economies.

### THE INSTITUTIONAL BASIS OF INEQUALITY

In the remainder of this chapter, our goal is to illuminate the basic economic structures and processes framework within which inequality is generated. We have chosen to stress the fundamental institutional basis of inequality because we believe that it is here that we are to locate the limits of egalitarian reform. Thus we make no attempt to present comprehensive or detailed theory or description of the income distribution process. We seek only to support our earlier assertion that the roots of unequal incomes and inequality of opportunity alike lie not in human nature, not in technology, not in the educational system itself, but in the dynamics of economic life.

The proposition that important sources of inequality are to be found in structural aspects of the economic system finds strong—but only prima facie—support in an international comparison of capitalist and socialist countries.[65] Using data from sixty-seven countries—sixty-two capitalist and five socialist—Cromwell found that the four most equal income distributions are in socialist countries. The most unequal socialist country in his sample, Yugoslavia, ranked eleventh. Overall, Cromwell found that the income inequality (as measured by the Gini coefficient) was, on the average, 40 percent less in socialist countries than in the sample as a whole.

To understand the relationship between market and property institutions and inequality in the United States, we must begin with a rather down-to-earth question: What are the empirical dimension of the income distribution? Income is the sum of wages or salaries, rent, interest, dividends, profits, and capital gains. (We abstract from gifts, pension payments, and government transfers.) We will call wages and salaries labor income; we will call interest, rent, dividends, and profits property income. For individuals with incomes less than $10,000 in 1971, labor income represented over 90 percent of the total income. For those in the $50,000 to $100,000 bracket, labor and property income were about equally important components of the total income; capital gains were relatively unimportant, constituting less than one-tenth of the total income. For the wealthiest individuals (those with incomes over $1,000,000), property income and capital gains (increases in the value of one's assets) accounted about equally for the total income; income from labor accounts for less than 5 percent of their income.[66]

Overall inequality of income is the sum of inequalities in labor income, inequalities in property incomes, and inequalities in capital gains, plus a substantial additional amount of inequality which arises because the very same people who receive large property incomes are also likely to earn substantial labor incomes and reap large capital gains. Grouping capital gains and income from property together, we may investigate the contribution of three distinct sources of inequality to the overall degree of inequality. The results are quite striking. Although roughly three-fourths of total income is received in the form of wages and salaries, inequalities in labor income account for less than half of the total inequality. A little less than one quarter of the overall inequality is attributed directly to inequalities in property income; slightly more than one quarter is attributed to the fact that the large property and capital gains income-recipients also tend to receive handsome salaries. If capital gains which have accrued to individuals but not yet realized through the sale of property (so-called unrealized capital gains) are included in this definition of income, the direct contribution of capital to income inequality rises to more than half.[67] Consideration of government transfers has little effect on these results.

Inequalities in income from property can be statistically accounted for by two facts. First, as we have already noted, property is very unequally owned. Second, the returns to capital (rent, interest, dividends, and profits as well as capital gains) are also unequal: the large owners in general receiving a higher return on each dollar of property owned. The contribution of property income to overall income inequality follows directly from the basic market and property institutions of capitalism—the private ownership of property. Uneven development is important here, too. The fact that big capitalists receive a higher return on their property may be accounted for, in large measure, by the concentration of capital in the dynamic and less competitive corporate sectors of the economy. Small property owners are much more likely to hold assets in small enterprises in highly competitive and relatively stagnant sectors, as well as in residential property.

But something like half of income inequality is due to the differences in labor incomes. How are those to be explained? They derive largely from the class structure and the structure of racial and sexual privilege. In a more proximate sense, differences in wages or salaries are associated with differing personal characteristics of workers and differing institutional, geographical, and sectional situations facing them. To illustrate these relationships, we draw on a study by Barry Bluestone on the determinants of hourly earnings.[68] Using data from the U.S. Government's Survey of Economic Opportunity and employing the technique of multiple linear regression analysis, Bluestone isolated a number of critical institutional and other variables which affect individual labor earnings. We present his results in the following way: First, we "construct" two hypothetical individuals: one is a white, experienced, male union member working in the primary segment of the labor market; the other hypothetical worker is a black female worker employed in the secondary segment. Using Bluestone's results, we predict the expected hourly earnings of these two workers.

The results indicate an expected hourly wage of the white male at about 3.1 times that of the black female. Of the hourly wage gap, 36 percent is due to sexual differences, 17 percent to race differences, and 22 percent to differences reflecting the primary/secondary labor market segmentation. These last relate to union membership and the profitability, capital intensity, monopolization, and degree of minority employment in the industry and occupation compared. The effects of differences in education and job experience between the two account for the remaining 25 percent of the wage gap.[69] These figures certainly support our contention that education and skill-related variables must be supplemented by class, sex, and race characteristics plus the aspects of uneven development in order to understand inequality in labor incomes.

Differences in conditions faced by workers in the primary and secondary segments of the labor force are not confined to inequalities in hourly earnings. Unemployment rates differ greatly as well. The high and fluctuating unemployment rates for workers in the secondary labor force allows the general level of business activity to move in its characteristic cycles without spreading serious unemployment to the more politically powerful and predominantly white male workers in the primary sector.

In fact, employment conditions are far more important than is schooling and experience as a determinant of annual earnings for female and black workers. For these workers, schooling and experience have little or no impact on annual income apart from their increasing the probability of being employed the year round. For white males facing less uncertain unemployment conditions and having access to job ladders and significant promotion possibilities, years of schooling and job experience play a much greater role in the determination of income.[70]

### INEQUALITY AND THE SOCIAL RELATIONS OF WORK

This survey of the income distribution process in the U.S. testifies to the importance of private property in the means of production and uneven development in the economy and labor force. The data also hint at the importance of our third characteristic of the capitalist economy: the social relations of the work process. However, the importance and complexity of this third basis of inequality in capitalist society warrants a more searching analysis.

How can the social relations of work affect inequality of incomes and inequality of economic opportunity? This is affected clearly by influencing the relative earnings of various jobs, the relative proportions of job categories, and the chances of individuals passing from one to the other. For example, if all individuals participated equally in communal enterprises and divided the proceeds equally, then no inequality would be due to the internal organization; all inequality would reflect differences in revenues among enterprises. As another example, we may consider an idealized guild economy. Each enterprise has a number of masters, a larger number of journeymen below them, and a larger number of apprentices below them. If each worker begins as an apprentice and progresses to the level of master, then guild organization would imply income inequality according to age; the degree of inequality depends on the wage differentials and the numerical proportions among the three age-related categories of workers. But incomes would be equalized over the lifetime of the workers.

In the United States, however, the social relations of work in the dominant private and state sectors is neither the communal nor the guild, but rather the hierarchical division of labor. With each level in the vertically ascending hierarchy of authority, there is associated a basic wage or salary. An individual enters the firm at a particular level in the hierarchy based on education, previous experience, social class, sex, race, age, and so forth— depending on the entrance criteria of employers. From there, the individual is faced with a job ladder of limited vertical length through which he or she is promoted. These job ladders are normally fairly short and mutually exclusive.[71] Thus entry to the job market as an unskilled worker reduces the chances of becoming a skilled worker; entry as a blue-collar worker reduces the chances of becoming a white-collar worker, and so on. Also the chances of moving up the job ladder are, beyond a certain point, quite limited. Thus only a few assembly line workers ever become supervisors; only a few steno-pool typists ever become personal secretaries; and so on. The worker's wage or salary depends on the particular job ladder, the rung on that ladder currently occupied, and the length of service.

Inequality is built into the hierarchical division of labor in several ways. First of all, positions of differential authority, prestige, and responsibility are endowed with commensurate differences in earnings. This is, in part, due to the operation of the labor market: In an economy of alienated work, the major inducement to the attainment of credentials and ability to exercise responsibility is pay. In part, wage differences in the enterprise flow from the employer's need to legitimate the authority structure and reduce worker solidarity by creating and maintaining different conditions of work and styles of life for different groups of workers.

Second, inequality is affected by the nature of job ladders and promotion. The pyramidal nature of the enterprise severely limits the chance of promotion, and the usual policy of segregating skilled and unskilled, blue- and white-collar and technical workers, and minimizing the opportunity of workers to obtain new skills keeps the job ladders relatively short. Moreover, the usual policy of rarely placing blacks over whites, women over men, or workers of lower "social class appearance and demeanor" over workers higher on these attributes, leads to important intergroup and intergenerational inequalities.

This last observation illustrates well that the bases of income inequality within the enterprise are not exhibited solely in the hierarchical structure of jobs and related-income differences; they are evidenced as much in the process by which people are selected for the available job slots. What individual attributes are entrance keys to the various levels in the hierarchy of the enterprise, and how do they relate to the class, sexual, racial, and other characteristics of the labor force? To answer this question, we develop our analysis of the social relationships of the enterprise at some length. For in addition to completing our treatment of income inequality, this analysis provides insight into the origins and economic meaning of the class-related differences in culture, consciousness, and social behavior which are so clearly part of the stratification process. We will use our model of the interaction of consciousness and the social relationships of production in this chapter to demonstrate the intimate relationship between inequality of income and inequality of opportunity. The same model will be the basis, in Chapters 4 and 5, of our understanding of the economic meaning of education.

One can think offhand of a host of individual attributes conceivably serving as occupational "entrance requirements." They include (at least) such features as ownership of physical implements (e.g., the medieval knight owned his horse, armor, and weapons), membership (e.g., the feudal guild master), traits acquired at birth (e.g., the houseworker is ordinarily female), and traits acquired through personal development (e.g., skills, motivation, attitudes, personality, credentials). In U.S. society, it is the last of these along with a few important ascriptive traits—sex, race, and age—that come to the fore. Thus we must focus on the supply and demand of those personal attributes and ascriptive traits that are relevant to getting ahead in the world of work.

While employers have certain restrictions on their hiring practices—child-labor and antidiscrimination laws, union regulations, social pressures for example—by and large, they employ those who can be expected to perform adequately in the work role in question. But what constitutes adequate performance in any job, of course, depends on the objectives of management. We have argued that the overriding objective of employers in organizing production and assigning workers to occupational slots is the perpetutation or enhancement of their class standing. The necessary condition for this is the profitability of the enterprise. Profitability, in turn, is sought through the complementary, but far from identical, strategies of efficiency and control.

This suggests several important types of worker characteristics which are demanded by employers. There are cognitive capacities (such as scholastic achievement) and concrete technical and operational skills (such as knowing how to do typing, accounting, chemical engineering, or carpentry). Second, there are personality traits (such as motivation, perseverance, docility) that enable the individual to operate effectively in a work role. Indeed, it is precisely these attributes that we will isolate as central to the educational process in Chapter 5. Third, there are traits that we have called modes of self-presentation (such as manner of speech and dress, patterns of peer identification, perceived "social distance" from individuals and groups of different social position). These traits do not necessarily contribute to the worker's execution of tasks, but may be valuable to employers in their effort to stabilize and legitimize the particular structure of power in the organization as a whole. Similar in function are our fourth set of traits: ascriptive characteristics such as race, sex, and age. Finally, we add to our list of attributes credentials, such as level and prestige of education. Credentials, like modes of self-presentation and ascriptive traits, are a resource used by employers to add to the overall legitimacy of the organization. All of these above-listed traits are the indices of adequate job performance, and we discuss each in turn.

The proper types of cognitive, physical, and operational skills are the most evident and widely discussed prerequisites to successful performance on the job. Their attainment represents a central function of the educational system. Discrepancies between skill "levels" and job "levels" are extremely dangerous to the operation of the hierarchical division of labor. Inadequate skills prohibit production from taking place; worker skills which exceed their level of status and authority threaten the legitimacy of the social division of labor within the enterprise. Thus the patterns of access to and denial of skill training in the firm are important parts of the reproduction of economic inequality. Yet there is little indication that inequality in such skills is an important cause of inequality. Indeed, in Chapter 4 we shall see that differences in measured mental abilities explain only a small portion of economic inequality. We demonstrate statistically that such differences explain neither the association of education with economic success nor the tendency for economic status to be passed on from generation to generation. Hence the association of cognitive achievement and access to higher level occupations must be largely a by-product of selection on the basis of other traits.

The personality traits and forms of consciousness required of workers are those which facilitate their harmonious integration into the hierarchical order of the enterprise. In the dominant corporate and state sectors, this order exhibits four essential characteristics.[72] First, the duties, responsibilities, and privileges of individuals are determined neither according to individual preference nor cooperative decision by workers, but rather by a system of formal and informal rules which guide the individual worker's participation in the work process and set limits on his or her actions. Second, the relationships among workers are characterized by hierarchical authority and interdependence. An individual's actions are closely tied to the wills of his or her superiors, and the results of these actions have repercussions on large numbers of other workers. Third, while control emanates ultimately from the top, the principle of hierarchical authority implies that middle-level workers have essential, though circumscribed, areas of decision and choice. Fourth, that jobs are determined on the basis not of workers' needs or interests, but rather in the interests of profitability implies that workers cannot be adequately motivated by the intrinsic rewards of the work process.

These characteristics of the hierarchical division of labor influence the personality traits required of workers. In Chapter 5, we will present a rather extensive empirical study of the personality traits of the "good worker." We are content here with a general survey. All workers must be dependable (i.e., follow orders) because of the strong emphasis on rules and the complex interrelations among tasks that define the enterprise. Similarly, all workers must be properly subordinate to authority (i.e., diligent in carrying out order as opposed to merely obeying orders). Furthermore, all workers, insofar as they have areas of personal initiative, must, to some extent, internalize the values of the organization. Lastly, all workers must respond to the external incentives of the organization—the crudest being threat of dismissal and the more subtle including the possibility of promotion to a higher status, authority, and pay.

While respect for rules, dependability, and internalization of norms are required to some extent by all workers, there are important qualitative differences between levels. These tend to follow directly from differences in the scope of independent decision-making which increases with hierarchical status. Thus the lowest level of worker must simply refrain from breaking rules. On the highest level, the worker must internalize the values of the organization, act out of personal initiative, and know when not to go by the book. In between, workers must be methodical, predictable, and persevering; at a somewhat higher level, they must respond flexibly to superiors whose directives acquire a complexity transcending the relatively few rules that apply directly to their tasks. As we move up in the hierarchy, the crucial determinants of job adequacy pass from rule-following to dependability-predictability to subordinateness to internalized values, all with an overlap of motivation according to external incentives and penalties. (Doubtless penalties play a larger role in the lower levels and incentives at the higher ones.)

It follows that the hierarchical division of labor affects inequality not only through wage differentials, but also through the divergent patterns of consciousness and motivation to which it gives rise. These patterns, as we will point out, tend to be transmitted through the family and impose severe limits on the functioning of the educational system.

We turn now to the importance of self-presentation as attributes relevant to the allocation of individuals to status positions. Numerous studies have shown these personal attributes to be definite (albeit often covert) criteria for hiring and promotion.[73] Three statistical studies seem germane. First, Hamilton and Roesner found that among employers of disadvantaged workers, personal appearance was between three and two times as important a selection criterion as any of the following: work experience, specific job training, high-school diploma, or test scores.[74] Second, Leland P. Deck, Director of Labor Relations at the University of Pittsburgh, found that among ". . . 1967 graduates of the University of Pittsburgh the height of the individual worker was more important as a determinant of earnings than either grade point average or *cum laude* degree."[75] Lastly, a recent survey of the salaries of 15,000 executives found that those who were "overweight" were paid significantly less than others, the penalty to the obese being in some cases as much as $1,000 a pound![76]

However, because most of the relevant studies are descriptive rather than statistical, they defy comparison with other data on personal attributes as to importance in the stratification process. We must content ourselves with a simple presentation of the arguments. Erving Goffman has documented the importance of self-presentation in a number of cases: doctors, nurses, waitresses, dentists, military personnel, mental patients, funeral directors, eighteenth-century noblemen, Indian castes, Chinese mandarins, junk peddlers, unionized workers, teachers, pharmacists, as well as in the relationships between men and women and blacks and whites.[77]

Central to Goffman's analysis of self-presentation is his concept of the "front" of a performance, defined as ". . . that part of the individual's performance which regularly functions in a general and fixed fashion to define the situation for those who view the performance." This front consists of personal behavior and characteristics (insignia of office or rank; clothing, sex, age, and racial characteristics; size and looks; posture; speech patterns; facial expressions; bodily gestures and the like) as well as physical setting (e.g., size, location, and amount of carpeting and/or windows in one's office). Moreover, argues Goffman, these fronts are not merely personal and idiosyncratic, but are socially regularized and channeled. Thus, on the one hand, modes of self-presentation take on a social class character, and on the other, physical settings are assigned not to individuals but to authority levels.

We may now consider the importance of our last two sets of employability traits: ascriptive characteristics (race, sex, and age) and acquired credentials (educational degrees and seniority). We have argued that the legitimacy as well as the smooth control over the work process requires that the authority structure of the enterprise respect the wider society's prejudices. In particular, socially acceptable power relationships must be respected. A recent national survey revealed, for example, that while few women become supervisors, almost all who do so supervise other women workers: Women workers are seventeen times more likely than male workers to have female supervisors.[78] In this, the economic system reinforces racial, sexual, and other distinctions of birth.

We make no claim that these distinctions originated as a capitalist contrivance, although a strong case could probably be made that the form and strength of both sexism and racism here are closely related to the particular historical development of class relations in the United States and Europe. Save credentialist distinctions, all predate the modern capitalist era. "Rational business practice" has reinforced and extended them, while consigning less useful prejudices to gradual extinction. The credentialist mentality, we believe, was, at least in part, contrived to perpetuate the concept of social rank in a society increasingly eschewing distinctions of birth. We will return to this point in future chapters.

The individual employer, acting singly, normally accepts social values and beliefs and will violate them only in the interest of long-term financial benefits. The broader prejudices of society are thus used as a resource by employers in their effort to control labor. In this way, the pursuit of profits and security of class position reinforces racist, sexist, and credentialist forms of status consciousness.

The importance of sex, age, race, and educational credentials in the determination of one's income is thus not an expression of irrational and uninformed employment policies, subject to correction by "enlightened" employment practices and social legislation. Less still are those distinctions likely to be eliminated by the competition for "good" workers among profit maximizing capitalists, as traditional economic theory would predict. Quite the opposite. The policy of basing pay on race, sex, credentials, and seniority is used by employers to control workers in the pursuit of profits.

Ideally, we could assess the importance of the social relationships of work in the income distribution process by conducting in depth surveys of the internal wage and authority structures of a large representative sample of firms. Not surprisingly, these studies are few and far between, so we are forced to rely on survey data. Fortunately, the last decade has produced a number of large representative samples of income recipients. We will rely particularly on the data provided by the University of Michigan's Panel Study of Income Dynamics, produced under contract with the U.S. Department of Health, Education and Welfare and the Survey of Economic Opportunity conducted by the U.S. Office of Economic Opportunity.[79]

These data, aside from lending support to the view outlined in the previous sections, tell a distressing story. Two of the most important avenues for getting ahead economically—education and job experience—work most effectively for the already economically advantaged, particularly white males. For most females, blacks, and white males of poorer family backgrounds, these avenues turn out to be rather short, dead-end streets.

While seniority and educational credentials are thought to be generally rewarded in the labor market, statistical evidence indicates that this is only partly the case. The acquisition of a college degree or a few gray hairs does indeed yield a substantial monetary return for white males. This economic payoff to aging and schooling is, of course, a complex phenomenon which involves the learning of productive skills in school and on the job. But far more important, we believe, is the symbolic value of seniority and educational credentials in allowing a person to be promoted to a position of authority over other workers. If we are correct, we should find that seniority and education have much less impact on earnings among those who for reasons of sex or race are excluded from consideration for positions of authority. Bluestone's data on the determinants of hourly earnings indicate that this is precisely the case: The economic return to schooling is twice as high for white males as for blacks or females. Moreover, Bluestone's results merely reiterate a finding consistently generated in studies of this type.[80]

Additional evidence for our view is found in the sample collected by the Institute of Social Research at the University of Michigan. These data support three conclusions. First, if individuals are classified according to their hierarchical position (using their responses to direct questions concerning their authority in the work place), the return to schooling among those classified as "managers" is substantially higher than among those classified as "workers." Those excluded from authority in the work place evidently benefit little from additional schooling. Second, among those classed as workers, the economic return to schooling is virtually the same for men and women, blacks and whites. Thus the differences in the monetary returns to schooling found in the Bluestone study likely reflect little more than differing access to positions of authority in the enterprise. Third, the economic return to schooling depends upon class origins as well as present class status. Preliminary results of Lee Rainwater's analysis[81] of the Institute of Social Research sample indicate that whites of high social class background enjoy economic returns to education that are 66 percent higher than those for either whites of low social class background or blacks.[82]

Turning to the economic payoff to aging and experience, a similar pattern emerges. Data from the U.S. government's Survey of Economic Opportunity clearly indicate race and sex differences in the economic effect of age: White males are more likely to earn higher incomes as they grow older than are blacks and females.[83] Data presented by the President's Council of Economic Advisors reveal that even among white males, it is predominantly the more educated who reap the gains from aging.[84] Finally, detailed evidence of the payoff to experience for white males indicates that only those in occupational categories involving the possibility of exercising significant control over other workers do white male workers reap any economic payoff to experience.[85]

Some economists have attempted to explain these data by differential learning on the job.[86] According to this view, income rises with age because productive skills are learned on the job, not because aging allows one access to positions of power or privilege. We do not doubt the importance of skills learned on the job. However, we are skeptical that on-the-job learning explains the relationship between age and income. Were this the case, we would expect that among workers of the same length of experience in a particular job differences in age would not be associated with differences in income. The data from the Institute for Social Research Survey show this to be decidedly not so. Age significantly affects income independently of job tenure. Indeed, the monetary returns to age are five times the returns to job tenure in this particular survey.[87]

To some extent, of course, these data on the economic return to aging and schooling reflect the segmentation of labor, the returns to education and age being significant only in the primary segment of the labor force. Yet, we find in the evidence striking support as well for our view of the role of the social relations of work in the process, whereby the pay of whites and blacks, of males and females is determined.

## Conclusion

> Men make their own history, but they do not make it just as they please; they do not make it under circumstances chosen by themselves, but under circumstances directly encountered, given and transmitted from the past.
>
> KARL MARX
> *Eighteenth Brumaire*

In 1913, John Dewey, doubtless the most penetrating of American educational philosophers, offered a most incisive observation. Education can foster personal development and economic equality while, at the same time, integrating youth into adult society only under one condition: a thorough extension of democracy to all parts of the social order.[88] For personal development consists in the acquisition of the full range of powers —physical, emotional, cognitive, spiritual, and aesthetic—to control one's life. Economic justice is built on a society of individuals capable of interpersonal relationships on the basis of equality and reciprocity.

Dewey's ideal society can only occur, we now see, when economic life itself is democraticized—when all relationships of power and authority are based on participation and democratic consent. But the social relations of economic life in the United States are by no means democratic and egalitarian. Starting from this fact, we have argued that alienated labor and income inequality are rooted in the social relations of the capitalist economy. These relations are embodied in the structure of property and market relations in the systems of control within the capitalist enterprise and in the dynamic of uneven development.

This analysis suggests, then, that the failure of liberal educational reform must be linked to fundamental characteristics of the economy. Also, that an adequate execution of the educational system's goal of integrating youth into adult society will conflict with its role in promoting equality and full human development. In the following chapters, we suggest that the basic outlines of the U.S. educational system and the conflicts which periodically shake its foundations and reroute its development are best understood through an analysis of the contradictory forces operating on the system. The struggle between working people and capital in the economy has its counterpart in educational conflict. On the one hand, employers and other social elites have sought to use the schools for the legitimation of inequality through an ostensibly meritocratic and rational mechanism for allocating individuals to economic positions; they have sought to use the schools for the reproduction of profitable types of worker consciousness and behavior through a correspondence between the social relationships of education and those of economic life. On the other hand, parents, students, worker organizations, blacks, ethnic minorities, women, and others have sought to use schools for their own objectives: material security, culture, a more just distribution of economic reward, and a path of personal development conducive not to profits but to a fuller, happier life.

# CHAPTER 4

•

# Education, Inequality, and the Meritocracy

It is the business of the school to help the child to acquire such an attitude toward the inequalities of life, whether in accomplishment or in reward, that he may adjust himself to its conditions with the least possible friction.

FRANK FREEMAN,
"Sorting the Students,"
*Education Review*, 1924

The humanity of a nation, it is said, can be gauged by the character of its prisons. No less can its humanity be inferred from the quality of its educational processes. In the initiation of youth, a society reveals its highest aspirations, tempered less by the weight of tradition than by the limits to which the social relationships of adult life can be pushed. We believe that in the contemporary United States, these limits are sufficiently narrow to preclude the educational system from simultaneously integrating youth into adult society and contributing significantly to economic equality. In promoting what John Dewey once called the "social continuity of life," by integrating new generations into the social order, the schools are constrained to justify and reproduce inequality rather than correct it.

The relative powerlessness of the educational system to promote equality is to be expected in light of the considerations of the previous chapter. The pattern of economic inequality is predominantly "set" in the economy itself—via market and property institutions which dictate wide inequalities in income from property, in the basic social relations of corporate enterprises, and in the tendency toward uneven development, which leads to regional, sectional, racial, sexual, and ethnic disparities. But the "legitimation hypothesis" which we hope to substantiate in this chapter goes considerably beyond this level of analysis. For it suggests that a major element in the integrative function of education is the legitimation of preexisting economic disparities. Thus efforts to realize egalitarian objectives are not simply weak; they are also, as we shall demonstrate, in substantial conflict with the integrative function of education.

The educational system legitimates economic inequality by providing an open, objective, and ostensibly meritocratic mechanism for assigning individuals to unequal economic positions. The educational system fosters and reinforces the belief that economic success depends essentially on the possession of technical and cognitive skills—skills which it is organized to provide in an efficient, equitable, and unbiased manner on the basis of meritocratic principle.

Of course the use of the educational system to legitimize inequality is not without its own problems. Ideologies and structures which serve to hide and preserve one form of injustice often provide the basis of an assault on another. The ideology of equal educational opportunity and meritocracy is precisely such a contradictory mechanism.

We shall argue that beneath the façade of meritocracy lies the reality of an educational system geared toward the reproduction of economic relations only partially explicable in terms of technical requirements and efficiency standards. Thus we shall first suggest that educational tracking based on competitive grading and objective test scores is only tangentially related to social efficiency. Then we shall confront the technocratic-meritocratic ideology headon by showing that the association between length of education and economic success cannot be accounted for in terms of the cognitive achievements of students. Thus the yardstick of the educational meritocracy—test scores—contribute surprisingly little to individual economic success. The educational meritocracy is largely symbolic.

Clearly, though, this symbolism is deeply etched in the American consciousness. Nothing exhibits this more clearly than the recent "IQ debate," where it has been generally assumed that IQ and other measures of cognitive performance are important indicators of economic success. Only the genetic or environmental determinants of IQ have been questioned. Yet we will argue that social class or racial differences in IQ are nearly irrelevant to the process of intergenerational status transmission.

## The Legitimation of Inequality

> . . . the fact is, [a] workman may have a ten year intelligence while you have a twenty. To demand of him such a home as you enjoy is as absurd as to insist that every laborer should receive a graduate fellowship. How can there be such a thing as social equality with this wide range of mental capacity?
>
> HENRY GODDARD, Lecture at Princeton, 1919

Throughout history, patterns of privilege have been justified by elaborate facades. Dominant classes seeking a stable social order have consistently nurtured and underwritten these ideological facades and, insofar as their power permitted, blocked the emergence of alternatives. This is what we mean by "legitimation": the fostering of a generalized consciousness among individuals which prevents the formation of the social bonds and critical understanding whereby existing social conditions might be transformed. Legitimation may be based on feelings of inevitability ("death and taxes") or moral desirability ("everyone gets what they deserve"). When the issue is that of social justice, these feelings are both present, with a dose of "custom" and "resignation" as well.

In U.S. economic life, legitimation has been intimately bound up with the technocratic-meritocratic ideology which we discussed in Chapter 2. Several related aspects of the social relations of production are legitimized, in part, by the meritocratic ideology. To begin with, there are the overall characteristics of work in advanced U.S. capitalism: bureaucratic organization, hierarchical lines of authority, job fragmentation, and unequal pay. It is essential that the individual accept and, indeed, come to see as natural, these undemocratic and unequal aspects of the workaday world. Moreover, the staffing of these positions must appear egalitarian in process and just in outcome, parallel to the formal principle of "equality of all before the law" in a liberal democracy.

This legitimation of capitalism as a social system has its counterpart in the individual's personal life. Thus, just as individuals must come to accept the overall social relations of production, so workers must respect the authority and competence of their own "supervisors" to direct their activities, and justify their own authority (however extensive or minimal) over others. That workers be resigned to their position in production is perhaps sufficient; that they be reconciled to their fate is even preferable.

The hallmark of the meritocratic perspective is its reduction of a complex web of social relationships in production to a few rules of technological efficiency. In this view, the hierarchical division of labor arises from its natural superiority as a device to coordinate collective activity and nurture expertise. To motivate the most able individuals to undertake the necessary training and preparation for occupation roles, salaries, and status must be clearly associated with level in the work hierarchy. Thus Davis and Moore, in their highly influential "functional theory of stratification," locate the "determinants of differential reward" in "differential functional importance" and "differential scarcity of personnel." "Social inequality," they conclude, "is thus an unconsciously evolved device by which societies insure that the most important positions are conscientiously filled by the most qualified persons."[1]

This meritocratic ideology has remained a dominant theme of the mainstream of social science since the rise of the factory system in the United States.[2] The robustness of this perspective (even those who reject it have nagging doubts) is due, in no small part, to its incorporation in major social institutions—factories, offices, government bureaus, and schools. For the technocratic justification of the hierarchical division of labor leads smoothly to a meritocratic view of the process whereby individuals are matched to jobs. An efficient and impersonal bureaucracy, so the story goes, assesses the individual purely in terms of his or her expected contribution to production. And the main determinants of job fitness are seen to be those cognitive and psychomotor capacities relevant to the worker's technical ability to do the job. The technocratic view of production, together with the meritocratic view of hiring, provides the strongest form of legitimation of alienated work and social stratification in capitalist society. Not only does it strongly reinforce the notion that the hierarchical division of labor is technically necessary (albeit politically totalitarian), but it also justifies the view that job assignment is objective and efficient and, therefore, just and egalitarian (albeit severely unequal). Moreover, the individual is resigned to, if not satisfied with, his or her own position in the hierarchy of production. The legitimacy of the authority of superiors flows not from social contrivance but from Science and Reason.

That this view does not strain the credulity of well-paid intellectuals is perhaps not surprising. But the meritocratic perspective would not be of much use in justifying the hierarchical division of labor if it counted among its adherents only the university elite and the technical and professional experts. But such is not the case. Despite the extensive evidence that IQ is not an important determinant of individual economic success, and despite the absence of evidence that technical skills have an important causal relationship to income inequality or intergenerational status transmission, the nearly exclusive importance of IQ and skills has captured the public mind. Numerous attitude surveys exhibit this fact.[3]

The linking of technical skills to economic success indirectly via the educational system strengthens rather than weakens the legitimation process. First, the day-to-day contact of parents and children with the competitive, cognitively oriented school environment, with clear connections to the economy, buttresses, in a very immediate and concrete way, the technocratic perspective on economic organization, to a degree that a sporadic and impersonal testing process divorced from the school environment could not accomplish. Second, by rendering the outcome (educational attainment) dependent not only on ability but also on motivation, drive to achieve, perseverance, and sacrifice, the status allocation mechanism acquires heightened legitimacy. Moreover, such personal attributes are tested and developed over a long period of time, underlining the apparent objectivity and achievement orientation of the stratification system. Third, frequent failures play an important role in gradually bringing a student's aspirations into line with his or her probable career opportunities. By the time most students terminate schooling, they have been put down enough to convince them of their inability to succeed at the next highest level. Through competition, success, and defeat in the classroom, students are reconciled to their social positions.[4]

So the objective educational system has etched the meritocratic perspective deeply into both popular culture and social science methodology. Nowhere is this seen more clearly than in the recent controversy over "open admissions" in colleges and universities. Open enrollment has been called on by militant minority groups to counteract the impediments of community deprivation, discrimination, and poor secondary education.[5] Both proponents and opponents of open admission have nearly uniformly assumed that the admission of students to higher education irrespective of IQ, test scores, or grades runs counter to efficiency and educational rationality.[6] Must not the principle of meritocracy in schools be efficient? Should not the most "able" be granted the right to further educational resources, since they will be the most capable of benefiting themselves and society? So goes the argument. But if social efficiency is the objective, the justification for a meritocratic admissions policy must rest on the assertion that "smart" people benefit more from college than those with lower test scores and grades. Stated more technically, the return from higher education, namely its impact on the individual's cognitive capacities, earning abilities, or productivity, must be positively related to prior test scores: The higher the test score the greater the expected return. If this is not the case, if low test scorers get as much out of college as high scorers, the argument that the policy of admitting the smartest must be maintained in the interest of social efficiency falls apart. And the evidence generally supports the view that the return from higher education is independent of prior test scores.

In a study exploring the cognitive "value added" in higher education, Alexander Astin, Director of the American Council on Education, found that there is no evidence that smart high-school seniors learn more in college, despite the fact that they tend to go to "better" institutions.[7] That is, education is something like physical exercise: Some people are more talented than others, but all benefit about equally from athletic involvement and instruction. But the more important question for our purposes is the way in which test scores affect the economic productivity of education, and, particularly, the predominant contemporary "sorting mechanism," higher education. The fact that for the past half century people have simply assumed the economic rationality of sorting by IQ and test scores in education speaks highly for the persuasiveness of the meritocratic perspective. Yet available evidence by no means substantiates this view. Of the six statistical studies which address this question, four indicate that schooling is *not* more productive for the higher-IQ individual; one produced mixed results; and only one supported the traditional view.[8]

For instance, Daniel C. Rogers[9] investigated the lifetime earnings of 1,827 males who were in the eighth or ninth grades in 1935, in various cities of Connecticut and Massachusetts, and who took an IQ test in that year. Rogers found that the economic productivity of a year of schooling is the same at all levels of IQ: The rate of return on the individual's "investment," including tuition and supply, costs as well as foregone earnings, toward attaining a higher degree, is more or less equal across a broad spectrum of IQ levels. At least from an economic point of view, higher education benefits all ability levels fairly equally, so the usual justification for selective enrollment is quite dubious.

But we do not propose to justify open admissions on grounds of pure economics or social efficiency. Rather, we wish to emphasize that the meritocratic orientation of higher education, far from serving "economic rationality," is actually a façade that facilitates the stratification of the labor force. Open admissions threatens this legitimation mechanism by rendering school success a less important factor in the opportunity to obtain higher education.

Experience with open enrollment seems to support our assertion that the ostensibly meritocratic and objective nature of selective admissions serves mainly the reproduction of the labor force through legitimation. The City

College of New York, which began an extensive program of open enrollment in 1970, asked Astin and his associates at the American Council on
Education to evaluate its first year of operation. They found that regular
and open-enrollment students improved their test scores at the same rate,
and there was no evidence that academic standards were lower in the first
year. Of course, the test scores of open-enrollment students were initially
lower than those of regulars (by the end of the freshman year, the test
scores of open-enrollment students had attained the level of entering regular students). Nonetheless, while 50 percent of the open-enrollment students progressed at the normal rate (i.e., had earned twenty-four college
credits), the proportion of regular students who did so was only slightly
higher than 60 percent. In their interim report, Astin and Rossman
conclude:

> Whether a student was regularly admitted or was an open-admissions student
> proved relatively unimportant in predicting his or her success in the first year.
> Although the two groups did indeed differ in many ways, it is clear that open-
> admissions students brought a number of personal characteristics besides past
> achievements that proved to be important for college.[10]

In summary, the ostensibly objective and meritocratic selection and reward system of U.S. education corresponds not to some abstract notion of
efficiency, rationality, and equity, but to the legitimization of economic inequality and the smooth staffing of unequal work roles. Every society must
and will reward some individual excellences. But which ones they reward,
in what manner, to what extent, and through what social process depend
critically on how economic life is organized. The predatory, competitive,
and personally destructive way in which intellectual achievement is rewarded in U.S. schools and colleges is a monument not to creative rationality, but to the need of a privileged class to justify an irrational, exploitative, and undemocratic system.

### Education, Income, and Cognitive Attainment

> I have never considered mere knowledge . . . as the only
> advantage derived from a good common school education.
> I have uniformly found the better educated as a class possess-
> ing a higher and better state of morals, more orderly and re-
> spectful in their deportment, and more ready to comply with
> the wholesome and necessary regulations of an establishment.

> And in times of agitation, on account of some change in regulations or wages, I have always looked to the most intelligent, best educated, and the most moral for support and have seldom been disappointed . . . they will generally acquiesce and exert a salutory influence upon their associates. But the ignorant and uneducated I have generally found most turbulent and troublesome, acting under the impulse of excited passion and jealousy.
>
> HOMER BARTLETT,
> a Massachusettes Industrialist writing
> to Horace Mann in 1841

Why does education increase people's income? The traditional explanation —which we have labeled the technocratic-meritocratic perspective— presents a simple and compelling answer. Earnings reflect economic productivity. In a technologically advanced society, an individual's economic productivity depends partly on the level of the cognitive skills he or she has attained. Each year of education increases cognitive skill levels, thus indirectly leading to higher income.

Were this view correct, our heavy emphasis on the legitimating role of education would be more than a little misleading. In that case, the competitive educational system would be a meritocratic "game" in which the stakes (economic success) would be directly related to the criteria (cognitive attainment) of winning or losing in a very rational and even technological way.[11] Again, were this view correct, it would be difficult to argue that there are fundamental contradictions among the integrative, egalitarian, and personal development functions of education in capitalist society. Education could be as egalitarian as people's innate biological capacities allowed—which would be pretty far. Moreover, were the technocratic-meritocratic perspective correct, the persistance of repressive education— in the face of alternatives which appear to offer both a more democratic and participatory environment and a more effective vehicle for the transmission of cognitive skills—would merely reflect an irrational institutional inertia on the part of the school system. If schools could be made more humane and more efficient producers of intellectual skills, why have not all parties concerned—educators, students, employers, parents, workers, school boards, everybody—celebrated the opportunity? The answer, we believe, lies in a simple, but often overlooked, fact: The role of schools in promoting cognitive growth by no means exhausts their social functions. Indeed, while skills are developed in schools and a skilled labor force is necessary in a technologically advanced society, a cognitive approach to the educational system which focuses on the production of mental skills cannot provide the basis for understanding the link between schools and the economy.

In particular, we shall demonstrate that although higher levels of schooling and economic success tend to go together, the intellectual abilities developed or certified in school make little *causal* contribution to getting ahead economically. Only a minor portion of the substantial statistical association between schooling and economic success can be accounted for by the school's role in producing or screening cognitive skills. The economic function of schools is thus not limited to the development or identification of these skills.

This assertion may strike some as curious. Many commentators on the educational scene—social scientists, educators, and employers among them —have mistakenly attributed overarching importance to the intellectual role of schooling. A mid-nineteenth-century industrialist, for example, wrote:

Whenever a mill or a room should fail to give the proper amount of work, my first inquiry . . . would be as to the character of the help, and if the deficiency remained any great length of time, I am sure I should find many who had made marks upon the payroll, being unable to write their names.[12]

Interestingly, the records of a mill virtually identical to that owned by this industrialist have been preserved, and a careful study of the number of pieces produced by each worker (paid according to piece rates) revealed absolutely no statistical relationship between worker productivity and literacy, as measured by the marking of the payroll receipt book with an "X" or a written signature.*

While our more general claim—that the primary economic function of schooling is not the production or selection of intellectual skills—can be verified through a wide variety of data sources,[13] our major illustration will be drawn from an extensive sample which we have subjected to close statistical analysis.[14]

We must first choose a convenient way to represent the statistical association between level of educational attainment in years and earnings in dollars. While our results are clearly independent of any particular representation, some representations can be more easily interpreted than others. We have chosen the top-quintile-by-decile method, already employed in Chapter 2.[15] We first order all individuals from lowest to highest in terms of level of educational attainment in years, dividing them into ten equal

* Hal Luft, "New England Textile Labor in the 1840's: From Yankee Farmgirl to Irish Immigrant," unpublished, Harvard University, January 1971.

parts ("deciles"). We then determine the percentage of individuals in each decile who are in the top fifth of the sample (the "top quintile") in income. We thus find the probability that an individual with a given level of education has of attaining the top 20 percent of the income distribution.[16]

For instance, the left-hand bars in Figure 4–1 illustrate that an individual in the ninth (next to highest) education decile has a 34.3 percent

FIGURE 4–1.
*Differences in Cognitive Test Scores do not Explain*
*the Association between Years of Schooling,*
*and Economic Success.*

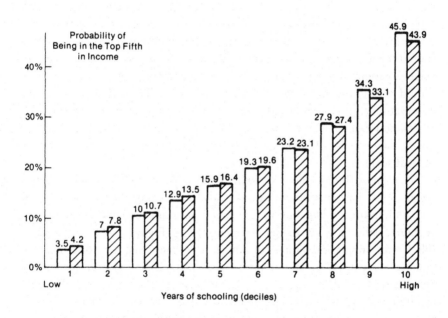

NOTES: The left-hand bar of each pair shows the estimated probability that a man is in the top fifth of the income distribution if he is in the given decile of education. The right-hand bar of each pair shows the estimated probability that a man is in the top fifth of the income distribution if he has an average adult cognitive test score and is in the given decile of education.

Note that the bars of any given pair are nearly the same height, showing that the income-education relationship is almost the same for individuals with the identical cognitive attainments as for all individuals.[18]

SAMPLE: Non-Negro white males of nonfarm background, 1962, aged 35–44 years.

SOURCE: Samuel Bowles and Valerie Nelson, "The 'Inheritance of IQ' and the Intergenerational Transmission of Economic Inequality," *The Review of Economics and Statistics*, Vol. 56 No. 1, February 1974.

chance of attaining a position in the top fifth of income earners, while an individual in the bottom decile in education has only a 3.5 percent chance. This illustrates the well-known importance of education in achieving economic success.

Just as the technocratic-meritocratic theory asserts, education is also closely associated with cognitive attainments. For instance, if the probability of attaining the top fifth in adult IQ is plotted against educational level, we find that a person in the top decile in education has a 57.7 percent chance of falling in the top fifth in cognitive scores, while a person in the bottom decile in education has less than a 1 percent chance.[17]

But is the higher average cognitive attainment of the more highly educated the *cause* of their greater likelihood of achieving economic success? This, of course, is the crucial question. If the cognitive theory is correct, two individuals with the same test scores but different levels of education should have, on the average, exactly the same expected incomes, and conversely people with different test scores but similar levels of education should on the average exhibit different incomes. Thus, if we restrict our observation to individuals with the same test scores, at whatever level, the association exhibited in the left-hand bars of Figure 4–1 should disappear —i.e., they should all have the same height at the 20-percent mark on the vertical scale.

To address this problem we will need to go beyond simple statistical associations and construct a causal model explaining the independent direct and indirect contribution of each important variable to individual economic success. Our model is illustrated in Figure 4–2. According to this figure, among individuals of similar age, race, and sex, differences in income are caused by differences in adult IQ, schooling, and socioeconomic background, as well as by other unmeasured differences. Differences in adult IQ and schooling are likewise due to the effects of the causally prior variables, socio-economic background and childhood IQ. Differences in childhood IQ are caused by differences in genetic inheritance, in socioeconomic background and their interaction. In the model, socioeconomic background influences income directly (arrow b) and indirectly through its effect both on educational attainments (arrows c and d; arrows e, g, and d) and on adult IQ (arrows e, j, and i; arrows e, g, j, and i; and arrows e, h, and i). Schooling influences income both directly (arrow d) and indirectly through its effect on adult IQ (arrows j and i). The direct and indirect effects of genetic inheritance may likewise be traced.

Our statistical technique for the estimation of these statistical relationships will be that of linear regression analysis. This technique allows us to

FIGURE 4–2.
*Causal Model of IQ, Socioeconomic Background,
Schooling and Economic Success*

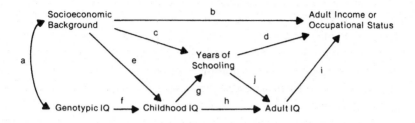

NOTES: The model applies to people of the same sex, race, and roughly the same age. Additional variables would be required to take account of these important aspects of the income determination process. Arrows indicate the assumed direction of causation. The one double-headed arrow represents statistical association with no implied causation. For a fuller discussion of the model, see Bowles and Nelson, "The 'Inheritance of IQ' and the Intergenerational Transmission of Economic Inequality," op. cit., 1974.

derive numerical estimates of the independent contribution of each of the separate but correlated influences (socioeconomic background, childhood IQ, years of schooling, adult cognitive attainment) on economic success, by answering the question: What is the magnitude of the association between any one of these influences among individuals who are equal with respect to some or all the others? Equivalently, it answers the question: What are the probabilities of attaining particular levels of economic success among individuals who are in the same decile in some or all of the above influences but one, and in varying deciles in this one variable alone?

The results of "holding constant" IQ at a particular level (e.g., average level) is exhibited in the right-hand bars of Figure 4–2. Rather than being of equal height, the right-hand bars are only slightly different from the left. For instance, in general a person from the ninth decile in education is nearly ten times as likely to be in the top quintile in income as is a person in the bottom education decile; but among people with identical adult cognitive test scores, the former is still eight times more likely to be in the top income quintile than the latter. Holding cognitive attainments constant barely changes the education-income relationship. Hardly comforting for those who assert the economic importance of mental skills in explaining inequality.[19]

Since the association between level of economic success and years of schooling is reduced only slightly when we look at individuals with the same level of adult cognitive skills, the association of schooling and economic success is largely unrelated to the differences in cognitive skills observed between workers with differing levels of education. Numerous other studies support these conclusions. A number of these are listed in Table A-2 of Appendix A.[20]

The reader may find our argument, despite its wide statistical support, not only counterintuitive, but actually incredible. For the figures seem to refute the manifest observation that the economy could not operate without the cognitive skills of workers, and these skills are acquired in school. This observation is eminently correct, and by no means contradicted by our data. What our argument suggests is merely that the mental-skill demands of work are sufficiently limited, the skills produced by our educational system sufficiently varied, and the possibilities for acquiring additional skills on the job sufficiently great so that skill differences among individuals who are acceptable for a given job on the basis of other criteria including race, sex, personality, and credentials are of little economic import. At most levels in the occupational hierarchy mental skills are productive, but are not scarce, and hence do not bear a direct monetary return. Indeed, we have suggested that the educational system serves to produce surpluses of skilled labor, thereby increasing the power of employers over workers. Thus the statistical evidence, far from being a striking curiosity, is an expected reflection of the class nature of the production process. Workers' skills are an absolutely fundamental element in economic growth, but skill differences do not explain the lack of progress toward social justice.

In sum, the available evidence seems to support our legitimization hypothesis. The meritocratic orientation of the educational system promotes not its egalitarian function, but rather its integrative role. Education reproduces inequality by justifying privilege and attributing poverty to personal failure.

## IQism: or "If You're So Smart, Why Aren't You Rich?"

One thing is clear—nature does not produce on the one side owners of money or commodities, and on the other, men possessing nothing but their own labor power. This relation has no natural basis, neither is its social basis one that is common to all historical periods. It is clearly the result of

> past historical development, the product of many economical
> revolutions, of the extinction of a whole series of older forms
> of social production.
>
> KARL MARX, *Capital*, 1867

> Poverty has many roots, but the tap-root is ignorance.
> PRESIDENT LYNDON B. JOHNSON,
> Educational Message to the 89th Congress, 1965

The technocratic-meritocratic ideology is also at the root of the currently popular "the-poor-are-dumb" theories of inequality. The notion that economic inequality is rooted in genetically determined differences in IQ has never lacked advocates. Yet the fortunes of this idea exhibit a curious ebb and flow; the economic and social importance of genetic differences never appears more obvious than in the aftermath of a series of unsuccessful liberal reforms. On the other hand, the three major periods of liberal educational reform—the two decades prior to the Civil War, the Progressive Era, and the 1960s—were all marked by a lack of concern with genetically inherited characteristics and a profound optimism concerning the malleability, even the perfectability, of youth. The main problem for reformers was to structure an environment in which individual development would be promoted rather than retarded. Not surprisingly, liberals have concentrated on those aspects of nurture which appeared susceptible to social intervention: schools, housing, medical care, and the like. Yet the demise of each liberal reform movement has been greeted by a genetic backlash: If improving the school environment does not achieve its elevated objectives, there must be something wrong with the kids. In the late 1960s, with the War on Poverty losing momentum and the dismal evaluation of the compensatory education programs accumulating, the historian, Michael Katz, predicted a counterattack by those who locate the roots of inequality in nature and, particularly, in genetically determined differences in IQ.[21]

The predicted reaction has since gathered force: The genetic interpretation of inequality had regained much of its tarnished academic respectability and has come to command the attention of social scientists and policymakers alike. The first major shot was Arthur Jensen's argument in the *Harvard Educational Review* that the failure of compensatory education to raise scholastic achievement levels must be attributed to the heritability of IQ.[22] Jensen's survey of the heredity research of Burtt and others was embraced and extended by Harvard psychologist Richard Herrnstein. The distribution of wealth, privilege, and social status, asserted Herrnstein, is determined to a major and increasing extent by the distribution of IQ. Because IQ is highly heritable, economic and social status is passed on within families from one generation to the next.[23]

These assertions by Jensen, Herrnstein, and others constituted a fundamental attack on the liberal reformist position. Yet the liberal defense has been curiously superficial: The putative economic importance of IQ has remained undocumented by the genetic school and unchallenged by their critics. Amidst a hundred-page statistical barrage relating to the genetic and environmental components of intelligence, Jensen saw fit to devote only three sparse and ambiguous pages to this issue. Later advocates of the "genetic school" have considered this "elemental fact," if anything, even less necessary of support.[24] Nor has their choice of battleground proved injudicious; to our knowledge, not one of their environmentalist critics has taken the economic importance of IQ any less for granted.[25]

This glaring lapse in the liberal defense is itself instructive. "The most important thing . . . that we can know about a man," says Louis Wirth, "is what he takes for granted, and the most elemental and important facts about a society are those that are seldom debated and generally regarded as settled." We are questioning here the undisputed assumption underlying both sides of the recently revived IQ controversy: that the distribution of IQ is a basic determinant of the structure of privilege.[26]

Our empirical results will reinforce our contention that the emphasis on IQ as the basis for economic success serves to legitimate an authoritarian, hierarchical, stratified, and unequal economic system, and to reconcile individuals to their objective position within this system. Legitimation is enhanced when people merely believe in the intrinsic importance of IQ. This belief is facilitated by the strong associations among all the economically desirable attributes—social class, education, cognitive skills, occupational status, and income—and is integrated into a pervasive ideological perspective. That IQ is not a major determinant of the social class structure also supports our argument in Chapter 3 that access to a particular job depends on the individual's pattern of noncognitive personality traits (motivation, orientation to authority, discipline, internalization of work norms), as well as on such personal attributes as sex, race, age, and educational credentials. These personality traits and personal attributes aid in legitimating and stabilizing the structure of authority in the modern enterprise itself. Thus, primarily because of the central economic role of the school system, the production of adequate intellectual skills becomes a spin-off, a by-product of a stratification mechanism grounded in the supply, demand, production, and certification of an entirely different set of personal attributes.

We must begin a discussion of genetic transmission of economic status by asking what "heritability" means. That IQ is highly heritable is merely to say that individuals with similar genes will exhibit similar IQs independent of differences in the social environments they might experience during their mental development. The main support for the genetic school are several studies of individuals with precisely the same genes (identical twins) raised in different environments (i.e., separated at birth and reared in different families). Their IQs tend to be fairly similar.[27] In addition, there are studies of individuals with no common genes (unrelated individuals) raised in the same environment (e.g., the same family) as well as studies of individuals with varying genetic similarities (e.g., fraternal twins, siblings, fathers and sons, aunts and nieces) and varying environments (e.g., siblings raised apart, cousins raised in their respective homes). The difference in IQs for these groups conform roughly to the genetic inheritance model suggested by the identical twin and unrelated individual studies.[28]

Leon Kamin recently presented extensive evidence casting strong doubt on the genetic position.[29] But by and large, environmentalists have been unable to convincingly disprove the central proposition of the genetic school. But then, they have emphasized that it bears no important social implications. They have argued, for example, that the genetic theory says nothing about the "necessary" degree of racial inequality or the limits of compensatory education.[30] First, environmentalists deny that there is any evidence that the average IQ difference between black and whites (amounting to about fifteen IQ points) is genetic in origin,[31] and second, they deny that any estimate of heritability tells us much about the capacity of enriched environments to lessen IQ differentials, either within or between racial groups.[32]

But the environmentalists' defense strategy has been costly. In their egalitarian zeal vis-à-vis racial differences, the environmentalists have sacrificed the modern liberal interpretation of social inequality. The modern liberal approach is to attribute social class differences to unequal opportunity. That is, while the criteria for economic success are objective and achievement-oriented, the failures and successes of parents are passed onto their children via distinct learning and cultural environments. From this it follows that the achievement of a more equal society merely requires that all youth be afforded the educational and other social conditions of the best and most successful.[33] But the liberal counterattack against the genetic position represented a significant retreat, for it did not successfully challenge the proposition that IQ differences among whites of differing social class backgrounds are rooted in differences in genetic endowments. Indeed, the genetic school's data come precisely from observed differences in the IQ of whites across socioeconomic levels! The liberal failure to question the causal role of IQ in getting ahead economically completes the rout. The fundamental tenet of modern liberal social theory—that progressive social welfare programs can gradually reduce and eliminate social class differences, cultures of poverty and affluence, and inequalities of opportunity—has been done in to a major extent by its erstwhile advocates. So the old belief—adhered to by present-day conservatives and liberals of past generations—that social classes sort themselves out on the basis of innate individual capacity to cope successfully in the social environment, and hence tend to reproduce themselves from generation to generation has been restored.[34]

The vigor of their reaction to Jensen's argument reflects the liberals' agreement that IQ is a basic determinant (at least ideally) of occupational status and intergenerational mobility. Indeed, the conceptual framework of the testers themselves would appear to insure this result. Jensen is thus merely stating what the testers had taken for granted: " . . . Psychologists' concept of the 'intelligence demands' of an occupation . . . is very much like the general public's concept of the prestige or 'social standing' of an occupation, and both are closely related to an independent measure of . . . occupational status."[35] Jensen continues, quoting the sociologist O. D. Duncan: ". . . 'Intelligence' . . . is not essentially different from that of achievement or status in the occupational sphere. . . . What we now mean by intelligence is something like the probability of acceptable performance [given the opportunity] in occupations varying in social status."[36] Moreover, Jensen argues that the purported trend toward making intelligence a requirement for occupational achievement will continue to grow.[37] This emphasis on intelligence as explaining social stratification is set even more clearly by Carl Bereiter: "The prospect is of a meritocratic caste system, based . . . on the natural consequences of inherited difference in intellectual potential. . . . It would tend to persist even though everyone at all levels of the hierarchy considered it a bad thing."[38]

Jensen and his associates cannot be accused of employing an overly complicated social theory. Thus Jensen's reason for the "inevitable" association of status and intelligence is that society "rewards talent and merit." And Herrnstein adds that:

If virtually anyone is smart enough to be a ditch digger, and only half the people are smart enough to be engineers, then society is, in effect, husbanding its intellectual resources by holding engineers in greater esteem and paying them more. . . . [S]ociety [thus] expresses its recognition, however imprecise, of the importance and scarcity of intellectual ability.[39]

Finally, according to Herrnstein, each generation is further refined into social strata on the basis of IQ:

. . . New gains of wealth . . . will increase the IQ gap between upper and lower classes, making the social ladder even steeper for those left at the bottom.

Herrnstein then proceeds to turn liberal social policy directly against itself, noting that the heritability of IQ and hence the pervasiveness of social stratification will increase, as our social policies become more progressive:

. . . The growth of a virtually hereditary meritocracy will arise out of the successful realization of contemporary political and social goals . . . as the environment becomes more favorable for the development of intelligence, its heritability will increase. . . .[40]

Similarly, the more we break down discriminatory and ascriptive criteria for hiring, the stronger will become the link between IQ and occupational success. And the development of modern technology, adds Herrnstein, can only quicken this process.

That such statements should be made by the "conservative" genetic school is hardly surprising. But why should liberals, who have contested the genetic hypothesis in the minutest detail, have so blindly accepted the genetic school's description of the social function of intelligence? The widespread assumption among all parties to the debate that IQ is an important determinant of economic success does not rest on compelling empirical evidence. Quite the contrary.

The most immediate support for the IQ theory of social inequality which we will call "IQism"—flows from two substantial relationships. The first is the significant association between socioeconomic background and childhood IQ. Thus, according to our research, having a parent in the top decile in socioeconomic status gives a child a 42 percent chance of being in the top fifth in IQ, while having a parent in the bottom socioeconomic status decile gives him only a 4.9 percent chance.[41] The second is the important association between childhood IQ and later economic success: An individual in the top childhood IQ decile is nearly four times as likely to achieve the highest income quintile as an individual from the bottom IQ decile.[42]

The proponent of IQism argues that higher social class leads to higher IQ, which, in turn, leads to a greater chance of economic success. We shall show, however, that this inference is simply erroneous. Specifically, we will demonstrate the truth of the following proposition, which constitutes the empirical basis of our thesis: the fact that economic success tends to run in the family arises almost completely independently from any inheritance of IQ, whether it be genetic or environmental. Thus, while one's economic status tends to resemble that of one's parents, only a minor portion of this association can be attributed to social class differences in childhood IQ, and a virtually negligible portion to social class differences in genetic endowments even if one were to accept the Jensen estimates of heritability. Thus a perfect (obviously hypothetical) equalization of IQs among individuals of differing social backgrounds would reduce the intergenerational transmission of economic status by only a negligible amount. We conclude that a family's position in the class structure is reproduced primarily by mechanisms operating *independently* of the inheritance, production, and certification of intellectual skills.

How are we to support this proposition? The correct way of posing the question is to ask the following: To what extent is the statistical association between socioeconomic background and economic success reduced when childhood IQ is held constant? If the proponents of IQism are correct, the reduction should be substantial. If the only source of intergenerational status transmission were the inheritance of IQ, there should be no relationship whatever between family background and economic success among individuals with the same IQ. The way to test this is again to use linear regression analysis on our basic data set. The left-hand bars in Figure 4–3 show the overall association between socioeconomic background and economic success. The results of holding constant IQ by linear regression, indicated in the right-hand bars of Figure 4–3, shows that the actual reduction in the relationship is practically nil.[43] Evidently, IQ—whether inherited or not—plays a negligible role in passing economic status from parent to child.

The unimportance of the specifically genetic mechanism operating via IQ in the intergenerational reproduction of economic inequality is even more striking. Figure 4–4 exhibits the degree of association between socioeconomic background and income which can be attributed to the genetic inheritance of IQ alone. This figure assumes that all direct influences of socioeconomic background upon income have been eliminated. On the other hand, it assumes Jensen's estimate for the degree of heritability of IQ. A glance at Figure 4–4 shows that the resulting level of intergenerational inequality in this highly hypothetical example would be negligible,[44] and contrasts sharply with the actual degree of inequality exhibited in the left-hand bars of Figure 4–3.

FIGURE 4–3.

*Relationship between Income and Inherited Social Status
cannot be Accounted for by Differences in I.Q.*

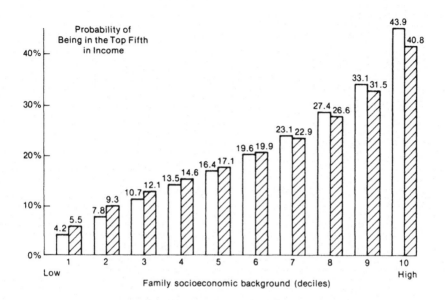

NOTES: The left-hand bar of each pair shows the estimated
probability that a man is in the top fifth of the income distribution if he is in a given decile of socioeconomic background.
The right-hand bar shows the estimated probability that a man
is in the top fifth of the income distribution if he has average
childhood IQ and is in a given decile of socioeconomic background.

Note that the bars of any given pair are very close, showing
that the income/socioeconomic background relationship is almost the same for individuals with identical IQs as for all
individuals.

SAMPLE: Non-Negro males of nonfarm background, 1962, aged
35–44 years.

SOURCE: Samuel Bowles and Valerie Nelson, "The 'Inheritance
of IQ' and the Intergenerational Transmission of Economic
Inequality," *The Review of Economics and Statistics,* Vol. 56,
No. 1, February 1974.

Our proposition is thus supported: The intergenerational transmission of
social and economic status operates primarily via noncognitive mechanisms, despite the fact that the school system rewards higher IQ, an attribute significantly associated with higher socioeconomic background.

The unimportance of IQ in explaining the relationship between socioeconomic background and economic success, together with the fact that
most of the association between IQ and income can be accounted for by

FIGURE 4-4.

*Family Background and Economic Success in the Hypothetical Meritocracy with Inheritable IQ.*

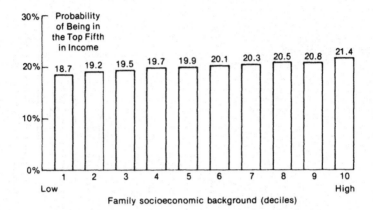

NOTES: Each bar shows the estimated probability that a man would be in the top fifth of the income distribution if he is in the given decile of socioeconomic background and the entire relationship between background and economic success worked through the genetic inheritance of IQ, so that no other sources of social inequality existed. All bars are close to the "random" probability of 20%.

SAMPLE: Non-Negro, nonfarm males, aged 35–44 years.

SOURCE: Samuel Bowles and Valerie Nelson, "The 'Inheritance of IQ' and the Intergenerational Transmission of Economic Inequality," *The Review of Economics and Statistics*, Vol. 56, No. 1, February 1974 (Table 3).

the common association of these variables with education and socioeconomic background, support our major assertion: IQ is not an important criterion for economic success. Our data thus hardly lends credence to Duncan's assertion that ". . . 'intelligence' . . . is not essentially different from that of achievement or status in the occupational sphere, . . ."[45] nor to Jensen's belief in the "inevitable" association of status and intelligence, based on society's "rewarding talent and merit,"[46] nor to Herrnstein's dismal prognostication of a virtually hereditary meritocracy as the fruit of successful liberal reform in an advanced industrial society.[47]

## Conclusion

> Their dullness seems to be racial, or at least inherent in the family stocks from which they come. The fact that one meets this type with such extraordinary frequency among Indians, Mexicans, and negroes suggests quite forcibly that the whole question of racial differences in mental traits will have to be taken up anew. . . . there will be discovered enormously significant racial differences . . . which cannot be wiped out by any schemes of mental culture.
>
> Children of this group should be segregated in special classes. . . . They cannot master abstractions, but they can often be made efficient workers.
>
> LEWIS TERMAN,
> *The Measurement of Intelligence*, 1916

The power and privilege of the capitalist class are often inherited, but not through superior genes. (Try asking David Rockefeller to hand over his capital in return for thirty more IQ points!) Differences in IQ, even were they genetically inherited, could not explain the historical pattern of economic and educational inequalities. The intractability of inequality of income and of economic opportunity cannot be attributed to genetically inherited differences in IQ. The disappointing results of the "War on Poverty" cannot be blamed on the genes of the poor. The failure of egalitarian school reforms reflects the fact that inequality under capitalism is rooted not in individual deficiencies, but in the structure of production and property relations.

In this chapter, we have suggested that education should be viewed as reproducing inequality by legitimating the allocation of individuals to economic positions on the basis of ostensibly objective merit. Moreover, the basis for assessing merit—competitive academic performance—is only weakly associated with the personal attributes indicative of individual success in economic life. Thus the legitimation process in education assumes a largely symbolic form.

This legitimation process, however, is fraught with its own contradictions. For the technocratic-meritocratic ideology progressively undermines the overt forms of discrimination which divide the work force into racially, sexually, and ethnically distinct segments. Ironically, the partial success of the meritocratic ideology has helped to create a political basis for working class unity. With the irrationality of these forms of discrimination increasingly exposed, the justification of inequality must increasingly rely on educational inequalities and IQism. Yet workers, minorities, and others have fought hard and to some extent successfully to reduce educational inequality, with little effect on economic inequality itself. This has tended to increase conflicts within education, to cast further doubt on the fairness of the income distribution process, and at the same time undercut traditional educational philosophy. Thus even the symbolism of meritocracy is threatened in the contemporary period.

Yet, as we have suggested, the reproduction function of education goes far beyond symbolic legitimation. In the next chapter, we shall show that the education system plays a central role in preparing individuals for the world of alienated and stratified work relationships. Such a class analysis of education is necessary, we believe, to understand the dynamics of educational change and also the structural relations among social class, education, and economic success—relationships which we have seen in this chapter to be inexplicable purely in terms of cognitive variables.

# CHAPTER 5

•

Education and

Personal Development:

The Long Shadow of Work

> Every child born into the world should be looked upon by society as so much raw material to be manufactured. Its quality is to be tested. It is the business of society, as an intelligent economist, to make the best of it.
>
> LESTER FRANK WARD,
> *Education, c.* 1872

It is not obvious why the U.S. educational system should be the way it is. Since the interpersonal relationships it fosters are so antithetical to the norms of freedom and equality prevalent in American society, the school system can hardly be viewed as a logical extension of our cultural heritage. If neither technological necessity nor the bungling mindlessness of educators explain the quality of the educational encounter, what does?

Reference to the educational system's legitimation function does not take us far toward enlightenment. For the formal, objective, and cognitively oriented aspects of schooling capture only a fragment of the day-to-day social relationships of the educational encounter. To approach an answer, we must consider schools in the light of the social relationships of economic life. In this chapter, we suggest that major aspects of educational organization replicate the relationships of dominance and subordinancy in the economic sphere. The correspondence between the social relation of schooling and work accounts for the ability of the educational system to produce an amenable and fragmented labor force. The experience of schooling, and not merely the content of formal learning, is central to this process.

In our view, it is pointless to ask if the net effect of U.S. education is to promote equality or inequality, repression or liberation. These issues pale into insignificance before the major fact: The educational system is an integral element in the reproduction of the prevailing class structure of society. The educational system certainly has a life of its own, but the experience of work and the nature of the class structure are the bases upon which educational values are formed, social justice assessed, the realm of the possible delineated in people's consciousness, and the social relations of the educational encounter historically transformed.

In short, and to return to a persistent theme of this book, the educational system's task of integrating young people into adult work roles constrains the types of personal development which it can foster in ways that are antithetical to the fulfillment of its personal developmental function.

## Reproducing Consciousness

> . . . children guessed (but only a few
> and down they forgot as up they grew
> autumn winter spring summer). . . .
> e e cummings, 1940

Economic life exhibits a complex and relatively stable pattern of power and property relationships. The perpetuation of these social relationships, even over relatively short periods, is by no means automatic. As with a living organism, stability in the economic sphere is the result of explicit mechanisms constituted to maintain and extend the dominant patterns of power and privilege. We call the sum total of these mechanisms and their actions the reproduction process.

Amidst the sundry social relations experienced in daily life, a few stand out as central to our analysis of education. These are precisely the social relationships which are necessary to the security of capitalist profits and the stability of the capitalist division of labor. They include the patterns of dominance and subordinacy in the production process, the distribution of ownership of productive resources, and the degrees of social distance and solidarity among various fragments of the working population—men and women, blacks and whites, and white- and blue-collar workers, to mention some of the most salient.

What are the mechanisms of reproduction of these aspects of the social relations of production in the United States? To an extent, stability is embodied in law and backed by the coercive power of the state. Our jails are filled with individuals who have operated outside the framework of the private-ownership market system. The modern urban police force as well as the National Guard originated, in large part, in response to the fear of social upheaval evoked by militant labor action. Legal sanction, within the framework of the laws of private property, also channels the actions of groups (e.g., unions) into conformity with dominant power relationships. Similarly, force is used to stabilize the division of labor and its rewards within an enterprise: Dissenting workers are subject to dismissal and directors failing to conform to "capitalist rationality" will be replaced.

But to attribute reproduction to force alone borders on the absurd. Under normal conditions, the effectiveness of coercion depends at the very least on the inability or unwillingness of those subjected to it to join together in opposing it. Laws generally considered illegitimate tend to lose their coercive power, and undisguised force too frequently applied tends to be self-defeating. The consolidation and extension of capitalism has engendered struggles of furious intensity. Yet instances of force deployed against a united and active opposition are sporadic and have usually given way to détente in one form or another through a combination of compromise, structural change, and ideological accommodation. Thus it is clear that the consciousness of workers—beliefs, values, self-concepts, types of solidarity and fragmentation, as well as modes of personal behavior and development—are integral to the perpetuation, validation, and smooth operation of economic institutions. The reproduction of the social relations of production depends on the reproduction of consciousness.

Under what conditions will individuals accept the pattern of social relationships that frame their lives? Believing that the long-term development of the existing system holds the prospect of fulfilling their needs, individuals and groups might actively embrace these social relationships. Failing this, and lacking a vision of an alternative that might significantly improve their situation, they might fatalistically accept their condition. Even with such a vision they might passively submit to the framework of economic life and seek individual solutions to social problems if they believe that the possibilities for realizing change are remote. The issue of the reproduction of consciousness enters each of these assessments.

The economic system will be embraced when, first, the perceived needs of individuals are congruent with the types of satisfaction the economic system can objectively provide. While perceived needs may be, in part, biologically determined, for the most part needs arise through the aggregate experiences of individuals in the society. Thus the social relations of production are reproduced in part through a harmony between the needs which the social system generates and the means at its disposal for satisfying these needs.

Second, the view that fundamental social change is not feasible, unoperational, and utopian is normally supported by a complex web of ideological perspectives deeply embedded in the cultural and scientific life of the community and reflected in the consciousness of its members. But fostering the "consciousness of inevitability" is not the office of the cultural system alone. There must also exist mechanisms that systematically thwart the spontaneous development of social experiences that would contradict these beliefs.

Belief in the futility of organizing for fundamental social change is further facilitated by social distinctions which fragment the conditions of life for subordinate classes. The strategy of "divide and conquer" has enabled dominant classes to maintain their power since the dawn of civilization. Once again, the splintered consciousness of a subordinate class is not the product of cultural phenomena alone, but must be reproduced through the experiences of daily life.

Consciousness develops through the individual's direct perception of and participation in social life.[1] Indeed, everyday experience itself often acts as an inertial stabilizing force. For instance, when the working population is effectively stratified, individual needs and self-concepts develop in a correspondingly fragmented manner. Youth of different racial, sexual, ethnic, or economic characteristics directly perceive the economic positions and prerogatives of "their kind of people." By adjusting their aspiration accordingly, they not only reproduce stratification on the level of personal consciousness, but bring their needs into (at least partial) harmony with the fragmented conditions of economic life. Similarly, individuals tend to channel the development of their personal powers—cognitive, emotional, physical, aesthetic, and spiritual—in directions where they will have an opportunity to exercise them. Thus the alienated character of work, for example, leads people to guide their creative potentials to areas outside of economic activity: consumption, travel, sexuality, and family life. So needs and need-satisfaction again tend to fall into congruence and alienated labor is reproduced on the level of personal consciousness.[2]

But this congruence is continually disrupted. For the satisfaction of needs gives rise to new needs. These new needs derive from the logic of personal development as well as from the evolving structure of material life, and in turn undercut the reproduction of consciousness. For this reason the reproduction of consciousness cannot be the simple unintended by-product of social experience. Rather, social relationships must be consciously organized to facilitate the reproduction of consciousness.

Take, for instance, the organization of the capitalist enterprise discussed in Chapter 3. Power relations and hiring criteria within the enterprise are organized so as to reproduce the workers' self-concepts, the legitimacy of their assignments within the hierarchy, a sense of the technological inevitability of the hierarchical division of labor itself, and the social distance among groups of workers in the organization. Indeed, while token gestures towards workers' self-management may be a successful motivational gimmick, any delegation of real power to workers becomes a threat to profits because it tends to undermine patterns of consciousness compatible with capitalist control. By generating new needs and possibilities, by demonstrating the feasibility of a more thoroughgoing economic democracy, by increasing worker solidarity, an integrated and politically conscious program of worker involvement in decision-making may undermine the power structure of the enterprise. Management will accede to such changes only under extreme duress of worker rebellion and rapidly disintegrating morale, if at all.

But the reproduction of consciousness cannot be insured by these direct mechanisms alone. The initiation of youth into the economic system is further facilitated by a series of institutions, including the family and the educational system, that are more immediately related to the formation of personality and consciousness. Education works primarily through the institutional relations to which students are subjected. Thus schooling fosters and rewards the development of certain capacities and the expression of certain needs, while thwarting and penalizing others. Through these institutional relationships, the educational system tailors the self-concepts, aspirations, and social class identifications of individuals to the requirements of the social division of labor.

The extent to which the educational system actually accomplishes these objectives varies considerably from one period to the next. We shall see in later chapters that recurrently through U.S. history these reproduction mechanisms have failed, sometimes quite spectacularly. In most periods—and the present is certainly no exception—efforts to use the schools to reproduce and extend capitalist production relations have been countered both by the internal dynamic of the educational system and by popular opposition.

In earlier chapters we have identified the two main objectives of dominant classes in educational policy: the production of labor power and the reproduction of those institutions and social relationships which facilitate the translation of labor power into profits. We may now be considerably more concrete about the way that educational institutions are structured to meet these objectives. First, schooling produces many of the technical and cognitive skills required for adequate job performance. Second, the educational system helps legitimate economic inequality. As we argued in the last chapter, the objective and meritocratic orientation of U.S. education, reduces discontent over both the hierarchical division of labor and the process through which individuals attain position in it. Third, the school produces, rewards, and labels personal characteristics relevant to the staffing of positions in the hierarchicy. Fourth, the educational system, through the pattern of status distinctions it fosters, reinforces the stratified consciousness on which the fragmentation of subordinate economic classes is based.

What aspects of the educational system allow it to serve these various functions? We shall suggest in the next section that the educational system's ability to reproduce the consciousness of workers lies in a straight-forward correspondence principle: For the past century at least, schooling has contributed to the reproduction of the social relations of production largely through the correspondence between school and class structure.

Upon the slightest reflection, this assertion is hardly surprising. All major institutions in a "stable" social system will direct personal development in a direction compatible with its reproduction. Of course, this is not, in itself, a critique of capitalism or of U.S. education. In any conceivable society, individuals are forced to develop their capacities in one direction or another. The idea of a social system which merely allows people to develop freely according to their "inner natures" is quite unthinkable, since human nature only acquires a concrete form through the interaction of the physical world and preestablished social relationships.

Our critique of education and other aspects of human development in the United States fully recognizes the necessity of some form of socialization. The critical question is: What for? In the United States the human development experience is dominated by an undemocratic, irrational, and exploitative economic structure. Young people have no recourse from the requirements of the system but a life of poverty, dependence, and economic insecurity. Our critique, not surprisingly, centers on the structure of jobs. In the U.S. economy work has become a fact of life to which individuals must by and large submit and over which they have no control. Like the weather, work "happens" to people. A liberated, participatory, democratic, and creative alternative can hardly be imagined, much less experienced. Work under capitalism is an alienated activity.

To reproduce the social relations of production, the educational system must try to teach people to be properly subordinate and render them suffi-ciently fragmented in consciousness to preclude their getting together to shape their own material existence. The forms of consciousness and behavior fostered by the educational system must themselves be alienated, in the sense that they conform neither to the dictates of technology in the struggle with nature, nor to the inherent developmental capacities of individuals, but rather to the needs of the capitalist class. It is the prerogatives of capital and the imperatives of profit, not human capacities and technical realities, which render U.S. schooling what it is. This is our charge.

## *The Correspondence Principle*

> In the social production which men carry on they enter into definite relations which are indispensible and independent of their will; . . . The sum total of these relations of production constitutes . . . the real foundation on which rise legal and political superstructures, and to which correspond definite forms of social consciousness.
>
> KARL MARX, *Contribution to a*
> *Critique of Political Economy*, 1857

The educational system helps integrate youth into the economic system, we believe, through a structural correspondence between its social relations and those of production. The structure of social relations in education not only inures the student to the discipline of the work place, but develops the types of personal demeanor, modes of self-presentation, self-image, and social-class identifications which are the crucial ingredients of job adequacy. Specifically, the social relationships of education—the relationships between administrators and teachers, teachers and students, students and students, and students and their work—replicate the hierarchical division of labor. Hierarchical relations are reflected in the vertical authority lines from administrators to teachers to students. Alienated labor is reflected in the student's lack of control over his or her education, the alienation of the student from the curriculum content, and the motivation of school work through a system of grades and other external rewards rather than the student's integration with either the process (learning) or the outcome (knowledge) of the educational "production process." Fragmentation in work is reflected in the institutionalized and often destructive competition among students through continual and ostensibly meritocratic ranking and evaluation. By attuning young people to a set of social relationships similar to those of the work place, schooling attempts to gear the development of personal needs to its requirements.

But the correspondence of schooling with the social relations of production goes beyond this aggregate level. Different levels of education feed workers into different levels within the occupational structure and, correspondingly, tend toward an internal organization comparable to levels in the hierarchical division of labor. As we have seen, the lowest levels in the hierarchy of the enterprise emphasize rule-following, middle levels, dependability, and the capacity to operate without direct and continuous supervision while the higher levels stress the internalization of the norms of the enterprise. Similarly, in education, lower levels (junior and senior high school) tend to severely limit and channel the activities of students. Somewhat higher up the educational ladder, teacher and community colleges allow for more independent activity and less overall supervision. At the top, the elite four-year colleges emphasize social relationships conformable with the higher levels in the production hierarchy.[3] Thus schools continually maintain their hold on students. As they "master" one type of behavioral regulation, they are either allowed to progress to the next or are channeled into the corresponding level in the hierarchy of production. Even within a single school, the social relationships of different tracks tend to conform to different behavioral norms. Thus in high school, vocational and general tracks emphasize rule-following and close supervision, while the college track tends toward a more open atmosphere emphasizing the internalization of norms.

These differences in the social relationships among and within schools, in part, reflect both the social backgrounds of the student body and their likely future economic positions. Thus blacks and other minorities are concentrated in schools whose repressive, arbitrary, generally chaotic internal order, coercive authority structures, and minimal possibilities for advancement mirror the characteristics of inferior job situations. Similarly, predominantly working-class schools tend to emphasize behavioral control and rule-following, while schools in well-to-do suburbs employ relatively open systems that favor greater student participation, less direct supervision, more student electives, and, in general, a value system stressing internalized standards of control.

The differential socialization patterns of schools attended by students of different social classes do not arise by accident. Rather, they reflect the fact that the educational objectives and expectations of administrators, teachers, and parents (as well as the responsiveness of students to various patterns of teaching and control) differ for students of different social classes. At crucial turning points in the history of U.S. education, changes in the social relations of schooling have been dictated in the interests of a more harmonious reproduction of the class structure. But in the day-to-day operation of the schools, the consciousness of different occupational strata, derived from their cultural milieu and work experience, is crucial to the maintenance of the correspondences we have described. That working-class parents seem to favor stricter educational methods is a reflection of their own work experiences, which have demonstrated that submission to authority is an essential ingredient in one's ability to get and hold a steady, well-paying job. That professional and self-employed parents prefer a more open atmosphere and a greater emphasis on motivational control is similarly a reflection of their position in the social division of labor. When given the opportunity, higher-status parents are far more likely than their lower-status neighbors to choose "open classrooms" for their children.[4]

Differences in the social relationships of schooling are further reinforced by inequalities in financial resources. The paucity of financial support for the education of children from minority groups and low-income families leaves more resources to be devoted to the children of those with more commanding roles in the economy; it also forces upon the teachers and school administrators in the working-class schools a type of social relationships that fairly closely mirrors that of the factory. Financial considerations in poorly supported schools militate against small intimate classes, multiple elective courses, and specialized teachers (except for disciplinary personnel). They preclude the amounts of free time for teachers and free space required for a more open, flexible educational environment. The well-financed schools attended by the children of the rich can offer much greater opportunities for the development of the capacity for sustained independent work and all the other characteristics required for adequate job performance in the upper levels of the occupational hierarchy.

Much of this description will most likely be familiar to the reader and has been documented many times.[5] But only recently has there been an attempt at statistical verification. We will review a number of excellent studies, covering both higher and secondary education. Jeanne Binstock investigated the different patterns of social relations of higher education by analyzing the college handbooks covering rules, regulations, and norms of fifty-two public junior colleges, state universities, teacher-training colleges, and private, secular, denominational, and Catholic colleges. Binstock rated each school along a host of dimensions,[6] including the looseness or strictness of academic structure, the extent of regulations governing personal and social conduct, and the degree of control of the students over their cultural affairs and extracurricular activities. Her general conclusion is quite simple:

The major variations of college experiences are linked to basic psychological differences in work perception and aspiration among the major social class (occupational) groups who are its major consumers. Each social class is different in its beliefs as to which technical and interpersonal skills, character traits, and work values are most valuable for economic survival (stability) or to gain economic advantage (mobility). Each class (with subvariations based on religion and level of urban-ness) has its own economic consciousness, based on its own work experiences and its own ideas (correct or not) of the expectations appropriate to positions on the economic ladder above their own. . . . Colleges compete over the various social class markets by specializing their offerings. Each different type of undergraduate college survives by providing circumscribed sets of "soft" and "hard" skill training that generally corresponds both to the expectations of a particular social class group of customers and to specific needs for sets of "soft" and "hard" skills at particular layers of the industrial system.[7]

Binstock isolated several organizational traits consistently related to the various educational institutions she studied. First, she distinguished between behavioral control which involves rules over the student's behavior rather than intentions and stresses external compliance rather than internalized norms, and motivational control which emphasizes unspecified, variable, and highly flexible task-orientation, and seeks to promote value systems that stress ambiguity and innovation over certainty, tradition, and conformity. Second, Binstock isolated a leader-versus-follower orientation with some schools stressing the future subordinate positions of its charges and teaching docility, and others stressing the need to develop "leadership" self-concepts.

Binstock found that institutions that enroll working-class students and are geared to staff lower-level jobs in the production hierarchy emphasize followership and behavioral control, while the more elite schools that tend to staff the higher-level jobs emphasize leadership and motivational control. Her conclusion is:

Although constantly in the process of reformation, the college industry remains a ranked hierarchy of goals and practices, responding to social class pressures, with graded access to the technical equipment, organizational skills, emotional perspectives and class (work) values needed for each stratified level of the industrial system.[8]

The evidence for the correspondence between the social relations of production and education, however, goes well beyond this structural level and also sheds light on the communality of motivational patterns fostered by these two spheres of social life. Juxtaposing the recent research of Gene Smith, Richard Edwards, Peter Meyer, and ourselves, the same types of behavior can be shown to be rewarded in both education and work. In an attempt to quantify aspects of personality and motivation, Gene Smith has employed a relatively sensitive testing procedure, which he has shown in a series of well-executed studies[9] to be an excellent predictor of educational success (grade-point average). Noting that personality inventories traditionally suffer because of their abstraction from real-life environments and their use of a single evaluative instrument, Smith turned to student-peer ratings of forty-two common personality traits, based on each student's observation of the actual classroom behavior of his or her classmates. A statistical technique called factor analysis then allowed for the identification of five general traits—agreeableness, extroversion, work orientation, emotionality and helpfulness—that proved stable across different samples. Of these five traits, only the work-orientation factor, which Smith calls "strength of character"—including such traits as ". . . not a quitter, conscientious, responsible, insistently orderly, not prone to daydreaming, determined, persevering . . ."—was related to school success. Smith then proceeded to show that, in several samples, this work-orientation trait was three times more successful in predicting post-high-school academic performance than any combination of thirteen cognitive variables, including SAT verbal, SAT mathematical, and high school class rank.

Our colleague Richard C. Edwards has further refined Smith's procedure. As part of his Ph.D. dissertation on the nature of the hierarchical division of labor, he prepared a set of sixteen pairs of personality measures relevant to work performance.[10] Edwards argued that since supervisor ratings of employees are a basic determinant of hirings, firings, and promotions, they are the best measure of job adequacy and, indeed, are the implements of the organization's motivational system. Edwards, therefore, compared supervisor ratings of worker performance with the set of sixteen personality measures as rated by the workers' peers. In a sample of several hundred Boston area workers, he found a cluster of three personality traits —summarized as rules orientation, dependability, and internationalization of the norms of the firm—strongly predicting supervisor ratings of workers in the same work group. This result, moreover, holds up even when the correlation of these traits with such attributes as age, sex, social class background, education, and IQ is corrected for by linear regression analysis. In conformance with our analysis in Chapter 3, Edwards found that rules orientation was relatively more important at the lowest levels of the hierarchy of production, internalization of norms was predominant at the highest level, while dependability was salient at intermediate levels.[11]

Edwards' success with this test in predicting supervisor ratings of workers convinced us that applying the same forms to high school students would provide a fairly direct link between personality development in school and the requirements of job performance.

This task we carried out with our colleague Peter Meyer.[12] He chose as his sample the 237 members of the senior class of a single New York State high school.[13] Following Edwards, he created sixteen pairs of personality traits,[14] and obtained individual grade-point averages, IQ scores, and college-entrance-examination SAT-verbal and SAT-mathematical scores from the official school records.[15]

As we expected, the cognitive scores provided the best single predictor of grade-point average—indeed, that grading is based significantly on cognitive performance is perhaps the most valid element in the "meritocratic ideology." But the sixteen personality measures possessed nearly comparable predictive value, having a multiple correlation of 0.63 compared to 0.77 for the cognitive variables.[16] More important than the overall predictive value of the personality traits, however, was the pattern of their contribution to grades. To reveal this pattern, we first eliminated the effect of differences in cognitive performance in individual grades and then calculated the correlation between grades and the personality traits.[17] The results are presented in Figure 5–1.

The pattern of resulting associations clearly supports the correspondence principle and strongly replicates our initial empirical study of grading presented in Chapter 2. The only significant penalized traits are precisely those which are incompatible with conformity to the hierarchical division of labor—creativity, independence, and aggressivity. On the other hand, all the personality traits which we would expect to be rewarded are, and significantly so. Finally, a glance at Figure 5–2 shows a truly remarkable correspondence between the personality traits rewarded or penalized by grades in Myer's study and the pattern of traits which Edwards found indicative of high or low supervisor ratings in industry.

As a second stage in our analysis of Meyer's data, we used factor analysis to consolidate the sixteen personality measures into three "personality factors." Factor analysis allows us to group together those measured traits which are normally associated with one another among all individuals in the sample. The first factor, which we call "submission to authority," includes these traits: consistent, identifies with school, punctual, dependable, externally motivated, and persistent. In addition, it includes independent and creative weighted negatively. The second, which we call temperament, includes: not aggressive, not temperamental, not frank, predictable, tactful, and not creative. The third we call internalized control, and it includes: empathizes orders and defers gratification.[18]

FIGURE 5–1.
*Personality Traits Rewarded and Penalized*
*(in a New York High School)*

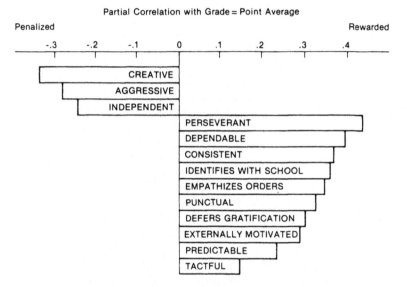

Partial Correlation with Grade = Point Average

Penalized                                                                    Rewarded

NOTES: Each bar shows the partial correlation between grade-point average and the indicated personality trait, controlling for IQ, SAT-Verbal, and SAT-Mathematical. The penalized traits (left) indicate creativity and autonomy, while the rewarded traits (right) indicate subordinacy and discipline. The data are from Samuel Bowles, Herbert Gintis, and Peter Meyer, "The Long Shadow of Work: Education, the Family, and the Reproduction of the Social Division of Labor," *The Insurgent Sociologist*, Summer 1975, and is described in Appendix B (see Bibliography Appendix B). All partial correlations are statistically significant at the 1 percent level. The results for English grades alone, and for a teacher-attitude rating in place of grade-point average, are similar and are presented in Appendix B.

These three factors are not perfectly comparable to Edwards' three factors. Thus our submission to authority seems to combine Edwards' rules and dependability factors, while our internalized control is comparable to Edwards' internalization factor. In the case of the latter, both Edwards and Meyer's data depict an individual who sensitively interprets the desires of his or her superior and operates adequately without direct supervision over considerable periods of time.

Our theory would predict that at the high school level submission to authority would be the best predictor of grades among personality traits, while internalization would be less important. (The temperament factor is essentially irrelevant to our theory and might be expected to be unimpor-

FIGURE 5–2.
*Personality Traits Approved by Supervisors.*

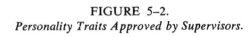

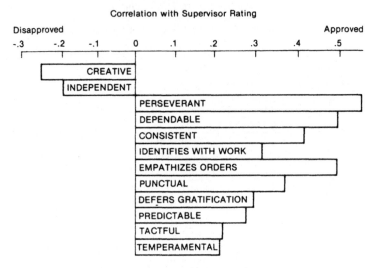

NOTES: The pattern of personality traits indicative of supervisor approval correspond to those rewarded in high school. Each bar shows the correlation between supervisor rating and the indicated personality trait. The results are similar to Figure 5–1, except that aggressive is insignificant and temperamental significant in the sample of workers. The data are from Richard C. Edwards, "Personal Traits and 'Success' in Schooling and Work," *Educational and Psychological Measurement,* in Press, 1976; "Individual Traits and Organizational Incentives: What Makes a "Good Worker?" *Journal of Human Resources,* Spring 1976, and are based on a sample of 240 workers in several government offices in the Boston area. All correlations are significant at the 1 percent level.

tant.) This prediction was confirmed. Assessing the independent contributions of both cognitive measures and personality factors to the prediction of grades, we found that SAT math were the most important, followed by submission to authority and SAT-verbal scores (each equally important). Internalized control proved to be significantly less important as predictors. The temperament and IQ variables made no independent contribution.

Thus, at least for this sample, the personality traits rewarded in schools seem to be rather similar to those indicative of good job performance in the capitalist economy. Since moreover both Edwards and Meyer used essentially the same measures of personality traits, we can test this assertion in yet another way. We can take the three general traits extracted by Edwards in his study of workers—rules orientation, dependability, and internalization of norms—and find the relationship between those traits

FIGURE 5–3.
*Predicting Job Performance and Grades in School
from the same Personality Traits*

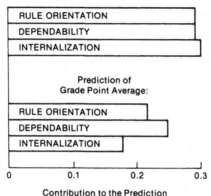

Contribution to the Prediction

NOTES: The top three bars show the estimated normalized regression coefficients of the personality factors in an equation predicting supervisor ratings. The bottom three bars show the coefficients of the same three factors in an equation predicting high-school grade-point average. All factors are significant at the 1 percent level. The regression equations are presented in our Appendix B.

SOURCES: Bowles, Gintis, and Meyer (1975); Edwards (See full citations in Figures 5–1 and 5–2).

and grades in Myer's school study. The results shown in Figure 5–3, exhibit a remarkable congruence.[19]

While the correspondence principle stands up well in the light of grading practices, we must stress that the empirical data on grading must not regarded as fully revealing the inner workings of the educational system's reproduction of the social division of labor. In the first place, it is the overall structure of social relations of the educational encounter which reproduces consciousness, not just grading practices. Nor are personality traits the only relevant personal attributes captured in this data; others are modes of self-presentation, self-image, aspirations, and class identifications. The measuring of personality traits moreover is complex and difficult, and these studies probably capture only a small part of the relevant dimensions. Finally, both traits rewarded in schools and relevant to job performance differ by educational level, class composition of schools, and the student's particular educational track. These subtleties are not reflected in this data.

For all these reasons, we would not expect student grades to be a good predictor of economic success. In addition, grades are clearly dominated by the cognitive performance of students, which we have seen is not highly relevant to economic success. Still, we might expect that in an adequately controlled study in which work performances of individuals on the same job and with comparable educational experience are compared, grades will be good predictors. We have managed to find only one study even approaching these requirements—a study which clearly supports our position, and is sufficiently interesting to present in some detail.[20] Marshall S. Brenner studied one hundred employees who had joined the Lockheed-California Company after obtaining a high school diploma in the Los Angeles City school districts. From the employees' high school transcripts, he obtained their grade-point averages, school absence rates, a teachers' "work habits" evaluation, and a teachers' "cooperation" evaluation. In addition to this data, he gathered three evaluations of job performance by employees' supervisors: a supervisors' "ability rating," "conduct rating," and "productivity rating." Brenner found a significant correlation between grades and all measures of supervisor evaluation.

We have reanalyzed Brenner's data to uncover the source of this correlation. One possibility is that grades measure cognitive performance and cognitive performance determines job performance. However, when the high school teachers' work habits and cooperation evaluations as well as school absences were controlled for by linear regression, grades had no power to predict either worker conduct or worker productivity. Hence, we may draw two conclusions: First, grades predict job adequacy only through their noncognitive component; and second, teachers' evaluations of behavior in the classroom are strikingly similar to supervisors' ratings of behavior on the job. The cognitive component of grades predicts only the supervisors' ability rating—which is not surprising in view of the probability that both are related to employee IQ.[21]

Why then the association between more schooling and higher incomes? In Chapter 3, we indicated the importance of four sets of noncognitive worker traits—work-related personality characteristics, modes of self-presentation, racial, sexual, and ethnic characteristics, and credentials. We believe that all of these traits are involved in the association between educational level and economic success. We have already shown how personality traits conducive to performance at different hierarchical levels are fostered and rewarded by the school system. A similar, but simpler, argument can be made with respect to modes of self-presentation. Individuals who have attained a certain educational level tend to identify with one another socially and to differentiate themselves from their "inferiors." They tend to adjust their aspirations and self-concepts accordingly, while acquiring manners of speech and demeanor more or less socially acceptable and appropriate to their level.[22] As such, they are correspondingly valuable to employers interested in preserving and reproducing the status differences on which the legitimacy and stability of the hierarchical division of labor is based. Moreover, insofar as educational credentials are an independent determinant of hiring and promotion, they will directly account for a portion of this association.[23]

Finally, family background also accounts for a significant portion of the association between schooling and economic attainment. Indeed, for white males, about a third of the correlation between education and income is due to the common association of both variables with socioeconomic background, even holding constant childhood IQ.[24] That is, people whose parents have higher-status economic positions tend to achieve more income themselves independent of their education, but they also tend to get more education. Hence the observed association is reinforced.

Indeed, there is a strong independent association between family background and economic success, illustrated in Figure 5–4. For the large national sample represented there, children of the poorest tenth of families have roughly a third the likelihood of winding up well-off as the children of the most well-to-do tenth, even if they have the same educational attainments and childhood IQ's. What is the origin of this effect? The inheritance of wealth, family connections, and other more or less direct advantages play an important role here. But there are more subtle if no less important influences at work here as well. We shall argue in the following section that the experiences of parents on the job tend to be reflected in the social relations of family life. Thus, through family socialization, children tend to acquire orientations toward work, aspirations, and self-concepts, preparing them for similar economic positions themselves.

## Family Structure and Job Structure

According to the materialist conception, the determining factor in history is, in the last resort, the production and reproduction of immediate life. But this itself is of a two-fold character. On the one hand, the production of the means of subsistence, of food, clothing, and shelter and the tools requisite therefore; on the other, the production of human beings themselves, the propagation of the species. The social institutions under which people of a particular historical epoch and a particular country live are conditioned by both kinds of production; by the stage of development of labor, on the one hand, and of the family on the other.

FRIEDRICH ENGELS, *The Origin*
*of the Family, Private Property, and the State*, 1884

FIGURE 5–4.

*The Effect of Socioeconomic Background on Economic Success
is Strong even for Individuals with Equal Education and I.Q.*

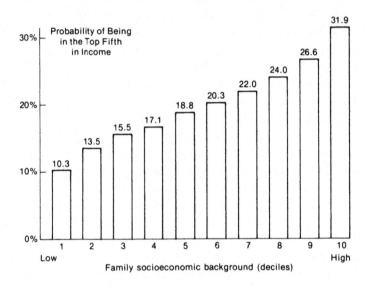

Low     Family socioeconomic background (deciles)     High

NOTES: Each bar shows the estimated probability that a man is in the top fifth of the income distribution if he is from the given decile of socioeconomic background (as a weighted average of his father's education, occupational status, and his parents' income), and if he has an average childhood IQ and average number of years of schooling. That is, it measures the effect of socioeconomic background on income, independent of any effects caused by education or IQ differences.[24]

SAMPLE: Non-Negro males from nonfarm backgrounds, aged 35–44.

SOURCE: Samuel Bowles and Valerie Nelson, "The 'Inheritance of IQ' and the Intergenerational Reproduction of Economic Inequality," *The Review of Economics and Statistics*, Vol. 56, No. I, February 1974.

Family experience has a significant impact on the well-being, behavior, and personal consciousness of individuals, both during maturation and in their daily adult lives. The social relationships of family life—relationships between husband and wife as well as between parents and children and among children—have undergone important changes in the course of U.S. economic development. The prospect for future changes is of crucial importance in the process of social transformation.[25]

Rather than attempt a broad analysis of family life, we shall limit our discussion to a few issues directly linked to our central concern: the reproduction of the social relations of production. Like the educational system, the family plays a major role in preparing the young for economic and social roles. Thus, the family's impact on the reproduction of the sexual division of labor, for example, is distinctly greater than that of the educational system.

This reproduction of consciousness is facilitated by a rough correspondence between the social relations of production and the social relations of family life, a correspondence that is greatly affected by the experiences of parents in the social division of labor. There is a tendency for families to reproduce in their offspring not only a consciousness tailored to the objective nature of the work world, but to prepare them for economic positions roughly comparable to their own. Although these tendencies can be countered by other social forces (schooling, media, shifts in aggregate occupational structure), they continue to account for a significant part of the observed intergenerational status-transmission processes.

This is particularly clear with respect to sexual division of labor. The social division of labor promotes the separation between wage and household labor, the latter being unpaid and performed almost exclusively by women. This separation is reflected within the family as a nearly complete division of labor between husband and wife. The occupational emphasis on full-time work, the dependence of promotion upon seniority, the career-oriented commitment of the worker, and the active discrimination against working women conspire to shackle the woman to the home while minimizing the likelihood of a joint sharing of domestic duties between husband and wife.

But how does the family help reproduce the sexual division of labor? First, wives and mothers themselves normally embrace their self-concepts as household workers. They then pass these onto their children through the differential sex role-typing of boys and girls within the family. Second, and perhaps more important, children tend to develop self-concepts based on the sexual divisions which they observe around them. Even families which attempt to treat boys and girls equally cannot avoid sex role-typing when the male parent is tangentially involved in household labor and child-rearing. In short, the family as a social as well as biological reproduction unit cannot but reflect its division of labor as a production unit. This sex typing, unless countered by other social forces, then facilitates the submission of the next generation of women to their inferior status in the wage-labor system and lends its alternative—child-rearing and domesticity—an aura of inevitability, if not desirability.

However, in essential respects, the family exhibits social patterns that are quite uncharacteristic of the social relations of production. The close personal and emotional relationships of family life are remote from the impersonal bureaucracy of the wage-labor system. Indeed, the family is often esteemed as a refuge from the alienation and psychic poverty of work life. Indeed, it is precisely because family structure and the capitalist relations of production differ in essential respects that our analysis sees schooling as performing such a necessary role in the integration of young people into the wage-labor system. We will return to this point in the next chapter.

Despite the tremendous structural disparity between family and economy—one which is never really overcome in capitalist society—there is a significant correspondence between the authority relationships in capitalist production and family child-rearing. In part, this is true of family life common at all social levels. The male-dominated family, with its characteristically age-graded patterns of power and privilege, replicates many aspects of the hierarchy of production in the firm. Yet here we shall be more concerned with the difference among families whose income-earners hold distinct positions in this hierarchy.

As we have seen, successful job performance at low hierarchical levels requires the worker's orientation toward rule-following and conformity to external authority, while successful performance at higher levels requires behavior according to internalized norms. It would be surprising, indeed, if these general orientations did not manifest themselves in parental priorities for the rearing of their children. Melvin Kohn's massive, ten-year study at the National Institute of Mental Health has documented important correspondences between authority in the social relationships of work and the social relationships of the family precisely of this type.

Kohn, in a series of papers and in his book, *Class and Conformity*, has advanced and tested the following hypothesis: Personality traits and values of individuals affect the economic positions they attain and, conversely, their job experiences strongly affect their personalities and values.[26] The most important values and behavior patterns in this interaction are those relating to self-direction and conformity,[27] with individuals of higher economic status more likely to value internal motivation and those of lower status more likely to value behavior that conforms with external authority. Thus, Kohn argues, individuals in higher-status jobs tend to value curiosity and self-reliance, to emphasize the intrinsic aspects of jobs such as freedom and choice, and to exhibit a high level of internalized motivation and a high degree of trust in interpersonal relationships. Conversely, people in lower-status jobs tend to value personal responsibility and the extrinsic aspects of jobs such as security, pay, and working conditions. Moreover, they exhibit more external motivations, a greater conformity to explicit social rules and they are less trustful of others.[28]

Kohn goes on to inquire which aspects of jobs produce these results and concludes that the statistically relevant job characteristic is the degree of occupational self-direction, including freedom from close supervision, the degree of initiative and independent judgment allowed, and the complexity and variety of the job.[29] Thus no matter what their economic status, whether white or blue collar, individuals with the same degree of occupational self-direction, tend to have similar values and traits. Self-direction versus close supervision and routinization on the job account for most of the status-related differences in personal preferences for self-direction, degree of internalized morality, trustfulness, self-confidence, self-esteem, and idea conformity.[30] He concludes:

> In industrial society, where occupation is central to men's lives, occupational experiences that facilitate or deter the exercise of self-direction come to permeate men's views, not only of work and their role in work, but of the world and of self. The conditions of occupational life at higher social class levels facilitate interest in the intrinsic qualities of the job, foster a view of self and society that is conducive to believing in the possibilities of rational action toward purposive goals, and promote the valuation of self-direction. The conditions of occupational life at lower social class levels limit men's view of the job primarily to the extrinsic benefits it provides, foster a narrowly circumscribed conception of self and society, and promote the positive valuation of conformity to authority.[31]

There remains, however, an important discrepancy between our interpretation and Kohn's. What Kohn calls "self-direction" we feel is usually better expressed as "internalized norms." That is, the vast majority of workers in higher levels of the hierarchy of production are by no means autonomous, self-actualizing, and creatively self-directed. Rather, they are probably supersocialized so as to internalize authority and act without direct and continuous supervision to implement goals and objectives relatively alienated from their own personal needs. This distinction must be kept clearly in mind to avoid the error of attributing "superior" values and behavior traits to higher strata in the capitalist division of labor.

Kohn then went on to investigate the impact of work-related values on child-rearing. He began, in 1956, with a sample of 339 white mothers of

145

children in the fifth grade, whose husbands held middle-class and working-class jobs.[32] He inquired into the values parents would most like to see in their children's behavior. He found that parents of lower-status children value obedience, neatness, and honesty in their children, while higher-status parents emphasize curiosity, self-control, consideration, and happiness. The fathers of these children who were interviewed showed a similar pattern of values. Kohn says:

Middle class parents are more likely to emphasize children's *self-direction*, and working class parents to emphasize their *conformity to external authority*. . . . The essential difference between the terms, as we use them, is that self-direction focuses on *internal* standards of direction for behavior; conformity focuses on *externally* imposed rules.[33]

Kohn further emphasized that these values translate directly into corresponding authority relationships between parents and children, with higher-status parents punishing breakdowns of internalized norms, and lower-status parents punishing transgressions of rules:

The principal difference between the classes is in the *specific conditions* under which parents—particularly mothers—punish children's misbehavior. Working class parents are more likely to punish or refrain from punishing on the basis of the direct and immediate consequences of children's actions, middle class parents on the basis of their interpretation of children's intent in acting as they do. . . . If self-direction is valued, transgressions must be judged in terms of the reasons why the children misbehave. If conformity is valued, transgressions must be judged in terms of whether or not the actions violate externally imposed proscriptions.[34]

In 1964, Kohn undertook to validate his findings with a national sample of 3,100 males, representative of the employed, male civilian labor force. His results clearly support his earlier interpretation: Higher-job-status fathers prefer consideration, curiosity, responsibility, and self-control in their children; low-status fathers prefer good manners, neatness, honesty, and obedience. Moreover, Kohn showed that about two-thirds of these social status-related differences are directly related to the extent of occupational self-direction. As a predictor of child-rearing values, the structure of work life clearly overshadows the other correlates of status such as occupational prestige or educational level.[35] He concludes:

Whether consciously or not parents tend to impact to their children lessons derived from the conditions of life of their own social class—and this helps to prepare their children for a similar class position. . . .
Class differences in parental values and child rearing practices influence the development of the capacities that children will someday need. . . . The family, then, functions as a mechanism for perpetuating inequality.[36]

Kohn's analysis provides a careful and compelling elucidation of one facet of what we consider to be a generalized social phenomenon: the reflection of economic life in all major spheres of social activity. The hierarchical division of labor, with the fragmentation of the work force which it engenders, is merely reflected in family life. The distinct quality of social relationships at different hierarchical levels in production are reflected in corresponding social relationships in the family. Families, in turn, reproduce the forms of consciousness required for the integration of a new generation into the economic system. Such differential patterns of child-rearing affect more than the worker's personality, as is exemplified in Kohn's study. They also pattern self-concepts, personal aspirations, styles of self-presentation, class loyalties, and modes of speech, dress, and interpersonal behavior. While such traits are by no means fixed into adulthood and must be reinforced at the workplace, their stability over the life cycle appears sufficient to account for a major portion of the observed degree of intergenerational status transmission.

## Conclusion

> You will still be here tomorrow,
> but your dreams may not.
> CAT STEVENS

The economic system is stable only if the consciousness of the strata and classes which compose it remains compatible with the social relations which characterize it as a mode of production. The perpetuation of the class structure requires that the hierarchical division of labor be reproduced in the consciousness of its participants. The educational system is one of the several reproduction mechanisms through which dominant elites seek to achieve this objective. By providing skills, legitimating inequalities in economic positions, and facilitating certain types of social intercourse among individuals, U.S. education patterns personal development around the requirements of alienated work. The educational system reproduces the capitalist social division of labor, in part, through a correspondence between its own internal social relationships and those of the workplace.

The tendency of the social relationships of economic life to be replicated in the educational system and in family life lies at the heart of the failure of the liberal educational creed. This fact must form the basis of a viable program for social change. Patterns of inequality, repression, and forms of class domination cannot be restricted to a single sphere of life, but reappear in substantially altered, yet structurally comparable, form in all spheres. Power and privilege in economic life surface not only in the core social institutions which pattern the formation of consciousness (e.g., school and family), but even in face-to-face personal encounters, leisure activities, cultural life, sexual relationships, and philosophies of the world. In particular, the liberal goal of employing the educational system as a corrective device for overcoming the "inadequacies" of the economic system is vain indeed. We will argue in our concluding chapter that the transformation of the educational system and the pattern of class relationships, power, and privilege in the economic sphere must go hand in hand as part of an integrated program for action.

To speak of social change is to speak of making history. Thus we are motivated to look into the historical roots of the present educational system in order to better understand the framework within which social change takes place. Our major question will be: What were the historical forces giving rise to the present correspondence between education and economic life and how have these been affected by changes in the class structure and by concrete people's struggles? How may we shape these forces so as to serve the goals of economic equality and liberated human development?

We shall show that the historical development of the educational system reflects a counterpoint of reproduction and contradiction. As we have already seen, capitalist economic development leads to continual shifts in the social relationships of production and the attendant class structure. These social relationships have involved class conflicts which, throughout U.S. history, have periodically changed in both form and content. In important respects the educational system has served to defuse and attenuate these conflicts. Thus the changing character of social conflict, rooted in shifts in the class structure and in other relations of power and privilege has resulted in periodic reorganizations of educational institutions. At the same time the educational system has evolved in ways which intensify and politicize the basic contradictions and conflicts of capitalist society.

# Part III

## THE DYNAMICS OF
## EDUCATIONAL CHANGE

# CHAPTER 6

•

# The Origins of
# Mass Public Education

> Most of you, indeed, cannot but have been part and parcel
> of one of those huge, mechanical, educational machines, or
> mills, as they might more properly be called. They are, I be-
> lieve, peculiar to our own time and country, and are so or-
> ganized as to combine as nearly as possible the principal
> characteristics of the cotton mill and the railroad with those
> of the model state's prison.
> CHARLES FRANCIS ADAMS,
> addressing the National Education Association, 1880

The evidence presented in the previous two chapters leaves little doubt that
the U.S. educational system works to justify economic inequality and to
produce a labor force whose capacities, credentials, and consciousness are
dictated in substantial measure by the requirements of profitable employment in the capitalist economy. Nor will there be much dissent from the
proposition that an essential structural characteristic of U.S. education is
what we have called the correspondence between the social organization of
schooling and that of work. An understanding of U.S. education, however,
requires that we know more than the dominant economic effects of schooling and the structural mechanisms which produce these effects. We must
discover how the school system changes. An analysis of the dynamics of
U.S. education may be helpful in two respects. First, it will enrich our
understanding of the correspondence between educational structure and
economic life. The fit between schooling and work described in the previous chapters is, in one sense, too neat. The ensuing study of historical
change in the U.S. school system reveals not a smooth adjustment of
educational structure to the evolution of economic life, but rather a jarring
and conflict-ridden course of struggle and accommodation. In this course,
the school system has, for substantial periods, been organized along lines
which, far from corresponding to the developing organization of economic
life, appear as bizarre or anachronistic throwbacks to earlier times. We

find, further, that the process of change, as exhibited in the history of educational reform movements, contributes significantly to the impact of schooling on consciousness, ideology, and the class structure itself. Particularly important in this respect is the discrepancy between the rhetoric and reality of educational reform. The popular objectives, slogans, and perspectives of reform movements have often imparted to the educational system an enduring veneer of egalitarian and humanistic ideology, while the highly selective implementation of reforms has tended to preserve the role of schooling in the perpetuation of economic order.

Our second reason for studying the dynamics of the school system is rather more political. The apparently smoothly functioning conveyor belt which carries young people from birth to adult work—the family, school, workplace machine—has faltered and then been readjusted in the past. As we watch the present stumbling performance of U.S. education, we witness the opportunity for radical change. An understanding of the dynamics of development in U.S. education, particularly of the sometimes harmonious and sometimes strained relationships between educational structure and economic forces, provides the indispensable foundations for a modern strategy for change. We must know how we arrived here so we may discover how we may move on.

Stepping back from the historical material, we are struck, first, by the sheer magnitude of educational change since the American War of Independence. Until quite recently, in no society did more than a tiny minority of children spend more than a small part of their youth in formal educational institutions. Even today, there are relatively few countries in which the majority of young people spend most of their youth in schools. In most societies throughout recorded history, schools have not played a major role in preparing children for adulthood. American colonial society was no exception.

Two centuries ago, the structure and scope of American education bore little resemblance to our current school system. Along the way, many and diverse alternatives were considered and tried. Looking backward, one might—and many educational historians do—see an inexorable march along a single line of ascent. But to educators, politicians, and others living in each historical period, the way forward did not seem so clear; education has reached and passed many crossroads.

Prior to the nineteenth century, the main job of upbringing and training of youth was carried by the family, occasionally supplemented by apprenticeship or the church.[1] The school played a rather marginal role in the process of child-rearing. Attendance, school reformers lamented, was sparse. Even for those attending, the school year was short. As recently as 1870, less than half of the children of age five to seventeen attended school; among those enrolled, the school year averaged seventy-eight days, or less than a quarter of a year.[2] Today, virtually all children in that age group attend school for an average of half of the days in the year.

The structure of schooling and not merely its extent has changed radically in the past two centuries. Early elementary schools in the United States were, not surprisingly, extension of the home. These "dame schools," conducted more often than not in the kitchen of a literate woman, provided most of the basic formal education available in the original thirteen colonies. Coexisting with the dame schools were the so-called "writing schools." These were ordinarily conducted outside the home but, like the dame schools, stressed basic literacy and computational skills. Like the dame schools, too, the internal structure of the writing schools was informal, bordering sometimes on the chaotic. At the other extreme, military discipline and drill prevailed in most of the charity schools for the poor.

Differing methods of instruction and student control, and the variety of structures of schooling do not exhaust the range of alternatives facing American educators a century and a half ago. Most seemed to accept the fact that different races and classes, and boys and girls, would attend quite different types of institutions. But even then, a substantial minority opinion in educational circles argued for the unification of all groups within the same school structure. Radically different proposals for the control and financing of education were also debated. Some would have left schooling in private hands, trusting to philanthropy to cater to the educational needs of the poor. Others promoted public schooling, but sought an extension of the prevalent "district system" which assured strict neighborhood control. Others, as we shall soon see, promoted a then thoroughly novel but now familiar educational structure. Public nonsectarian compulsory and tax-supported schooling was far from a foregone conclusion in the early years of the nineteenth century.[3]

But as the United States entered the last quarter of the nineteenth century, the modern school system, more or less as we know it, had taken form most completely in the urban Northeast. By 1880, asserts the educational historian Michael Katz:

... American education had acquired its fundamental structural characteristics, they have not altered since. Public education was universal, tax-supported, free, compulsory, bureaucratically arranged, class based, and racist.[4]

Rapid growth in attendance paralleled these dramatic changes in the legal, financial and social structure of U.S. education. Twenty years before the Civil War, just under 38 percent of white children aged five–nineteen were attending schools.[5] By 1860, the figure had risen to 59 percent. Thus the few decades of educational change, which may be dated from Horace Mann's ascendency to the newly created Massachusetts State Board of Education in 1837, marked a major turning point in U.S. social history. For a period of comparable importance, we must await the evolution of corporate capitalist production and the closely associated Progressive Education movement around the turn of the present century.

In this chapter, we propose to answer the question: How did the present structure of U.S. education arise out of the political and economic conflicts of the mid-nineteenth century? In Chapters 7 and 8, we will extend our analysis to cover two other turning points in U.S. educational history: the years 1890–1930 and the period extending from roughly 1960 to the present. In Chapter 9, we will present an overview and interpretation of the results of our historical research.

In the second part of this chapter we treat, in rather broad terms, the joint evolution of economic structure and schooling in the antebellum period. Though essential, a broad survey of this type hardly does justice to the complexity of the material. Nor, we suspect, will it satisfy the critical reader. The available primary historical materials allow a considerably more searching investigation of our interpretations. We will draw upon these materials in three ways. First we will study the evolution of economic life and schooling in a particular town. Second we will examine the mid-nineteenth-century reform movement through the work of its greatest exponent, Horace Mann. Lastly, we will use detailed statistical evidence from town-by-town and state-by-state records to present our analysis of the economic bases for the rise of mass education. Our three types of evidence —detailed studies of a single town, a major reformer, and the available quantitative data—cannot, of course, demonstrate beyond a shadow of doubt the validity of our interpretation. The most we claim is that our detailed studies provide compelling support for our view and are, in important respects, contradictory to alternative explanations.

A word must be said about what may seem to the reader to be a peculiar geographic narrow-mindedness on our part. Most of our evidence in this chapter comes from Massachusetts. The emphasis on Massachusetts is no accident. The educational reform movement which marked the first turning point in U.S. educational history originated in the burgeoning industrial cities and towns of this state and was dominated throughout its course by the example of Massachusetts and its educational leaders.[6] Needless to say, the experience of Massachusetts was not perfectly replicated elsewhere, but we believe (and present some evidence) that the course of educational change in this state is not atypical of the rest of the country.

## The Expansion of Capital and the Origins of Public Education

> Whereas our employers have robbed us of certain rights . . .
> we feel bound to rise unitedly in our strength and burst
> asunder as Freemen ought the shackles and fetters with which
> they have long been chaining and binding us, by an unjust
> and unchristian use of power . . . which the possession of
> capital and superior knowledge furnishes.
> "Declaration of Independence"
> Beverly, Massachusetts shoe workers, 1844

On March 6, 1824, Kirk Boott, manager of the Merrimack Manufacturing Company in Lowell, Massachusetts, drove his carriage to South Boston to pick up Theodore Edson, a young Episcopal minister. Edson had accepted Boott's offer to move to the booming mill town fifteen miles north of Boston to preach and establish a school. "Conversation," Edson later recalled, "was easy, various and unconstrained as we drove on together." They arrived in time for Edson to tour the cotton mills before they closed down for the night.[7] Edson was to become the leading educator of the soon-to-be-flourishing city. His zeal to establish a modern and well-financed system of public education brought him into conflict, at one time or another, with just about every major political group in town, including his old friend Kirk Boott and the other employers.

At the March 1860 Town Meeting of Beverly, just a few miles from Lowell, the shoemakers, farmers, sailors, and laborers of the town outvoted the professional and business people and closed down the town's brand new public high school. Few of them had or were likely to have children in the school; the high school tax seemed to be little more than a gift to the well-to-do. Beverly's artisans were just about evenly split on the vote. But the professional and business groups voted to retain the school by a two to one margin; more than three-quarters of the working people of the town voted against it.[8]

The shoe workers played a particularly important part in the defeat of the school, casting over half of the "no" votes. But to many of them, the school must have been a rather minor concern: That very week, after months of angry discussion and protest at the loss of independence to the capitalist employers who had come to dominate the shoe trade, most of them went out on strike. The strike, which spread to surrounding towns, was to become the largest in the U.S. prior to the Civil War.

The development of mass public education in the United States was the work of people like Kirk Boott, Theodore Edson, and ironically, the shoe workers of Beverly. As we shall soon see, it was because of—if not on behalf of—groups such as the striking shoe workers of Beverly that Edson, Boott, and others had forged an unequal and often uneasy alliance of reformers and capitalists for the purpose of establishing mass public education.

In colonial America, the basic productive unit was the family. Most families owned the tools of their trade and worked their own land. Transmitting the necessary productive skills to the children as they grew up proved to be a simple task, not because the work was devoid of skill, but because the quite substantial skills required were virtually unchanging from generation to generation, and because the transition to the work world did not require that the child adapt to a wholly new set of social relationships. The child learned the concrete skills and adapted to the social relations of production within the family. To put the point more technically: Production and reproduction were unified in a single institution—the family. Preparation for life in the larger community was facilitated by the child's experience with the family. While the nuclear, rather than the extended, family was the norm, people did not move around much.[9] Relatives tended to live fairly close to one another; children had ample opportunity to learn to deal with complex relationships among adults other than their parents and with children other than their brothers and sisters.[10]

It was not required that children learn a complex set of political principles or ideologies, as political participation was limited. The only major cultural institution outside the family was the church, which sought to inculcate the accepted spiritual values and attitudes. In addition, a small number of children learned craft skills outside the family as apprentices. Elementary schools focused on literacy training to facilitate a familiarity with the Scriptures. Above this level, education tended to be narrowly vocational, restricted to preparation of children for a career in the church, the "learned professions," or the still inconsequential state bureaucracy.[11] The curriculum of the few universities reflected the aristocratic penchant for conspicuous intellectual consumption.

Rapid economic change following the War for Independence set into motion forces which would radically alter the relationship between the family and the system of production. Commerce expanded dramatically: In the fifteen years before 1807, the value of foreign trade increased fourfold.[12] Larger commercial interests profited from the expansion of trade, amassed substantial concentrations of capital, and sought new arenas for profitable investment. Increasingly, capital was used for the direct employment of labor in production rather than remaining confined to the buying and selling of commodities and related commercial activities. The expansion of capitalist production, particularly the factory system as well as the continuing concentration of commercial capital, undermined the role of the family as the major unit of both child-rearing and production. Small shopkeepers and farmers were competed out of business. Cottage industry and artisan production were gradually destroyed. Ownership of the means of production became heavily concentrated in the hands of landlords and capitalists. Faced with declining opportunities for an independent livelihood, workers were forced to relinquish control over their labor in return for wages, or piece rates. The pay workers received increasingly took the form of a "wage" rather than a "price."[13]

The statistics for New York City for the years 1795 to 1855 illustrate these trends: A fourfold increase in the relative number of wage workers and a reduction by two-thirds in the relative number of independent merchants and proprietors.[14] In the country as a whole, agricultural pursuits —the stronghold of independent production—lost ground to manufacturing. In 1820, for every person working in manufacturing and distribution, there were six people engaged in agriculture; by 1860, this figure had fallen to three.[15] By the Civil War, the family no longer constituted the dominant unit of production. Increasingly, production was carried on in large organizations in which an employer directed the activities of the entire work force and owned the products of their labor. The social relations of production became increasingly distinct from the social relations of reproduction.

The emerging class structure evolved in accord with these new social relations of production: An ascendant and self-conscious capitalist class came to dominate the political, legal, and cultural superstructure of society. The needs of this class were to profoundly shape the evolution of the educational system.

The expansion and continuing transformation of the system of capitalist production led to unprecedented shifts in the occupational distribution of the labor force and constant changes in the skills requirement for jobs. Training within the family became increasingly inadequate; the productive skills of the parents were no longer adequate for the needs of the children during their lifetime. The apprentice system of training, which, by custom, committed masters for a period of as much as seven years to supply apprentices with room and board as well as (sometimes) minimal levels of training in return for labor services, became a costly liability as the growing severity of depressions made the demand for the products of the apprentices' labor more uncertain. The further expansion of capital increasingly required a system of labor training which would allow the costs of training to be borne by the public. Equally important, the dynamism of the capitalist growth process required a training system which would facilitate a more rapid adjustment of employment to the business cycle and allow the constantly changing dictates of profitability to govern the allocation of labor.

While undermining the economic role of the family and the adequacy of the apprenticeship system, the expansion of capital created, at the same time, an environment—both social and intellectual—which would ultimately challenge the political order. Workers were thrown together in large factories. The isolation, which had helped to maintain quiescence in earlier, widely dispersed farming populations, was broken down. With an increasing number of families uprooted from the land, the workers' search for a living resulted in large-scale labor migrations. Labor scarcity induced by an abundance of land and rapid capital accumulation led employers in the expanding sectors of the economy to rely increasingly on an influx of foreigners to staff the lowest-paying jobs. In the ten-year period beginning in 1846, the United States absorbed 3.1 million immigrants—a number equal to an eighth of the entire population at that date. (The better-known massive immigration of the pre-World-War-I decade constituted a somewhat lesser fraction of the total population.) Most immigrants, arriving with few resources other than their labor power, became part of the growing urban proletariat. Others, less fortunate, swelled the ranks of the "reserve army" of the unemployed, ready to take up jobs at near subsistence wages. They were a constant threat to the job security and livelihood of the employed workers. Transient—often foreign—elements came to constitute a major segment of the urban population and began to pose seemingly insurmountable problems of assimilation, integration, and control.[16] Cultural diversity came to be seen as a social problem. Ethnic conflicts shattered the calm and threatened the political stability of many towns.

With the rapid expansion of both industrial and commercial capital, inequalities in wealth increased. Using data from New York City, Brooklyn, and Boston, we estimate that, early in the nineteenth century, the wealthiest 1 percent of urban residents in the Northeast owned something like a quarter of all tangible wealth. By midcentury, the figure had risen to about two-fifths. Moreover, fragmentary evidence suggests a drastic reduction of general mobility into the ranks of the very wealthy.[17] Significantly, only the economically stagnant towns appear to be exceptions to this trend toward wealth concentration.[18]

Inequality was increasingly difficult to justify and was less readily accepted. The simple legitimizing ideologies of the earlier periods—the divine origin of social rank, for example—had fallen under the capitalist attack on royalty, royal monopoly, and the traditional landed interests. The broadening of the electorate and of political participation generally—first sought by the propertied and commercial classes in their struggle against the British Crown—threatened soon to become a powerful instrument in the hands of farmers and workers. Common people did not limit their political efforts to the ballot box alone. Since the end of the War of Independence, Shays' Rebellion, the Whiskey Rebellion, the Dorr War, and a host of minor insurrections had erupted, often led by Revolutionary War heroes and supported by thousands of poor and debt-ridden farmers and workers. These rebellions seemed to portend an era of social upheaval.

The process of capital accumulation drastically changed the structure of society: The role of the family in production was greatly reduced; its role in reproduction was increasingly out of touch with economic reality. A permanent proletariat and an impoverished and, for the most part, ethnically distinct, reserve army of the unemployed had been created. Economic inequality had increased. Small manufacturing towns had become urban areas almost overnight. The expansion of capitalist production had at once greatly enhanced the power of the capitalist class and had inexorably generated a condition which challenged their continued domination. With increasing urgency, economic leaders sought a mechanism to insure political stability and the continued profitability of their enterprises.

Confronted with novel and rapidly changing economic conditions, working people, too, sought new solutions to the age-old problems of security, independence, and material welfare. The stakes of the economic game had greatly increased. As farmers and artisans became wage workers, they sought a means by which they or their children might recoup their lost status. Some—surely a small minority—proposed to attack the wage-labor system. Many saved what meager amounts they could afford in hopes of eventually getting back into business on their own. Others followed the lure of independence and cheap land and moved West. But for many, education seemed to promise the respectability and security which they sought.

A similar response to the expansion of capitalist production—though with important variations reflecting differing economic, political, and cultural conditions—occurred in other countries. In England, both working people and employers supported some kind of educational expansion, although their objectives were radically different. An effective stalemate among the proeducational strategies of capitalist employers, the powerful and more conservative Church of England, and land-owning interests postponed the implementation of public education on a national scale until the 1870s.[19] In a few areas—such as Prussia and Scotland—where military or religious purposes dominated educational policy, mass instruction was implemented considerably before the impact of capitalist expansion was felt.[20] In the remainder of this chapter, we illustrate how this process of economic expansion and educational change came about in the United States.

## The School System of Lowell, Massachusetts, 1824–1860

> . . . Let then the influence of our Common Schools become *universal*, for they are the main pillars of the permanency of our free institutions; a protection from our enemies abroad, and our surest safety against internal commotions.
>
> Lowell Massachusetts School Committee Report, 1846

The growing pressure for public education which marked the early nineteenth century reflected an increasing concern with production and with the conditions of labor. This concern took a variety of forms. In Boston, the cessation of overseas trade during the embargo of 1807 and the closing of the port during the War of 1812 shifted the interests of the propertied classes from a preoccupation with mercantile trade to a consideration of the opportunities of profit through direct employment of labor. The economic distress of this period intensified economic concerns among artisans and other workers. Both concerns were reflected in a petition which was presented in 1817 to the Boston Town Meeting calling for, among other things, the establishment of a system of free public primary schools. As this petition is something of a landmark, it may be worth investigating who signed it. Fortunately, William Weber has carefully analyzed the occupations and classes of these petitioners.[21] While the vast majority of the townspeople fall within Weber's category, "laborers," only 21 percent of the petitioners came from this class. The bulk of support (56 percent) is found among the well-to-do artisans and shopkeepers. Large merchants and entrepreneurs, a minute percent of the populace, provided 23 percent of the signatures and over half of what Weber has classed as the educational leadership of the period.

The demand for elementary schooling in Boston apparently originated with the large propertied class and what might today be called the middle class. Not too much should be read into these data, however, for Boston was clearly an atypical case, representing as it did one of the major mercantile centers of the young nation. Boston would escape much of the social distress and turmoil which would accompany the Industrial Revolution soon to sweep over the Northeast. The wealth of the Boston rich, however, was intimately involved in both industrialization and educational "modernization." We may learn more about this complex story by looking into the educational and economic history of the booming industrial community of Lowell, Massachusetts, during the first four decades of its existence.

When the representatives of the Boston Manufacturing Company began buying up farmland along the Merrimack River in East Chelmsford in 1821, the district had a population of about 200.[22] Though according to school board records, the town—soon to become Lowell—had boasted at least one "Righting School" for over a century, most of the children were not in attendance. Within two decades, Lowell was to become the third largest city in the state, a center of the textile trade, and a leader in establishing one of the first modern school systems in the country.

The owners of the new mills which sprung up in Lowell sought to usher in a new era of industrialization, one which would ensure the profitability of their enterprise without spawning the poverty and human degradation which typified the English manufacturing centers. For the women recruited from the surrounding farms, work in the mills would be well-paying and their leisure hours would be spent in cultural activities and other moral recreation. A literary magazine would soon be formed for the mill women. As a more permanent work force was recruited, particularly from the ranks of Irish immigrants, schooling would play an increasing role in the overall social strategy of the mill owners. During the period of growth of the Lowell economy, the "respectable" members of the community articulated the arguments for a universal public school system which were later to become common throughout the United States.

Educated workers, they noted, would be better workers. Homer Bartlett, agent of the Massachusetts Cotton Mills, wrote in 1841:

From my observations and experience, I am perfectly satisfied that the owners of manufacturing property have a deep pecuniary interest in the education and morals of their help; and I believe the time is not distant when the truth of this will appear more and more clear. And as competition becomes more close, and small circumstances of more importance in turning the scale in favor of one establishment over another, I believe it will be seen that the establishment, other things being equal, which has the best educated and most moral help will give the greatest production at the least cost per pound.[23]

George Boutwell, who succeeded Horace Mann as Secretary of the Massachusetts Board of Education, summarizing the views of employers interviewed during his visit in 1859, wrote:

In Lowell, and in many other places, the proprietors find the training of the schools admirably adapted to prepare the children for the labors of the mills.[24]

Upbringing in the family, evidently, was not adequate training for work in the rising industrial sector. Particularly after the mass influx of Irish workers in the late 1840s, the school committee saw the schools as a partial substitute for the home. Many of the city's children, lamented the committee in 1851:

. . . Have to receive their first lessons of subordination and obedience in the school room. At home, they are either left wholly to their own control, or, what is almost equally bad, the discipline to which they are subjected alternates between foolish indulgence, and exasperated tyranny. . . .[25]

The mill owners echoed these concerns. Boutwell's summary reflects the writings of numerous employers:

The owners of factories are more concerned than other classes and interests in the intelligence of their laborers. When the latter are well-educated and the former are disposed to deal justly, controversies and *strikes* can never occur, nor can the minds of the masses be prejudiced by demagogues and controlled by temporary and factious considerations.[26]

These and other salutory effects of schooling could hardly have been fully appreciated by either Theodore Edson or Kirk Boott—textile capitalist and soon-to-be schoolmaster—as they rode together in 1824 from South Boston to Lowell. But Edson's arrival in Lowell signaled a new departure for the educational system of the city. The changes in the structure and scope of schooling over the next generation were to become a pattern for the rest of the state.

The numerous and scattered district schools were consolidated and brought under the control of the central school board. This centralized body, unlike the decentralized district boards, articulated the concerns of teachers, lawyers, doctors and other professionals, and through them the large property-owning elite of the town. Alexander Field's study of the social composition of the school board reveals that, over the first three decades of the Lowell school committee's existence, 85 percent of the membership was drawn from business and the professions; less than 5 percent were workers. The remainder, those with unknown occupations, were presumably farmers and perhaps workers whose occupation had not been thought important enough to record.[27]

Under the leadership of the centralized school board, the fraction of children attending school grew. The term was substantially lengthened. The larger numbers of children in school allowed the school committee, for the first time, to place students in separate classrooms graded according to age and scholastic proficiency. The curriculum was broadened. The "hidden curriculum" of the school came increasingly to stress "heart culture over brain culture," as the school superintendent of neighboring Lawrence put it.

Not all of the citizens of Lowell endorsed these changes. The first major source of opposition came from the farming families in the outlying districts who resented the growing elite domination of school policy through the town school board and the increasing restriction of the powers of the district school boards. The conflict over centralization came to a head at the 1832 Annual Town Meeting. That night, the citizens of Lowell reversed the decision of the central school board to disqualify a popular district teacher and later voted out the entire school committee.

As production expanded in the mid-1830s, the prices of textile goods began to fall.[28] By the mid-1840s, prices had fallen by between a third and a half. Real wages of textile workers were roughly constant over the years 1835 to 1855, so company profits could be maintained only by drastically increasing the amount of work extracted from the operatives. Despite the lack of significant improvement in the technology of production, output per worker rose, probably by something like 50 percent over the two decades beginning in 1835.[29] The increased pressure on labor coincided with, and was partly responsible for, the gradual replacement of "Yankee" workers by immigrant labor during the 1840s and 1850s. Now even the pretentions of a humane paternalistic industrial system were discarded. The antagonistic relations between capital and labor were revealed in undisguised form as the piecerates which paid workers were lowered year after year.

During the first two decades of Lowell's history when mill hands were recruited on a temporary basis from the surrounding rural towns, the major capitalists remained divided on the question of educational expenditure. On balance, even in these early days, the corporations placed their weight on the side of public education. The two schools most highly regarded by the school committee were located on corporation property and served directly the children and workers in the adjacent mills. However, many manufacturers opposed taxation of their properties for expensive school construction. Kirk Boott himself opposed one of Edson's plans for a new construction on the grounds that it was too lavish. But as the problem of creating, controlling, and extracting ever-increasing amounts of work from a permanent labor force became more pressing, the support for public educaton among employers became virtually unanimous. Significantly, it was in the depression years of the early 1840s that Horace Mann, too, became convinced of the economic value of education.[30]

Irish parents and children evidently did not share the employers' enthusiasm for schooling. Though the precise causes are obscure, the Lowell School Board reports document a sustained school boycott by the Irish community and a number of attempts to burn down the school in the Irish neighborhood.[31]

By the outbreak of the Civil War, the outlines of a modern system of elementary education had taken shape in Lowell. Truant officers were employed to enforce compulsory schooling. Most school-age children, in fact, attended school for a good part of the year. The curriculum and classroom structure, now barely recognizable as descendant from the chaotic rural "writing schools," had begun to assume a form all too familiar to most schoolchildren in the present century.

These developments in Lowell were hardly unique. They were, indeed, repeated all over the state. Moreover, the changing position of the state government on the question of schooling had a major bearing on the turn of events in Lowell and elsewhere. We turn now to investigate the school reform movement at the state level.

*Horace Mann's "Balance Wheel of the Social Machinery"*

> . . . Education is not only a moral renovator and a multiplier of intellectual power, but . . . also the most prolific parent of material riches. . . . It is not only the most honest and honorable, but the surest means of amassing property.
>
> HORACE MANN,
> Fifth Annual Report of the Secretary
> of State Board of Education, 1842

One evening in May 1837, Edmund Dwight took Horace Mann aside at a social gathering and urged that he consider accepting the Secretaryship of the newly formed State Board of Education.* Dwight, a major industrialist from Springfield, had persuaded Governor Everett that the post was too important to be given to an educator. Mann seemed an ideal choice. As Secretary of the Massachusetts Senate, he had a substantial statewide reputation; his effectiveness as a politician had been amply demonstrated in his advocacy of railway construction, insane asylums, debtor law reforms, and numerous other humanitarian reforms. The formation of the Board itself reflected a growing recognition among industrialists such as Dwight and other respectable members of the society that the problems of labor and urbanization required strong action at the state level. Few persons, Dwight told Mann, could match his qualification, to meet such a challenge. Should Mann accept, Dwight was prepared to privately supplement Mann's salary in the new post.

The Board would have no administrative authority; its responsibilities were to be confined to gathering statistics and writing occasional reports on the status of education. To leave the Senate for this post must, initially, have seemed to Mann a political error. The very limited powers of the Board were hardly up to the task of dealing effectively with the rapid transformation of the Massachusetts economy and the growth of urban poverty and unrest.

The structure of employment was changing drastically: Between 1820 and 1840, the percentage of the work force engaged in agriculture fell from 58 to 40 percent; by 1850, the percentage would fall to 15 percent.[32] Employment in manufacturing was growing correspondingly. Cities were springing up in the once-rural state. Population grew from less than half a million in 1820 to over a million and a quarter in 1865. Many of the new Massachusetts residents were foreign born.

Led by the textiles and shoe industries, Massachusetts was experiencing its industrial revolution. Increasingly, the factory replaced the home production of the putting-out system or the small artisan shops. Housed in dormitories or urban slum dwellings, the new industrial labor force constituted a new and, to many of the well-to-do, a threatening element in the

* We have relied heavily on Jonathan Messerli, *Horace Mann: A Biography* (New York: Alfred A. Knopf, 1972), and Mann's Annual State Board of Education Reports which are found in both *Horace Mann*, and *Life and Works of Horace Mann* (Boston: Walker and Fuller Co., 1865–1868); and Alexander J. Field, "Skill Requirements in Early Industrialization: The Case of Massachusetts," working paper in Economics, University of California at Berkeley, December 1973.

social structure. Already fearing the thrust of Jacksonian democracy, the respectable members of society were beginning to realize that industrialization was undermining the once-stable and deferential communities of the state, and rapidly ushering in an era of conflict, contention, and possible social disruption.

Horace Mann viewed these developments with dismay. Some years earlier, he had been persuaded to reenter the political sphere after a long absence following the death of his first wife. His mission was to counter the political aspirations of what a Whig editor referred to as ". . . a coalition consisting of Jackson men, Anti-Masons, workeys [Workingmen's Party people], Fanny Wright men and infidels of all description."[33] The destruction and desecration of a convent by an anti-Catholic mob in Charlestown in 1834 was, Horace Mann noted, "a horrible outrage." While Mann was considering Dwight's suggestion, a riot, sparked by a collision of a Yankee fire-engine crew and Irish funeral procession, destroyed much of Broad Street in Boston. Reflecting on the Broad Street riot, Mann feared that the social fabric was weakening and that chaos would ensue unless strong state action was taken. After almost a month of deliberation, he told Dwight that he was ready to accept the post.

Mann was a supporter of the industrial system. His advocacy of railroads in the state was based on a conviction that the expansion of wealth through industrialization could provide the basis for a fuller and more abundant life for all citizens. However, Mann was distressed by the growing ". . . domination of capital and the servility of labor . . ." which renders the ". . . latter . . . the servile dependents and subjects of the former."

The structure of the society and economy would not long bear up under the strain. The problem facing Mann, as he assumed office, was how to amend the existing structures to insure their permanence. His objective, he wrote a friend, was ". . . the removal of vile and rotten parts from the structure of society as fast as salutory and sound ones can be prepared to take their place."[34] But how to prepare these new parts? He flatly rejected the notion that there was any necessary antagonism between classes; class conflict would have no place in his program. Unlike many reformers of his day, he did not support the rights of workers to organize. The idea of "some revolutionizers" that "some people are poor because others are rich," he labeled as dangerous.[35] An early supporter of temperance, he estimated that fully four-fifths of the pauperism in the state could be attributed to liquor.[36] It was education, he wrote, that would become "the balance wheel of the social machinery." Properly reformed and administered schools could provide a generation of:

. . . Sober, wise, good men to prepare for coming events, to adjust society to the new relations it is to fill, to remove the old, and to substitute a new social edifice, without overwhelming the present occupants in ruin.[37]

The formulation of concrete educational objectives by Mann and the other reformers took time. Nonetheless, the years that Mann occupied the secretaryship of the State Board of Education saw the evolution of a comprehensive educational strategy, involving both the structure of elementary education as a whole and the internal structure of the school.

Mann sought an overall school system which would be public, tax-supported, and nonsectarian. In addition, the heavy demands of social reform and amelioration now being placed on the educational system required that virtually all children be induced, if possible, and forced, if necessary, to attend school. The school term would be expanded to increase the impact of education. Particularly important was Mann's conviction that children of diverse backgrounds should attend the same elementary school. By developing Common Schools, as they were called, Massachusetts would achieve:

. . . a Free school system. It knows no distinction of rich and poor, of bond and free, or between those who, in the imperfect light of this world, are seeking through different avenues, to reach the gate of heaven. Without money and without price, it throws open its doors, and spreads the table of its bounty, for all the children of the State. Like the sun, it shines, not only upon the good, but upon the evil, that they may become good; and, like the rain, its blessings descend not only upon the just, but upon the unjust, that their injustices may depart from them and be known no more.[38]

Such a system, a writer in the *American Annals of Education and Instruction* had earlier argued, would enable the poor ". . . to look upon the distinctions of society without envy . . ." and to be ". . . taught to understand that they are open to him as well as to others and to respect them for this reason."[39]

But the internal structure of the school would have to change, too. One of the more important innovations, as we have already seen, was the graded school in which children were grouped according to age and proficiency rather than assembled in a single room, as they had been in the dame schools and writing schools. The graded school allowed a more standardized curriculum, graded texts, and the establishment of standards of individual progress or productivity. The Lowell School Committee was quick to perceive the advantages of this plan. In 1852, they wrote:

The principle of the division of labor holds good in schools, as in mechanical industry. One might as justly demand that all operations of carding, spinning and weaving be carried out in the same room, and by the same hands, as insist that children of different ages and attainments should go to the same school, and be instructed by the same teacher. . . . What a school system requires is that it *be* systematic; that each grade, from the lowest to the highest, be distinctly marked, and afford a thorough preparation for each advanced grade.[40]

Moreover, they noted after a number of years, experimentation with the system:

The expense of instruction has been materially lessened . . . a great deal of disorder has been checked; punishments are almost abolished; and a marked progress in study has been made. The change thus made is nothing less than a public benefaction.[41]

The curriculum was to be broadened; the three R's—bread and butter of the writing schools' offerings—were not sufficient intellectual training for the modern era. An understanding of political economy would surely make better citizens.[42] Not surprisingly, the other new subjects introduced often had an ostensible bearing on the world of industry or commerce. Foreign languages, geography, and even surveying were introduced. But one is struck more by the irrelevance of the material than by its utilitarian value. Consider the entrance examination for the Lowell High School in 1850. Applicants were expected to be able to name:

. . . The capital of Abbyssinia, two lakes in the Sudan, the river that runs through the country of the Hottentots, and of the desert lying between the Nile and the Red Sea, as well as to locate Bombetok Bay, the Gulf of Sidra, and the Lupata Mountains.[43]

Even such evidently useful training as sewing was introduced less for its vocational value than for its moral effect. The Boston School Committee reported:

The industrious habits which sewing tends to form and the consequent high moral influence which it exerts upon society at large may cause its introduction more extensively in all the schools.[44]

That those involved in education were more interested in the high moral influence of the school than in the intellectual product of education seems quite true.

Although we have no direct evidence on this point, it appears likely that employers shared the educators' viewpoint. Intellectual skills were not required for most workers on the job. Luft's study of piece-rate productivity records of thousands of mid-nineteenth-century Lowell millworkers indicated no statistical relationship between individual worker productivity and literacy.[45] The elementary educational system was already much larger than necessary to train the minority of clerical and professional workers who would need literacy in their work. In 1840, roughly three-quarters of the adult U.S. population (including slaves) could read and write; the literacy rate in Massachusetts was substantially higher. The fraction of jobs requiring literacy could not possibly have exceeded 20 percent.[46]

Concerning cognitive skills more advanced than literacy, we doubt that any employer familiar with the daily workings of their textile mills or other similar factories would seriously entertain the notion that the curriculum taught in the schools of the day had much connection to the productive capacities of the workers. The reasons why most larger employers supported public education apparently related to the noncognitive effects of schooling—in more modern terms, to the hidden curriculum. On this, we have ample testimony from the mill owners themselves.[47] Some school committees were quite explicit about what they termed their moral objectives. In 1854, for example, the Springfield School Committee wrote:

> The object of education is by no means accomplished by mere intellectual instruction. It has other aims of equal if not higher importance. The character and habits are to be formed for life. . . .[48]

They go on to designate a few of the prominent points that a teacher should inculcate in the formation of character: ". . . the habit of attention, self-reliance, habits of order and neatness, politeness and courtesy . . . habits of punctuality."

The connections between moral training in school and the needs of the business world were not missed by educators. A writer in the proreform *Massachusetts Teacher* wrote:

> That the habit of prompt action in the performance of the duty required of the boy, by the teacher at school, becomes in the man of business confirmed; thus system and order characterize the employment of the day laborer. He must begin each half day with as much promptness as he drops his tools at the close of it; and he must meet every appointment and order during the hours of the day with no less precision. It is in this way that regularity and economy of time have become characteristic of our community, as appears in the running "on time" of long trains on our great network of railways; the strict regulations of all large manufacturing establishments; as well as the daily arrangements of our school duties. . . . Thus, what has been instilled in the mind of the pupil, as a principle, becomes thoroughly recognized by the man as of the first importance in the transaction of business.[49]

In Lowell, Theodore Edson designed a special clock for classroom use which divided the school day neatly into thirty-two ten-minute recitation periods.

But neither Mann nor most of the school committees or manufacturers confined their objectives to the inculcation of mere obedience. The schools must train young people, argued Mann, so that the citizen of tomorrow will ". . . think of duty rather than of the policeman."[50] A stable body politic and a smoothly functioning factory alike required citizens and workers who had embraced and taken on as their own the values and objectives of those in authority. Schools might do better than to instill obedience; they might promote self-control.

Widely practiced teaching methods of the period were hardly conducive to this purpose. The Lancasterian system, though not in general use, had captured the imagination of numerous educators. Intended primarily for the children of the poor, this approach to education was modeled after the factory rather than the family. Under this system, literally hundreds of children were instructed in a single hall, the main task of instruction and drill being done by more advanced children—monitors—under the direction of a single teacher. The Lancaster system, said DeWitt Clinton in 1809, ". . . is in education what . . . machines for abridging labor and expense are in the mechanic arts."[51] The monitorial system never found much favor with the well-to-do, but according to the early twentieth-century educator, Ellwood Cubberly, it served a useful purpose:

> In place of their idleness, inattention and disorder, Lancaster introduced activity, emulation, and a kind of military discipline which was of much value to the type of children attending these schools.[52]

The Lancasterian system was practiced almost exclusively in charity schools, particularly in New York, but methods of teaching in the public schools in Massachusetts and elsewhere were only slightly less regimented.

Disagreement on the relative importance of external and internal control provided the fundamental conflict which fired the heated debate concerning pedagogy between Mann and the Boston schoolmasters in 1844. The masters, in a pamphlet entitled "School Discipline," had attacked Mann's *Seventh Annual Report* as proposing methods which were dangerously permissive. Here is part of Mann's reply:

> . . . Here, then, is the philosophy of *School Discipline*. Authority, Force, Fear, Pain! The ideas of Childhood and Punishment indissolubly associated together. . . .
>
> Authority, Force, Fear, Pain! These motives, taken from the nethermost part of the nethermost end of the scale of influences, are to be inscribed on the lintels and doorposts of our school houses and embroidered on the phylacteries of the teachers' garments. . . . *Conscience* is nowhere referred to as one of the motive powers in the conduct of children. . . . That powerful class of motives which consists of affection for parents, love for brothers and sisters, . . . justice and the social sentiment toward schoolmates, respect for

elders, the pleasures of acquiring knowledge, the duty of doing as we would be done by, the connection between present conduct and success, estimation, eminence in future life, the presence of an unseen eye—not a syllable of all these is set forth with any earnestness or insisted upon as the true source and spring of human actions.[53]

Through his newly formed normal schools for teacher training, Mann strongly urged a modification of classroom methods to tap the affection, loyalty, and other higher motives of students. The replacement of male by female elementary school teachers during this period constituted a step in the right direction. The fact that female teachers were much cheaper to hire than males may have provided the main impetus for the feminization of the teaching staff. But the shift in hiring policy was probably at least as much a reflection of the view that schools should increasingly become an extension of the family or, when necessary, even its substitute.

Not surprisingly, reforms of this magnitude generated opposition. The rural population, not yet awakened to the social distress, explosive potential, and commercial needs of the new industrial order, found the State Board of Education meddlesome and a likely source of increased taxation. Mann never looked forward to his speaking tours in the rural Berkshires. Those associated with private schools found the common school a threat to their eminent positions. Many of the unincorporated private academies did close down during this period, though the more prestigious incorporated academies prospered. A few critics could not swallow Mann's rigid insistence on the separation of church and school. The Boston masters and other old school pedagogues felt that permissiveness in the classroom was an invitation to anarchy in the streets. Abolitionists' attacks were spurred by Mann's acceptance of racially segregated education, as well, perhaps, as his attempts to curb abolitionist-minded schoolmasters from speaking publically on the subject.[54] (Later, as a member of the U.S. House of Representatives, Mann would himself adopt the antislavery cause.)

Mann did everything possible to portray himself as an embattled crusader. "When I took my circuit last year," Mann reported to Barnard, "I mounted on top of a horse, and went Paul Prying along the way, and diverging off to the right or left, wherever I scented any improvement. I believe that was substantially the way that Peter the Hermit got up the Crusades."[55]

But the history of the period reveals more Mann's overwhelming political power stemming from enthusiastic support from virtually all influential quarters. The one serious challenge to his position reflects the political climate of the day, and deserves brief mention.

In 1838, the Temperance reformers succeeded in gaining passage of a bill which would limit the sale of alcoholic beverages to those who could purchase it in lots of fifteen gallons or more. For the Whig governor who signed the measure, this attempt to close down the saloons and limit drinking to the well-to-do was not much of an asset at the polls. The new Democratic governor, in his inaugural address, announced his intention to abolish the State Board of Education and its secretary. A committee of the House quickly reported favorably on a measure to halt the development of normal schools and close down the State Board. Though Mann marshaled his forces and managed to get to enough state legislators to defeat the impending legislation, the incident does suggest that the most serious threat to the new educational order came more from the party of Jackson than from the reactionary churchmen or narrow-minded business interests.

At its base, the incident reflected a conflict between proponents of the older decentralized community-controlled school system and those who, like Mann, sought to centralize control over the schools in the hands of enlightened and specially trained professionals. We have seen, earlier, the temporary success of the Lowell town meeting protest against the centralization of the school system. The same conflict—between proponents of what the historian Michael Katz calls "democratic localism" and "incipient bureaucracy"—is, indeed, a continuing theme in the U.S. educational history extending right down to current conflicts over "community control" of schools. Similar conflicts erupted over this period throughout the New England states and formed the basis of a major debate at the Pennsylvania Constitutional Convention of 1837–1838. New York City's "first great school war," extending over most of the first half of the nineteenth century, was fought—partly along ethnic lines—over this issue of school centralization.[56]

We now turn to the difficult task of investigating to what extent Mann succeeded in transforming the structure of education.

Ordinarily, we learn about reform movements through the writings of the reformers and their opponents and, later, from their apologists and detractors. It is wise, however, to go beyond what was said and attempt to assess what was done. This is no easy task, but it is essential to understand the thrust of the reform movement. Educational reform movements usually espouse a wide variety of objectives; yet, more often than not, the actual implementation of these programs in the schools is highly selective. The differing fates of reform programs in practice is frequently at least as revealing of what the reform movement was about as is a study of the writings of the main actors. This will be particularly the case when we come to study the Progressive education movement of the early decades of the present century. But a study of the impact of Mann and the other reformers on the schools of nineteenth-century Massachusetts is also instructive. As it turns out, the reformers did not make progress toward all of their objectives. Considering Massachusetts as a whole, the percentage of people under the age of twenty enrolled in school (both public and private) fell slightly from 46 percent in 1837 to 43 percent in 1860. Even taking into account the gradual increase in the length of the school session, the amount of schooling afforded to young people did not increase over this period.[57] As we shall see shortly, in this respect Massachusetts was atypical.

What did change? We are indebted to Mann's passion for numbers for our ability to answer this question with some confidence. The reformers did accomplish a significant increase in the percentage of school-age children enrolled in public as opposed to private schools. Attendance at private institutions fell both absolutely and relatively. The common school was coming to be a reality. The amount of resources devoted to public schooling increased dramatically, not only due to the expanding numbers of children in public school, but through a marked increase in per-pupil expenditures. Taking account of changes in the level of prices over this period, the rate of increase of per-pupil expenditure amounts to well over 2 percent per annum. The consolidation of district schools is reflected in a modest increase in the average size of schools: from twenty-seven in 1839 to thirty in 1859. Moreover, by the end of this period, women teachers had come to predominate in primary schools. They constituted roughly seven-eighths of all public school teachers.[58]

How are we to assess the impact of Mann's reforms? That some of Mann's contemporaries pictured him a radical is, perhaps, not surprising; his reforms were at once progressive and conservative. Sensing its productive potential, he embraced the new capitalist order and sought through social amelioration and structural change to adjust the social institutions and the people of Massachusetts to its needs. At the same time, Mann's reforms had the intent (and most likely the effect as well) of forestalling the development of class consciousness among the working people of the state and preserving the legal and economic foundations of the society in which he had been raised. The reformed school system of Massachusetts was Mann's crowning achievement. It was truly an innovative solution to the problem of conservative adaption to change. It was soon to be duplicated around the country.

## The Spread of Public Education

> Let your common school system go hand in hand with the
> employment of your people; you may be quite certain that
> the adaption of these systems at once will aid each other.
>
> Letter from Abbott Lawrence of Massachusetts
> to William Rives of Virginia, 1846

We have argued that the expansion of the industrial capitalist system was a major force promoting educational reform and expansion in the antebellum period. Our evidence from the town of Lowell and from the study of Horace Mann's reforms certainly point in this direction. Yet, the reader may object that these are exceptional cases. Would a detailed study of another industrial town or another reformer support these conclusions? We suspect that as more detailed case studies are conducted, our interpretation will be supported. In the meantime, we must content ourselves with the less detailed, but quite comprehensive, statistical evidence available in state educational reports and in the U.S. Census. A number of excellent studies are at our disposal. We will consider first a statewide study of Massachusetts before considering national data.

The argument that there was an intimate connection between economic and educational change is supported by the recent research of Alexander Field on mid-nineteenth-century Massachusetts.[59] Drawing upon town-by-town statistics and on both schooling and economic and demographic structure, and using the technique of multiple regression, his work supports the view that the impetus behind the implementation of school reforms was not from urbanization itself, not the introduction of capital intensive machinery, but rather the rise of the factory as the dominant production unit. He found that school boards were most likely to press for educational expansion in those towns characterized by a large percentage of workers employed in large establishments and a low level of capital per worker. A more detailed consideration of Field's results reveals that it was crowded conditions (measured by inhabitants per dwelling) and the relative size of the Irish community, not the size of the town itself, which was associated with school-board attempts to lengthen the school year.

Field's study is unusual in that it allows us to distinguish between the intent of the town school boards and the response of parents and students. The school board determined the length of the school session; its attempts to expand education are perhaps best measured by this variable. But the levels of actual attendance were, for the most part, out of their hands. The percentage of school-age children attending school reflected the complex interplay of factors involving parents, children, social pressures, and the employment situation. Using Field's results, we can develop a quantitative picture of the conflicting interests at work in the process of educational reform. Significantly, despite the demonstrated positive relationship between the length of the school session and the presence of a large Irish community, school attendance was no higher in towns with large Irish populations. This evidence is consistent with the interpretations that the Irish influx provoked school boards to expand the school system, but their attempts, at least prior to the Civil War, were effectively offset by the indifference or resistance of Irish parents and children.

Numerous quantitative studies support the view that resistance to public schooling among the foreign-born was widespread. In their multiple regression study of attendance levels in New York State counties in 1845, Kaestle and Vanovskis found a strong negative relationship between school attendance and the percentage of the population born outside the United States. Also negatively related to school attendance was a variable measuring the extent of poverty in the county.[60] Kaestle and Vanovskis found a positive but statistically insignificant relationship between attendance on the one hand and degree of urbanization and per capita tax valuation on the other. Of 1,066 truants in Boston in 1849, 963 (or 90 percent) had foreign-born parents.[61] Thernstrom's study of Newberryport, Massachusetts, shows that native-born workers tended to send their children to school while Irish-born workers resisted schooling. Irish-born preferred, if possible, to use whatever savings would result from their children's labor to buy property.[62]

Though useful in identifying gross relationships, the above quantitative data are not adequately complex to capture the ethnic dimension of the conflict over school expansion. The foreign-born did not oppose education itself, but rather public schooling controlled by others. In New York and elsewhere, the Irish community fought hard for its own schools. The professional and business elite did not attempt to force the children of all foreign-born families into school. Their "target populations" were the foreign-born in the potentially explosive urban proletariat and reserve army. They were concerned not so much with cultural diversity as with the threat of social unrest. The evident cultural diversity in late eighteenth-century New York City, which included significant numbers of economically independent Dutch, Huguenot, and other non-english-speaking people, did not concern the well-to-do nearly as much as the growth of the English-speaking but impoverished Irish community in the early nineteenth century.[63]

The economic transformation of Massachusetts during this period was more thoroughgoing and dramatic than that experienced in most states, but the conditions existing in neighboring Connecticut, New York, Pennsylvania, and wherever the wage-labor system was coming to dominate the social relations of production were not so different from those which had prodded the capitalist and professional classes of Massachusetts to action. The spread of public education outside Massachusetts was hardly uniform, or universal; both before and after the Civil War, the states exhibited dramatic differences in the pace at which public elementary education was expanded. Nor were the particularly urban or wealthy states in the lead. Albert Fishlow has demonstrated that school attendance in the mid- and late nineteenth century appears to be unrelated to the level of income or the degree of urbanization in the state.[64]

In the South, prior to the Civil War, the well-to-do saw little value in public schooling, particularly in those states with large slave populations and relatively few wage workers. Where manufacturing did employ any significant numbers of people, public schools followed. A study of state-by-state education and employment statistics for the period of 1840–1860, conducted by one of us in conjunction with Janice Weiss, revealed, for example, that attendance at public schools was positively related to the percentage of the labor force employed in manufacturing and negatively related to the importance of slaves in the state's economy. Extending our study to cover the years 1860–1880, we found that the demise of slavery and the Reconstruction Period brought with it an expansion of schooling, again following closely the evolution of the labor force in manufacturing.[65]

At least as important in this period, we suspect, was the vigorous struggle of blacks for more education in the postslave South. However, the educational development of the Southern states was not, as these results might suggest, determined solely—or even primarily—by forces internal to the states. The rest of the country, and particularly the Northeast, had a major influence on the Southern school system: The carpetbagger and the Northern capitalist were quickly followed by the schoolmaster. Starting in 1866, Northern capitalists exerted their influences directly through early educational foundations such as the Peabody Fund and the Slater Fund.[66] By the turn of the century, John D. Rockefeller and other major financial figures had begun to sense the importance of Southern agricultural productivity and of black labor in the continued profitability of capitalist enterprises. The early trickle of capitalist philanthropy to Southern education grew to a flood. Over its first decade of existence (1901–1911), the newly formed General Education Board—a private body channeling corporate funds into school reform—would receive $50 million from Rockefeller alone. This gave the Board an annual operating income far in excess of the education budgets of most Southern states.[67] Always working within the framework of Southern power and race relations, these Northern philanthropists sought to eradicate the educational backwardness of the South with the support of the blacks themselves. They met with only mixed success. Between the Civil War and World War I, enrollments and expenditures in Southern education expanded dramatically, and the dual system of school with its separate, and increasingly unequal, facilities for blacks and whites was firmly established.[68]

In the farming areas of the West, the spread of public education appears to have been associated not, as some would have it, with the strength of an independent farming class, but with its opposite, the development of a wage-labor force in agriculture. The study by Medoff and Buchele indicates that public educational expenditures were significantly and positively related to the mechanization and increasing use of wage labor in agriculture. No relationship whatever was found between educational expansion and per-capita income or urbanization.[69]

Interestingly, Buchele and Medoff found that, taking account of the apparently relevant dimensions of the economic structure of each state, those which were the centers of the Populist revolt (Minnesota, the Dakotas, Nebraska, Kansas, North Carolina, and Alabama) devoted significantly less resources to public education during this period. This finding, of course, invites a variety of interpretations. But it is hardly surprising in view of the fact that, unlike Horace Mann and the other reformers, the Populists identified the structure of the economy and not the lack of schooling as the source of poverty, economic insecurity, and inequality. While supporting public education, Populist leaders had emphasized a more immediate and more direct economic objective. "With the collapse of political Populism," observed Lawrence Cremin, one of the foremost educational historians of this period, "educational reform seemed to gain new vigor."[70] Yet Populism would, in the end, make a major, if unexpected, contribution to the growth of education in the West and South, for it was precisely the fear of Populist revival that led many major capitalist organizations—the Rockefeller-endowed General Education Board, the American Bankers Association, at least four major railroad companies, the National Implement and Vehicle Association among them—to lend their political and financial support to the fledgling agricultural education and extension movement.[71] Education was not an objective of Populist agitation. But it was certainly one result. Increasingly, business leaders came to see schooling and extension work as a safe alternative to the "agrarianism" and economic transformation espoused by so many late nineteenth-century farmers.

## Conclusion

> Education universally extended throughout the community will tend to disabuse the working class of people in respect of a notion that has crept into the minds of our mechanics and is gradually prevailing, that manual labor is at present very inadequately rewarded, owing to combinations of the rich against the poor; that mere mental labor is comparatively worthless; that property or wealth ought not be accumulated or transmitted; that to take interest on money lent or profit on capital employed is unjust. . . . The mistaken and ignorant people who entertain these fallacies as truths will learn, when they have the opportunity of learning, that the institution of political society originated in the protection of property.
>
> THOMAS COOPER, *Elements of Political Economy*, 1828

The statistical studies reviewed in the previous section are not, of course, all that we would like to evaluate critically in our interpretation of educational history. In our attempt to get a broader picture, we have lost much of the detail of our earlier case studies. Measures such as capital per worker, or workers per farm, or slaves as a percentage of the working population do not adequately capture the relevant data on the class structure and mode of production. Statistics on the growth of enrollments or school expenditures fail to capture much of what was important in the nineteenth-century educational reform movements.

Despite these drawbacks, however, these large-scale statistical studies, in conjunction with our earlier evidence, present a dramatic if sketchy picture of educational change. There can be little doubt that educational reform and expansion in the nineteenth century was associated with the growing ascendancy of the capitalist mode of production. Particularly striking is the recurring pattern of capital accumulation in the dynamic advanced sectors of the economy, the resulting integration of new workers into the wage-labor system, the expansion of the proletariat and the reserve army, social unrest and the emergence of political protest movements, and the development of movements for educational expansion and reform. We find also a recurring pattern of political and financial support for educational change: While the impetus for educational reform sometimes came from disgruntled farmers or workers, the leadership of the movements—which succeeded in stamping its unmistakable imprint on the form and direction of educational innovation—was without exception in the hands of a coalition of professionals and capitalists from the leading sectors of the economy.

We note in closing, however, that no very simple or mechanistic relationship between economic structure and educational development is likely to fit the available historical evidence. As we saw in our study of Lowell, Massachusetts, and of Horace Mann's work, political factors have intervened between economic structures and educational outcomes in complex and sometimes, apparently, contradictory, ways. In the next chapter, we expand our analysis to cover the Progressive reforms of the first part of the twentieth century.

# CHAPTER 7

•

# Corporate Capital
# and Progressive Education

> Confronted with a "heterogeneous high school population destined to enter all sorts of occupations," high school teachers and administrators and professors of education needed some justification for a complete overhauling of a high school curriculum originally designed for a homogeneous student body. . . . After closing John Dewey's volume, *Democracy and Education*, I had the feeling that, like the Austro-Hungarian Empire of the nineteenth century, if John Dewey hadn't existed he would have had to be invented. In a sense perhaps he was. . . .
>
> JAMES CONANT, *The Child, the Parent, and the State*, 1959

The period 1890–1930, extending from the early years of the Progressive Era to the Great Depression, constitutes our second major turning point in the history of U.S. education. Like the reform movement of the mid-nineteenth century, Progressive education was born in a decade of labor strife and was fueled throughout its course by social unrest and the specter of political upheaval. Like the earlier movement, Progressivism coincided with a dramatic shift in the structure of the economy and the integration of masses of new workers into the wage labor system. The Progressive Movement, like the common school revival, gave birth to a radically new educational philosophy. It stressed diversity, unity of the school with community, and what is now called "child-centered" instruction. Forcefully articulated by John Dewey and others, the precepts of Progressive education were selectively implemented by Ellwood Cubberly and the small army of "education executives" trained and deployed across the country. This period again witnessed the familiar coalition of liberal professionals and business leaders, often working through philanthropic foundations, who pressed the cause of educational reforms.

During these years, the public high school became a mass institution: In 1890, high-school graduates constituted less than 4 percent of all seventeen-year-olds; by 1930, 29 percent of seventeen-year-olds were graduates of high school. In 1890, high-school students represented 1 percent of all children enrolled in elementary and secondary education (86 percent were in public primary schools and the rest were in private schools); by 1930, this figure had risen to 15 percent.[1] In 1890, there were 6.8 times as many fourteen- to nineteen-year-olds at work as at school. In 1930, 1.8 times as many were in school as were at work.[2] Between those two dates, the percentage of all fourteen- to seventeen-year-olds attending public high schools rose from 4 percent to 47 percent. By 1930, private secondary schools enrolled only 7 percent of all secondary school students.[3]

Like the earlier common school reformers, the Progressives left their mark on U.S. education. We have examined the educational philosophy of Progressivism at some length in Chapter 2. The educational practice of Progressivism brought us the comprehensive high school, tracking, educational testing, home economics, the junior high school, the student council, the daily flag pledge, high-school athletics, the school assembly, vocational education and guidance, clubs, school, newspapers and monopolization of executive authority by superintendents and other professionals.[4]

The legacy of this period, the reader may suspect, is not exactly what John Dewey had in mind. The Progressive Movement lacked the ideological unity and the fusion of educational theory and practice of the common school revival. The name embraced such self-proclaimed socialists as Dewey, businessmen, and major capitalist foundations, upper-crust "good government" groups, and even a few trade unionists. From the ideological and political crosscurrents of this movement emerged a radically transformed school system, one which has set the pattern for elementary and secondary education today and which—as we argue in Chapter 8—is increasingly invoked as the model for mass higher education as well.

In the selective implementation of reformers' ideas, the reader will detect the practical force of the contradictions of progressive educational theory which we outlined in Chapter 2. The imperative of producing a labor force for corporate enterprises is starkly revealed in the mixed record of progressive success and failure. The objective of social equalization and full human development, so central to the thinking of John Dewey and his followers, were pursued within the constraints set by this imperative. Indeed, Dewey himself seems to have been aware of the nature of these constraints. True to his philosophy of pragmatism, he operated consciously and knowledgeably within them.[5] In the end, the role of education in capitalist expansion and the integration of new workers into the wage-labor system came to dominate the potential role of schooling as the great equalizer and the instrument of full human development.

We cannot, of course, in this limited space provide a detailed history of education in this period. As in the previous chapter, we outline the main economic and social trends in the first section and offer a somewhat more detailed treatment of three important cases. In the second section we investigate the politics of urban school reform; in the third section the vocational education movement; and in the fourth section the emergence of educational testing. We turn first to the economic background of the Progressive Movement.

## The Expansion of Corporate Capital

> I can say, without the slightest hesitation, that the science of handling pig-iron is so great that the man who is fit to handle pig-iron as his daily work cannot possibly understand that science; the man who is physically able to handle pig-iron and is sufficiently phlegmatic and stupid to choose this for his occupation is rarely able to comprehend the science of handling pig-iron. . . . The man who is fit to work at any particular trade is unable to understand the science of that trade without the kindly help and cooperation of men of a totally different kind of education. . . .
>
> FREDERICK WINSLOW TAYLOR,
> in Congressional Testimony, 1912

Throughout the latter nineteenth century and into the twentieth, the accumulation of capital and the extension of the wage-labor system marked the continued expansion of the capitalist economy. By 1890, almost two-thirds of all economically active people were employees.[6] Family farming continued to lose ground to large-scale capitalist agriculture and to manufacturing; simple manufacturing gave way to production involving complex interrelated processes; an increasing fraction of the labor force was employed in producing services rather than goods. The small shop gave way to the corporation employing thousands of workers. Domestic, craft, and entrepreneurial production were giving way to the corporate capitalist sector. Self-employed workers and entrepreneurs constituted a third of the economically active individuals in 1890, and only a fifth in 1930. In a few critical industries—steel, for example—a handful of giant firms predominated.

The counterpoint of uneven development—stagnation in some spheres and economic dynamism in others—continued. The South remained underdeveloped, but was soon to become a source of cheap labor for the booming industrial Northeast and Midwest. Spurred by the decline in ocean freight rates and the completion of the continental railroad network, the U.S. became part of the world economy. Millions of Europeans, many of them peasants driven out of business by cheap U.S. grain imports, came to the U.S. in search of a living wage. In 1910, 16 percent of the U.S. population was foreign-born; another 40 percent had foreign-born parents.[7] Until immigration was effectively cut off in 1924, the ever-increasing numbers of foreign-born workers played a major role in keeping wages low and profits high.

The integration of farmers into the world market and the attendant fluctuations in farm incomes as well as the growing monopolization of agricultural trade and transportation was challenged in the 1880s and 1890s by an increasingly powerful Populist Movement. In a like manner, the growth of wage employment, the increasing similarity among workers in the conditions of employment, and the hardship of three major depressions in the course of two decades spurred the development of organized resistance. Radical thrusts against the evolving capitalist relations of production broke out during the latter part of the nineteenth century. A series of major strikes—Homestead in 1892, Pullman in 1894, and others—signaled a growing militancy among workers. Labor organizations proliferated; membership in labor unions grew fourfold between 1897 and 1904.[8]

The objectives of the labor movement, like the objectives of the earlier radicals of the 1840s, were somewhat backward-looking. The labor historian, Gerald Grob, has noted that, to the extent that working people's organizations challenged the social relations of production, they tended to take as their norm ". . . the vision of a past society [perhaps one that existed only in their own minds] where the independent artisan combined in his own person both employer and employee functions. . . ."[9] With the significant exceptions of the Socialist Party and the International Workers of the World, most workers' organizations lacked a political perspective consistent with the forces of production under corporate capitalism. They did not espouse any comprehensive and viable alternative to capitalism. The potentially radical thrust of these movements was deflected and their force eventually either crushed or harnessed to the pursuit of more manageable objectives such as higher wages: "In return for labor non-support of revolutionary theories, industry promised the worker a rising standard of living and a respected, though subordinate, position in the community."[10] Yet for a period which extended from the late 1870s to the First World War, the perpetuation and extension of the capitalist system had become problematic.

The problem of controlling labor presented itself to capitalists within their own enterprises as well as in the social system as a whole.[11] Labor organizations and more or less spontaneous collective action by workers jeopardized profits. With the increasing centralization of capital and the associated increase in the size of firms, the simple, direct control mechanisms which had served to extract the maximum work at the least price became inadequate. The sheer size of the turn-of-the-century corporation required, in some cases, hundreds of foremen, office employees, and other nonproduction workers. The personalized authority and direct overseeing of the boss was no longer up to the task of controlling even the supervisory personnel, much less production workers.

The response by corporate employers to this new reality was to develop a complicated vertical segmentation of the labor force. In the new corporate division of labor, power was bureaucratically—not personally—sanctioned. It was wielded in the context of a hierarchically ordered structure of jobs. A large middle group of employees was created which comprised clerical, sales, bookkeeping, and low-level supervisory workers. These workers ordinarily exercised a modicum of control over their own work, and in some cases directed the work of others while themselves falling under the direction of higher management. The division of labor within the enterprise had become a finely articulated system dominated at the top by a small group with control over work processes and a high degree of personal autonomy in their work activities. The hierarchy descended by finely differentiated stages down the chain of bureaucratic command to those who worked within the narrow confines of the "company rules and regulations" and under the close supervision of the next higher-up. The bureaucratic hierarchy of the modern corporation replaced the simple boss-worker hierarchy of older entrepreneurial firms. Whenever possible, ethnic, racial, sexual, and, increasingly, differences in educational credentials among workers were used to divide workers against one another. The use of black strike breakers against white unions became a common employer strategy.

The structure of jobs, as much as the size of the work force, made the control of labor increasingly difficult. The new structure of production provided little built-in motivation. There were fewer jobs like self-employed craft work, farming, and piece-rate work in manufacturing in which material reward was tied directly to effort. As work became more complicated and interrelated and as the output shifted toward intangible services rather than material goods, the evaluation of an individual worker's performance became increasingly difficult. Employers in the most rapidly growing sectors of the economy began to require more than obedience and punctuality from their workers; they began to look for workers who had internalized the production-related values of the firm's managers. A change in motivation outlook was required.

Frederick Winslow Taylor's newly launched school of scientific management captured the attention of employers, whose concerns increasingly turned to the motivation and control of labor.[12] A central tenet of Taylor's approach was the concentration of the relevant production knowledge and skills in the hands of management. Taylor urged the reduction of most jobs to the carrying out of simple and highly explicit directives. The position of foreman came to occupy a central role in the corporate strategy of deepening control over the work force and usurping the power of the skilled workers. The problem of insuring that the foremen identify with the employer rather than with the workers increasingly commanded the attention of the corporate leadership.

Beyond the confines of the corporate enterprise, the forces serving to perpetuate the dominance of the capitalist class were formidable. The bureaucratically sanctioned power and privilege of the corporate elite within their own establishment was buttressed by a legal and political structure reflecting the power of the corporate sector in the society at large. State and Federal legislatures, the courts and—if all else failed, as it often did—the National Guard and the private armies of Pinkerton men were readily called upon to preserve the prerogatives of capital.

In response to the strains induced by the continuing integration of once-independent workers into the capitalist relations of production, the state began to take a larger role in the regulation of social and economic activity. Increasingly, the state intervened with positive programs of pacification.[13] Changes in the structure of employment reflected the growth of the corporate sector and the corporate elite's strategy for social control and maintenance of profits. The number of nonmanual employees grew rapidly. Clerical and sales workers, only 5 percent of the labor force in 1900, accounted for a quarter of the increase in total employment over the next three decades. The number of foremen in manufacturing and construction grew from 90,000 to 336,000 between 1890 and 1930. In 1900, employers hired, on the average, one foreman for every eighty-nine workers; by 1930, they were hiring a foreman for every thirty-four workers. Between 1890 and 1930, government employment (excluding education) grew fivefold, well over twice the rate of total employment.[14]

The changing division of labor within the corporation, the conflict between capital and labor both within the enterprise and in the larger society, and the changing occupational structure all had a major bearing on the educational system. The expansion of schooling and the implementation of Progressive educational reforms were an expression of these developments.

The expansion of education was pressed by elites alarmed by growing labor militancy. These elites found new urgency in the social-control arguments popular among the proponents of education in the antebellum period. Again, schooling was seen as a means of producing the new forms of motivation and discipline required in the emerging corporate order. Schooling would Americanize immigrant groups with a dangerous penchant for European radicalism and socialism. It would discipline a new proletariat, fragment it and eventually stratify it along racial, ethnic, and sexual lines. The expansion of education was also pressed by Progressives who hoped it would prove an effective antidote to urban poverty, so much on the liberal conscience through the efforts of muckraking journalists like Jacob Riis. Finally, with the closing of the Western frontier and the declining prospects for workers going into self-employment, small business, or cooperative trades, labor itself often stood behind educational expansion as the only remaining path toward mobility, security, and social respectability.

## Class Politics of Urban School Reform

> There is no more need for oratory in the conduct of a school system than there would be in the conduct of a national bank.
> ELLWOOD CUBBERLY,
> *Public School Administration*, 1916

The schools of the late nineteenth century were hardly up to the tasks which were heaped upon them. Muckrakers from Joseph Rice in the 1890s to Upton Sinclair in the 1920s attacked their corrupt administration and mindless routines.[15] Others noted structural weaknesses, the most striking of which was the incompatibility between the democratic ideology of the common school and the social reality of the class structure. The strategy for the reform of schools emerged piecemeal and, at first, without apparent coherent direction. The first item on the reformers' agenda, not surprisingly, was to gain control of the schools. Most interesting for our purpose is the process whereby reformers gained the upper hand over what they considered the "narrow-minded" and corrupt political machines which had come to dominate the politics of many cities.

The urban school reform movement was an integral part of the broader municipal reform movement, aimed at reducing the political power of the "ethnic enclaves" of the urban working class and small property owners. Under the banner of honesty and good government, small groups of big businessmen, newspaper editors, and professionals in city after city succeeded in altering the structure of urban government. According to historian Samuel Hays:

> Available evidence indicates that the source of support for reform in municipal government did not come from the lower or middle classes, but from the upper class. . . . The drama of reform lay in the competition for supremacy between two systems of decision-making. One system based on ward representation . . . involved wide latitude for the expression of grass roots impulses. . . . [In] the other . . . decisions arose from expert analysis and flowed from fewer and smaller centers outward to the rest of society.[16]

The objective of the school reformers was to centralize control of urban education in the hands of experts. They sought to replace ward elections for school boards by citywide at-large elections, to grant autonomy to the superintendent, and to develop a more specialized and well-defined hierarchical bureaucratic order for the improvement and control of the schools. Schools were to be as far removed as possible from the sordid world of politics.

Democratic pluralism, we have emphasized, generally has had little place in erecting new institutional forms. However well a system of grass-roots democracy might succeed in reproducing and stabilizing existing social arrangements, at the "crucial turning points" in social life, a clear process of economic elite control of the decision-making process can be seen. Nowhere was the elite nature of the municipal reform movement more evident than in the struggle for the schools. Proponents of reform tended to be lawyers, businessmen—particularly the new and rising corporate elite—upper-class women's groups, school superintendents, university professors, and presidents. Almost all were white anglo-saxon Protestants. Though locally based, these reformers used the National Education Association, the Chambers of Commerce, newspapers, professional journals, and businessmen's clubs to forge what one of their foremost historians termed a "nationwide interlocking directorate."[17] On the other hand, teachers' unions in New York, San Francisco, and other cities stood opposed to centralization.[18] Substantial opposition arose from urban ethnic communities as well.

In a few cities, we have detailed evidence on the occupations of the main reformers, and, in one case, of those who opposed the reforms. These data, summarized in Figure 7–1, are worthy of at least brief mention. In New

York City and Philadelphia, the pro-reform Committee of One Hundred, the Public Education Association, and the Civic Club were dominated by the social elite. In addition, we know that the membership of the two major reform groups in the first decade of this century in Pittsburgh were composed exclusively from members of two occupational groups: professionals (48 percent) and large businessmen (52 percent).[19] Perhaps more striking is the comparison—also in Figure 7–1—of the elite nature of an

FIGURE 7–1.
*Supporters and Opponents of Urban School Reform:*
*Percent of Members from Social Elite.*

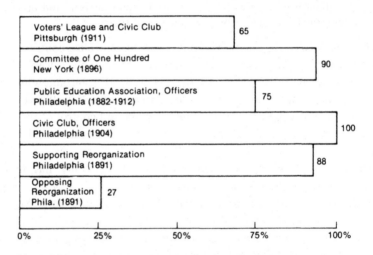

NOTES: Social elite is defined by appearance of one's name in the Social Register (for New York) or either the Social Register or the Blue Book (for Philadelphia) or what Hays calls ". . . upper-class directories which contain the names of only 2 percent of the city's families."
SOURCE: Samuel P. Hays, "The Politics of Reform in Municipal Government in the Progressive Era," *Pacific Northwest Quarterly*, October 1964; William Issel. "Modernization in Philadelphia School Reform, 1882–1905," *The Pennsylvania Magazine of History and Biographies*, Vol. 94, No. 3, July 1970.

earlier Philadelphia reform effort, the Delegation Supporting the 1891 Reorganization Bill, with the popular basis of its opposition. The reformers had very clear ideas, not only about the ideal structure of power relationships within the school system, but also about who should occupy the positions of power. A clear statement of their position is contained in the 1911 Statement of the Voters' League of Pittsburgh. Noting that ". . . a man's occupation ought to give a strong indication of his qualifications for membership on a school board, . . ." they summarized their position:

Employment as ordinary laborer and in the lowest class of mill worker would naturally lead to the conclusion that such men did not have sufficient education or business training to act as school directors. . . . Objection might also be made to small shopkeepers, clerks, workmen at many trades, who by lack of educational advantages and business training, could not, no matter how honest, be expected to administer properly the affairs of an educational system, requiring special knowledge, and where millions are spent each year.[20]

The victory of the school reformers is evident from the size of school boards from 1893 to 1913. In the twenty-eight largest cities in the United States, the average number of central school board members was cut in half. Ward-board members, who in many cities numbered in the hundreds, were all but eliminated.[21] But their true success is nowhere more clearly indicated than in the statistics of school board membership before and after the early twentieth-century reforms. Figure 7–2 presents the available evidence. In both cases, there is a decisive shift toward elite control of the schools. Evidence for the postreform domination of school boards is not

FIGURE 7–2.
*Social Composition of School Boards
Before and After Reform.*

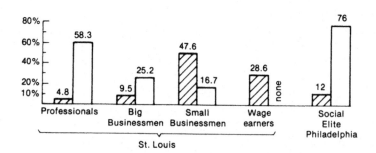

NOTES: The shaded column refers to the pre-reform composition, and unshaded column is the post-reform composition of school boards. The last two columns show the percent of social elites (in Social Register or Blue Book) on ward boards before their abolition in 1905, and on the Central Board of Education after the Philadelphia reform in 1906.
SOURCE: David Tyack "City Schools: Centralization and Control at the Turn of the Century" in J. Israel, *Building the Organizational Society* (New York: Free Press, 1972); William Issel, "Modernization in Philadelphia School Reform, 1882–1905," *The Pennsylvania Magazine of History and Biographies*, Vol. 94, No. 3, July 1970.

limited to these few cities. Scott Nearing, after his dismissal from the University of Pennsylvania, in 1915, was moved to investigate the structure of control in U.S. education. Included in his extensive research is a study of urban school boards. The occupational composition of these boards, presented in Table 7-1, reveals the same pattern as in our earlier studies. Business and professional groups predominate with doctors, dentists, and lawyers comprising over two-thirds of these professionals. Clerical workers, sales people, mechanics, and wage earners comprise the vast majority

TABLE 7-1.
*Composition of Boards of Education by Occupation*

| OCCUPATION | % MEM- BERSHIP ON SCHOOL BOARD IN 1916 | % IN NON-AGRIC. LABOR FORCE IN 1920 | DEGREE OF REPRESEN- TATION* |
|---|---|---|---|
| BUSINESSMEN | | | 5.1 |
| Merchants | 14.8 | 4.0 | 3.7 |
| Bankers, Brokers, Real Estate, and Insurance | 10.8 | .5 | 21.6 |
| Manufacturers | 8.1 | | |
| Other Businessmen | 11.1 | 4.2 | 2.6 |
| | 44.8 | 8.7 | |
| PROFESSIONALS | | | 4.7 |
| Doctors | 12.2 | .5 | 24.4 |
| Lawyers | 14.9 | .4 | 34.7 |
| Other Professionals | 7.3 | 6.5 | 1.1 |
| | 34.4 | 7.4 | |
| FOREMEN | 2.6 | 1.7 | 1.5 |
| WORKERS | | | .1 |
| Clerks and Sales | 5.0 | 17.7 | .28 |
| Mechanics and Wage Earners (All Manual Workers) | 4.0 | 64.0 | .06 |
| | 9.0 | 81.7 | |
| MISCELLANEOUS | 9.2 | .5 | 18.4 |

SOURCE: Scott Nearing, "Who's Who on Our Boards of Education" *School and Society*, vol. 5, No. 108, January 1917, from a sample of 104 U.S. cities in 1916; and U.S. Bureau of Census, (1960), sample: U.S. Census, 1920.

* The degree of representation to the percentage of school board membership divided by the percentage in the non-agricultural labor force.

of the urban working population, yet are represented by only one-tenth of the school board members.

To a remarkable extent, the reformers got their way in the running of the schools as well. Following the reform of the Boston school system, the superintendent enthusiastically reported that ". . . the work of the board is conducted in a conversational tone."[22] Their reforms, so well described in Callahan's *Education and the Cult of Efficiency*, ushered in an era of tight top-down control, paramilitary discipline, and substantial independence from popular control. Bureaucracy became the watchword of the schools. While the older, decentralized village pattern of schooling was viewed by some reformers as an impossible ideal of bygone days, all agreed that the sheer increase in numbers of students alone necessitated bureaucratic control in the modern era.[23] Thus Taylorism in the school was justified in the same technocratic terms that were increasingly employed by proponents of the hierarchical division of labor in the workplace.

For many of the perhaps naive supporters of reform, these results were hardly intended. The practice of the reform movement was clearly out of step with the democratic and open education advocated by John Dewey and other Progressive educational theorists. Those who understood "the integration of the community into the school" to mean neighborhood involvement, after-hours use of the school as a community center and the like found their efforts constantly frustrated and circumscribed by the centralization and professionalization of the control of urban education. In fact, the urban school was far less a neighborhood institution on the eve of World War I than it had been two decades earlier.

## Vocational Education and the Demise of the Common School

> Until very recently [the schools] have offered equal opportunity for all to receive *one kind* of education, but what will make them democratic is to provide opportunity for all to receive such education as will fit them *equally well* for their particular life work.
>
> Superintendent of Boston Schools, 1908

As large numbers of working-class and particularly immigrant children began attending high schools, educational reformers began to propose a system of stratification within secondary education. The older ideology of the common school—that the same curriculum should be offered to all children—increasingly came under attack. The uniform curriculum sym-

*191*

bolized, for liberal reformers, an elitist and anachronistic holdover from the nineteenth century. The high school could not remain as a minority institution designed, in the words of an 1893 Declaration of the National Education Association Committee of Ten:

> To prepare for the duties of life that small proportion of all the children in the country . . . who show themselves able to profit by an education prolonged to the eighteenth year, and whose parents are able to support them while they remain so long in school.[24]

Education, the Progressives argued, should be tailored to the "needs of the child." Progressive indeed was the demand for flexible programs to handle ethnic diversity in language skills. Progressive too was the demand for a curriculum sensitive to the later life and family surroundings of the students. Indeed, the uniform curriculum made the teacher's task next to impossible. The expansion of public secondary education, and its transformation from an upper class preserve to a mass institution was eminently consistent with democratic and egalitarian traditions.[25] In the context of a rapidly developing corporate division of labor, however, such demands spelled not equality and democracy, but stratification and bureaucracy.

Special curricula were developed for the children of working families. The academic curriculum was preserved for those who might later have the opportunity to make use of book learning, either in college or in white-collar employment. Typical of the arguments then given for educational stratification is the following by a Superintendent of Schools of Cleveland:

> It is obvious that the educational needs of children in a district where the streets are well paved and clean, where the homes are spacious and surrounded by lawns and trees, where the language of the child's playfellows is pure, and where life in general is permeated with the spirit and ideals of America—it is obvious that the educational needs of such a child are radically different from those of the child who lives in a foreign and tenement section.[26]

Nowhere are the arguments for and against educational stratification more clearly exhibited than in the course of the vocational education movement.[27] Building on the quite distinct manual training movement of the 1880s, the vocational education movement during the 1890s gathered the political support of major educators and the financial backing of a number of leading capitalists—J. P. Morgan and John D. Rockefeller among them.[28] With the founding of the National Association of Manufacturers in 1896, the movement gained what would become its most important advocates and acquired a strong antiunion orientation. From the late 1890s until World War I virtually every national N.A.M. conference passed resolutions advocating vocational education.

The reasons for this widespread support among employers are simple enough. As late as the 1890s, skilled workers exercised considerable power within the enterprise. In many industries, they collectively retained control of the shop floor, often hired their own assistants, and, most important for this story, substantially influenced the recruitment of new skilled workers through their control over the apprenticeship system.[29] The employers' strategy to break the power of the skilled workers was spearheaded by a largely successful attempt to destroy their unions. The ideological rationale for limiting the power of the skilled workers was propagated by the school of scientific management, which held that the behavior of workers, down to the very movements involved in a mechanical operation, must be controlled and dictated by technicians and managers according to scientific principle.

Employers seized upon vocational education as a means of breaking the workers' control over skills training. In 1906, the N.A.M. committee on Industrial Education reported: "It is plain to see that trade schools properly protected from the domination and withering blight of organized labor are the one and only remedy for the present intolerable conditions."[30] Moreover, vocational education offered a useful method of training and labeling the growing strata of foremen so as to set them above and apart from other production workers.

Until the turn of the century, organized labor took little part in the discussions of vocational education. A survey of labor organizations in New York, in 1886, revealed substantial support for manual training and trade schools. Opposition, while a minority position, was vociferous. The Secretary of Cigarmakers Union No. 144 called trade schools "breeding schools for scabs" and the Secretary of the Twist and Warp Lace Makers Association warned that vocational education ". . . would be rather a curse than a blessing by placing at the disposal of every capitalist bent on grinding down wages to the lowest point an unlimited number of skilled out of work, to supercede those who might resist his tyranny."[31] The flagrantly antiunion advocacy of vocational education by the N.A.M. hardened labor's opposition and, by the turn of the century, Samuel Gompers and the A.F. of L. had taken a firm position against the movement.

However, with the growing momentum of the vocational education movement, labor's position shifted. Faced with the virtual certainty of a federally funded vocational education program, organized labor sought, by joining the movement, to gain some influence over its direction. By the eve of World War I, there was virtually no organized opposition to federal aid to vocational education. The movement culminated in 1917 with the successful passage of the Smith-Hughes Act, providing federal support for vocational education. While in most respects reflecting the views of N.A.M., the final legislation was not all that some employers had hoped for. Federal aid was to be restricted to those over fourteen years of age, thus dampening the hopes of some advocates that the newly formed junior high school could become "the vocational preparatory school of the future."

Labor was successful in preventing the development of dual school systems. In Massachusetts, a partially implemented plan for the housing of vocational education in separate trade schools incurred substantial opposition from educators as well as organized labor and was ultimately rejected. In Chicago, a similar proposal arrayed the Chicago Federation of Labor, supported by most of the city's teachers and its most renowned educator—John Dewey—against a coalition built around the Chicago Association of Commerce and including virtually every major business organization in the state of Illinois.[32] At issue was the Cooley Bill, which would have provided a dual vocational and academic secondary-education system for the state. Introduced in 1913 and in subsequent years, the bill was defeated. As the 1920s progressed, it became clear that the impact of the vocational education movement would not be—as many of its early business backers had hoped—separate school systems, but rather the development of vocationally oriented tracking within the comprehensive high school.

By the time the Smith-Hughes Act was passed, the original claims of both labor and capital were probably somewhat outdated. The power of the skilled workers had been decisively broken in a number of major lockouts and unsuccessful strikes; apprenticeship was clearly on the wane. But one detects a more contemporary ring in the Chicago Federation of Labor's opposition to the Cooley Bill, and its continuing opposition to other mechanisms of early selection and educational stratification—the junior high school and educational testing. They claimed, as did the more radical of the progressive educators, that vocationalism would have the effect of channeling working-class, immigrant, and black children into manual jobs. Indeed, we believe that the evidence strongly supports the thesis that the vocational education movement was less a response to the specific job training needs of the rapidly expanding corporate sector than an accommodation of a previously elite educational institution—the high school—to the changing needs of reproducing the class structure. Particularly important in this respect was the use of the ideology of vocationalism to justify a tracking system which would separate and stratify young people loosely according to race, ethnic origins, and class backgrounds.[33]

The history of the vocational education movement illustrates well the contradictions of Progressive education described in Chapter 2. For while Dewey and other Progressive educators sought to replicate the community in the school and to build a sense of unity and common experience among students, the stratification of the high school—pressed by those more concerned with processing future workers—advanced apace. As we have seen, those who opposed stratification gained important concessions. Yet they could not resist tracking within the high school. Within the school, the reformers' attempts to bring students together and to forestall differentiation were limited to the more or less peripheral sphere of extracurricular activities. But no amount of schoolwide assemblies, clubs, or athletics—all of which were institutionalized during this period—could bridge racial, ethnic, and class divisions which were symbolized and reinforced by curriculum tracking. True to form, the Progressive thrust of educational reform turned out to be little more than a Band-Aid remedy.

## *Testing and Tracking: Streamlining the Meritocracy*

> The alleged "mental levels," representing natural ability, it will be seen, correspond in a most startling way to the social levels of the groups named. It is as though the relative social positions of each group are determined by an irresistible natural law.
>
> Attack on IQ Testing
> by Chicago Federation of Labor, 1924

The frankness with which students were channeled into curriculum tracks on the basis of their ethnic, racial, and economic background in the early twentieth century raised serious doubts about the "openness" of the social class structure. By the end of the 1920s, the relationship between social background and a child's chances of promotion or tracking assignments would be disguised—though not mitigated much—by another reform: "objective" educational testing.[34] Particularly after World War I, the capitulation of the schools to business values and concepts of efficiency led to the increased use of "intelligence" and scholastic-achievement testing as an ostensibly unbiased means of measuring the product of schooling and classifying students.[35] The complementary growth of the vocational guidance profession allowed much of the channeling to proceed from the student's own well-counseled choices, thus adding a welcome element of voluntaryism to the system.[36]

If the rhetoric of the educational response to the economic changes after

the turn of the century was "progressive," much of its content and consciousness was supplied by the new science of "evolutionary genetics." Of
course, as Clarence Karier notes:

> . . . The nativism, racism, elitism and social class bias which were so much a
> part of the testing and Eugenics Movement in America were, in a broader
> sense, part of the *Zeitgeist* which was America.[37]

Yet its grounding in Mendel's laws, Darwin, and the sophisticated statistical methodologies of Pearson, Terman, and Thorndike lent it the air of
exacting rigor previously accorded only to the Newtonian sciences. IQ tests
captured the imagination of high-level policy-makers and were seized upon
by school administrators. In the years 1921–1936, over 4,000 articles on
testing appeared in print; by 1939, no less than 4,279 mental tests were in
circulation; a survey of 150 city school systems, in 1932, revealed that
three-quarters were using "intelligence" tests to assign students to curriculum tracks.[38]

An essential theme of the testing movement was the uniting constitutional character of human excellence, as rooted in genetic endowment.
Moral character, intelligence, and social worth were inextricably connected
and biologically rooted. In the words of the eminent psychologist, Edward
L. Thorndike, ". . . to him that a superior intellect is given also on the
average a superior character."[39] Study after study exhibited the "low intelligence" of "wards of the state" and social deviants. In Albany, New York,
it was reported that 85 percent of the city's prostitutes were feeble-minded;
69 percent of the white inmates and 90 percent of the black inmates in a
Kansas prison were found to be morons; a study revealed that 98 percent
of unmarried mothers were feeble-minded.[40] Immigrants, tests showed,
were particularly prone to low intelligence. Professor Henry Goddard's
1912 study, sponsored by the U.S. Immigration Service, found that 83
percent of Jews, 80 percent of Hungarians, 79 percent of Italians, and 87
percent of Russians were feeble-minded, based on "culture-free" tests.[41]
These test results would shortly become powerful ammunition in the movement to restrict immigration. But of greater interest here is their eventual
use in educational selection.

Although Alfred Binet's original "intelligence" test had been developed
for use in the French school system, its possible application to a broader
range of social problems is clearly suggested by the assumptions Binet
attempted to build into the test:

> An individual is normal when he is able to conduct himself in life without need
> of the guardianship of another, and is able to perform work sufficiently re-

numerative to supply his personal needs, and finally when his intelligence does not exclude him from the social rank of his parents.[42]

The translation of his 1905 test and its early growth in popularity in this country is to be explained largely by interest in military classification and immigration restriction. Many of the early U.S. testers were quick to perceive the potential use of the tests for achieving a more efficient and rationally ordered society. The major capitalist foundations concurred. Much of the early work on testing was financed by the Carnegie Corporation of New York.[43] Later, they would support Thorndike's research to the extent of $325,000. Lewis Terman, likewise, received substantial foundation grants, totaling almost a quarter of a million dollars for work on gifted children alone.[44]

Possible applications of the tests to the school system were quickly perceived. Terman put the view as clearly as any of the early proponents of educational testing:

> At every step in the child's progress the school should take account of his vocational possibilities. Preliminary investigations indicate that an IQ below 70 rarely permits anything better than unskilled labor; that the range from 70 to 80 is pre-eminently that of semi-skilled labor, from 80 to 100 that of the skilled or ordinary clerical labor, from 100 to 110 or 115 that of the semi-professional pursuits; and that above all these are the grades of intelligence which permit one to enter the professions or the larger fields of business. . . . This information will be a great value in planning the education of a particular child and also in planning the differentiated curriculum here recommended.[45]

Proponents of the use of tests for educational tracking found support in John Dewey's writings. In 1900, he had written, ". . . in the great majority of human beings the distinctively intellectual interest is not dominant. They have the so-called practical impulse and disposition."[46]

At the end of World War I, the Rockefeller Foundation began its support of research to investigate possible educational uses of the tests.[47] The Carnegie Corporation would, over the next two decades, pour over $3 million into the effort.[48] The most important of the Carnegie educational testing studies was carried out in Pennsylvania. In their 1931 annual report to the Carnegie Corporation, they drew these then obvious conclusions:

> The conspicuous lesson of the Pennsylvania study thus far is the dependence of all successful education on adequate provision for proved differences in individual interests and capacities. . . . It is probable, however, that on both the secondary and the higher levels much more than this can be done, and that certain groups having similar abilities can be segregated and given a more appropriate curriculum.[49]

The results of IQ tests could be used to justify tracking by race, ethnic origin, and class background. While IQ tests were standardized to produce equal results for boys and girls, the testers provided an equally "scientific" justification for sexual channeling in the schools. This is how Thorndike put it:

> The most striking differences in instinctive equipment consists in the strength of the fighting instinct in the male and of the nursing instinct in the female. . . . And probably no serious student of human nature will doubt that these are matters of original nature. The out-and-out physical fighting for the sake of combat is preeminently a male instinct and the resentment at mastery, the zeal to surpass and the general joy at activity in mental as well as physical matters seem to be closely correlated with it. It has been common talk of women's "dependence," This is, I am sure, only an awkward name for less resentment at mastery. The actual nursing of the young seems likewise to involve equally unreasoning tenderness to pet, coddle, and "do for" others.[50]

Boys and girls, Thorndike concluded, should not share an identical curriculum: Boys should be subjected to educational environments which, by evoking their competitive and fighting instincts, would prepare them for adult positions of "mastery"; girls should be encouraged to develop their "unreasoning" instinct to ". . . pet, coddle, and 'do for' others."[51]

The last stage in the implementation of testing as the basis of tracking was the institutionalization of the testing system. Carl Brigham, whose foundation-supported research had earlier confirmed Goddard's study of immigrant feeble-mindedness, went on to develop the Scholastic Aptitude test in his capacity as the secretary of the newly formed College Entrance Examination Board. In 1930, Rockefeller's General Education Board gave half a million dollars for the founding of the Cooperative Test Service to the American Council of Education (itself established in 1918 by Rockefeller and Carnegie money). In addition to the Cooperative Test Service, Carnegie and Rockefeller supported the Educational Records Bureau, the Graduate Records Office, the National Committee on Teachers Examinations, and the College Entrance Examination Board. Prodding and a substantial grant from the Carnegie Foundation achieved the consolidation of these testing units under the aegis of the Educational Testing Service in 1948. In the first half of the twentieth century, these organizations alone received over $7 million from the Rockefeller and Carnegie foundations.[52]

## *Conclusion*

> Our schools are, in a sense, factories in which the raw materials are to be shaped and fashioned into products to meet the various demands of life. The specifications for manufacturing come from the demands of the twentieth century civilization, and it is the business of the school to build its pupils to the specifications laid down. This demands good tools, specialized machinery, continuous measurement of production to see if it is according to specifications, the elimination of waste in manufacture and a large variety of output.
>
> ELLWOOD CUBBERLY

Major periods of educational change are responses to alternatives in the structure of economic life associated with the process of capital accumulation. The common school movement of the nineteenth century, we have seen, developed to complement a burgeoning factory system increasingly rendering the family inadequate to the task of reproducing the capitalist division of labor. The Progressive Era accompanied the transition to corporate capitalism, in light of which the small decentralized common school was manifestly anachronistic, both in its internal social relationships and in the degree to which it could be centrally controlled through enlightened social policy.

The legacy of the urban school reform movement in this period reflects both its strongly upper-class basis and its commitment to social control as the overriding objective of schooling. Social amelioration, open education, equalization of opportunity, and all the democratic forms could have been pursued only insofar as they contributed to—or at least did not contradict —the role of the school in reproducing the class system and extending the capitalist mode of production. The essence of Progressivism in education was the rationalization of the process of reproducing the social classes of modern industrial life. The Progressives viewed the growing corporatization of economic activity as desirable and forward-looking—indeed, the best antidote to the provincialism and elitism of U.S. culture. For some, Taylorism in the schools was, in turn, seen as an ideal. For others, the unified and centralized high school with the differentiated curriculum represented the most efficient accommodation to the new exigencies of economic life.

As a force for qualitatively new types of social stability, the Progressive Movement must be judged an eminent success. As a force for equality and human development, however, it went little beyond the progressive elements in the organizational revolution of turn-of-the-century economic life. The counterpoint of success and failure in this period of change highlights the general contradictions of liberal educational reform discussed in Chapter 2: the incompatibility of the egalitarian, developmental, and integrative functions of education within the context of capitalist relations of production.

That a school system geared toward "moral development" and toward domesticating a labor force for the rising corporate order might readily embrace standardization and testing—to the benefit of the leaders as well as the led—seems in retrospect to have been almost inevitable. Lacking any strong grass-roots support, and self-consciously eschewing any systemic critique of the evolving economic order, it is not surprising that the idealistic Progressives worked in vain for a humanistic and egalitarian education. More in tune with immediate economic realities, the bureaucratization, tracking, and test-orientation of the school system proceeded smoothly, promoted by seed money from large private foundations, articulated by social scientists at prestigious schools of education, and enthusiastically implemented by business-controlled local school boards.[53] Only a mass-based organization of working people powerfully articulating a clear alternative to corporate capitalism as the basis for a progressive educational system could have prevented this outcome.

# CHAPTER 8

•

# The Transformation of Higher Education and the Emerging White-Collar Proletariat

At least there is tolerably general agreement about what a university is not. It is not a place of professional education. Universities are not intended to teach the knowledge required to fit men for some special mode of gaining their livelihood.

J. S. MILL

More knowledge has resulted from and led to service (by the university) for government and industry and agriculture. . . . All of this is natural. None of it can be reversed. . . . The campus has evolved consistently with society. . . . The university and segments of industry are becoming more and more alike. . . . The two worlds are merging. . . .

CLARK KERR

## Introduction: From Ivory Tower to Service Station

Two hundred years ago, the college existed as an elevated cultural community on the periphery of the social and economic mainstream. At such aristocratic bastions as Harvard, Yale, and William and Mary, many who would enter the learned professions were trained and certified. The tradition of classical scholarship was maintained. Even among the economic elite of the day, college attendance was the exception rather than the rule, a cultural luxury rather than a social necessity. As late as 1870, only 1.7 percent of eighteen- to twenty-one-year-olds were enrolled in higher education.[1] Higher education was of only marginal importance to the processes by which the economic order was reproduced and extended.

No longer. At the end of World War II, slightly under one-fifth of the eighteen- to twenty-one-year-olds were enrolled; now, roughly half of the relevant age group go on to postsecondary educational institutions.[2] Colleges and universities play a crucial role in the production of labor power, in the reproduction of the class structure, and in the perpetuation of the dominant values of the social order.

Higher education has taken its place alongside other types of schooling and the family as part of the process by which the class structure of advanced capitalism is reproduced: Higher education has been integrated into the wage-labor system.

In this chapter we describe the ways in which recent structural changes in economic life are manifested in the current evolution of U.S. higher education. In brief, we suggest that the character of recent conflicts and reform efforts in this sphere may be explained by the concurrence of three historical tendencies: the vastly expanded demand for technical, clerical, and other white collar skills by employers in the corporate and state sectors in the post-World-War II period; the proletarianization of white-collar labor, whose privileges and prerogatives are being brought into line with the profit and control objectives of corporate enterprise; and the demand for expanded access to higher education by minority- and working-class youth.

As in the case of previous historical periods, traditional liberal theory is ill-equipped to handle contemporary educational dynamics. The technocratic version might explain some of the quantitative expansion of the past quarter century in terms of technological demands, but ignores the critical social issues: Why have the social relations of higher education developed as they have; why the tremendous politicization of student life and culture in recent years; and why the dramatic overexpansion of the supply of skilled labor, creating a veritable reserve army of underemployed white-collar labor? The democratic version of traditional theory, on the other hand, cannot explain the complex stratification of higher education now crystallizing, and the clear retreat from liberal education to the fragmentation and vocationalization of college life.

We analyze these phenomena in terms of our correspondence principles and the contradictions of the capitalist growth process. The recent expansion of the state and corporate sectors of the economy—at the expense of family agriculture and entrepreneurial, craft, and household production— has worked in two directions. On the one hand, parallel to the dynamic of previous periods, this expansion has required the integration of blacks, women, and middle-class youth into the corporate wage-labor system. On the other, it has fostered a tremendously increased stratification of the white-collar labor force, and relied on educational credentials to legitimate the stratification process; hence, a contradiction between the social relations of higher education and the emerging economic order. First, the traditional system of higher education is a relatively homogeneous four-year college structure with a dedication to the liberal ideals of expression and inquiry. This structure, while suitable for training an economic elite, was hard-pressed to accommodate a wave of students who are highly politicized by the rapid changes in their class status, and destined for the alienated labor of the new corporate order. Second, the heightened degree of consciousness and struggle on the part of minority groups tends toward an intensified disparity between the number of "credentialed" workers and the number of high-status and rewarding jobs. Underlying these strains is a fundamental contradiction between the two dominant capitalist objectives for education: the augmentation of labor power, and the reproduction of the conditions for its exploitation. In recent years, pursuit of the former objective—historically progressive and dynamic—has tended, as we shall see, to undermine efforts to meet the latter—conservative and inertial—objective.

This emergent contradiction between the educational system and the new conditions of economic life underlie the political dynamics of the past fifteen years. As in previous periods of rapid integration of new groups of workers into the wage-labor system, the modern period is marked by class and other group conflict. And as in previous periods, we witness a proliferation of analyses and proposals for educational change, only some of which are compatible with the further consolidation of the corporate capitalist system.

In the second section of this chapter we survey the recent evolution of the social relations of production in the U.S. economy and higher education's accommodation to these changes. In the third section, we explore the ways in which these changes impinge on student life, suggesting that the strains associated with the transformation of higher education are manifestations of fundamental contradictions emanating from the structure of economic life. The student response—at once radical and backward-looking—is analyzed, and the possibilities for radical change are assessed in the concluding section.

## *The Proletarianization of White-Collar Labor and the Stratification of Higher Education*

> If we can no longer keep the floodgates closed at the admissions office, it at least seems wise to channel the general flow away from four-year colleges and toward two-year extensions of high school in the junior and community colleges.
> AMITAI ETZIONI,
> *Wall Street Journal*, March 17, 1970

The continued expansion of the corporate and state sectors of the economy has had two major effects: The self-employed have become increasingly peripheral to the economy, and, at the same time, entire new cadres—technical, lower supervisory, and white-collar service workers—have come to occupy a central role in production. Recent changes in U.S. higher education, we believe, are, in important measure, an accommodation to these trends.

The expansion of capital—largely through accumulation by large corporations—has hastened the integration of workers into the wage-labor system. Over the past century, the percentage of self-employed professionals and entrepreneurs has fallen from about two-fifths to less than one-tenth of all economically active individuals. The percentage of salaried managers and professionals have multiplied sevenfold. And the proportion of wage earners to the labor force has continued its steady rise.[3]

The integration of white-collar labor into the dominant wage-labor system has required changes in the quality of work similar to those which blue collar workers experienced in a previous era.[4] Prominent is the fragmentation of white-collar skills, which mirrors the process whereby capitalists wrested control over the production process from the highly skilled craft workers in the late nineteenth century.[5] The compartmentalization of white-collar skills has become an essential aspect of the capitalist "divide and rule" strategy for the control of the labor force. Even in well-paid and high-status jobs the worker's discretion and participation is increasingly limited. Equally important, the creation of a reserve army of underemployed skilled white-collar workers whose jobs by no means exhausts the limits of their skills or abilities has increased the pool of available labor. By reducing job security this reserve army acts as a critical buttress to the power of employers over their workers.

The case of teaching provides a good example of this shift. It is easy to imagine teaching as relatively integrated, unalienated labor. The teacher is in direct contact with his or her material and has at least a modicum of control over his or her work. Given a sufficiently vivid imagination, he or she may even entertain illusions of social usefulness. However, the teacher's job has undergone subtle change. The educational efficiency binge of the 1920s led to the application of business management methods to the high schools.[6] The concentration of decision-making power in the hands of administrators and the quest for economic rationalization had the same disastrous consequences for teachers that bureaucracy and rationalization of production had on most other workers. In the interests of scientific management, control of curriculum, evaluation, counseling, selection of texts, and methods of teaching was placed in the hands of experts. A host of specialists arose to deal with minute fragments of the teaching job. The tasks of thinking, making decisions, and understanding the goals of education were placed in the hands of high-level administrators. Ostensibly to facilitate administrative efficiency, schools became larger and more impersonal. The possibility of intimate or complicated classroom relationships gave way to the social relations of the production line.[7]

The fragmentation of tasks and the demise of intimate personal contact has not been limited to teaching but, rather, has pervaded the "service" professions. The medical sector, for example, has seen the rise of large, impersonal medical bureaucracies, the ascendancy of specialists, the proliferation of subprofessionals, and the demise of the general practitioner who once administered to the health of the whole body and the whole family. None of these developments is inherent in medical science.

Along with the virtual demise of the self-employed worker and the integration of white-collar labor into fragmented and hierarchical work roles, the expansion of corporate capital has brought the rapid growth of new kinds of work. These new cadres—for a lack of a shorter expression, we call "skilled subprofessional white-collar workers"—include technicians, lower-level supervisory personnel, secretaries, nonretail sales workers, dental assistants, draftsmen, and paraprofessional personnel in medicine and education. These are just a few of the rapidly growing occupational titles in this group.

The expansion and indeed overexpansion of college enrollments has been, in part, a response to the needs generated by this changing occupational structure. Increased enrollments in the 1950s and 1960s have, in turn, effected two critical changes in the social position of higher education. First is the increasing scientific, cultural, and social role of the college community. Second is the frank recognition that colleges must become the training ground for much more than the economic elite; community colleges and many four-year institutions have taken up the task of training the middle-level office and technical workers of the future.

The transformed social and economic role of higher education has rendered the traditional university structure inadequate to the needs of reproducing the contemporary corporate capitalist system. Yet the mobilization of the professional and capitalist elites for structural change in higher education over the past decade was provoked by more immediate concerns: the rise of student radicalism in the late 1960s and the deepening financial crisis. By the early 1970s, Clark Kerr's "social service station" was running out of gas. With colleges and universities wracked by internal dissention and an unaccustomed financial squeeze, the battered ex-chancellor of the University of California at Berkeley, who had a decade earlier likened U.S. higher education to the blooming early twentieth-century auto industry, was now wondering if it might be, instead, more like the presently floundering railroads.[8]

By far the most important effort to restructure U.S. higher education is the work of the Carnegie Commission on Higher Education, chaired by Clark Kerr. Between 1967 and 1973, this group, representing the commanding heights of the educational establishment, produced twenty-one monographs, over eighty other publications, and a highly influential *Final Report*.[9] We draw on these documents to elucidate the evolving strategy for the restructuring of higher education to meet the needs of stable capitalist expansion. Two related aspects of this strategy emerge as central. The first is a concerted attempt to fragment the culture of the college community. The second is the advocacy of community colleges and other means to stratify and vocationalize higher education. The third is an effort to curb the rate of growth of the total postsecondary educational system to restrict the size of the reserve army of white-collar workers to politically acceptable levels.

The issue of the culture of the college community is particularly difficult. For the process of college study undermines much of the legitimacy of the capitalist system. It is simply impossible for higher education to conserve its traditional liberal arts structure and to transmit useful high-level skills to students without, at the same time, developing some of the students' critical capacities and transmitting some of the truth about how society operates. Over a century ago, Marx foresaw that the continued expansion of the forces of production under capitalism might necessitate the development of a labor force whose skills and outlook would bring it into conflict with the social relations of production. Will such a labor force acquiesce to the social relations of corporate capitalist production? Andre Gorz expresses the contradiction between the augmentation of labor power and the reproduction of capitalist class relations succinctly:

Big Business, in short, is seeking to reconcile two opposites: on the one hand, the need created by the modern process of production for a higher development of human capabilities; and on the other hand, the political need to prevent this development from leading to an increased autonomy of the individual which would threaten the existing division of social functions and the distribution of power.[10]

As long as college students were destined for positions of leadership, the tradition of scholarship and unfettered inquiry was probably an appropriate context for college training. Yet with half of each age cohort continuing schooling after high school, it is clear that both leaders and followers are being trained. The educational processes best suited to training an elite are less successful in fostering quiescence among followers. This contradiction in the objectives of higher education seems likely to intensify as the system is forced to combine the teaching of intellectual and leadership skills with an increased role in the mass propagation of the folklore of capitalism and the reproduction of a fragmented and submissive consciousness among middle level workers. Moreover, the contradictions of the larger society increasingly impinge on the classroom. The struggles of blacks, women, Third World peoples, welfare recipients, and others expose the seamy side of American reality and are rapidly serving to explode the legitimating ideologies taught in our college and high schools.

The political consequences of a failure to adapt the structure and objectives of the university community to its new diversity of social functions are fairly obvious. The economic consequences are no less important. Skilled and professional labor power—like all labor power—is embodied in people. But skills are not learned in a vacuum. Because of the cultural environment of the traditional college community and the nature of technical skills themselves, the educational process seems increasingly to provide the means, but not the motivation, to be a useful cog in the economic system.

As a result, there have been barriers to the development of a market in skills and ideas in which services flow readily to the highest bidder. Teachers, researchers, and other college graduates increasingly impose qualitative as well as monetary conditions upon the rental of their services to business and the government.

Recent tendencies in college teaching and research may be seen as an only partially successful attempt to deal with the problem. With the specialization of jobs in the economy has come a fragmentation of studies and research. Increasingly, students and researchers are discouraged from dealing with a whole problem, just as a worker is forbidden to produce a whole product. The artificial compartmentalization of intellectual pursuits allows the development of advanced technique within each area and simultaneously militates against the application of comprehensive moral standards or the consideration of the larger social consequences of one's work. The narrowing effect of academic specialization is furthered by the modern conception of professionalism, in which the intellectual is seen as a technician whose success depends upon his skill in devising technical solutions to technical problems.[11] In addition, the research functions of the intellectual community are increasingly severed from their university base. These functions are now carried out in large private or government laboratories and institutes where the cultural climate is more favorable to the pursuit of profit.

Other developments are aimed at fragmenting not the intellectual, but the cultural unity of the college community. The Carnegie Commission supports the extension of alternatives to four-year college study: The "two-year planning module" should be the basis for higher education, new educational policies should enhance ". . . other channels—on-the-job training, proprietary schools, apprenticeship programs, education in the military . . . off-campus extension work, and national service opportunities." The ". . . mixing of persons from different groups both in classes and in out-of-class contacts . . ." will provide a ". . . more constructive environment on campus." Graduate education should be divided into a ". . . Doctor of Arts degree more oriented toward teaching broad subject matter, and the Ph.D." Lest there be any mistaking the likely impact of these changes, the Carnegie Commission concludes:

> We recognize that some of these options reduce the chances of a common culture among college graduates within which people communicate, but this has been happening anyway, and we believe the gains will outweigh the losses.[12]

The increasing fragmentation of educational pursuits is but one outgrowth of the conflict between the traditional elite-training function of the university and the greatly expanded numbers of students enrolled. The growth of two-year colleges and postsecondary technical institutes is another. In what follows, we suggest that the booming community college movement has created a class stratification within higher education parallel to the hierarchical relationships of production in the modern corporation. An expansion of the number of students in higher education has thus been facilitated without undermining the elite status and function of the established institutions. Again, the Carnegie Commission states the intent clearly:

> "Elite" institutions of all types—colleges and universities—should be protected and encouraged as a source of scholarship and leadership training at the highest levels. They should not be homogenized in the name of egalitarianism. Such institutions, whether public or private, should be given special support for instruction and research, and for the ablest of graduate students; they should be protected by policies on differentiation of functions.

and quoting Sir Eric Ashby, they conclude:

> All civilized countries . . . depend upon a thin clear stream of excellence to provide new ideas, new techniques, and the statesmanlike treatment of complex social and political problems.[13]

Whatever became of equality of educational opportunity? Or to the idea that a public and common educational experience was an essential ingredient to the perpetuation and extension of the democratic process? K. Patricia Cross, an influential writer on education, provides the now dominant answer. It is starkly reminiscent of the arguments made for high-school stratification during the Progressive Era:

> . . . The time is past when a single type of institution can hope to serve the needs of the diverse population now seeking higher education. The notion that universities provide the best in the way of education for New Students is not only a perpetuation of an elitist philosophy in an egalitarian era; it is also probably wrong. . . .
>
> Surely quality education consists not in offering the same things to all people in a token gesture toward equality but in maximizing the match between the talents of the individual and the teaching resources of the institution. Educational quality is not unidimensional. Colleges can be *different* and *excellent* too. . . .[14]

Underlying this rhetoric is, of course, the specter of a vastly expanded student enrollment.

Concerns about poverty and racial discrimination, and the increasing use of access to higher education to placate previously excluded middle- and lower-income families have given increased impetus to the movement for a stratified system of higher education. In 1972, enrollments on two-year colleges were over eight times what they were in 1947, and over three times what they were in 1962. Two-year college enrollments are, by far, the most rapidly growing body of college students. Public institutions now dominate the two-year college system. Since 1947, the number of private junior colleges has fallen while the number of public community colleges has almost tripled. In 1972, enrollments in community colleges constituted 95 percent of all two-year college enrollments.[15] In a period of educational retrenchment, the Carnegie Commission has proposed the creation of roughly 200 new public community colleges by 1980.

Higher education has developed a multitiered system dominated at the top by Ivy League institutions and the great state universities, followed by the less prestigious state universities, state colleges, and ending with the community colleges.[16] This system reflects both the social status of the families of the students and the hierarchy of work relationships into which each type of student will move after graduation.

Comprehensive national data collected by the American Council on Education—presented in Figure 8–1—reveal sharp disparities between the social origins of students and attendance at various types of institutions.

FIGURE 8–1.
*Stratification of Higher Education by Family Income
in 1971.*

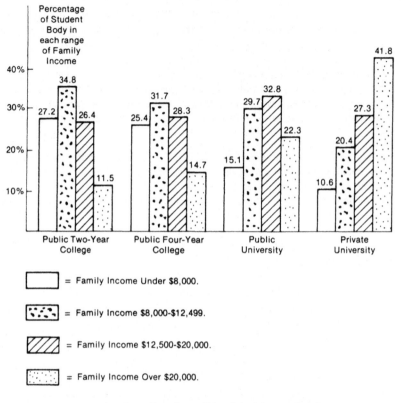

= Family Income Under $8,000.

= Family Income $8,000-$12,499.

= Family Income $12,500-$20,000.

= Family Income Over $20,000.

SOURCE: American Council on Education data as cited by Jerome Karabel, "Community Colleges and Social Stratification" *Harvard Educational Review*, Vol. 42, No. 4, November 1972.

Even the more egalitarian state systems exhibit this stratified pattern. Data are available from California. Over 18 percent of the students at the Universities of California in the mid-1960s came from families earning $20,000 or more. Less than 7 percent of the students in community colleges, on the other hand, came from such families. (Less than 4 percent of the children not attending higher education came from such families.) Similarly, while only 12.5 percent of the students attending the Universities of California came from families earning less than $6,000, 24 percent of the students attending community colleges and 32 percent of the children not enrolled in higher education came from such families.[17]

The segregation of students not destined for the top has allowed the development of procedures and curricula more appropriate to their future "needs," as defined by their actual occupational opportunities.[18] The vast majority of students in community colleges are programed for failure. Great efforts are made—through testing and counseling—to convince students that their lack of success is objectively attributable to their own inadequacies. Burton Clark, the sociologist, acutely describes the process:

. . . In the junior college, the student does not so clearly fail, unless he himself wishes to define it that way, but rather transfers to terminal work . . . The terminal student can be made to appear not so radically different from the transfer student, e.g., an "engineering aide" instead of an "engineer" and hence he goes to something with a status of his own. This reflects less unfavorably on the person's capacities. . . . The provision of readily available alternative achievements in itself is an important device for alleviating the stress consequent on failure. . . . The general result of "cooling out" processes is that society can continue to encourage maximum effort without major disturbance from unfulfilled promises and expectations.[19]

Bringing student hopes into line with the realities of the job market is facilitated by a tracking system within the community college much like the channeling system for high schools: four-year college transfer programs for the "promising," vocational programs for the "dead-enders." The magnitude of the task of lowering student expectations can hardly be exaggerated: At least three times as many entering community college students want to complete four or more years of college as actually succeed in doing so. Less than half of community-college entrants receive even the two-year Associate of Arts degree. Thus we can hardly share the surprise voiced by the authors of the influential Folger Report:

Paradoxically, the community colleges appear to have increased college opportunity for low-status youth and at the same time to have increased socioeconomic differentials in college completion.[20]

For those who stay, studies at community colleges are—much more often than in four-year colleges—explicitly vocational, emphasizing such middle-level training as nursing, computer work, and office skills. The connection between the needs of business and the curricula of community colleges is fostered by business representation on advisory boards. Community-college presidents are more than willing to help out. When ". . . corporate managers announce a need for skilled workers, . . ." writes Arthur Cohen, Director of the ERIC Clearing House for Junior Colleges, ". . . college administrators trip over each other in their haste to develop a new technical curriculum."[21] The continuing vocationalization of the community-college curriculum is now actively being pushed by the business community, the Federal Government, and major private foundations.[22]

The structure of production in the corporate sector is reflected in the social relationships of education at the community colleges as much as in the curriculum. To accommodate the expanded enrollments, the former president of a Chicago community college contends, a more differentiated approach is needed:

> Community college students . . . need more guidance and control. If students are properly motivated, the programmed-learning approach seems to provide an ideal amount of specific direction. Course outlines, specific assignments, clear lectures, deadlines for turning in assignments, and other allegedly high school practices are recommended.[23]

The student is allowed little discretion in selecting courses or pursuing a liberal education. Systems of discipline and student management resemble those of secondary education more than those of the elite universities; some have called community colleges "high schools with ashtrays." Pressures from state legislatures seek to increase teaching loads and class sizes, and, in some cases, even to standardize curriculum and teaching methods.[24] The social relationships of the community-college classroom increasingly resemble the formal hierarchical impersonality of the office or the uniform processing of the production line.[25]

All of this, of course, must not be seen as a failure of the community-college movement, but rather as a successful adaption to the tasks which they were set up to perform: processing large numbers of students to attain that particular combination of technical competence and social acquiescence required in the skilled but powerless upper-middle positions in the occupational hierarchy of the corporate capitalist economy.

The vocational orientation of the community colleges is becoming more typical of the system of U.S. higher education as a whole. This process is occurring, in large part, through the rapidly increasing fraction of all college students who are enrolled in community colleges. Nor is the fraction likely to level off: Current projections are for the community-college enrollment to continue its rapid rise, while the total enrollment in all colleges slowly moves toward a plateau in the late 1970s or early 1980s. In the absence of drastic changes in student financial support, four-year institutions thus stand to lose enrollments over the next decade. Moreover, the four-year institutions are likely to come under pressure for a rationalization of curriculum and educational method as the financial crisis of the colleges and universities intensifies.

The expansion of state universities and community colleges has generated severe financial problems for the elite private institutions. The preservation of the small liberal arts colleges and perhaps even the Ivy League institutions requires more than the provision of alternative channels for the less fortunate; it is precisely the low-tuition state universities which are threatening to drive the elite colleges out of business. Thus the Carnegie commitment to preserve the elite institutions involves more than the stratification of higher education; it necessitates a retreat from the principle of public education. The Carnegie Commission favors a "market model" for higher education, and urges sharply increased tuition at public institutions to ". . . narrow the . . . tuition gap with private institutions."[26] The financial recommendations of the Carnegie Commission recently have been enthusiastically supported and extended by an influential mouthpiece for the corporate capitalist class, the Committee on Economic Development. They propose fee increases which would result in a doubling of tuition at universities, an increase of two and a half times at four-year colleges, and a tripling of tuition at two-year colleges.[27]

## The Expansion of Corporate Capital and the Contradictions of Student Life

> Modern industry compels society . . . to replace the detail worker of today, crippled by life long repetition of one and the same trivial operation, and thus reduced to a mere fragment of a man, by the fully developed individual, fit for a variety of labors ready to face any change in production and to whom the different social functions he performs are but so many modes of giving free scope to his own natural and acquired powers.
>
> KARL MARX, *Capital*, Vol. I

Student life has already been radically changed by the transformation of higher education. The rapid increase in enrollments over the past half century, the central role of university research and personnel in the domestic and international expansion of corporate capital, the stratification of higher education, the vocationalization of the curriculum, the rationalization of methods in order to process more students more cheaply—all have impinged on students' daily life. The process of change, though carefully engineered by top university administrators and adroitly sold by apologists for the new order, has not been a placid one. Since the Berkeley uprising of the early 1960s, students in revolt against mechanized, mass-produced education have announced that they will not be spindled, folded, or mutilated. Attempts to hitch up the college community in more direct service to the state and the business community were met with ever-more direct resistance. Attacks on ROTC and other campus war-related establishments have been widespread. The protest has extended to graduate students and young professionals. Dozens of radical professional organizations have sprung up in medicine; sociology; the physical sciences; economics; psychiatry; literature and the languages; engineering; law; city planning; and Asian, African, and Latin American studies—to mention just a few. These groups give tangible political expression to a growing commitment among students, young teachers, and other professionals that their function is not to administer society, but to change it drastically. During the late 1960s, radical sentiment among students grew rapidly. In 1968, an opinion poll reported that 4 percent of U.S. students identified themselves as "radical or far left." Two years later, the same poll reported 11 percent as radical.[28] Dr. Edward Teller's assessment of the strength of the movement at its height was clearly extravagant, but indicative of the new trend nonetheless. He told a Presidential commission that events in universities in 1969 and 1970 have ". . . practically cut the connection between universities and defense-related industries. . . . In twenty years," he warned, "the United States will be disarmed."[29] Protest activity peaked in May 1970, following the U.S. invasion of Cambodia. For the four days following the Kent State killings, there were a hundred or more strikes a day. A week later, on May 10, almost one-fifth of the nation's 2,500 colleges and universities were still affected by a strike or completely shut down.[30]

At least, during full-employment periods, campus recruiters for big business and the government find a cooler reception than in the past. Direct political action, originally focused against companies in the war business, is now aimed at a much broader range of targets—General Motors, General Electric, Polaroid, and the Peace Corps, for example. Student attacks on campus recruitment by the United States Information Service, Department of State, and companies with substantial international operations are indications of the repugnance felt by many students at being trained to administer the U.S. world empire.

Assaults against the multitiered educational stratification system, pressures for open enrollment, and demands for access to prestigious institutions among students already enrolled have mounted. In New York City, black and Puerto Rican students took the lead in "opening up" the previously highly selective city colleges. In Seattle and elsewhere, minority students have resisted being shunted into the newly formed vocational tracks at the bottom of the educational pyramid.[31] Other students have fought against hierarchy in the classroom, in many institutions successfully demanding an open classroom approach to teaching and undermining the grading system.

Some analysts, seeking a structural explanation, have located the roots of the crisis in higher education itself in the "industrialization of the university" and in the eclipse of liberal education in the new "knowledge factories."[32] While much student protest is undoubtedly an outcry against the immediate concerns of college life, the pattern of student radicalism is hardly consistent with the industrialization of the university hypothesis. The most liberal institutions were not spared their share of radical protests. Many large state universities—perhaps the best representatives of the archetypal knowledge factory—weathered the late 1960s and early 1970s without serious disruptions. Karabel's survey of the student protest activity indicated that measures of college environment were only weakly associated with the incidence of protests and, further, that students at large institutions were not more likely to be involved in protest than those at medium or small institutions.[33]

In our view, the origins of the student movement and youth radicalism may be traced, not so much to the university itself, as to fundamental contradictions in the larger society. The nature of contradiction may be briefly summarized. First, the expansion of enrollments, like the expansion of capital, continues to be essential in legitimizing the class structure and allowing its reproduction. Yet the material well-being and transformed social relations of production induced by the expansion of capital have produced an incongruence between the aspirations of college students on the one hand and the labor requirements of the economy on the other. In short, colleges can no longer make good their promises: Most students are simply not getting enough of what they want out of higher education.

Second, the rapid transformation of the U.S. economy is from entrepreneurial capitalism, in which the middle classes maintain the privilege of controlling their work lives, to a corporate capitalism in which white-collar labor is proletarianized and bureaucratized. This transformation leaves children from relatively well-off families essentially declassed—part of a new wave of workers integrated into the wage-labor system. A result is the already mentioned discrepancy between the beleaguered but deeply entrenched liberal ideal in education and the one dimensional patterns of human development appropriate to the alienated work situations into which most of today's college students are moving.

To the extent that students see college as an investment toward a better job, three broad types of objectives may be identified: money, status, and rewarding work. Of the three, the expectation of a monetary payoff is most likely to be fulfilled, at least for those—the minority—who manage to receive a four-year degree. Although the average return of higher education has fallen in recent years, a college degree continues to be a well paying investment. No doubt this helps to explain the tenacious hold that colleges exercise on the public imagination. yet even here the diploma is no longer a simple union card to a better paying job. Increasingly, with the growth of surpluses of skilled labor, it has become a glorified lottery ticket, paying off only for the lucky. Moreover, increasingly students see their education not in purely monetary terms, but as a means of access to rewarding work. Like the dispossessed artisan and farmer of the nineteenth century, students increasingly reject the fragmentation of tasks and the hierarchy of production in the modern corporation; they want to be their own bosses. One survey strikingly documents the shifting attitude toward work. Daniel Yankelovich reports that, in 1968, over half of his sample of students did not mind the future prospect of being "bossed around" on the job. By 1971, only one in three expressed willingness to submit to this treatment.[34] In this, students are hardly different from workers, as we have seen in Chapter 4. Desirable jobs are coming to be seen as those which make a contribution to social betterment and which are an aid, not an obstacle, to the continuous development of one's creative, aesthetic, emotional, and intellectual capacities.

The increasing discrepancy between jobs and expectations is not a passing phenomenon. Both the change in student consciousness and the declining opportunities for rewarding and high-status work are firmly rooted in three aspects of the process of capitalist expansion: the level of material affluence, the stratified and alienating social relationships of production, and the pervasiveness of waste and irrational production necessary to absorb the surplus productive capacity of the economy.

The ever-increasing level of material well-being—both of the students' families and that which they reasonably expect to enjoy after they leave college—has reduced the urgency of immediate consumption needs. Thus, the success of the economic growth process has itself undermined much of the monetary rationale for getting a college degree, for it has changed the way in which many students value the economic payoff to their studies. With the lure of the external monetary reward on the wane, students—particularly the most affluent—demand that education be intrinsically rewarding: College study must be interesting and enjoyable, and must contribute to the individual's personal development.

The social relations of production under corporate capitalism represent

*216*

a major obstacle to meeting student aspirations for either rewarding work or status. Alienated labor now characterizes most of the occupational slots open to college graduates. Most now move into jobs in which they exercise little control over the disposition of their own labor power; they neither own nor identify personally with the products of their labor. Thus, work tasks tend to be repetitive, fragmented, and meaningless. The time spent on the job is not only physically and emotionally draining; it is worse, for it stunts the creative and personal development of an individual. Time on the job channels energies into the development of those skills and capacities which are valued only insofar as they bring a little more job security or a slightly larger pay check. This condition is felt particularly poignantly by students of traditionally middle-class entrepreneurial, professional, and technical backgrounds, for these students have been imbued with the "bourgeois" culture of autonomy, creativity, and self-definition.

The social relations of production thwart the status aspirations of students as much as they curb the opportunity for rewarding work. The continued expansion of corporate capital has altered the system of status differentiation. Many of the high-status occupations—the independent businessman, the self-employed professional—are losing numbers. The jobs open to college people are now found in the well-paying but lackluster middle rungs of the corporate hierarchy. Even without changes in the availability of high-status jobs, there would be not enough status to go around. The nature of the status objective itself—based as it is on invidious distinctions—makes it unattainable to most of the vast numbers of students now enrolled in two- and four-year institutions. The promise of high status seemingly offered by admission to community colleges is a particularly cruel hoax. The occupational opportunities and likely incomes of workers with less than four years of college fall far short of the opportunities open to four-year college graduates.[35] Four-year college graduates are over twice as likely to end up in the high-status professional or technical jobs as those who have less than four years of college. Those without four-year degrees are over twice as likely to end up in clerical jobs.[36] As of 1972, the expected lifetime income of four-year college graduates (as calculated by the U.S. Census Bureau) exceeded that of high-school graduates by 50 percent; for those who have been to college, but for less than four years, the advantage over high-school graduates is a paltry 14 percent.[37]

The waste and irrationality which characterize production under corporate capitalism also limit the opportunities for rewarding work. The alienated white-collar worker lacks a personal identification with the product of her or his labor not simply because the product is owned by the capitalist, but because, in many cases, the product does not meet any real human need. Teachers are a good example: Preparing youth for alienated jobs is hardly calculated to produce a feeling of integration of teachers with their labors. The product of work may be as alienating as the process. Ecology and consumer protection movements, the pervasive demands for more adequate social services, the energy crisis, and the Third World liberation movements have all helped to reveal the massive waste and irrationality of what is produced in the U.S. Having a hand in producing it has less and less appeal to young people. The growing numbers who feel that too many commodities for private consumption are produced already—and for the wrong people—balk at most work prospects available in the present capitalist economy. Others, sensitive to concerns such as environmental issues, can feel nothing better than ambivalence about their work. And while employment in military and war-related work was not long ago seen as a social contribution, it is now more often taken on with only a sense of humiliation, embarrassment, or even contempt. The new armies of workers involved in packaging, product design and redesign, advertising, and other aspects of the sales effort are face to face with the fact that the object of their labor is capitalists' profits, not the satisfaction of consumer needs. Even work in education itself has lost much of its appeal. The smug ideology which once celebrated the enlightening and equalizing mission of the teaching profession has given way under the pressure of political movements and radical critiques to a more persuasive, though less inspiring, view of education which stresses its inegalitarian and repressive features.

The uninviting job prospects for college students are thus a manifestation of contradictions in the evolving structure of the corporate capitalist economy. On the one hand, the expansion of corporate capital has provided much of the impetus for the increase in enrollments. On the other, the changing class structure and the growing waste and irrationality associated with corporate capitalist expansion have so altered work as to thwart student aspirations. Student protests of the past decade reflected this basic contradiction, but discontent has its roots in other contradictions of the larger society as well. Attacks on institutional racism arise less from the peculiarities of college life than from the nationwide movement for racial self-determination. The women's movement on the campus, though often concentrating on such college-related objectives as women's studies programs, is an assault on female oppression in all forms. The fight against ROTC and campus military recruiters is just a small part of the worldwide anti-imperialism struggle. Likewise, the radicalism of many young teachers, technicians, social workers, and other professionals is, in part, a response to the continuing failure to place the nation's productive capacities and fiscal resources in the service of the people.[38]

What we have witnessed over the past decade is nothing less than a massive undermining of the legitimacy of U.S. social institutions. Between 1966 and 1971—long before Watergate—the percentage of Americans expressing confidence in the Federal Executive branch fell from 41 to 23 percent. The fall from grace of other major institutions was even more drastic. "Banks and financial institutions" fell from 67 to 36 percent; "major companies," from 55 to 27 percent; the "military," from 62 to 27 percent; and "education" itself fell from 61 to 37 percent.[40]

The fact that the political manifestations of this shift in opinion are more acutely felt on the campuses and in the professional organizations should not obscure their broader social importance. Today's students are tomorrow's workers. Even today's young workers are increasingly sharing the antiauthoritarian values of the students. A massive six-year survey by Daniel Yankelovich involving 3,522 respondents found that the values of college youth changed radically during the years 1966 to 1971, increasingly reflecting humanistic, antimaterialist, and antiauthoritarian perspectives.[40] While the political expression of these views (for example, the percent classifying themselves politically as "radical") declined between 1971 and 1973, a far more significant finding of the Yankelovich survey is the fact that the change in the underlying values continued. Equally important is the finding that antiauthoritarian goals are increasingly shared by all youth. "The enduring heritage of the 1960s," this survey concludes, "is the new social values that grew up on the nation's campuses during that same period and have now grown stronger and more powerful."[41] These survey results, we believe, strongly support our contention that the student movement is not the result solely of events confined to the campus; nor can it be understood as a unique episode to be explained by the accidental confluence of the antiwar and civil rights movements. The relative absence of political expressions of student radicalism in the early 1970s has been accompanied by the continued radicalization of student consciousness and the dramatic radicalization of the consciousness of working young people. The student movement and the continuing radicalization of young people's values is an expression of the changing class structure and the increasingly obvious conflicts between the imperatives of profit and the requirements of human welfare and progress.

This is not to say that the structure of higher education and the conditions of student life are unimportant in the analysis of radical change. Quite the opposite. The weakening of the reproductive role of higher education represents an opportunity for radical change, not only on the campuses, where these contradictions are now most acutely felt, but also in other sections of the society where the crisis in higher education will help destroy the mythology of opportunity and progress and thus reveal the shortcomings of the social institutions which regulate our lives.

## The Consequences of Contradictory Development: Backward-Looking Consciousness and Revolutionary Potential

> "Four years of college and they move me right into the driver's seat."
>
> University of Massachusetts student
> now driving a pick-up truck

Like the nineteenth-century labor movement, the student and radical educational reform movements are, in large measure, a product of the proletarianization of labor which accompanies the accumulation of capital. Like the early labor movement, too, they have combined militant action and a sometimes radical rhetoric with a backward-looking consciousness.

The skilled factory hands who sought to regain a freedom they lost with the demise of craft production, the agricultural workers and farm tenants who bemoaned the bygone respectability and independence of the family farmer find their twentieth-century echo in the college student who despises the thought of salaried work in the corporate bureaucracy and longs for the free-wheeling personal independence of the self-employed professional or owner-entrepreneur. The same backward-looking consciousness finds expression in the teachers or engineers who agonize at the loss of status and independence as they are absorbed into large bureaucracies.

The Jeffersonian ideal—the small community of independent property owners—which captured the imagination of dispossessed farmers and craftsmen a century ago, was gradually extinguished, for it had been bypassed by the growth of the competitive capitalist system. Today, the competitive capitalist ideal—the individuality and respectability of the individual entrepreneur or professional—is expressed in slightly altered form in student definitions of a good job and in their desire to "do their own thing." Like the Jeffersonian ideal, this competitive capitalist vision is sharply in conflict with the reality of the corporate capitalist economy. The underlying aspirations which unify major segments of the student movement, contemporary youth culture, and the malaise of many young white-collar workers is thus a hip version of petty bourgeois consciousness.

Unlike the nineteenth-century workers and farmers, whose consciousness was often rooted in their own experience as independent producers, the backward-looking consciousness of today's discontented students is borrowed largely from their parents. The student values of independence, initiative, individuality, and social service reflect the often unrealized aspirations of a parental generation of social service workers, independent professionals, and small business people.[42] These values were passed on to the younger generation through patterns of "progressive" child-rearing as well as by more formal "indoctrination."[43] Well before the decade of the 1960s, the accumulation of corporate capital had undermined the economic base of the parents' entrepreneurial values. The social relations of production of corporate capitalism had been radically transformed, leaving the parents of the college generation more often than not in wage or salary employment and drastically altering the occupational structure open to their children. The result was a massive discrepancy between the entrepreneurial consciousness of the college generation and the contemporary and future structure of jobs and work for which the students were preparing.

For all the discontent that has been generated, the contradiction between the structure and growth of higher education on the one hand and the expansion of corporate capital on the other has thus not produced a revolutionary consciousness save among a small minority of students. Yet the contradictions underlying student protest are likely to intensify, for they are deeply rooted in the process of capitalist expansion. As the proletarianization of white-collar work continues to propel the vocationalization and stratification of U.S. higher education, the political expression of the contradictions in higher education may begin to take a more radical form. Two tendencies, though of seemingly minor importance at the present, are likely to increase over the next decade.

First, by escalating serious class and racial inequalities from secondary to higher education, the expansion of enrollments has done much more than increase the awareness of the degree of inequality in our school system. It has created in the mass of nonelite college students a group of people who have had at least a taste of inequality and hardship, who are old enough to be politically active and yet young enough to have dreams and take chances, and who are brought together on a day-to-day basis through common experiences and, in some cases, common residence.

The growth of campus political discontent outside the elite colleges is a reflection of a broad struggle for greater equality in higher education. By the early 1970s, protest activity in community colleges was on the rise, and state colleges were experiencing more protest than the more exclusive private nonsectarian institutions.[44] Events such as the strike at San Francisco State College in 1968 and the struggle for open enrollment in New York and elsewhere have revealed the short-sighted and narrow limits within which the corporate elite and other privileged groups are willing to make concessions to Third World and less affluent students. These conflicts have thus helped to clarify the fundamental role of the community colleges and some state colleges in the class hierarchy of higher education, thereby undermining one of the central legitimizing beliefs of the capitalist order.

A second source of potential radicalization arises from parallel contradictions in U.S. higher education and in the evolution of the class structure. Until recently, professional workers and white-collar labor had smugly accepted the comforting view that they constituted a privileged group —a modern aristocracy of labor. They had greater job security, greater control over their work, and of course, more money. They had little reason to be critical of the hierarchical social division of labor. Along with the substantially overlapping group of property owners, they were the main beneficiaries of the capitalist system and constituted the foundation of its political defense.

While the earnings of professional and other white-collar workers continue to exceed those of blue-collar workers by a good margin,[45] the resulting consumption privileges accruing to this labor elite have left many less than satisfied. At the same time, highly valued privileges in production are rapidly being withdrawn. The working conditions of office and "brain" labor are increasingly coming to resemble those of the production line. The widespread unemployment and job insecurity of engineers, teachers, and technicians is symptomatic of these changes.[46]

Consciousness, of course, does not change in automatic response to a changing economic reality. Yet it is possible that over the next decades workers in all occupational categories, as well as students, will increasingly trace their frustrations to a common set of obstacles barring their pursuit of rewarding work and a better life. The corporate capitalist economy—with its bias toward hierarchy, waste and alienation in production, and its mandate for a school system attuned to the reproduction and legitimation of the associated hierarchical division of labor—may then be seen as a source of the problem.

As the individual salvation once seemingly offered through access to higher education is shown to be an empty promise, the appeal of political rather than private solutions will increase. With much of the legitimizing ideology of the capitalist system destroyed by everyday experience, the ground would be laid for a broad-based movement demanding participatory control of our productive and educational institutions, a movement demanding development of a liberating education and its complement: a humane and efficient social technology of production.

The contradictions of corporate capitalism will not by themselves create a revolutionary movement, but they do give birth to a revolutionary potential. The contradictions now manifest in higher education provide us with the opportunity to organize, and to bring that revolutionary potential to fruition.

# CHAPTER 9

•

# Capital Accumulation, Class Conflict, and Educational Change

> Now the whole earth had one language and few words . . .
> They said, "Come, let us build ourselves a city and a tower
> with its top in the heavens, and let us make a name for our-
> selves, lest we be scattered upon the face of the whole earth."
> And the Lord came down to see the city and the tower,
> which the sons of men had built. And the Lord said, "Behold,
> they are one people, and they have all one language; and this
> is only the beginning of what they will do; and nothing that
> they propose to do will now be impossible for them. Come,
> let us go down, and there confuse their language that they
> may not understand one another's speech." So the Lord scat-
> tered them abroad from there over the face of all the earth,
> and they left off building the city.
>
> *Genesis*, 11

In the previous three chapters we surveyed the evolution of primary, secondary, and higher education over the last century and a half. We presented a picture closely parallel in its historical dimensions to our analysis
of the articulation of education and economic life in Chapters 4 and 5. Our
historical interpretation, however, goes considerably beyond our earlier
more statistical and structural analysis. For we have been able to show
more than a correspondence between the social relations of production and
the social relations of education at a particular moment: We have shown
that changes in the structure of education are associated historically with
changes in the social organization of production. The fact that changes in
the structure of production have preceded parallel changes in schooling
establishes a strong prima facie case for the causal importance of economic
structure as a major determinant of educational structure.

Our analysis of the correspondence between the uneven development and the changing social relationships of the capitalist economy on the one hand and the changing scope and structure of the U.S. school system on the other provides a critical and—we hope—constructive perspective on the educational alternatives before us today. We will consider these in the next chapter. But the knowledge that educational and economic structures have evolved in parallel fashion does not tell us much about how to change either. A description of educational development adequate to inform a strategy for radical change in the U.S. today must go beyond the description of the historical correspondences to depict the political and other mechanisms by which these correspondences have been achieved and maintained. We would like, in short, to answer the question: What forces govern the process of educational change?

## How Does Education Change?

> The school is to fit us for the world, and life is more a season of discipline than of amusement. Discipline is the rule, pleasure the exception . . . .
> From a statement by the Boston School Masters, 1844

Not surprisingly, historians and other students of the subject offer different —and often sharply contrasting—interpretations of the process of educational change.

Some, like the prominent educational historian, R. Freeman Butts, have described the development of U.S. education as an ". . . unflagging search for freedom."[1] According to Butts, the question dominating U.S. educational history is: "What kind of education will best develop the free citizen and the free person?" As the leaders of the new nation ". . . set up and operated a republican form of government dedicated to equality, democracy and freedom, they found that they needed an educational system appropriate to such a government."[2] The problem of control of the schools was settled in favor of democracy: "The only institution of a free society which serves everyone equally and is controlled by everyone is the government. So the government should control the common schools."[3] The shift from the mid-nineteenth-century common school ideology to the class stratification of education at the turn of the present century fits neatly into this analysis. While the contribution of the early educators to freedom was significant, it was not, according to Butts, complete:

> Their primary concern was to design a universal, free, public school that would promote free institutions and free citizenship. For the first one hundred years of the Republic, the need for creating the common bonds and loyalties of a free community was paramount.
>
> Less attention was given to the claims of diversity and difference as the essence of freedom for individuals. This came later when the Union had been established, made secure against internal opposition, defended against outside invaders, and preserved despite a war between the states themselves.[4]

Ordinarily troublesome for libertarian thinkers is the problem of compulsory attendance. But not for Butts:

> A smaller freedom must be limited in the interests of a greater freedom. And to guarantee the larger freedom, the state must exert its authority to see to it not only that schools were available to all but that all children actually attended school. Massachusetts led the way by passing its compulsory attendance law in 1852. The solution was a genuinely creative one.[5]

This widely held view, which we refer to as the "democratic imperative" interpretation, does not so much explain educational change as posit for the school system an evolutionary process by which it progressed along some unexplained and predetermined, but evidently universally endorsed path, toward freedom. The only role for conflict in this theory is in the pace of movement, not the direction of change.

Other writers, stressing the role of conflict in the development of U.S. schooling, have seen the present system as the monument to the triumph of the little people over the powerful. Typical of this view is that expressed by Ellwood Cubberly. "The second quarter of the nineteenth century may be said to have witnessed the battle for tax-supported, publicly controlled and directed, and non-sectarian common schools. Excepting the battle for the abolition of slavery, perhaps no question has ever been before the American people for settlement which caused so much feeling or aroused such bitter antagonism."[6]

Naturally, such a bitter discussion of a public question forced a division of the people for or against publicly supported and controlled schools. This ". . . alignment of interests . . .," according to Cubberly, saw ". . . philanthropists, humanists, public men of large vision, New England men and intelligent working men in the cities . . ." pitted against the forces of reaction—". . . politicians of small vision, the ignorant, narrow-minded and penurious, the old aristocratic class and the non-English speaking classes . . ."—in a battle for progress.[7]

226

Frank Tracy Carleton, a historian, stressed, in particular, the role of labor in the struggle:

Practically every workingmen's meeting . . . took up the cry. Horace Mann, Henry Barnard, James G. Carter, Robert Dale Owen, George H. Evans, and others directed the movement, but the potent push came from the firm demand of an aroused and insistent wage earning class armed with the ballot.

The rural districts, employers, and men of wealth were rarely favorable to the tax-supported schools; and often their voices were raised against it in bitter protest or stinging invective. A careful study of the development of a free school system in the different states—and the utter lack of a free school system in the slaveholding South, confirm these general statements.[8]

We refer to Cubberly and Carleton's view as the "popular demand for education" interpretation, recently espoused by S. M. Lipset as the "democratic class struggle theory."[9]

Others have put forward a view at once less inspiring than that of Butts and less exciting than that of Cubberly and Carleton: This is what may be called the technological interpretation. According to this interpretation, the growth and structure of U.S. education has represented an accommodation to the labor-training needs generated by the growth and structure of skill requirements in the economy. Typical of this view is the following statement by Martin Trow:

The mass public secondary school system as we know it has its roots in the transformation of the economy and society that took place after the Civil War. . . . The growth of the secondary school system after 1870 was in large part a response to the pull of the economy for a mass of white collar employees with more than an elementary school education.[10]

These three interpretations—the democratic imperative, the popular demand for education, and the technological—were, until very recently, dominant theories of the rise of U.S. mass education. The reader will not be surprised to find that we hold them to be fundamentally deficient. We present them not simply because they are standard academic arguments which must be considered, but also because we feel that many readers, upon reflection, will find they subscribe to one of them.

Both the democratic imperative and the technological perspectives fail because they are based on false premises. The inspirational interpretation of historians such as Butts is confounded by the fact that the history of the structure, content, and control of U.S. education reveals a striking constancy in its self-conscious repression of youth. Control, not liberation, is the word on the lips of our most influential educational leaders.[11] While secondary education has promoted tolerance, broad-mindedness, and

227

cosmopolitan values to a significant extent, and while the elite remnants of U.S. higher education have fostered an increased social awareness on the part of many students, these seem like oases of freedom in a desert of authoritarianism. Writers of the democratic imperative persuasion are in the unenviable position of having explained the historical genesis of something that never occurred!

The technological perspective finds little support in the history of mass elementary education. There is no evidence of a growth of skill requirements in the nineteenth-century economy.[12] Nor did the proponents of mass education embrace the notion that schools would teach occupationally relevant skills. Indeed, the fragmentary evidence available, while suggesting that educated workers may have been "better behaved" in the eyes of the employers, suggests that, in a technical sense, they were no more productive than unschooled workers.[13] It is particularly difficult to make the case that the objective of early school reform movements was mass literacy in view of the fact that literacy was already very high—about 90 percent of adult whites—prior to the common school revival.[14] For secondary and higher education, the occupational skills perspective explains the need for an educational system to foster cognitive development, but leaves untouched the really crucial issue as to why the resulting school system took the form that it did. For we have shown in previous chapters that the social relations of today's schools cannot be deduced from the technical requisites of imparting cognitive skills. Moreover, we have shown that cognitive skills imparted do not account for the association between educational attainment and economic success.[15]

The evidence in favor of Carleton's and Cubberly's "popular demand" interpretation of educational progress appears, at first glance, rather more convincing. Workers' organizations and citizens' groups often demanded more schooling and, in due course, the school system expanded. A closer look, however, reveals a number of difficulties with this view. First, working people's organizations made a large variety of demands throughout the periods we have studied. Educational reform and expansion tended to be a rather minor concern compared to more direct economic demands—for land reform, co-ops, job security, and the like. Accepting for the moment the view that they were responsible for the expansion in enrollments, what explains their ability to achieve a larger school system when their other demands were not met with such conspicuous success? The answer, we believe, is that the expansion of public education was supported by employers and other powerful people as well as by organized labor. Where the educational demands of organized labor diverged from that of business elites—as in the turn-of-the-century struggle for control of vocational education—labor generally lost. (But not always, as the successful battle against vocational tracking by the Chicago Federation of Labor reveals.)

A second problem with this interpretation is that the evidence of working-class support for educational expansion is not altogether persuasive. Educational demands by working people's organizations are hardly indicative of the perspectives of the majority of workers. In the nineteenth and twentieth centuries alike, only a small minority of workers have been in unions. The nineteenth-century unions whose educational demands provided the prime evidence for Carleton's view were comprised primarily of relatively well-off skilled workers. The educational demands of unorganized common people—farmers and workers—are almost impossible to discover. Nonetheless, the available evidence is hardly supportive of the popular-demand approach. Substantial opposition to educational consolidation and expansion is evident both in the rural small farmers' opposition to the demise of the district school and in the widespread nonattendance, and later truancy, of Irish children as well as rural children generally. The evidence from the turn of this century is similarly ambiguous. Opposition to the school reformers came primarily from popular urban machines and, to some extent, from teachers. Educational reform in rural areas was almost always imposed from the outside.[16]

Third, Carleton's interpretation prompts us to ask: Did working people get what they wanted from education? This is an impossible question to answer satisfactorily. However, the available evidence on the timing and content of educational change does not support an affirmative answer. The periods of pre-Civil War educational ferment in New England and New York most likely were prompted in large measure by the growing militance of workers and other less well-off people.

Workers spoke out for universal education and local control. What they got was quite a different matter: Taking New England as a whole, the percentage of all children attending school fell slightly from 1840 to 1860.[17] Local control was gradually undermined by the formation of centralized school systems, by professionalization of teaching, and the gradual assertion of state government authority over education. In New York City, the available evidence suggests that neither the level of enrollment nor class composition changed much between 1795 and 1860.[18] The antebellum period in the Northeast was one of educational reorganization, not expansion. Other regions—the upper Midwest, in particular—witnessed substantial educational expansions. But these were not areas of working-class organization or strength.

Enrollment did expand in New England, New York, and throughout the country after the Civil War. We do not question the important role of popular pressure in opening up the school system. Particularly in recent years, widespread demands for open enrollments in college have further propelled the development of a mass educational system. But here again, we see a familiar pattern in the relationship between popular demands and educational change. Working-class and poor families have demanded and, to some extent, gained access to postsecondary education. But did they ask to be channeled into dead-end community college programs? Did they ask for "high schools with ashtrays?" Was theirs the vision of stratification in higher education?

We find little support for the view that our educational system took its shape from the demands of common people. There can be little doubt that popular demands have had an important influence on the evolution of U.S. schools and colleges. Yet we are struck by the fact that working people have managed, over the years, to get more education. However, they have, by and large, managed to get the kind of education demanded only when their needs coincided with those of economic elites. We doubt that even the most generous treatment of evidence can invoke popular pressure as an explanation of the structure of control—from the classroom to the school board to the private foundation—of U.S. education. Nor can the popular-pressure argument deal effectively with the extensive need for truancy officers, nor the nearly universal tracking and labeling of working-class and minority youth.

Even the more limited analysis of the popular-pressure interpretation—that focusing on political mechanisms involved in educational change—has recently been shown to be largely incorrect. A "revisionist" viewpoint of educational history has challenged the putative importance of working-class pressure as an agent in educational change. In the course of less than a decade, the path-breaking work of Michael Katz, Clarence Karier, Marvin Lazerson, Carl Kaestle, Joel Spring, David Tyack, Colin Greer, and others has offered a dramatically different picture of educational history.[19] With painstaking care, these and other authors have gone back to the early school-committee reports, the personal letters of the major reformers, the relevant business and foundation reports. Employing both traditional historical arguments and sophisticated statistical treatments they have put forward a new view—too diverse to be called a "school" but coherent enough to loosely summarize. The expansion of mass education and the evolution of its structural forms, they have argued, was sparked by demographic changes associated with the industrialization and urbanization of economic and social activity. The main impetus for educational change was not, however, the occupational skills demanded by the increasingly complex and growing industrial sector, nor was it primarily the desire for the elimination of urban squalor. Rather, in their view, schools were promoted first and foremost as agents for the social control of an increasingly culturally heterogeneous and poverty-stricken urban population in an increasingly unstable and threatening economic and political system. Katz, perhaps the most prominent of the revisionists, suggested that schools, far from being won by workers over the opposition of capitalists and other entrenched interests, were imposed upon the workers.[20]

As our footnotes amply testify, we have learned much from the revisionist historians. Yet our reading of the history of U.S. education has led us to an alternative interpretation—one which, while generally supportive of the revisionist view, differs in essential respects from theirs as well.

## Contradiction and Educational Change: An Overview

> ... The whole battle with the slum is fought out around the public school ...
>
> JACOB RIIS, *How the Other Half Lives*, 1902.
> The clash of cultures in the classroom is essentially a class war, a socio-economic and racial warfare being waged on the battleground of the schools . . . This is an uneven balance, particularly since, like most battles, it comes under the guise of righteousness.
>
> KENNETH CLARK, *Dark Ghettos*, 1965

Our interpretation of the process of educational change is a straightforward extension of our analysis (in Chapter 3) of the the capitalist economy. The role of education (outlined in Chapters 4 and 5) in legitimizing the class structure and in fostering forms of consciousness consistent with its reproduction also figure prominently in our analysis.

Capital accumulation has been the driving force behind the transformation and growth of the U.S. economy. Labor is combined in production with increasing amounts of machinery and other capital goods. At the same time, labor power is itself augmented by schooling and training. Two important aspects of the process of capital accumulation may be identified. The first is the expansion of the forces of production with a consequent rapid and sustained increase in the output of goods and services per worker.[21] The second is an equally dramatic transformation of the social relations of production. The sphere of capitalist control over production is widened through the reduction of ever-increasing segments of the population to the status of wage labor. At the same time, capitalist control has deepened through the gradual extension and refinement of the hierarchical division of labor in the enterprise.

The accumulation of capital and the associated extension of the wage-labor system are essential aspects of the expanded reproduction of the capitalist system. The capitalist economy and bicycle riding have this in common: stability requires forward motion. Yet the accumulation of capital and the widening of capitalist control over production also undermines the reproduction of the capitalist order. It inevitably involves the creation of a growing class of wage laborers and the growth of a reserve army of unemployed or marginally employed workers. The antagonistic relationship between capital and labor, and the increased potential for working-class action against capital afforded by the agglomeration of workers into large enterprises and urban areas have threatened the perpetuation of the capitalist system. We refer to this tension between growth and stability as the contradiction between the accumulation of capital and the reproduction of the capitalist relations of production.[22] This basic contradiction has constituted one of the major underlying forces propelling U.S. history for the past century and a half.

At times, the contradiction between accumulation and reproduction has been expressed in militant class struggle and other forms of political activity—examples are the mass strikes which paralyzed the economy in the last quarter of the nineteenth century and again following the First World War, in the Populist revolt of the 1880s and 1890s, in the sit-down strikes and mass labor organizing drives of the late 1930s, and in the urban uprisings of the 1960s. Equally important, however, is the fact that, through much of U.S. history, dominant elites have successfully confined class conflict to the isolated daily struggles of workers in the factories, offices, and shops across the country. The ever-present contradiction between accumulation and reproduction has been submerged or channeled into demands which could be contained within the outlines of capitalist society. The contradiction has been temporarily resolved or suppressed in a variety of ways: through ameliorative social reforms; through the coercive force of the state; through racist, sexist, ageist, credentialist, and other strategies used by employers to divide and rule; and through an ideological perspective which served to hide rather than clarify the sources of exploitation and alienation of the capitalist order. The expansion of mass education, embodying each of the above means, has been a central element in resolving—at least temporarily—the contradiction between accumulation and reproduction.

It is thus hardly accidental that many of the manifestations of this contradiction in the U.S. economy have appeared in the state sector, and particularly in the educational system. Reformers have consistently believed that our most pressing social problems could be solved, or at least significantly attenuated, through the benign offices of the state. Yet the types of social distress which excite the reformers' conscience result from the most basic workings of the capitalist economy. They are not readily alleviated through a strategy of reforms which leaves untouched the property and market institutions that characterize capitalism as a system. The problem of inequality provides a telling example. The intervention of the state in the income-distribution process—through welfare assistance, social security, unemployment insurance, and progressive taxation, for example —has probably helped to forestall the outbreak of open class conflict in the economic sphere. Yet the problems to which they are addressed are not solved. Rather, we observe a welfare crisis, or a conflict over taxes; or a struggle within the school system over resource transfers. Increasingly, the classroom and the admissions office, as well as the factory floor and the office, are arenas in which basic social conflicts are fought out.

The reformers' optimism has not been rewarded: The problem of inequality is not solved. Rather, its form is changed. But the reform strategy can hardly be considered a failure from the standpoint of the capitalist class. The displacement of social problems into the state sector plays a central role in the reproduction of the capitalist order. The form in which a social problem manifests itself and the arena in which the resulting conflicts are fought out are matters of no small importance. Conflicts within the state sector, even if bitter and enduring, appear to be much less threatening to capital and less disruptive to profits than those which take place on the shop floor or in the office. The class nature of social problems is often obscured when the manifestations of the underlying contradictions are displaced into the state sector.

The overarching role of the state in social reproduction is a relatively recent development. Prior to the expansion of capitalist production in the era of commercial capitalism extending into the early decades of the nineteenth century, the nuclear family successfully unified the functions of accumulation and reproduction. The demise of the family as the primary unit of production, the growing preponderance of wage labor, and the evolution of large-scale business organizations posed problems which shattered the unity of accumulation and reproduction. Both the expansion of capitalist production and the reproduction of the capitalist relations of production required a radically new nexus of social institutions. The school was increasingly looked to by the capitalist class as an institution which could enhance the labor power of working people and at the same time reproduce the social conditions for the transformation of the fruits of labor into capitalist profits. We have attempted to show that the main periods of educational reform coincided with, or immediately followed, periods of deep social unrest and political conflict. The major reform periods have been preceded by the opening up of a significant divergence between the ever-changing social organization of production and the structure of education. Lastly, each major reform period has been associated with the integration into the dynamic capitalist wage-labor system of successive waves of workers. These workers have emerged from the relatively stagnant sectors of the economy or from abroad. More concretely, the uneven expansion of the school system has played the role alternatively of recruiter and of gate-keeper—depending on the level of labor needs—of the dynamic sectors. Schools at once supply labor to the dominant enterprises and reinforce the racial, ethnic, sexual, and class segmentation of the labor force.

The evolving social relationships of the classroom and school, too, were a response to the pattern of capitalist development primarily as manifested in the ever-changing social organization of work in enterprises of the dynamic sectors of the economy. The system of class, race, and sex relations which was continually shaped and reshaped by the evolving structure of production plus the uneven development of the capitalist economy has been reflected in the segmented, hierarchically structured, racist, sexist, and nativist structure of U.S. education. The emergence and evolution of this educational system, we contend, represented an outgrowth of the political and economic conflict arising from this continued widening and deepening of capitalist control over production, and the contradictions inherent in this process.

The three turning points in U.S. educational history which we have identified all correspond to particularly intense periods of struggle around the expansion of capitalist production relations. Thus the decades prior to the Civil War—the era of the common school reform—was a period of labor militancy associated with the rise of the factory system, growing economic inequality, and the creation and vast expansion of a permanent wage-labor force. The Progressive education movement—beginning at the turn of the present century—grew out of the class conflicts associated with the joint rise of organized labor and corporate capital. At least as much so, Progressive education was a response to the social unrest and dislocation stemming from the integration of rural labor—both immigrant and native —into the burgeoning corporate wage-labor system. The particular concerns of the Progressives—efficiency, cooperation, internalization of bureaucratic norms, and preparation for variegated adult roles—reflect the changing social organization of production in the giant corporate enterprises. The Progressive reforms represented in their implementation little more than an echo of the corporate managers' growing commitment to scientific-management and the control of production and personnel.

The recent period of educational change and ferment—covering the Sixties to the present—is, in large measure, a response to the post-World-War-II integration of three major groups into the wage-labor system: uprooted Southern blacks, women, and the once-respectable, "solid" members of the precorporate capitalist community—the small business people, independent professionals, and other white-collar workers.

## *The Process of Educational Reform: Conflict and Accommodation*

> Education is the property of no one. It belongs to the people as a whole. And if education is not given to the people, they will have to take it.
>
> CHE GUEVARA, 1964

The idea that the dynamics of the capitalist economy and the pattern of change in the educational system are intimately related will not strike the reader as either novel or particularly controversial. Nor will the proposition that educational change is the product of intense social conflict provoke adverse comment from any but the most committed advocate of a consensus view of history. A more likely reaction to our overview will be frustration. We have described the process of educational change without identifying the mechanisms whereby economic interests are translated into educational programs. We turn now to this critical last step in our interpretation.

We have argued that the moving force behind educational change is the contradictory nature of capital accumulation and the reproduction of the capitalist order. Conflicts in the educational sphere often reflect muted or open conflicts in the economic sphere. Thus, analysis of the process of educational reform must consider the shifting arenas of class conflict and the mechanisms which the capitalist class has developed to mediate and deflect class conflict. This is a tall order. Indeed, a thorough treatment would require—as a bare minimum—an extended investigation of the bureaucratization and professionalization of education, the role of the major private foundations and quasi-public institutions, the composition of major public decision-making bodies, the crucial process of educational finance and resource allocation, the impact of parental and student opinion, and the role of teachers' associations. Historical and contemporary research into these areas is at best rudimentary. Our interpretation is necessarily somewhat tentative.

First, the economic and educational systems possess fairly distinct and independent internal dynamics of reproduction and development. The process of incessant change within the economic system is a basic characteristic of capitalism. The educational system is rather less dynamic: Our schools and colleges, foundations and schools of education tend to promote a set of cultural values and to support an educational elite which reproduces and stabilizes these institutions through time.

Second, the independent internal dynamics of the two systems present the ever-present possibility of a significant mismatch arising between economy and education. We have seen in the previous three chapters that the educational system acquires its economic importance and contributes to the reproduction of the class structure through a correspondence of its social relationships with the social relations of economic life. Yet the historical dynamic of the capitalist economy involves continual change in the social relations of production and transformation of the class structure. Thus, the relatively static educational system periodically falls out of correspondence with the social relations of production and becomes a force antithetical to capitalist development. This disjunction between an economic dynamic which extends the wage-labor system and incessantly alters the organization of work and the class structure on the one hand, and the educational system which tends to stabilize it in a given form on the other, is, we believe, an essential aspect of the process of educational change.

Third, the accommodation of the educational system to new economic conditions proceeds by two distinct but parallel processes. One operates through the relatively uncoordinated pursuit of interests by millions of individuals and groups as mediated by local school boards, the market for private educational services, and other decentralized decision-making arenas. This process, which we shall call "pluralist accommodation," involves a more or less automatic reorientation of educational perspectives in the face of a changing economic reality. Historical experience exhibits the strong tendency of educators, in periods of economic change, to alter their educational values and goals in progressive directions—i.e., directions conforming to the new economic rationality emerging in the social relations of production.[23] Parents desirous of a secure economic future for their children often support moves toward a more "vocationally relevant education."[24] The several governmental inputs into the educational decision-making process seek to tailor education to the perceived needs of their various political constituencies. These elements of pluralist accommodation in education provide a strong latent force for re-establishing a "natural" correspondence between the social relations of education and production. Periodic financial crisis can play an important role in this process of educational rationalization. When budgets are ample and the demand by employers for the products of the school system is high, educators have a relatively independent hand in developing new programs and approaches to instruction. Students, also, are freer to pursue their own interests. This was certainly the case for higher education during the late 1960s. But a budget squeeze and the threat of unemployment serve to weed out both the opportunity and the student demand for educational experiences that do not contribute directly to employability. Financial hardship thus operates in educational evolution somewhat as famine or drought does in Darwin's "survival of the fittest."

The day-to-day operations of these pluralist forces—the "free market" choices of students, the school bond-issue referenda, the deliberations of elected school boards and the like—reinforce the image of an educational system whose open and decentralized structure defies control or even significant influence by an elite. Indeed, it is absolutely essential for the school system to appear to be democratically controlled if it is successfully to contribute to the legitimation and reproduction of the U.S. capitalist order.

What is less often noted is that the accommodation by the educational system to a changing economic reality, however pluralistic, is, in essence, a process led by a changing structure of production. And, as we have suggested in Chapter 3, the evolution of the structure of production is governed by the pursuit of profit and class privilege by the small minority of capitalists and managers who dominate the dynamic sectors of the economy. The process of pluralist accommodation thus operates within an economic framework determined almost entirely outside of the democratic political arena. Decentralized administration, democratically elected and representative school boards, and local control over school finance thus do not inhibit the process of establishing and continually re-establishing the correspondence between school structure and the social relations of production.

It is only during the crisis periods—which appear in retrospect as the major turning points in U.S. educational history—that control over the relevant decision-making institutions makes a major difference. It is here that our second process of adjustment—concrete political struggle along the lines of class interest—comes to the fore. Particularly in periods of serious disjuncture between the school system and the economy—the 1840s and the 1850s, the first two decades of the present century, and the 1960s and early 1970s—the school system appears less as a cipher impartially recording and tallying the choices of millions of independent actors and more as an arena for struggle among major social groups. The response of forward-looking capitalists to popular unrest is typically dual: material amelioration and educational expansion or reform. Thus the response to the strikes of the 1840s was higher wages for organized workers and the consolidation of the common school. The fruits of Populism as a political movement were somewhat higher farm incomes and the development of agricultural extension and education. The response to the Civil Rights Movement and black urban rebellions of the 1960s was an attempt to ameliorate the economic condition of blacks and a massive program in so-called compensatory education.

In each case, the capitalist class—through its use of the police power of the state in suppressing anticapitalist alternatives, through more generalized political power naturally attending its control over production and investment, and through its extensive control over the financial resources for educational research, innovation, and training—has been able to loosely define a feasible model of educational change, one which has appeared reasonable and necessary in light of the "economic realities" of the day. Forces for educational reform can coalesce only around a common and forcefully articulated social philosophy and program of action. Yet the ideological framework for educational reform is determined in what, with embarrassing accuracy, is called the "free marketplace in ideas." In a relatively decentralized decision-making framework, this preponderant control over information, educational values, and the articulation of programatic ideas—exercised by the capitalist class in large measure through its foundations—has played a crucial role in directing the process of educational accommodation to economic change.

In the absence of any clearly spelled out alternative to the evolving capitalist system, and lacking a political vehicle for the transformation of social life, those who have proposed school reforms which would have significantly undermined the profitability or stability of the economy have been more or less easily swept aside as Utopians. The only feasible counterforce to the capitalist domination of the educational reform process would have been—indeed is today—a party representing all working people and articulating both concrete educational reforms and a general ideological and programatic alterntive to capitalism. Only the Socialist Party during the second decade of this century came remotely close to providing such a real alternative. In general, then, popular forces have had no recourse from the capitalist dominated strategy of educational reforms save chaos.

Partly as a result, the accommodation of working people's educational objectives to changing economic conditions has tended to betray a partially regressive character. Groups have struggled against a change in economic status—for instance, proletarianization—that they are more or less powerless to prevent, rather than against the system imposing the change. Thus struggle has frequently taken the form of attempts to restore the irretrievable past. Such has been the case with farmers in the 1840s, workers' organizations in the mid-nineteenth century, craft unions in the early twentieth century, and the student movement of the 1960s.

## Conclusion

> By the infirmity of human nature, it happens that the more skillful the workman, the more self-willed and intractable he is apt to become, and of course the less fit a component of a mechanical system in which . . . he may do great damage to the whole.
>
> ANDREW URE, *The Philosophy of Manufactures*, 1835

The development of mass education—now extending up through the college level—was, in many respects, a genuinely progressive development. A larger fraction of U.S. youth is now enrolled in college than was enrolled in elementary school 135 years ago. Illiteracy has been virtually eliminated: In 1870, one-tenth of whites and four-fifths of blacks could not read or write.[25] This massive expansion of schooling and the structural forms which it assumed were not simply an imposition on the working class, though workers and their children did sometimes resist attendance. Less still was it a victory for the working class, though the benefits of literacy, access to more advanced learning, custodial care of children and the like are real enough. Rather, the spread of mass education can best be seen as an outcome of class conflict, not class domination. The impetus for educational reform and expansion was provided by the growing class consciousness and political militancy of working people. While working people's groups have, at least for the past hundred and fifty years, demanded more and better education for their children, demands for economic reform and material betterment have been both more urgent and more strongly pressed. In supporting greater access to education, the progressive elements in the capitalist class were not so much giving workers what they wanted as giving what would minimize the erosion of their power and privilege within the structure of production. Educational change has historically played the role not of a complement to economic reform, but as a substitute for it.

The evolution of U.S. education over the last century and a half was the result of a compromise—granted an unequal one—between the capitalist class and the very social classes it had unintentionally but nonetheless inexorably created. Though the business interests often struck their compromise under severe duress, and—as we have seen in numerous cases—did not always prevail, they were highly successful in maintaining ultimate control over the administration of educational reform. Working people got more schooling, but the form and content of schooling was more often than not effectively out of their hands.

The liberal professionals and enlightened school reformers—from Horace Mann and Henry Barnard, John Dewey and Ellwood Cubberly to Clark Kerr and Charles Silberman—were essential mediators of this compromise. These professional educators developed and propagated its ideological rationale, articulated its objectives, and helped shape its programs. Always involved in the implementation of educational change but never independent of its ultimate financial dependence on the business elite, the educational elite has not been able to mount an independent and sustained movement for overall reform.

The major actors with independent power in the educational arena were, and continue to be, labor and capital. We conclude that the structure and scope of the modern U.S. educational system cannot be explained without reference to both the demands of working people—for literacy, for the possibility of greater occupational mobility, for financial security, for personal growth, for social respect—and to the imperative of the capitalist class to construct an institution which would both enhance the labor power of working people and help to reproduce the conditions for its exploitation. To a major extent the schools did successfully weld together the functions of accumulation and reproduction. By obscuring the underlying contradiction between accumulation and reproduction, the school system has played an important role in preserving the capitalist order; within that order, it has also brought tangible, if limited, benefits to the working people of the United States.

The expansion of schooling, like the expansion of the wage-labor system, has had consequences not only unanticipated by the capitalist and professional elites, but unwanted as well. The schools have been used to smother discontent. By embracing potentially radical elements in the society, the school system has helped to extract the political sting from fundamental social conflicts. Yet the basis for these conflicts continues in the underlying contradictions of the capitalist economy. Educational reformers have partially succeeded in displacing these conflicts out of the workplace and into the classroom. Thus, as we shall see in our next chapter, the contradictions of capitalism frequently surface as contradictions within the educational system. And what Charles Silberman has labeled the "crisis in the classroom" has opened up a host of educational alternatives. To these, we now turn.

# Part IV

## GETTING THERE

# CHAPTER 10

•

# Educational Alternatives

> The social revolution . . . cannot draw its poetry from the past, but only from the future.
>
> KARL MARX
> *The Eighteenth Brumaire*
> *of Louis Napoleon* (1852)

The 1960s and 1970s, like other periods of social dislocation in U.S. history, have spawned a host of proposals for restructuring the educational system. In response to the struggles of blacks, women, Chicanos, and other oppressed groups for a more just share of the economic pie have come proposals for racially integrated schooling, compensatory education, open enrollment, voucher systems, and other reforms aimed at creating a more equal educational system. In response to job dissatisfaction, a growing sense of powerlessness among even the relatively privileged, and the spread of a do-your-own-thing youth culture, reformers have offered the open classroom, unstructured learning environments, the open campus, pass-fail options, and other changes directed toward a more liberating educational experience. Some have proposed that we do away with schools altogether and carry on the task of education in decentralized and voluntary skill exchanges, reference services, and "learning webs." Some of these proposals go little beyond social tinkering; others are quite radical. Most of the proposals have existed in some form for at least half a century; a few are genuinely new. Some have been proferred in the hopes of preserving the status quo; others embody distinctly revolutionary objectives. Many modern progressive educators have seen a more equal and liberating school system as the major instrument for the construction of a just and humane society.

The reader will not be surprised to find that we are more than a little skeptical of these claims. The social problems to which these reforms are addressed have their roots not primarily in the school system itself, but rather in the normal functioning of the economic system. Educational alternatives which fail to address this basic fact join a club of venerable lineage: the legion of school reforms which, at times against the better intentions of its leading proponents, have served to deflect discontent, depoliticize social distress, and thereby have helped to stabilize the prevailing structures of privilege.

Schools and educational reforms play a central role in the reproduction of the social order. Yet this need not be the case. The character of reform depends, not only on the content of the reform itself, but on the programatic context in which the reform is advocated and the process by which it is won as well. Many of the above proposals could be welded into a powerful and progressive program. Such a program would have as its overriding objective the ultimate dismantling of the capitalist system and its replacement by a more progressive social order. Yet its most immediate objectives would certainly include many of those espoused by today's social reformers. The unifying theme of a program of revolutionary reforms is that short-run successes yield concrete gains for those participating in the struggle and, at the same time, strengthen the movement for further change.[1] In the context of a general strategy for social change, we include proposals for a more equal and less repressive education as revolutionary reforms.

Revolutionary school reformers must recognize, and take advantage of, the critical role of education in reproducing the economic order. It is precisely this role of education which both offers the opportunity for using schools to promote revolutionary change and, at the same time, presents the danger of co-optation and assimilation into a counterstrategy to stabilize the social order. Nothing in our analysis suggests that equal schooling or open education is impossible in the U.S. But we are firmly convinced that, if these alternatives are to contribute to a better social order, they must be part of a more general revolutionary movement—a movement which is not confined to schooling, but embraces all spheres of social life. In this chapter, we will consider some of the proposed educational alternatives. In each case, we ask: In what sense can these proposals meet their ostensible objectives and promote a movement for the thoroughgoing transformation of the U.S. social and economic order?

## Equal Education

> ... if the children ... are to go every evening, the one to his wealthy parents' soft-carpeted drawing room, the other to its poor father's or widowed mother's comfortless cabin, will

> they return [to school] the next day as friends and equals? He
> knows little of human nature who thinks they will.
>
> ROBERT OWEN,
> *The Working Man's Advocate*, 1830

Proposals for a more equal education may be grouped under three headings. First are those—such as open enrollment in colleges—which would reduce the inequality in the number of years of schooling attained by individuals. Second are the programs which seek to reduce the degree of inequality in educational resources—such as the attempt to render school finance independent of the local property-tax base and other programs for resource transfers among school districts. Last are the custom-tailored programs for children with special needs, of which Project Headstart is, perhaps, the best example.

Without exception the ostensible objective of these programs is to reduce inequality of educational opportunity, that is, to render one's educational chances independent of race, sex, and parental status. The programs are aimed at reducing inequality in the amount of schooling attained by individuals only insofar as this is essential to achieving greater equality of educational opportunity. The rationale behind these programs is fairly simple. Income, occupational attainment, or some other measure of economic success, it is argued, is related to educational attainments. Differences in educational attainments cause differences in income. If inequalities in educational attainments can be reduced, then inequalities in income will be reduced. Similarly inequality of economic opportunity operates, in part, through the effect of race, sex, or parental status upon educational attainments which thus indirectly affect incomes. If the correlation between race, sex, and parental status on the one hand and educational attainments on the other could be reduced (even without reducing inequality in years of schooling attained), the total correlation between these background characteristics and income would be reduced.

This simple model has been the intellectual arena for the major debates over strategies toward achieving greater economic equality through more equal schooling. Far from clarifying the main issues, this model has helped to cloud the discussion with competing and equally erroneous interpretations of empirical data. Evidence presented in the late 1950s and the early 1960s by Becker, Schultz, and others, showing a strong statistical relationship between education and income, appeared to bolster the case for using school equalization to move toward social equality or equality of economic opportunity.[2] More recent writers—Jencks in particular—have stressed the fact that, while the more educated do receive, on the average, substantially more income than the less schooled, educational differences account statistically for only a very small portion of overall income inequality.[3] Jencks concluded that even a completely equal school system (i.e., no differences in years of schooling attained) would leave income equality substantially untouched.

A simple enough argument, but less than compelling. The case which social scientists have made both for and against education as an instrument toward greater equality of opportunity or greater economic equality is based on a simple fallacy: the assumption that statistical relationships between schooling and income can be used to predict the consequences of social changes which would create situations drastically different from the social experiences reflected in our currently available data. Indeed, we expect that significant changes toward a more equal educational system— or toward one less class-, sex-, and race-biased—would be associated with equally significant changes in the statistical relationship between education and the distribution of economic rewards. Thus the simple models based on the assumption that current relationships among the main variables will remain unchanged even if the distribution of these variables changes in heretofore unprecedented ways are simply inappropriate. The convenient assumption of holding other things constant is a misleading guide to the analysis of any but the most trivial educational changes.

The error in Jencks' method and the main shortcoming of the entire debate on the efficacy of equal education to achieve economic goals may be traced to the theory of education which places it outside of society, an instrument to be independently manipulated for the better or ill by enlightened reformers, selfish, elites or mindless bureaucrats. Against this naive view, we have argued that schooling is very much a part of the production and reproduction of the class structure. The evidence of the previous four chapters suggests that the structure of schooling has changed over time to accommodate the shifting conflicts associated with the transformation of the capitalist relations of production. The primary relationship between schooling and inequality cannot be discovered in a model which assumes that schools cause inequality. Rather, unequal schooling perpetuates a structure of economic inequality which originates outside the school system in the social relationships of the capitalist economy.

Does this mean that a more equal school system has no role to play in creating a more equal society? Not at all.

The reduction of economic inequality is ultimately a political, not an economic question. The legitimation of economic inequality is critical to the political defense of the fundamental institutions which regulate the U.S. economy. An educational system purged of its social biases would hardly contribute to the legitimation of inequality. Given the current emphasis on meritocratic process, an equal school system would substantially undermine the defenses of hierarchical privileges. Indeed, we believe that the movement for racial equality and the widespread dissatisfaction among increasingly well-educated workers is, to a degree, the result of the increasing equality of educational attainments.[4] But a more equal school system will not create a more equal society simply through equalizing the distribution of human resources. It will only create the political opportunity for organizing a strong movement dedicated to achieving greater economic equality. Egalitarian school reform must be explicitly political; its aim must be to undermine the capacity of the system to perpetuate inequality. This entails at least three objectives. An egalitarian program of educational reforms must make it perfectly clear that equality is not a question of subcultural values, nor is it a biological issue, nor is it a narrowly economic issue. Equality is a political issue, and the only route to a more equal society lies through political struggle. Second, egalitarian reforms in education must seek to disable the myths which make inequality appear beneficial, just, or unavoidable. Finally, a program of egalitarian reforms in education must seek to unify diverse groups and combat attempts to segment workers of different social circumstance.

Let us consider how these principles might apply in the case of a particular egalitarian reform: open enrollment in higher education. This reform could very well meet the first objective—the politicization of inequality. If youth of minority and blue-collar families gained their share of higher education credentials, the legitimacy of organizing production and social life hierarchically along class and race lines would be drastically undermined. The continued exploitation of labor and social oppression of minorities would increasingly come to be seen as rooted in the political power of dominant elites rather than in any cultural, biological, or skill deficiencies of workers. But open enrollment does not necessarily generate a more equal distribution of educational credentials. Along with freer admissions policies have come a stronger internal tracking system within higher education and the proliferation of sub-B.A. degrees. These symbolize the new educational stratification.[5]

The relationship between open enrollment and the second objective—undermining antiegalitarian myths—is similarly ambiguous. Certainly, open enrollment can, and has, in important cases, laid to rest the notion that only a select few can benefit from higher education.[6] The presence of increasing numbers of black, Chicano, and blue-collar youth in college has also made it increasingly difficult for college teachers to propagate the racist and elitist myths of conventional social sciences without incurring protest. Yet, in many institutions, large numbers of students with drastically deficient high-school backgrounds have been confronted by a hostile or indifferent faculty who are committed to a traditional academic curriculum. In these cases, widespread failure among the new students has probably reinforced discriminatory ideologies.

Lastly, we believe that open enrollment can play a significant role in unifying workers of diverse social circumstances. The universalization of higher education breaks down artificial cultural distinctions among working people. More concretely, by vastly increasing the potential numbers of beneficiaries of higher education, it strengthens public higher education in the political arena. This can yield direct material benefits to faculty as well as to students already enrolled. Yet this is often not the case. If state legislatures and university administrations opt for open enrollment without augmenting the available resources, the increased size of the student body will be reflected in heavier course loads for teachers, larger and more impersonal classes for students, and a heightened probability of blaming the new students for the "decline in educational quality."

It turns out, then, that this reform—indeed, any reform—cannot be evaluated in the abstract. It could have strongly inertial consequences, but it need not. A program of open enrollment, free tuition, no tracking, curriculum and evaluation procedures appropriate to all students' needs, significantly increased finances, and a critique of ideologies which celebrate the status quo would indeed constitute a revolutionary reform program. Essential to the success of the program would be a functioning coalition of students, teachers, community groups, and workers' organizations. A similar analysis of other egalitarian reforms would reveal, at least in some, a genuinely revolutionary potential.

## Free Schools

> We refuse to buy the right not to die of hunger by running the risk of dying of boredom.
>
> Student Slogan, Paris, 1968

Why saddle our youth with the burden of authoritarian schools? Why ought the better part of a young person's days pass in an atmosphere of powerlessness, of demeaning and dictatorial rigidity, perpetual boredom, and behavior modification? Why, in a democratic society, should an individual's first real contact with a formal institution be so profoundly anti-democratic?

Many people have been asking these questions in recent years. Whence the birth of a new movement: free school reform. With a heavy intellectual debt to such venerable thinkers as Paul Goodman and Abraham Maslow,[7] a host of poignant interpreters and critics of modern education have emerged in the past decade with creative alternatives to the dismal countenance of the school. Ranging from the personal diaries of George Dennison, James Herndon, Herbert Kohl, and Jonathan Kozol through the programatic writings of John Holt to the full-fledged social analysis of Charles Silberman,[8] the ideas and strategies of these critics have left scarcely a person involved in education untouched and unmoved.

Indeed, who but the reactionary or ill-informed could disagree with the ideal of liberated education? Evidently no one. Indeed the politics of free schools and open classrooms have made strange bedfellows. Ex-hippies and well-to-do suburbanites; refugees from the radical student movement and editors of *Fortune* magazine, T-group psychotherapists, and the Secretary of the U.S. Department of Health, Education and Welfare; and from various other segments of the political spectrum educational liberators find themselves united by a common vision: a democratic, cooperative, and unstructured education—a vision of schools that promotes rather than retards personal development.

Almost too good to be true! Indeed, we believe that the perception of unity of purpose and clarity of vision is profoundly illusory. The illusion has taken the reform movement some distance. But at a price: failure to develop a realistic analysis of the class basis of educational repression and a viable long-range strategy to combat it. We believe that these deficiencies may be overcome—indeed, as they are in the recent writings of Kozol, Graubard, and other radicals in the movement, for example[9]—and that the free-school movement can be transformed into a powerful progressive force. What this requires is the development within the movement of an analysis which rejects any notion that schools are independent of society, an analysis which places schools concretely in their social and economic context. The unavoidable outcome of such an analysis, we believe, is a commitment to the transformation of the capitalist economy as the guiding principle of a revolutionary program for a liberated education.

We will argue for a rejection of the present free-school movement's economics, its philosophy, and its politics. Our critique of the implicit economics of the movement is exceedingly simple and flows directly from the analysis presented in this book. The educational system trains people to take positions in economic life by patterning its own social relationships after those of the office and factory. Thus, the repressive aspects of schooling are by no means irrational or perverse but are, rather, systematic and pervasive reflections of economic reality. By itself a liberated education will produce occupational misfits and a proliferation of the job blues. It will not by itself contribute to a freer existence because the sources of repression lie outside the school system. If schools are to assume a more humane form, so, too, must jobs.

This economic reality has implications for the philosophy of education: The free-school movement must develop an educational philosophy which recognizes that a liberated educational system must prepare youth for democracy and participation in economic life. This educational philosophy —in order to avoid the failures and distortions of earlier Progressive movements—must be revolutionary and egalitarian. Here we find the prevalent ideology of free school reform, with its emphasis on the abolition of authority and its ideal of the unsullied flowering of the child's "true inner self," to be barren and naively individualistic. Democracy—particularly economic democracy—involves both authority and an intrinsically social consciousness on the part of individuals. Above all, socialism involves the will to struggle as well as the capacity to cooperate. A realistic educational philosophy must reflect this.

A further shortcoming of the free-school movement concerns the manner in which it treats (or, to be more precise, ignores) its own class composition. Its supporters among teachers, students, and parents are drawn from a rather limited and privileged segment of the population. Yet the movement has presented its ideals as universal; it has remained puzzled by its lack of acceptance by other social groupings—among which oppressed minorities and the traditional working class are only the most obvious. One political error in this approach is to orient strategy uniquely around gaining recruits to its ideology, rather than recruiting within itself while developing working alliances with other classes and groups which have distinct immediate needs and objectives. A revolutionary transformation and democratization of economic life clearly requires united action of diverse social groups and classes—e.g., minority groups; white- and blue-collar, and technical workers; public sector employees; and the women's movement. Each of these groups has specific and diverse immediate educational needs and aspirations. It is hardly surprising that the educational liberation movement must also take the form of a cooperative (not to say conflict-free) alliance among groups. What is valid and just for one, may be irrelevant—at least here and now—for another. This leads to a fundamental strategic error in a movement which does not recognize its class basis: By

252

treating its ideas as universally valid and by ignoring its emergence as a particular sociohistorical event, the educational liberation movement loses perspective on the social forces which gave rise to it and which may promote or hinder its further development.

In previous chapters, we have suggested a framework for analyzing educational change which we believe applicable to the contemporary movement for school reform. According to this historical interpretation of the corresponding processes of economic and educational change, every major transformation of the educational system and ideology has been precipitated by a shift in the structure of production, in the class composition of the work force, and in the identity of oppressed groups. The beginnings of factory life gave rise to radical workers' movements, to the nineteenth-century common school, and to the ideology of mass education. The rise of corporate capitalism at the turn of the present century gave birth to the Progressive Movement and the bureaucratic stratification of education. The modern period involves another basic economic shift with educational implications: the proletarianization of the once-independent nonmanual producers. The massive increase in employment in the corporate, state, and nonprofit sectors of the economy has eclipsed the self-employed professional and the traditional, small-scale entrepreneurial enterprise—the historical niche of the independent producer. Thus traditionally elite independent jobs—entrepreneurial, privileged white-collar, professional, and technical occupations—are reduced to the condition of wage labor. No longer can professional and small-business people look confidently to a future of controlling their work processes, finding creative outlets in work, or holding decision-making power. Some, experiencing a loss in objective power and status, tend to become radicalized. They seek to regain the lost ideal of independence and personal control in some sphere of life. Much of the student movement and youth culture has embraced a kind of retrospective radicalism vaunting the ideals of spontaneity and unfettered personal independence. Some young professionals, too, have elevated work autonomy and life-style individualism to a commanding position among their personal and social objectives. These ideals may be traced to the aspirations of the property-owning class in the epoch of petty capitalism. In the corporate era, they constitute an anachronism—granted an inspiring and evocative one—unless altered in ways compatible with the political needs for a radical transformation of the U.S. economic and social structure.

But what does all this imply for educational change? What is the potential of the free-school movement both to achieve a more humane education and to contribute to the radical transformation of the structure of economic life? As in the case of egalitarian reforms, our evaluation must be ambiguous.

There is a considerable potential for the assimilation of the free-school movement into a program for the streamlining and rationalization of the advanced capitalist order. The new corporate organization itself requires a shift in the social relationships of education. Direct discipline and emphasis on external rewards, characteristic of the assembly line and the factory system, have given way for a major segment of the work force to motivation by internalized norms characteristic of the service and office worker. Cooperative rather than individually competitive work relationships are increasingly emphasized. Entrepreneurial capitalism, which brought us the chairs-nailed-to-the-floor classroom, has given way to corporate capitalism. It may belatedly usher in the era of the open classroom, minimization of grading, and internalized behavior norms contemplated for at least a century by so many educational reformers. Thus the free-school movement contains elements thoroughly consistent with the modern corporate capitalist imperative for the "soft" socialization of at least a substantial minority of the workers: whence the strange coalition of corporate and political leaders with free school "radicals." The very rhetoric of educational liberation—genuinely put forth by radicals—can quite easily become the concrete practice of recasting much of the school system into the mold of advanced corporate capitalism. As in the case of its inspirational progenitor, the Progressive Movement, the ideology of educational liberation can become a tool of domination.

Yet the revolutionary potential of the free-school movement is substantial. While much of the rhetoric and results of free schooling will be easily assimilated by the modern corporate and state bureaucracies, much of it will be difficult to digest. Young people, whose dominant experiences in school have been cooperative, democratic, and substantially participatory, will find integration into the world of work a wrenching experience. Students emerging from genuinely free schools already know that hierarchical organization is not the natural, best, or only form of productive human relationships.

But it takes more than personal discontent and job blues to create a movement capable of transforming the structure of society. The incompatibility of the antiauthoritarian and spontaneous ethic of the free schools with alienated labor, by itself, hardly provides the basis for a revolutionary politics. Some turn to drugs and self-indulgent consumption, some to counterculture, some seek a back-to-the-earth or craft solution, and others develop a personally and politically destructive self-hatred and cynicism.

The potential revolutionary impact of the free school movement will depend not so much on its capacity to create miniutopias in our schools as on its ability to create an awareness among its participants of why the ideals of the movement cannot be generally realized. To be an effective tool for human liberation, free schools must create, not a temporary and privileged oasis of freedom, but an understanding of oppression and how to fight it in capitalist society. Lacking a political understanding of their predicament, graduates of free schools may well attribute their discontent to their own failings, to human nature, or to the inevitable requisites of production. Yet a politically radical free-school movement could well provide a seed bed for revolutionaries. The content as well as the process of free schooling has an important role to play. The free-school movement must go beyond life-style radicalism and a preoccupation with educational form and begin to teach the tools of liberation. Much depends on the development of a political self-understanding by the movement itself.

Far from bidding the call of a timeless universal moral imperative, the relatively well-off are erecting utopian educational alternatives in response to particular historical contradictions in their own lives. These contradictions may not extend to all parts of the working class and to other potentially revolutionary groups. It is for this reason that the ideals of free-school reform may not be embraced by oppressed minorities and groups of workers proletarianized in earlier periods in U.S. history. The once-independent professionals and small business people are now part and parcel of the working class. But they must understand that however compatible the types of educational reform they envisage are with the long-run objectives of other potentially revolutionary groups, they are neither moral imperatives nor even necessarily attractive to potential allies.

The political impact of the free-school movement will depend, in large measure, on the objectives pursued by school reformers, students and organizations of young white-collar and professional workers. If they act out the retrospective consciousness of the newly proletarianized nonmanual workers, if they seek to restore their lost privileges in the hierarchy of production—as independent decision-makers and directors of the labor of others—they will isolate themselves from other workers. Should they embrace a set of educational goals in reaction only to their own class predicament, even if in the names of freedom and humanity, this isolation will be complete. Conversely, an explicitly politicization of the free-school movement, an espousal of a participatory and egalitarian workers' democracy, and a strategy for alliance with all oppressed groups may indeed provide a dynamic basis for the liberation of the schools.

## De-Schooling

> . . . out, out brief candle. . . .
> SHAKESPEARE'S *Macbeth*

The most drastic recent proposal for education, and one with a growing number of adherents, is that schools be abolished. The popularity of this idea owes much to an eloquent and incisive book, *De-Schooling Society* by Ivan Illich.[10] In it, Illich confronts the full spectrum of the modern crisis in values by rejecting the basic tenets of progressive liberalism. He dismisses what he calls the "myth of consumption" as a cruel and illusory ideology foisted upon the populace by a manipulative bureaucratic system. He treats welfare and service institutions as part of the problem, not as part of the solution. He rejects the belief that education constitutes the great equalizer and the path to personal liberation. Schools, says Illich, simply must be eliminated.

Illich does more than merely criticize; he conceptualizes constructive technological alternatives to repressive education. Moreover, he sees the present age as revolutionary because the existing social relationships of economic and political life, including the dominant institutional structure of schooling, have become impediments to the development of liberating, socially productive technologies. Here Illich is relevant indeed, for the tension between technological possibility and social reality pervades all advanced industrial societies today. Illich's response is a forthright vision of participatory, decentralized, and liberating learning technologies, and a radically altered vision of social relationships in education.

Yet, while his description of modern society is sufficiently incisive, his analysis is, we believe, inadequate, and his program, consequently, is a diversion from the immensely complex and demanding political, organization, intellectual, and personal demands of revolutionary reconstruction in the coming decades. It is crucial that educators and students who have been attracted to him—for his message does correspond to our personal frustration and disillusionment—move beyond this program.

Educational reformers commonly err by treating the system of schools as if it existed in a social vacuum. Illich does not make this mistake. Rather, he views the internal irrationalities of modern education as reflections of the larger society. The key to understanding the problems of advanced industrial economies, he argues, lies in the character of its consumption activities and the ideology which supports them. The schools, in turn, are exemplary models of bureaucracies geared toward the indoctrination of docile and manipulable consumers.

Guiding modern social life and interpersonal behavior, says Illich, is a destructive system of "institutionalized values" which determines how one perceives one's needs and defines instruments for one's satisfaction. The process which creates institutional values insures that all individual needs —physical, psychological, social, intellectual, emotional, and spiritual— are transformed into demands for goods and services. In contrast to the "psychological impotence" which results from institutionalized values, Illich envisages the "psychic health" which emerges from self-realization— both personal and social. Guided by institutionalized values, one's well-being lies not in what one does but in what one has—the status of one's job and the level of material consumption. For the active person, goods are merely means to, or instruments in, the performance of activities; for the passive consumer, however, goods are ends in themselves and activity is merely the means toward sustaining or displaying a desired level of consumption. Thus, institutionalized values manifest themselves psychologically in a rigid fetishism of commodities and public services. Illich's vision rests on the negation of commodity fetishism:[11]

I believe that a desirable future depends on our deliberately . . . engendering a life style which will enable us to be spontaneous, independent, yet related to each other, rather than maintaining a life style which only allows us to make and unmake, produce and consume.[12]

Commodity fetishism is institutionalized in two senses. First, the "delivery systems" in modern industrial economies (i.e., the suppliers of goods and services) are huge, bureaucratic institutions which treat individuals as mere receptors for their products. Goods are supplied by hierarchical and impersonal corporate enterprises, while services are provided by welfare bureaucracies which enjoy ". . . a professional, political and financial monopoly over the social imagination, setting standards of what is valuable and what is feasible. . . . A whole society is initiated into the Myth of Unending Consumption of Services."[13]

Second, commodity fetishism is institutionalized in the sense that the values of passive consumerism are induced and reinforced by the same delivery systems whose ministrations are substitutes for self-initiated activities.

. . . Manipulative institutions . . . are either socially or psychologically "addictive." Social addiction . . . consists in the tendency to prescribe increased treatment if smaller quantities have not yielded the desired results. Psychological addiction . . . results when consumers become hooked on the need for more and more of the process or product.[14]

These delivery systems, moreover, ". . . both invite compulsively repetitive use and frustrate alternative ways of achieving similar results." For example, General Motors and Ford:

. . . produce means of transportation, but they also, and more importantly, manipulate public taste in such a way that the need for transportation is expressed as a demand for private cars rather than public buses. They sell the desire to control a machine, to race at high speeds in luxurious comfort, while also offering the fantasy at the end of the road.[15]

This analysis of addictive manipulation in private production is, of course, well-developed in the literature. Illich's contribution is to extend it to the sphere of service and welfare bureaucracies:

Finally, teachers, doctors and social workers realize that their distinct professional ministrations have one aspect—at least—in common. They create further demands for the institutional treatments they provide, faster than they can provide service institutions.[16]

The well-socialized naturally react to these failures simply by increasing the power and jurisdiction of welfare institutions. Illich's reaction, of course, is precisely the contrary.

As the basis for his educational proposals, Illich's overall framework bears close attention. Since commodity fetishism is basically a psychological stance, it must first be attacked on an individual rather than a political level. For Illich, each individual is responsible for his or her own demystification. The institutionalization of values occurs, not through external coercion, but through psychic manipulation, so its rejection is an apolitical act of individual will. The movement for social change thus becomes a cultural one of raising consciousness.

But even on this level, political action in the form of negating psychic manipulation is crucial. Goods and services as well as welfare bureaucracies must be prohibited from disseminating fetishistic values. Indeed, this is the basis for a political program of de-schooling. The educational system, as a coercive source of institutionalized values, must be denied its preferred status. Presumably, this politics of negation would extend to advertising and all other types of psychic manipulation.

Since the concrete social manifestation of commodity fetishism is a grossly inflated level of production and consumption, the second step in Illich's political program is the substitution of leisure for work. Work is evil for Illich—unrewarding by its very nature—and not to be granted the status of "activity":

. . . "making and acting" are different, so different, in fact that one never includes the other. . . . Modern technology has increased the ability of man to
relinquish the "making" of things to machines, and his potential time for
"acting" has increased. . . . Unemployment is the sad idleness of a man who,
contrary to Aristotle, believes that making things, or working, is virtuous
and that idleness is bad.[17]

Again, Illich's shift in the work-leisure choice is basically apolitical and
will follow naturally from the abolition of value indoctrination. People
work so hard and long because they are taught to believe the fruits of their
activities—consumption—are intrinsically worthy. Elimination of the
"hard sell pitch" of bureaucratic institutions will allow individuals to discover within themselves the falsity of the doctrine.

The third stage in Illich's political program envisages the necessity of
concrete change in social delivery systems. Manipulative institutions must
be dismantled and replaced by organizational forms which allow for the
free development of individuals. Illich calls such institutions "convivial"
and associates them with leftist political orientation.

The regulation of convivial institutions sets limits to their use; as one moves
from the convivial to the manipulative end of the spectrum, the rules progressively call for unwilling consumption or participation. . . . Toward, but
not at, the left on the institutional spectrum, we can locate enterprises which
compete with others in their own field, but have not begun notably to engage
in advertising. Here we find hand laundries, small bakeries, hairdressers,
and—to speak of professionals—some lawyers and music teachers. . . . They
acquire clients through their personal touch and the comparative quality of
their services.[18]

In short, Illich's Good Society is based on small-scale entrepreneurial
(as opposed to corporate) capitalism, with competitive markets in goods
and services. The role of government in this society is the prevention of
manipulative advertising; the development of left-convivial technologies
compatible with self-initiating, small-group welfare institutions (education,
health and medical services, crime prevention and rehabilitation, community development, and so on); and the provisioning of the social infrastructure (e.g., public transportation). Illich's proposal for "learning
webs" and "skill exchanges" in education is only a particular application of
this vision of left-convivial technologies.

Illich's model of consumption manipulation is crucial at every stage of
his political argument. But it is substantially incorrect. First, Illich locates
the source of social decay in the autonomous, manipulative behavior of
corporate bureaucracies. However, as we have argued, the source must be
sought in the normal operation of the basic economic institutions of capitalism which consistently sacrifice the healthy development of work, educa-

tion, and social equality to the accumulation of capital and the requisites of the hierarchical division of labor. Moreover, given that individuals must participate in economic activity, these social outcomes are quite insensitive to the preferences or values of individuals, and are certainly in no sense a reflection of the autonomous wills of manipulating bureaucrats or gullible consumers. Hence, merely ending manipulation while maintaining basic economic institutions will affect social life only minimally.

Second, Illich locates the source of consumer consciousness in the manipulative socialization of individuals by agencies controlled by corporate and welfare bureaucracies. This institutionalized consciousness induces individuals to choose outcomes not in conformity with their real needs. Yet a causal analysis can never take socialization agencies as basic explanatory variables in assessing the overall behavior of the social system. In particular, consumer consciousness is generated through the day-to-day activities and observations of individuals in capitalist society. The sales pitches of manipulative institutions do not produce the values of commodity fetishism, but rather capitalize on and reinforce the values and anxieties derived from and reconfirmed by daily personal experience in the social system. In fact, while consumer behavior may seem irrational and fetishistic, it is a reasonable accommodation to the options for meaningful social outlets in the context of capitalist institutions. Driving an oversized car may be one of the few experiences of personal power available in a world of alienated labor and fragmented community. Owning a late model convertible probably does enhance one's love life, or at least provide a substitute for one. Therefore the abolition of addictive propaganda cannot liberate the individual to "free choice" of personal goals. Such choice is still conditioned by the pattern of social processes which have historically rendered individuals amenable to "institutionalized values." In fact, the likely outcome of demanipulation of values would be no significant alteration of these values at all.

Moreover, the ideology of commodity fetishism reflects not only the day-to-day operations of the economy. It is also a necessary condition for the profitability of capitalism as a system in the long run. Commodity fetishism motivates men and women to accept and participate in the system of alienated production, to peddle their (potentially) creative activities to the highest bidder through the market in labor, to accept and participate in the destruction of their communities, and to bear allegiance to an economic system whose market institutions and patterns of control of work and community systematically subordinate all social goals to the criteria of profit. Thus, the weakening in institutionalized values would, in itself, lead logically either to unproductive and undirected social chaos or to a rejection of the social relations of capitalist production along with commodity fetishism.

Third, Illich argues that the goal of social change is to transform institutions according to the criterion of nonaddictiveness, or left-convivality. However, since manipulation and addictiveness are not the sources of social problems, their elimination offers no cure. Certainly, the implementation of left-convivial forms in welfare and service agencies—however desirable in itself—will not counter the effects of capitalist development on social life. More important, Illich's criterion explicitly accepts those basic economic institutions which structure decision-making power, lead to the growth of corporate and welfare bureaucracies, and lie at the root of social decay. Illich's criterion must be replaced by one of democratic and participatory, control over social outcomes in factory, office, community, schools, and media.

If sources of social problems lay in consumer manipulation of which schooling is both an exemplary instance and a crucial preparation for future manipulation, then a political movement for de-schooling might be, as Illich says, ". . . at the root of any movement for human liberation." But if schooling is a preparation for work and a central aspect of the reproduction of the social relationships of production, the elimination of school without the transformation of economic life would inevitably lead to a situation of social chaos, but probably not to a viable mass movement toward constructive social change. In this case, the correspondence principle simply fails to hold, producing, at best, a temporary breakdown in the social fabric, if elites can find an alternative mode of work socialization, or ultimately fatal, if they cannot. But only if we posit some essential pre-social human nature on which individuals draw when normal paths of individual development are abolished, might this lead in itself to liberating alternatives.

Illich's analysis is no more persuasive when applied to societies in the process of building a socialist order. Indeed, the inadequacy of Illich's conception of education is striking in his treatment of China and Cuba.[19] It is quite evident that these countries are following new and historically unprecedented directions in social development. But Illich argues the necessity of their failure from the simple fact that they have not de-schooled. That they were essentially de-schooled before the revolution (with no appreciable social benefits) does not faze him. While we may welcome and embrace Illich's emphasis on the social relationships of education as a crucial variable in their internal development toward new social forms, his own criterion is without practical application.

In our society, the argument over the sufficiency of de-schooling is nearly irrelevant. For schools are so important to the reproduction of capitalist society that they are unlikely to crumble under any but the most massive political onslaughts. "Each of us," says Illich, "is personally responsible for his or her own de-schooling, and only we have the power to do it." This is not true. Schooling is legally obligatory, and is the major means of access to a livelihood. The political consciousness behind a frontal attack on institutionalized education would necessarily spill over to attacks on other major institutions. "The risks of a revolt against school," says Illich,

> . . . are unforeseeable, but they are not as horrible as those of a revolution starting in any other major institution. School is not yet organized for self-protection as effectively as a nation-state, or even a large corporation. Liberation from the grip of schools could be bloodless.[20]

This is no more than whistling in the dark.

Although schools neither can nor should be eliminated, the social relationships of education can be altered through genuine struggle. Moreover, the experience of both struggle and control prepares the student for a future of political activity in factory and office.


## Conclusion

> Pray for the dead and fight like hell for the living.
> MOTHER JONES,
> turn-of-the-century labor organizer

Many of the reforms discussed in this chapter are feasible within the context of present-day U.S. society. There are also a host of others of great interest we have not discussed. Some, like local control of schools, would extend to urban areas some of the privileges of the relatively class- and race-homogeneous suburbs. At the same time, however, local control would further the fragmentation of working people. Others, like educational vouchers which would offer parents a fixed sum of money per child to spend on education any way they see fit, might equalize educational resources and foster the proliferation of alternative educational settings. All would, with hard work, have the effect of improving, to some degree, the future lives and present comforts of our youth. As such, they are desirable indeed. However, we have argued that none, within its own framework, is capable of addressing the major problems facing U.S. society today. None utilizes the full potential of the educational system for contributing to social change. Only revolutionary reforms, we believe, have this potential. Implicit in the need for such reforms is the understanding that educational change must contribute to a fundamental democratization of economic life.

The possibility of revolutionary reforms in education arises from the contradiction both within the school system and in the society as a whole. The open conflict between the objectives of corporate employers and other privileged elites—to use schools to perpetuate the capitalist system and its structure of wealth and power—and the needs of just about everyone else for a school system dedicated to greater equality and fuller human development has shattered much of the liberal educational ideology. The notion that the U.S. school system does—or ever can, under capitalism—effectively serve the interests of equality or human growth is going by the boards. Fast fading, too, is the idea that schools are—or should be—"above politics," more or less like foreign policy and Federal regulation of the supply of money. The confidence and power of the liberal educational establishment has been severely shaken by persistent conflict and failure during the 1960s and 1970s.

The evident potential for revolutionary reforms in education presents a great opportunity for progressive social change. As in other eras of educational ferment, the outcome over the next decade or so will depend, in large measure, on the political will and skill of the opposing forces. Success in the protracted educational struggle will require an acute awareness of both the dynamics of contemporary social change and an alternative to the contemporary social order. In the final chapter, we suggest that a strategy of revolutionary reforms must be based on an analysis of the contradictions in modern capitalist society, and must offer a vision of a socialist education and society sufficiently well-articulated to draw together the various groups which, however diverse their immediate needs, stand to gain from a radical transformation of social life.

# CHAPTER 11

•

# Education, Socialism,

# and Revolution

> The tradition of all the dead generations weighs like a night-mare on the brain of the living. And just when they seem en-gaged in revolutionizing themselves and things, in creating something that has never yet existed, precisely in such periods of revolutionary crisis they anxiously conjure up the spirits of the past to their service and borrow from them names, battle cries and costumes, in order to present the new scene of world history in this time-honored disguise and this bor-rowed language.
>
> KARL MARX,
> *The Eighteenth Brumaire*
> *of Louis Napoleon* (1852)

Venereal disease ravaged the population of prerevolutionary China, attack-ing one in ten in urban areas. The colonial administration in the British-held ports was concerned indeed, and went to great lengths to battle the dread disease. In 1920, the wife of a High Court judge, as part of a concerted effort, collected the names of all 900 brothels owners in Shang-hai. They were invited to a grand ball where they would be given paper carnations and Christian Bibles; one hundred eighty, chosen at random, would be "invited" to close their establishments. Only twenty of the flour-ishing businessmen showed up, and none saw fit to restrict their activities. In Shanghai alone 150,000 prostitutes were working. Their number was continually swelled by the poverty and famine to which prostitution was a welcome alternative. It was not surprising that the colonial administration, despite its good will, made no headway. Venereal disease was simply a fact of life. Yet after the revolution, progress was so rapid that, in 1969, Dr. Joshua Horn could say: "Active venereal disease has been completely eradicated from most areas and completely controlled throughout China."[1] The British administration should not have been so pessimistic. Often the best social policy is a revolutionary policy. But how could they have sus-pected that?

Education and venereal disease are social problems of a different order. But our analysis of the dynamics of liberal educational reform and the weakness of its successes urges upon us a correspondingly radical alternative. What we demand of U.S. schools is perfectly straightforward. We envision an educational system which, in the process of reproducing society, vigorously promotes personal development and social equality. What we have shown in this book is equally straightforward: The major characteristics of the educational system in the United States today flow directly from its role in producing a work force able and willing to staff occupational positions in the capitalist system. We conclude that the creation of an equal and liberating school system requires a revolutionary transformation of economic life.

The most critical aspect of U.S. capitalism is that a few people own and control the bulk of productive resources, while most—aside from personal possessions—own only their labor power. The U.S. economy exhibits the most extensive and complete wage-labor system in the history of civilization. This system, which emerged historically as a progressive force in the service of economic productivity and the ethos of individuality and personal freedom, has long become repressive and anachronistic, an obstacle to further human progress. The many must daily acquiesce to domination by the few, giving rise to the systemic perpetuation of extensive inequalities —not only between capital and wage labor, but among working people as well. The stability and security of these economic power relationships require the creation and reinforcement of distinctions based on sex, race, ethnic origin, social class, and hierarchical status.

The educational system, basically, neither adds to nor subtracts from the degree of inequality and repression originating in the economic sphere. Rather, it reproduces and legitimates a preexisting pattern in the process of training and stratifying the work force. How does this occur? The heart of the process is to be found not in the content of the educational encounter— or the process of information transfer—but in the form: the social relations of the educational encounter. These correspond closely to the social relations of dominance, subordination, and motivation in the economic sphere. Through the educational encounter, individuals are induced to accept the degree of powerlessness with which they will be faced as mature workers.

The central prerequisite for personal development—be it physical, emotional, aesthetic, cognitive, or spiritual—lies in the capacity to control the conditions of one's life. Thus a society can foster personal development roughly to the extent that it allows and requires personal interaction along the lines of equal, unified, participatory, and democratic cooperation and struggle.* Needless to say, these very conditions are those most conducive to social and economic equality. The U.S. educational system, in the present nexus of economic power relationships, cannot foster such patterns of personal development and social equality. To reproduce the labor force, the schools are destined to legitimate inequality, limit personal development to forms compatible with submission to arbitrary authority, and aid in the process whereby youth are resigned to their fate.

Hence we believe—indeed, it follows logically from our analysis—that an equal and liberating educational system can only emerge from a broad-based movement dedicated to the transformation of economic life. Such a movement is socialist in the sense that private ownership of essential productive resources must be abolished, and control over the production process must be placed in the hands of working people.

The goals of such a revolutionary socialism go beyond the achievement of the Soviet Union and countries of Eastern Europe. These countries have abolished private ownership of the means of production, while replicating the relationships of economic control, dominance, and subordination characteristic of capitalism. While the abolition of private property in the means of production has been associated with a significant reduction in economic inequality, it has failed to address the other problems with which we have dealt in this book. The socialism to which we aspire goes beyond the legal question of property to the concrete social question of economic democracy as a set of egalitarian and participatory power relationships. While we may learn much about the process of building a socialist society from the experiences of the Soviet, Cuban, Chinese, and other socialist peoples—and indeed, may find some aspects of their work downright inspiring—there is no foreign model for the economic transformation we seek. Socialism in the United States will be a distinctly American product growing out of our history, culture, and struggle for a better life.

What would socialism in the United States look like?[2] Socialism is not an event; it is a process. Socialism is a system of economic and political democracy in which individuals have the right and obligation to structure their work lives through direct participatory control. Our vision of socialism does not require as a precondition that we all be altruistic, selfless people. Rather, the social and economic conditions of socialism will facilitate the full development of human capacities. These capacities are for cooperative, democratic, equal, and participatory human relationships; for cultural, emotional, and sensual fulfillment. We can ascribe to a prospec-

* Here we could not be in closer agreement with John Dewey's philosophy; see chapter 2.

tive U.S. socialism no fixed form, nor is socialism a solution to all the problems we have discussed here. Socialism directly solves many social problems, but, in many respects, it is merely a more auspicious arena in which to carry on the struggle for personal and social growth. Its form will be determined by practical activity more than abstract theorizing. Nevertheless, some reasonable aspects of socialism in the United States of direct relevance to the transformation of education can be suggested.

The core of a socialist society is the development of an alternative to the wage-labor system. This involves the progressive democratization of the workplace, thus freeing the educational system to foster a more felicitous pattern of human development and social interaction. The ironclad relationship between the division of labor and the division of social product must also be broken: Individuals must possess, as a basic social right, an adequate income and equal access to food, shelter, medical care, and social services independent of their economic position. Conversely, with the whip of material necessity no longer forcing participation in economic life, a more balanced pattern of material, symbolic, and collective incentives can, indeed must be developed. Essential in this respect is the legal obligation of all to share equitably in performing those socially necessary jobs which are, on balance, personally unrewarding and would not be voluntarily filled. An educational system thus freed from the legitimation of privilege could turn its energies toward rendering the development of work skills a pleasant and desirable complement to an individual's life plans.

The object of these changes in the social division of labor is not abstract equality, but the elimination of relationships of dominance and subordinacy in the economic sphere. There will certainly always be individual differences in ability, talent, creativity, and initiative, and all should be encouraged to develop these capacities to their fullest. But in a socialist system, they need not translate into power and subordinacy in control of economic resources. For similar reasons, historical patterns of racial, sexual, and ethnic discriminations must be actively redressed as socially divisive and unjust. What is now called household work will also be deemed, at least in part, socially necessary labor. This work, whether done in collective units or individual homes, must be equitably shared by all individuals.

Another central goal of socialism in the United States must be the progressive democratization of political life. From production planning, the organization of social services, and the determination of consumption needs at the local level right up to national economic planning and other aspects of national policy, decisions will be made in bodies consisting of or delegated by those affected by the result. We envisage a significant role for the national government: assuring regional economic equality; integrating and rationalizing local production, service and consumption plans; and, directly implementing other social and economic policies which are infeasible at the local level. The egalitarian and democratic nature of economic life should vastly increase the responsiveness and flexibility of governmental institutions. While mediating disputes between groups and regions will remain a central political function, economic equality will eliminate the need of the state to pander to interests and powers of a small minority who control production. Though political activity will not be a major preoccupation of most, the process of participation in work and community should dramatically increase the political sophistication, participation, and knowledgeability of citizens. Indeed, we venture to suggest that all of the glaring inadequacies of political democracy in the United States are attributable to the private ownership of the means of production and the lack of a real economic democracy.[3]

It is a tenet of liberal thought that social equality can be purchased only at the expense of economic efficiency. Yet the evidence is less than persuasive. Democratic social relationships in production lead to highly motivated and productive workers, who will turn their creative powers toward the improvement of work and the satisfaction of consumer needs rather than profit. Moreover, democratic control of work can reorient technology toward the elimination of brutalizing jobs, toward a progressive expansion of the opportunity of attaining skills through on-the-job and recurrent education, and toward a breakdown of the division between mental and physical labor. The elimination of racial and sexual discriminations would liberate a vast pool of relatively untapped talents, abilities, and human resources for productive purposes. Comprehensive and rational economic planning leads to heightened efficiency through elimination of wasteful competition and redundancy in the provision of services (e.g., insurance, banking, and finance), the elimination of unemployment, rational programs of research and development, and a balanced policy of resource development with environmental stability.

The increased efficiency of socialist economic life should quickly reduce the workweek devoted to the production of social necessities, thus freeing individuals for creative leisure and more informal production. Indeed, this aspect of individual development in U.S. socialism will represent one of its most central successes—a veritable new stage in the history of humankind. Under capitalism, a true dedication to the fostering of individual capacities for creative leisure and craft production is incompatible with generating a properly subservient labor force. We expect the creative production and consumption of social amenities to form an ever-increasing portion of economic activity in socialist society. Thus, there must be a stress on the development of a vital craft and artistic sector in production as a voluntary supplement to socially necessary work. It can be organized on a master-apprentice or group-control line and open to all individuals. Far from being a neglected afterthought in socialist society, this sector will be a major instrument in channeling the creative energies unleashed by liberated education and unalienated work toward socially beneficial ends.

To those of us who envision economic equality and a social system dedicated to fostering personal growth, democratic and participatory socialism is clearly desirable. But is such a system of economic democracy feasible? The conventional wisdom in academic social science supports a negative reply. Yet in this book we have shown that the cynicism bred by modern mainstream economics, sociology, and political science is based on a series of myths: that inequality is due to unequal abilities; that hierarchical authority is necessitated by modern technology; that capitalism is already meritocratic; and that the existing situation corresponds to people's needs and is the product of their wills.

Just as the philosophers of ancient Greece could not conceive of society without master and slave and the Scholastics of medieval times without lord and serf, so, today, many cannot conceive of society without a controlling managerial hierarchy and a subservient working class. Yet neither technology nor human nature bar the way to democratic socialism as the next stage in the process of civilization. Unalienated work and an equal distribution of its products is neither romantic nostalgia nor postindustrial Luddism. The means of achieving social justice and of rendering work personally meaningful and compatible with healthy personal development are as American as apple pie: democracy and equality.

What is the role of education in this process? In the context of U.S. capitalism, a socialist education is a revolutionary education. Our objective for U.S. schools and colleges here and now is not that they should become the embryo of the good society but that struggles around these institutions, and the educational process itself, should contribute to the development of a revolutionary, democratic socialist movement. An ideal education for a socialist society may, in some respects, be irrelevant to the task of bringing that society into existence. This danger is not intrinsically great, however, for the struggle to liberate education and the struggle to democratize economic life are inextricably related. The social relations of education can be altered through genuine struggle for a democratic and participatory classroom, and for a reorganization of power in education. The process of creating a socialist educational system for the United States, if successful, render the contradictions among administrators, teachers, and students nonantagonistic in the sense that the day-to-day outcomes of their struggles may be the positive, healthy development of both structures and individuals beneficial to all parties concerned. The experience of struggle and control promotes personal growth, forges solidarity, and prepares the student for a future of political activity in factory and office. The consciousness nurtured in such an integrated educational encounter is one of self-worth, cooperation, and an implacable hostility to arbitrary authority.

Even following a successful transformation of formal power relationships in the economic sphere, education will be part of the struggle for democratization of substantive social relationships. The educational system will be set the task of preparing youth for a society which, while geared toward the progressive realization of revolutionary goals, still bears the technological and cultural heritage of the present system. In this setting, the social relations of education will themselves be transitional in nature. For instance, the elimination of boring, unhealthy, fragmented, uncreative, constraining, and otherwise alienated but socially necessary labor requires an extended process of technological and organizational change in a transitional phase. The shift to automated, decentralized, and worker-controlled technologies requires the continuous supervision and cooperation of the workers themselves. Any form this takes in a transitional society will include a constant struggle among three groups whose ultimate interests may converge, but whose daily concerns remain distinct: managers concerned with the development of the enterprise, technicians concerned with the scientific rationality of production, and workers concerned with the impact of innovation and management on job satisfaction and material welfare. The present educational system does not develop in an individual the capacities of cooperation, struggle, autonomy, and judgment appropriate to this task. The need for developing innovative educational forms is here paramount.

## Revolutionary Education

> We must force the frozen circumstances to dance by singing
> to them their own melody.
>
> KARL MARX

A revolutionary education must be guided by a revolutionary educational philosophy. In this section, we tentatively suggest what such a philosophy might look like. We have been motivated by several concerns. First, educational goals must recognize the correspondence between the social relationships of economic life and those of the educational encounter. Work and personal development are intimately related not only in capitalist, but in any conceivable society. Second, we want to embrace the élan of the contemporary egalitarian and antiauthoritarian critique of U.S. education while avoiding the pitfalls described in the previous chapter.

Hence, we shall develop a dialectical humanism, largely inspired by the Marxist concept of personal development through the dialectical interaction between individuals and their environments. In this approach, the educational system is judged by the way it resolves the basic contradition between the reproduction needs of the community and the self-actualizing needs of students and, more narrowly, its inevitable reflection in the contradiction between teacher and student.

The development of simple forms of life, from birth to death, is governed by the unfolding of genetic potential. The organism's natural and social environment can promote, retard, or even end this unfolding but has little effect on the forms that it may assume. Complex forms of life, in contrast, exhibit learned components of behavior. That is, the organism's path of maturation depends on its particular interaction with its environment. The higher on the evolutionary ladder, the greater the tendency for the individual organism to be the product of its social experience and less of its genetic unfolding. In the case of human beings, the staggering variety of past and present patterns of social interaction attests to the importance of learned components of behavior.

The primacy of social experience in human maturation implies a basic contradiction to which all educational theory must relate: the contradiction between individual and community. Among the manifold potential paths of individual development, only certain ones are compatible with the reproduction of the community. At each point in one's personal development, the individual acts on the basis of interest, inclinations, and personal codes. The final result of this is submission to the requirements of social life or, failing this, the destruction of either individual or community as constituted. The contradiction is an inescapable aspect of modern life whether the community is slave or "free," class or classless, democratic or totalitarian, purgatory or utopia.

Of course, this contradiction has its realm of freedom as well as its realm of necessity: the poles of the individual/community dichotomy depend on one another for the very existence of each. Personal development is inconceivable outside a structured social context, and no community can transcend the individuals participating in its reproduction. Or more pointedly, we have the potential to choose paths of personal development more conducive to our needs by reorganizing the institutions which frame our social experience toward forms we embrace but within which we struggle for autonomy and solidarity, individuality and acceptance, free space and social security.

The contradiction between individual and community is mediated by formal and informal institutions—kinship and peer group, rites of passage, churches and armies, guild and factories, town meetings, prisons and asylums. In American society, one of these institutions is the school. The essence of the school (or of its social surrogate) lies in its counterposition to the student, who is taken with manifest needs and interests and turned against his or her will into a product of society.

Schools cannot be considered repressive merely because they induce children to undergo experiences they would not choose on their own, or because they impose forms of regimentation which stifle immediate spontaneity. Schools, or any other institution that mediates the passage to full adult social participation, are intrinsically constraining. Schools which deny this role, or claim compatibility with a society in which this role is unnecessary, are hypocritical and misleading. Worse, they are positively harmful. They thereby forfeit their roles as historical agents. To wish away this contradiction between individual and community is quickly to be pushed aside in the historical struggle for human liberation.

Nor would this stance be desirable were it possible. Human development is not the simple "unfolding of innate humanity." Human potential is realized only through the confrontation of genetic constitution and social experience. Dogma consists precisely in suppressing one pole of a contradiction.[4] The dogma of repressive education is the dogma of necessity which denies freedom. But we must avoid the alternative dogma of freedom which denies necessity. Indeed freedom and individuality arise only through a confrontation with necessity, and personal powers develop only when pitted against a recalcitrant reality. Accordingly, most individuals seek environments which they not only draw on and interact with, but also react against in furthering the development of their personal powers. Independence, creativity, individuality, and physical prowess are, in this sense, developed in institutionalized settings, as are docility, subservience, conformity, and weakness. Differences must not lie in the presence or absence of authority but in the type of authority relations governing activity.

272

If authority alone were the culprit, the cure would be its abolition—a quick and painless excision—as advocated, for example, by Theodore Roszak:

> . . . to teach in freedom, in complete freedom, in response to the native inclination of the student; to be a teacher only when and where and insofar as the student authorizes us to be.[5]

But to assert authority as the culprit is to suppress the inevitable contradiction between individual and community. Too often, this is done and, frequently, by the most sensitive and poignant interpreters of youth's predicament. Thus, Peter Marin can write:

> [In education] the individual is central; the individual in the deepest sense, *is* the culture, not the institution. His culture resides in him, in experience and memory, and what is needed is an education that has at its base the sanctity of the individual's experience and leaves it intact.[6]

Of course, education can recognize the sanctity of the individual's experience, but it cannot leave it intact.

The teacher is delegated by society to mediate the passage to adulthood, and his or her obligation is dispatched only when society's trip is successfully laid on its new members. The student, on the other hand, seeks the power—within the constraints placed on him or her by society and its coercive instruments—to use the educational encounter toward personal ends. This contradiction is pervasive and inevitable, independent from the wills of the individuals involved, and independent as well from the formality or informality of the teacher-student relationship. It stands above whatever warmth and personal regard these adversaries have for one another as human beings. By denying the necessary conflict between teacher and student, the radical teacher is suppressing a most manifest, and personally destructive contradiction: that his or her personal interests, goals, and ideals often involve the negation of his or her social role. Personally expedient, perhaps, but socially irrelevant. Society cannot be suppressed as easily as the consciousness of contradictions in our lives. The majority of individuals with senses tuned to the realities of everyday life will take pleas for a release from the bonds of authority for what they are: poetic fancy. The creators of valid educational values must begin by affirming this contradiction and proceed to ask whether its process of resolution, reappearance, and reresolution in the educational encounter promotes or retards our personal development, cultivates or stunts our potential for equal and cooperative relationships, fosters or hinders the growth of our capacities to control the conditions of our lives.

The immediate implication is that education need distort human development only to the extent demanded by the repressiveness of the social relationships of adult life. The educator must represent society in mediating the contradiction between individual and community in order to fulfill his or her institutional role. Or unwilling, he or she must make war on social institutions and, by opposing them, change them. Even within the individual classroom, the dissident teacher can become an effective subversive through teaching the truth about society; through inspiring a sense of collective power and mutual respect; through demonstrating that alternatives superior to capitalism exist; through fighting racist, sexist, and other ideologies of privilege through criticizing and providing alternatives to a culture that, in Woody Guthrie's words:

> . . . makes you feel you're not any good . . . just born to lose, bound to lose . . . because you're too old or too young or too fat or too thin or too ugly or too this or too that, that runs you down, that pokes fun at you on account of your bad luck or your hard traveling. . . .

But institutional change in education, unless itself random and chaotic, is the culmination of the coordinated activity of social classes. The politics of a revolutionary education like its philosophy are grounded in dialectics. They must proceed from a commitment to a revolutionary transformation of our entire society. We have argued both the desirability and the feasibility of a socialist society. But is it possible to get from here to there? And if so, what form might a democratic socialist revolution take?

### The Contradictions of Capitalism

> Turning and turning in the widening gyre
> The falcon cannot hear the falconer;
> Things fall apart; the centre cannot hold . . .
> Surely the Second Coming is at hand.
> WILLIAM BUTLER YEATS, *The Second Coming*, 1921

A revolutionary transformation of both education and economic life in the United States is possible because the advanced capitalist society cannot solve the problems it creates. A social system which generates or awakens needs in people which it cannot fulfill is surely vulnerable to social upheaval. This is all the more true when the means to the satisfaction of people's felt needs are clearly available. Capitalism in the U.S. is indeed such a system. It both awakens and thwarts people's needs—needs for economic security, for mutual respect, and for control over one's life. Capitalism has, at the same time, developed a technological and material base which could successfully address these needs, though under a radically different social order. Both the desirability and the possibility of democratic socialism flow from a basic contradiction in the capitalist system: While capitalism vigorously promotes the development of production, its basic social institutions are not geared to translating this development into balanced social development for fostering general human fulfillment and growth. The power, class, and institutional arrangements of capitalist society do not permit the full exploitation of the benefits of those productive forces that the capitalist growth process has brought into being. Modern capitalism is characterized by a set of highly advanced technological possiblities played out in the confines of a backward and retarding set of social relationships. Transportation engineers are laid off, while urban mass transit systems decay. Astronauts circle the globe eating their fill, while farmers die of hunger. Capitalism is an irrational system, standing in the way of further social progress. It must be replaced.

Progress and welfare in capitalist society is highly uneven. Americans believe in progress. We believe that the United States is the most advanced country in the world. We mark our achievements by the wondrous development of science, technology, and organization that can potentially benefit all areas of social life: power, transportation, television, computers, wonder drugs, automation, synthetic materials, and so on. But the only area in which we measure real, clear-cut progress is in the area of commodity production: Per capita gross national product (corrected for inflation) has quadrupled since the close of the nineteenth century.

Where else should we expect social progress to be equally evident? In greater community integrity, better environment, more meaningful work, greater equality? In each of these areas, however, we see that U.S. capitalism is not fulfilling people's needs. Progress, when perceivable, is absurdly slow; more often, it is nonexistent. In fact, many of these aspects of life are deteriorating in the United States. But this is not necessary or inevitable.

Without the benefit of advanced technology, many societies have developed socially integrated communities which are architecturally pleasing and well-engineered to relate work, family life, play, and social activity into a meaningful unity. Capitalism has produced only the urban nightmare, the opprobrious dormitory suburb, the fragmented megalopolis, and the depressed rural ghetto.

Why should science and technology destroy the natural environment?

Modern technology should draw us into an ever more perfect union with nature. Instead, capitalist society destroys nature. This is true not only for air and water pollution. It applies equally to the more general balance between people and nature. Even if there were no pollution, the inexorable growth of sprawling megalopolises would eliminate the last vestiges of nature. Our places of natural beauty are being overrun and—far from being brought into harmony with social life—are slowly being destroyed.

Since the dawn of humanity, men and women have been condemned to "earn their bread by the sweat of their brow." Perhaps there is no better clear-cut indication of the success of modern society than its ability to reduce the brute physical toll of work. While millions of workers still ruin their bodies and shorten their lives in unnecessary and often dangerous work in America, more and more are liberated from this condition. But in scarcely any other respect has progress extended to the social sphere of work. Within capitalism, progress has not made work meaningful—indeed, it is not hard to argue that in the olden days of independent farming and small crafts, work offered an incomparably more vital outlet for independence, creativity, craft, and pride.

Because of the class nature of production under capitalism, there is no progress in this sphere of social life. The ideals of the French revolution and the American War of Independence were visions of equality. Certainly, any notion of progress includes movement toward a society of evermore equal economic outcomes. Yet capitalist society exhibits no movement toward more equality in such vital spheres as income, wealth, and power. Most efforts in this direction have failed miserably.

But we cannot stop here in our assessment of progress. What about people? Mose Allison once said, "Things are getting better and better. It's people I'm worried about!" The paradox of progress is that there are more and more "things" around (higher GNP), but this does not seem to lead to progress in the sphere of human development. The social relationships of economic life, despite a vast extension of productive technology, render impossible a qualitative and society-wide expansion of people's capacities to function physically, cognitively, emotionally, aesthetically, and spiritually.

Emotional progress? Capitalism and the "Anxious Society" are one. Drugs, suicide, mental instability, personal insecurity, predatory sexuality, depression, loneliness, bigotry, and hatred mark the perennial fears of Americans. Psychology has made advances; why cannot progress include emotional health?

Even physical capacities are left out of the march of progress. People live longer with modern medical practice—they are less prone to crippling diseases—but we certainly expect much more than this from progress. Why are we weak, uncoordinated, flabby, and unathletic—in short, unphysical? Why must we get our physical pleasures vicariously, watching superstars on television, without moving a muscle?

Why is progress so uneven? The answer, important elements of which have been developed in this book, is that the uneven development of social progress results from the inability of the social relationships of economic life in U.S. capitalism to harness for social ends the productive forces to which it gives rise. This contradiction between the forces and social relations of production under advanced capitalism not only renders democratic socialism a progressive transformation of social life, but gives rise to some of the basic preconditions of such a transformation. We believe that the political and social upheavals of the 1960s—including the black and women's movements, radical student revolts, rank-and-file unrest in the labor movement, the rise of the counterculture, and a new mood of equality among youth—have ushered in a growing consciousness directed against the power relationships of the U.S. society. These are but manifestations of the contradictions that inevitably arise out of the system's own successes—contradictions that lead to social dislocation and require structural change in the social relations of production for the further development of the social system.

Central to our optimism that social revolution is indeed possible in the United States is the ever-widening gulf between human needs—what people want—and the imperatives of further capitalist expansion and production. This position may seem out of place in a book which has laid such stress on the reproduction of consciousness and skills consistent with capitalist expansion. The preponderant influence of the capitalist class, not only on the structure of the workplace but on schools and other institutions central to the process of human development, is well documented. Why then do the needs of workers diverge from those of capital? We can only outline an answer.

The work process produces people as well as commodities. But people, unlike commodities, can never be produced exactly to capitalist specifications. The product—including the experienced needs of people—depends both upon the raw material with which the production process begins, and the "treatment" it receives. Neither is by any means under the full control of the capitalist class.

What people become, the consciousness they exhibit, the needs they feel depends on the joint interaction of human genetic potential and the social

277

environments experienced by the developing person. It matters not that the patterns of development consistent with human genetic constitution display an impressive variety. What is critical here is that people bring to the process of personal development something independent of the wills of the capitalist class.

Equally important, the social experiences through which genetic potential is developed are not determined solely by the capitalist class. To paraphrase Marx in a different context: the capitalist class produces people, but not exactly as it chooses and under conditions inherited from the past. It is equally true that people produce themselves. Just as labor is an active agent in the process of production and never a passive commodity, so too, human beings are active agents in their own reproduction, pursuing their own ends and resisting the designs of others.

The institutions which govern the process of human development—families and schools as well as the workplace—have evolved historically in response to struggles among competing groups, of which the capitalist class has been dominant but by no means unchallenged. In the school system, as we have emphasized, contradictory forces meet: capital expressing its objective—a well trained and well-behaved work force—and students and their families pursuing their own objectives—material security, intellectual and cultural development, and the like. The outcome, today's school system, cannot be understood without reference to these partially successful attempts over a century and a half by working people to capture some control over the process of human development.

The conditions of human development are inherited from the past and are, for this reason as well, never perfectly attuned to the changing needs of capital. Values, needs, and consciousness which may once have been consistent with the objectives of capital often become anachronistic barriers to the further accumulation of capital and the reproduction of the class structure. Perhaps no better example of this can be given than the spread of democratic ideology in the eighteenth and nineteenth centuries. Initially propagated by bourgeois ideologists in the struggle between capital and the Crown, the "Rights of Man" quickly became a potentially powerful weapon in the hands of the working class.

The felt needs of working people may diverge from the requirements of capital for other reasons as well. Most fundamental, perhaps, is the now familiar fact that the capitalists' objectives for the development of a labor force may be internally inconsistent. Thus, contradictions between the progressive, growth-oriented tendencies of the capitalist accumulation process and the conservative, inertial tendencies of the capitalist social relations of production are evident within the school system itself. The imperative of enhancing labor power consistent with the evolving forces of production often, as we have seen, clashes with the objective of reproducing the social, political, and economic conditions for the perpetuation of capitalism as a system.

This contradiction between accumulation and reproduction is, of course, quite general, reaching far beyond the school system, and giving rise to a broad range of revolutionary possibilities.

At the base of these contradictions lies the irreconcilable and repeatedly erupting antagonisms between capital and labor. Yet the fundamental character of these antagonisms has changed in several significant ways in recent history. First, the legitimacy of the capitalist system has been historically based, in no small part, on its proven ability to satisfy people's consumption needs. The ever-increasing mass of consumer goods and services seemed to promise constant improvement in levels of well-being for all. Yet the very success of the process has underminded the urgency of consumer wants. Other needs—for community, for security, for a more integral and self-initiated work and social life—are coming to the fore and indeed are the product of U.S. society's very failures. These needs are unified by a common characteristic: They cannot be met simply by producing more consumer goods and services. On the contrary, the economic foundations of capital accumulation are set firmly in the destruction of the social basis for the satisfaction of these needs. Thus through economic development itself, needs are generated that the advanced capitalist system is not geared to satisfy. The legitimacy of the capitalist order must increasingly be handled by other social mechanisms, of which the educational system is a major element. It is not clear that the latter can bear this strain.

Second, the concentration of capital and the continuing separation of workers—white collar and professional as well as manual—from control over the production process have reduced the natural defenders of the capitalist order to a small minority. Two hundred years ago, over three-fourths of white families owned land, tools, or other productive property; this figure has fallen to about a third and, even among this group, a tiny minority owns the lion's share of all productive property. Similarly, two hundred years ago, most white male workers were their own bosses. The demise of the family farm, the artisan shop, and the small store plus the rise of the modern corporation has reduced the figure to less than 10 percent. Even for the relatively well-off, white, male American worker, the capitalist system has come to mean what it has meant all along for most

women, blacks, and other oppressed peoples: someone else's right to profits, someone else's right to work unbossed and in pursuit of one's own
objectives. The decline of groups outside the wage-labor system—farmer,
artisan, entrepreneur, and independent professional—has eliminated a ballast of capitalist support, leaving the legitimation system alone to divide
workers against one another.

Third, developments in technology and work organization have begun to
undermine a main line of defense of the capitalist system; namely, the idea
that the capitalist relations of production—private property and the hierarchical organization of work—are the most conducive to the rapid expansion of productivity. We have suggested that in those complex work
tasks that increasingly dominate modern production, participatory control
by workers is a more productive form of work organization. The boredom
and stultification of the production line and the steno pool, the shackled
creativity of technical workers and teachers, the personal frustration of the
bureaucratic office routine increasingly lose their claim as the price of
material comfort. The ensuing attacks on bureaucratic oppression go hand
in hand with dymystification of the system as a whole. Support for capitalist institutions—once firmly rooted in their superiority in meeting urgent
consumption needs and squarely based on a broad mass of property-
owning independent workers—is thus weakened by the process of capitalist
development itself. At the same time, powerful anticapitalist forces are
brought into being. The accumulation of capital—the engine of growth
under capitalism—has as its necessary companion the proletarianization of
labor, and the constant increase in the size of the working class.

Fourth, the international expansion of capital has fueled nationalist and
anticapitalist movements in many of the poor countries. The strains associated with the world-wide integration of the capitalist system are manifested
in heightened divisions and competition among the capitalist powers the
resistance of the people of Vietnam, in the socialist revolutions in China
and Cuba, and in the political instability and guerrilla movements in
Asia, Africa, and Latin America. The U.S. role in opposition to wars of
national liberation—particularly in Vietnam—has brought part of the
struggle back home and exacerbated many of the domestic contradictions
of advanced capitalism.

Fifth, and cutting across all of the above, with the return of comparatively smooth capitalist development in the United States in the mid-1950s
after the tumultuous decades of the 1930s and 1940s, the impact of far-
reaching cumulative changes in the class structure is increasingly reflected
in crises of public consciousness. The corporatization of agriculture and

reduction of the farm population has particularly affected blacks; they are subjugated to the painful process of forceful integration into the urban wage-labor system. The resulting political instabilities are not unlike those following the vast wave of immigrants in the early decades of the century. Changes in the technology of household production and the increase in female labor in the service industries also portend a radically altered economic position for women. Finally, the large corporation and the state bureaucracies have replaced entrepreneurial, elite, white-collar, and independent professional jobs as the locus of middle-class economic activity. This effective proletarianization of white-collar labor marks the already advanced integration of these groups into the wage-labor system. In each case, the contradictions have arisen between the traditional consciousness of these groups and their new objective economic situations. This has provided much of the impetus for radical movements among blacks, women, students, and counterculture youth.

Sixth, even the vaunted material productivity of capitalism—its ability to deliver the goods—seems increasingly open to question. Inflation, commodity shortages, unemployed workers, and unmet social needs all attest to the growing inability of capitalism to meet people's needs for material comfort, economic security, and social amenity.

Lastly, in response to the unsolved—and we believe unsolvable—problems of capitalism, modern liberals have advocated, and won, significant extensions of the role of government in our society. Indeed, the expansion of education is a prime example of this process. Increasingly, the government has taken responsibility for the attainment of social objectives unattainable within the capitalist economic framework: full employment, clean air, equality of opportunity, stable prices, and the elimination of poverty, to name only a few. The result: Social problems are increasingly politicized. People are increasingly coming both to understand the political origins of social and economic distress and to sense the possibility of political solution to these problems.

The assault on economic inequality and hierarchical control of work appears likely to intensify. Along with other social strains endemic to advanced capitalism, the growing tension between people's needs for self-realization and material welfare through work and the drive of capitalists and managers for profits opens up the possibility of powerful social movements dedicated to the construction of economic democracy.

*Strategies for Social Change*

> Wandering between two worlds, one dead
> the other powerless to be born.
> MATTHEW ARNOLD,
> *Stanzas from the Grand Chartreuse*

Revolutionary social change is a serious affair. Responsible individuals and social groups with a sober respect for the inertial pace of historical progress do well to consider the tumultuous dislocation and uncertainties of revolutionary change only as a last resort. Gradualism and piecemeal reform represent normal and healthy responses to social problems, to be rejected only in the face of compelling evidence of their failure or unfeasibility.

Nonetheless, we support the development of a revolutionary socialist movement in the United States. However arduous the path to success, a socialist alternative can provide the sole access to a future of real progress in terms of justice, personal liberation, and social welfare. Revolutionary—even violent—changes have unleashed massive progressive forces in the past. Witness the French, Russian, Chinese, Cuban, Revolutions and the American War of Independence. They will continue to do so in the future. At least in areas of education, human development, and social equality—which we have treated extensively in this book—the socialist alternative is both necessary and feasible on technological and political grounds. We believe this to be true in other areas as well. We need, in short, a second American revolution—and a more democratic, egalitarian, and participatory one at that.

How do we get there? This is the central question of political strategy. We have not approached this problem with anywhere near the degree of focus and intensity that we have devoted to the analysis of education and the class structure in U.S. capitalism. Indeed, we have no firm, strongly held, overall, and intellectually coherent answer to the central issue. We consider this a major task of socialists in the coming years—one to be dealt with in terms of both social theory and concrete political practice.[7] In this section, we will restrict our remarks to those aspects of socialist strategy of most immediate relevance to the issues raised in this book.

Our analysis is inspired by three basic principles. First, socialism is the progressive strengthening and extending of the process of economic democracy, with its attendant continual transformation of the process of interpersonal relationships in work, community, education, and cultural life. Economic democracy includes such "events" as a change in the patterns of ownership of the means of production, or the adoption of particular institutional forms in work or education, but merely as aspects in the development process. Second, the nature of socialism will depend on the content of revolutionary struggle in this society. A socialist movement cannot subordinate means to ends and cannot manipulate and deceive to achieve success precisely because socialism is not an event. The consciousness developed in struggle is the very same consciousness which, for better or worse, will guide the process of socialist development itself. Thus a socialist movement, while striving to obtain power, must do so through means which inexorably promote democracy, participation, and a sense of solidarity and equality. Third, a socialist movement must be based on the recognition of class struggle as its organizing principle. A revolution is a fundamental shift in the structure of power in the social system and, with it, a shift in those aspects of social life on which power is based and by means of which it is reproduced. A socialist revolution is the shift of control over the process of production from the minority of capitalists, managers, and bureaucrats to the producers themselves. The move toward democratic and participatory economic relationships makes possible the breakdown of the hierarchical division of labor and the antagonistic relationships among groups of workers vying for positions in the stratification system (e.g., between blacks and whites, men and women, white- and blue-collar workers). It unleashes the possibility of turning technology and organization toward unalienated social relationships. By undermining the social subordination of working people, it allows the emergence of a truly democratic consciousness—both political and economic—of the citizenry. By removing the economic base of class oppression, it permits the construction of social institutions—such as schools —which foster rather than repress the individual's struggle for autonomy and personal development while providing the social framework for making this a truly cooperative struggle.

A revolutionary shift in power renders all this possible but not inevitable. A change which formally transfers power to workers but is not based on a spirit of socialist consciousness around the goals of economic democracy will merely reproduce the old power relationships in new forms. This is true also for the elimination of racism, sexism, and the fetishism of hierarchical authority.

A revolution may be violent or peaceful; it may succeed with the aid of existing political channels or in spite of them. Which characteristics predominate is of central strategic importance, but cannot be prejudged in one way or another as intrinsic to a revolutionary movement. Nevertheless, we must forcefully reject the notion that a revolution is a bloody putsch by a minority of political zealots. A socialist revolution in the United States cannot be a coup in which one small ruling minority replaces another. Nor can it be a result of the insurgency of a Messianic "vanguard." We have argued that those who will benefit from socialism are workers in all walks of life. We have also argued that, at the present time, the overwhelming majority of individuals are workers, and increasingly proletarianized workers at that. Hence, the new American revolution cannot succeed without being a truly democratic movement which ultimately captures the hearts of the majority of the people.

The question of violence, while clearly a weighty tactical consideration, must also be assigned to a position of secondary importance. A majoritarian revolution has no use for terrorism. The socialist alternative involves a struggle for power and the struggle will be bitter and hard-fought. It is almost inconceivable that a socialist revolution in the United States would not involve violence at some stage. But there is little reason to depend on violence as a basic strategic weapon. Rather, socialists must be prepared to counter violent measures taken against them; they must deploy all their resources to deflect and expose any such violent measures. Strong local and national victories, electoral or otherwise by the socialist movement raise a strong probability that dominant elites will subvert the democratic process and attempt to draw on the might of the armed forces and the National Guard to restore order. This tactic can be countered only if military rank and file are on the side of the socialists and refuse to exercise a repressive role. The question of violence recedes into the background, for the only viable socialist strategy is to disable the military capacity of the capitalist class, rather than to develop the force to combat it on its own terms.

As we have suggested, the socialist movement is a social, not merely a political, movement as it deals with the transformation of daily life rather than the mere reorientation of political power. As such, the diversity of the U.S. working class lends a socialist movement immense potential for vitality and creativity. We expect socialist manual workers to use their extensive knowledge in reorganizing production and training others to do their share of manual work. We expect socialist women to be in the forefront of eliminating oppression in the home and demanding vital alternatives to traditional domestic patterns. We expect socialist artisans, architects, and planners to heighten the artistic and aesthetic powers of the rest of us in the process of pursuing their own struggles. We expect revolutionary health workers to open new horizons in health-care delivery, and revolutionary

284

teachers to forge the liberating schools of tomorrow as major tactics in their struggles for power. Revolutionary athletes must teach us all to respect our bodies, and teachers our minds—all this and more the creative potential of the revolutionary movement derives from the diversity and resourcefulness of American workers.

The other side of the diversity of the U.S. working class is its lack of a unified consciousness. We have argued that major aspects of U.S. society can best be understood in terms of the need of the dominant classes to fragment the work force and by dividing, conquer them. The strategy is as old as civilization itself. In the United States today, the fragmentation of consciousness is facilitated by racial, sexual, and socioeconomic antagonisms.

The overriding strategic goal of a socialist movement is the creation of working-class consciousness. Too frequently, this task is seen as simply making people aware of their oppression. Far from it! Most people are all too well aware of the fact of their oppression; what is lacking is a strategy to overcome it. The conviction that a change for the better is possible will arise only where the divisive and fragmented consciousness of U.S. working people is progressively replaced by an understanding that, beneath the all too real differences in needs, desires, and social prerogatives, all suffer oppression from the same source and stand to gain similarly from the socialist alternative. Toward the end, each group struggling for control over its conditions of production must deploy its forces to overcome immediate conflicts among the people. In part this can be done by each group extending its demands to embrace other potential allies and to protect their interests. Workers seeking higher pay and control of the enterprise must fight also to promote consumers' rights, to reduce pay differentials on the job, to eliminate the demeaning secondary-status jobs and discriminatory hiring, and to create free day-care centers for the children of employees. Pursuit of an integrated set of objectives broad enough to encompass most elements in the working class will of course require some form of co-ordination among popular groups. In the absence of a unfied theoretical and programmatic framework, radical spontaneity may result in less rather than more unity among oppressed peoples.

Capitalism is by no means the sole source of oppression in the United States, nor is socialism the solution to all forms of oppression. Racial and sexual oppression are part and parcel of the capitalist system; yet, they have quite distinct sources as well. The struggle against racism and sexism, while part of the socialist revolutionary movement, will take distinct forms.

The evolution of economic life in the United States, by undermining the mechanisms which reproduce and legitimate the class structure, has already done much to create a common consciousness of capitalist oppression. We expect this process of disintegration to continue. Constructive ideological work must be based on the evolving, concrete, and material experiences of all segments of the population. Political work by radical and other groups can considerably hasten or retard the potential afforded by changing material circumstance.

A major strategic element of a socialist movement is the continual interjection of a broader vision of a socialist alternative into concrete struggles of all types. All too often, those with utopian visions of the Good Society have neither the capacity nor the inclination to engage in real social struggle. Conversely, those with an earthy sense of the arduous task of day-to-day struggle have either cynically or opportunistically buried their vision of the larger goals. Yet the propagation of a socialist vision in the context of down-to-earth politics is essential. Few in the United States will opt for a revolutionary change as a nothing-to-lose desperation assault on a literally unbearable status quo; life for most people is simply not that bad. People must choose, and choose to fight for, socialism as a positive alternative based on a serious, desirable, and feasible vision. This vision must develop in the course of struggle, but the struggle will not develop without it. Moreover, vague notions of socialism and economic democracy, however effective in producing change, will by no means insure that change will take desirable and ultimately progressive forms. As we are often reminded by our more conservative friends, revolutionary change can be a disaster, too—a disaster which buries the fondest hopes of the strongest supporters. Only a vigorous and creative effort at defining the course of socialist development before its ultimate victory, however extensively this course must be altered through the practical experience of people involved in the struggle, can minimize this possibility. Finally, the fragmentation of consciousness of working people can be overcome only by offering an alternative in which the disparate objectives of different groups are simultaneously met.

The final strategic consideration we have in mind is the sober recognition that the preparatory phase of a revolutionary movement involves working in, and through, existing capitalist institutions. We cannot sit around and wait for a political cataclysm. We cannot rely solely on creating alternative institutions as ". . . little islands of socialism in a sea of capitalism." Rather, we must think in terms of building up working-class and popular power; creating arenas of social management and direct democracy in the major branches of production; conquering positions of strength in bodies such as unions, schools, the media, and government. In short, proper strategy requires what Rudi Dutschke called the ". . . long march through the institutions." This crucial aspect of movement strategy is necessary to prepare people for taking power in every area of their lives. It has two aims: (1) to weaken progressively the power of those who control economic life and undermine the functioning of oppressive capitalist institutions, and (2) to develop in people the facility for making cooperative decisions and for exercising power, an experience normally denied us in a capitalist society.[8]

The drive for an egalitarian and liberating educational system must be an essential element of a socialist movement. Indeed, the process-oriented nature of the educational encounter can render political activity in the school system exemplary for the rest of society. We offer five guidelines toward a socialist strategy for education. First, revolutionary educators—teachers, students, and others involved in education—should vigorously press for the democratization of schools and colleges by working toward a system of participatory power in which students, teachers, parents, and other members of the community can pursue their common interests and rationally resolve their conflicts. Second, the struggle for democratization should be viewed as part of an effort to undermine the correspondence between the social relations of education and the social relations of production in capitalist economic life. Socialist educational reform must consciously move toward equating liberated education with education for economic democracy, along lines sketched earlier in this chapter. Third, a movement for socialist education must reject simple antiauthoritarianism and spontaneity as its guiding principles. We must develop and apply a dialectical educational philosophy of personal development, authority, and interpersonal relationships as sketched above. Fourth, revolutionary educators must be in the forefront of the movement to create a unified class consciousness. Socialist teachers must not only demand control over their activities; we must also extend this control to students and to the broader community. We must fight for curriculum which is personally liberating and politically enlightening; we much reject our pretentions as professionals—pretentions which lead only to a defeatist quietism and isolation—and ally with other members of the working class. We must expand their demands to include the use of educational resources by parents, workers, community groups, and the elderly; and finally, we must fight for egalitarian educational practices which reduce the power of the schools to fragment the labor force. Fifth, socialist educators should take seriously the need to combine a long-range vision with winning victories here and now. In the long march through the institutions, reforms must be sought which satisfy the immediate needs of students, teachers, and parents. Pie-in-the-sky politics must be rejected in favor of a program of revolutionary reforms built around such issues as democracy, free classrooms, open enrollment, adequate financial aid for needy students, and development of a critical antidiscriminatory and socialist content of education.

We cannot move forward through the band-aid remedies of liberal educational reform. The people of the United States do not need a doctor for the moribund capitalist order; we need an undertaker. Nor can the political challenge facing us be met through the spontaneous efforts of individuals or groups working in isolation. The development and articulation of the vision of a socialist alternative, as much as the ability to meet today's concrete human needs requires a mass based party able to aid in the daily struggles of working people throughout the United States and committed to a revolutionary transformation of the U.S. economy.

# APPENDIX A

•

The figures, calculated from data presented in Bowles and Nelson (1974), rely on the correlation matrices from that article reproduced in Table A-1. This Appendix will explain the construction of that table and then present the regression equations calculated from it for the figures.

1. The correlation coefficients above the diagonal of Part A of Table A-1 are for ages 25–34, below for ages 35–44, above the diagonal of Part B for ages 45–54, below for ages 55–64.

These estimated true correlation coefficients were found by correcting the original observed coefficients using the relationship:

$$r_{jk}' = r_{jk}r_jr_k + r_{ujk}[(1 - r_j^2)\,(1 - r_k^2)]^{\frac{1}{2}}$$

where $r_{jk}$ and $r_{jk}'$ are the true and observed correlations between variables j and k, respectively, $r_j$ is the correlation between true and observed values of variable j, and $r_{ujk}$ is the correlation of the error terms between variables j and k.

The values of $r_j$ appear along the diagonal of Part A of Table A-1., and their estimation is described in detail in Bowles (1972). In general, they depend on the 1950 Post-Enumeration Survey, U.S. Bureau of the Census. However for occupation and education (years of schooling), we have relied on a match of the 1960 Census with the Current Population Survey (*see* Hodge and Siegel [1968]). This procedure yields correlations of 0.91 and 0.958, respectively, instead of the .92 and .91 derivable from the Post-Enumeration Survey. Also, for childhood IQ and adult IQ, we have relied on the test-retest correlations presented in the Personnel Research Section (1945). The reliability of the IQ tests from the California Guidance Study used here is .90 (see Jencks et al. [1972]).

The values of $r_{ujk}$ do not appear in Table A-1. Using estimates of the reliabilities of the respondents' retrospective recall of fathers' occupational status based on Blau and Duncan (1967) and on procedures described in Bowles (1972), we estimate $r_{ujk} = .04$ for income $\times$ occupation, income $\times$ education, and occupation $\times$ education. We have assumed the same value of $r_{ujk} = .04$ is also the best estimate for the same variables applied to the parents' generation (variables 3, 6, and 7). Variables are numbered as in Table A-1. Elsewhere, $r_{ujk}$ is taken to be zero.

Unless otherwise indicated, the original uncorrected correlation coefficients are from Duncan, Featherman, and Duncan (1968). The number of people surveyed from each age group is 3,141 (25–34), 3,214 (35–44), 2,596 (45–54), and 1,482 (55–64). The sample sizes for the actual correlation coefficient calculations vary with the number of people responding to both relevant questionnaire items.

The correlation between childhood IQ and income is estimated from the correlations of childhood IQ with those variables which influence income, and the normalized regression coefficients of those variables on income. Thus:

$$r_{51} = b_{14}r_{45} + b_{18}r_{85} + b_{13}r_{35}.$$

The correlation between childhood IQ and occupation is calculated in a similar manner:

$$r_{52} = b_{24}r_{45} + b_{26}r_{65} + b_{27}r_{75} + b_{23}r_{35}.$$

The correlation between childhood IQ and father's education can be calculated from an equation predicting adult IQ, whose correlation with father's education is already known:

$$r_{86} = b_{83}r_{36} + b_{84}r_{46} + b_{85}r_{56}.$$

Thus we have:

$$r_{56} = [r_{86} - b_{83}r_{36} - b_{84}r_{46}]/b_{85}.$$

To estimate the correlation between childhood IQ and father's occupation, we use the same method, finding

$$r_{57} = [r_{87} - b_{83}r_{37} - b_{84}r_{47}]/b_{85}.$$

The correlation between adult IQ and income, occupation, education, father's education, and father's occupation are derived from the National Opinion Research Center's 1966 Veteran sample, reported in Griliches and Mason (1972). Correction for restricted variance follows Gulliken (1950). The correlation between childhood IQ and adult IQ is taken from Bloom (1964), Ch. 3. See Bowles (1972) and Bowles and Nelson (1974) for further sources and assumptions.

The variable socioeconomic background is the equally weighted normalized sum of parents' income, father's education, and father's occupation. The correlation between socioeconomic background and another variable j is then calculated to be:

$$r_{9j} = [r_{j3} + r_{j6} + r_{j7}]/[3 + 2(r_{36} + r_{37} + r_{67})]^{\frac{1}{2}}.$$

2. Figure 4.1 based on a normalized regression equation predicting income from education (years of schooling) and adult IQ. Our estimates of the equation for four age groups are:

| AGE GROUP | EDUCATION | ADULT IQ | $R^2$ |
|---|---|---|---|
| 25–34 | .222 (8.38) | .174 (6.48) | .13 |
| 35–44 | .431 (17.07) | .045 (1.58) | .21 |
| 45–54 | .406 (15.95) | .060 (2.37) | .20 |
| 55–64 | .293 (11.16) | .130 (4.98) | .15 |

Figure 4.1 constructed using the 35–44 age group, as were all the others. The simple correlations between education and income, from which the comparison in the figure is drawn are 0.33, 0.46, 0.44, and 0.37, respectively, for the four age groups. T-statistics are in parentheses.

3. Figure 4.2 based on a normalized regression equation predicting income from socioeconomic background and childhood IQ. Our estimates of the regression equation for the four age groups are:

| AGE GROUP | SOCIOECONOMIC BACKGROUND | CHILDHOOD IQ | $R^2$ |
|---|---|---|---|
| 25–34 | .251 (10.97) | .180 (7.87) | .13 |
| 35–44 | .384 (17.59) | .122 (5.59) | .20 |
| 45–54 | .413 (19.14) | .125 (5.81) | .23 |
| 55–64 | .235 (10.11) | .171 (7.34) | .12 |

The simple correlations between income and socioeconomic background, from which the comparison in the figure is drawn are: .324, .433, .464, and .308, respectively, for the four age groups. T-statistics are in parentheses.

4. Figure 4.3 based on two normalized regression equations. Our estimates of the first equation, which predicts education (years of schooling) from childhood IQ and socioeconomic background, for the four age groups are:

| AGE GROUP | SOCIOECONOMIC BACKGROUND | CHILDHOOD IQ | $R^2$ |
|---|---|---|---|
| 25–34 | .536 (29.84) | .253 (14.10) | .46 |
| 35–44 | .544 (30.68) | .256 (14.45) | .47 |
| 45–54 | .536 (29.80) | .253 (14.09) | .46 |
| 55–64 | .482 (25.49) | .268 (14.14) | .41 |

Our estimates of the second equation, which predicts income from childhood IQ, education, and socioeconomic background, are:

| AGE GROUP | SOCIOECONOMIC BACKGROUND | CHILDHOOD IQ | EDUCATION | $R^2$ |
|---|---|---|---|---|
| 25–34 | .166 (6.08) | .140 (5.87) | .158 (5.60) | .15 |
| 35–44 | .226 (8.77) | .048 (2.12) | .291 (10.86) | .24 |
| 45–54 | .292 (11.48) | .068 (3.07) | .225 (8.52) | .26 |
| 55–64 | .109 (4.17) | .101 (4.23) | .261 (9.74) | .16 |

## TABLE A-1.

Estimated "True" Zero Order Correlations among the Variables for Non-Negro Males with Non-Farm Backgrounds in Experienced Labor Force, 1962.

### A. AGE GROUPS 25–34 AND 35–44

| | 1 | 2 | 3 | 4 | 5 | 6 | 7 | 8 | 9 |
|---|---|---|---|---|---|---|---|---|---|
| 1. Income | .840 | .429 | .300 | .330 | .283 | .228 | .300 | .312 | .324 |
| 2. Occupation | .566 | .910 | .485 | .740 | .367 | .470 | .485 | .470 | .564 |
| 3. Parents' Income | .385 | .580 | .840 | .573 | .299 | .459 | .566 | .228 | |
| 4. Education | .459 | .732 | .573 | .958 | .473 | .524 | .539 | .618 | .640 |
| 5. Childhood IQ | .275 | .404 | .299 | .473 | .900 | .348 | .400 | .850 | .410 |
| 6. Father's Education | .347 | .475 | .459 | .528 | .346 | .800 | .740 | .362 | |
| 7. Father's Occupation | .385 | .580 | .566 | .566 | .385 | .806 | .800 | .383 | |
| 8. Adult IQ | .312 | .470 | .228 | .619 | .850 | .862 | .383 | .950 | |
| 9. Socioeconomic Background | .433 | .634 | | .646 | .399 | | | | |

### B. AGE GROUPS 45–54 AND 55–64

| | 1 | 2 | 3 | 4 | 5 | 6 | 7 | 8 | 9 |
|---|---|---|---|---|---|---|---|---|---|
| 1. Income | | .561 | .451 | .444 | .294 | .283 | .451 | .312 | .464 |
| 2. Occupation | .485 | | .519 | .677 | .402 | .346 | .519 | .470 | .541 |
| 3. Parents' Income | .278 | .487 | | .573 | .299 | .459 | .566 | .228 | |
| 4. Education | .374 | .634 | .573 | | .473 | .481 | .581 | .619 | .640 |
| 5. Childhood IQ | .271 | .410 | .299 | .473 | | .372 | .377 | .850 | .410 |
| 6. Father's Education | .237 | .415 | .459 | .461 | .383 | | .737 | .362 | |
| 7. Father's Occupation | .278 | .487 | .566 | .506 | .419 | .808 | | .383 | |
| 8. Adult IQ | .312 | .470 | .228 | .619 | .850 | .862 | .383 | | |
| 9. Socioeconomic Background | .308 | .538 | | .597 | .426 | | | | |

SOURCE: Bowles and Nelson (1974).

## TABLE A-2.
### The Role of Cognitive Attainment in the Relationship Between Education and Economic Success

| STUDY | SAMPLE | MEASURE OF ECONOMIC SUCCESS | COGNITIVE TEST SCORE | OTHER CONTROLLED VARIABLES | PROPORTION OF EDUCATION—ECONOMIC SUCCESS CORRELATION DUE TO COGNITIVE TEST SCORE |
|---|---|---|---|---|---|
| Conlisk (1971) | 75 males over a 30 year observation period | Occupational status scaled by census average income for the occupation | IQ, taken at various ages 1–18 | Parental income | Less than 10% |
| Duncan (1968) | CPS–NORC, 10/64, white, ages 24–34; CPS–OCG, 3/62, non-black, nonfarm | 1964 earnings; 1964 occupational status | Early IQ; later IQ | | 10%–25% |
| Cutwright (1969) | 1% random sample of men registered with Selective Service 4/30/53 | Earnings | AFQT | | 22%–35% |
| Duncan, Featherman, and Duncan (1968) | OCG study, all men ages 20–64 | Status of first job | IQ, Army general qualification test | | 20% |

TABLE A-2. (*Continued*)

| STUDY | SAMPLE | MEASURE OF ECONOMIC SUCCESS | COGNITIVE TEST SCORE | OTHER CONTROLLED VARIABLES | PROPORTION OF EDUCATION—ECONOMIC SUCCESS CORRELATION DUE TO COGNITIVE TEST SCORE |
|---|---|---|---|---|---|
| Bajema (1969) | 437 males | Occupational status, NORC prestige index at age 45 | Early IQ Terman Group Intelligence in sixth grade | | 13% |
| Griliches and Mason (1972) | 1964 CPS–NORC veterans file, males ages 25–34 who have been in the Army | Log actual income | AFQT | Age, race, sex, SES regional location | 12%–25% depending on which other variables entered |
| Sewell, Haller, and Ohlendorf (1970) | one-third random sample of Wisconsin high school seniors of 1957, follow-up in 1968 | Occupational attainment using Duncan (1961) socioeconomic index of occupational status in 1964–1965 | IQ, Henman-Nelson Test of Mental Ability | | 7% |
| Taubman and Wales (1969) | All Minnesota high school graduates of 1936 | Income in 1953 | IQ | | 4% |

TABLE A-2. (*Continued*)

| STUDY | SAMPLE | MEASURE OF ECONOMIC SUCCESS | COGNITIVE TEST SCORE | OTHER CONTROLLED VARIABLES | PROPORTION OF EDUCATION—ECONOMIC SUCCESS CORRELATION DUE TO COGNITIVE TEST SCORE |
|---|---|---|---|---|---|
| Fisher, Lutterman, and Ellegard (1973) | 2,400 Wisconsin males who attended college in 1958 | Earnings | Henman-Nelson Mental Ability | | Insignificant |
| Porter (1974) | 14,891 white males from Project Talent Sample | Socioeconomic status (Duncan scale) | IQ | Socioeconomic status, "creativity," "conformity," "grades," "ambition" | 19% |
| Porter (1974) | 495 black males from Project Talent Sample | Socioeconomic status (Duncan scale) | IQ | Same as above | Insignificant |

## Bibliography for Appendix A

C. J. Bajema, "Interrelations Among Intellectual Ability, Educational Attainment and Occupational Achievement," *Sociology of Education*, 1969.

Peter Blau and Otis D. Duncan, *The American Occupational Structure*, New York: John Wiley, 1967.

Benjamin Bloom, *Stability and Change in Human Characteristics*, New York: John Wiley and Sons Inc., 1964.

Samuel Bowles, "Schooling and Inequality from Generation to Generation," *The Journal of Political Economy*, Vol. 80, No. 3, Part II, May/June 1972.

Samuel Bowles and Valerie Nelson, "The 'Inheritance of IQ' and the Intergenerational Reproduction of Economic Inequality," *The Review of Economics and Statistics*, Vol. LVI, No. 1, February 1974.

John Conlisk, "A Bit of Evidence on the Income-Education-Ability Interaction," *Journal of Human Resources*, Vol. VI, Summer 1971.

Phillips Cutwright, *Achievement, Military Service and Earnings*, Social Security Administration, Contract No. SSA 67–2051, May 21, 1969.

Otis D. Duncan, "Achievement and Ability," *Eugenics Quarterly*, March 1968.

Otis D. Duncan, D. C. Featherman and Beverly Duncan, *Socioeconomic Background and Occupational Achievement, Final Report*, Project No. S-0074 (E0-191), Washington, D.C.: Department of Health, Education and Welfare, Office of Education, 1968.

Janet A. Fisher, Kenneth G. Lutterman and Dorothy M. Ellegard, "Post-High School Earnings: When and For Whom Does 'Ability' Seem to Matter?" University of Wisconsin: Social Systems Research Institute, April, 1973.

Zvi Griliches and William M. Mason, "Education, Income and Ability," *Journal of Political Economy*, Vol. 80, May/June 1972.

H. Gullikson, *The Theory of Mental Tests*, New York: John Wiley and Sons Inc., 1950.

R. Hodge and P. Siegel, "A Causal Approach to the Study of Measurement Error," in Herbert Blalock and Ann Blalock (eds.), *Methodology in Social Research*, New York: McGraw-Hill, 1968.

Christopher Jencks, Marshall Smith, Henry Acland, Mary Jo Bane, David Cohen, Herbert Gintis, Barbara Heyns and Stephen Michelson, *Inequality: A Reassessment of the Effects of Family and Schooling in America*, New York: Basic Books, 1972.

Personnel Research Section, "The Army General Classification Test," *Psychological Bulletin*, Vol. 42, 1945.

James N. Porter, "Race, Socialization and Mobility in Education and Early Occupational Attainment," in *American Sociological Review*, Vol. 39, June 1974.

Paul Taubman and Terance Wales, *Higher Education and Earnings*, New York: McGraw-Hill, 1974.

W. H. Sewell, A. P. Haller and G. W. Ohlendorf, "The Educational and Early Occupational Status Achievement Process," *American Sociological Review*, Vol. 35, December, 1970.

# APPENDIX B

•

# Personality Traits Associated with School and Work Success

The following results are derived from Edwards (1975); Meyer (1972); and Bowles, Gintis, and Meyer (1975). Listed in Table B–1 are the sixteen pairs of personality traits appearing on the Meyer questionnaire, taken from his Table A–4. The Edwards questionnaire is similar, with work-related terms replacing school-related ones.

TABLE B-1.
*Personality Traits.*

|  | POSITIVE | NEGATIVE |
|---|---|---|
| Not temperamental | Rarely shows emotions; calm, stable while in school; remains calm even during an argument; shows few signs of excitement. | Sometimes lets emotions get in the way of doing schoolwork; emotional; temperamental; often gets excited; shows affection, anger, all emotions. |
| Punctual | Is always punctual; comes to class, school, etc. on time; is always aware of whether other people are on time or not. | Is not especially concerned about being on time; often comes late to meetings or classes. |
| Perseverant | Does not quit easily; determined, persevering; this person sticks at anything until the goal is achieved or the assignment is done. | Sometimes gives up before thoroughly finishing something; often quits before the job is done; is easily distracted. |
| Externally motived | Is very concerned about getting good grades; tries hard to win the teacher's approval; seems to be motivated mainly | Does not seem to care about getting high grades; when this person works hard, it is because he or she wants to do |

TABLE B-1 (*Continued*):
*Personality Traits.*

| | POSITIVE | NEGATIVE |
|---|---|---|
| | by the prospect of high grades and good recommendation. | the assignment well. |
| Independent | Likes to be independent and wants to arrange his or her own activities; dislikes being told what to do. | Is able to accept directions easily; follows the teacher's directions, even if doing things another way seems better. |
| Consistent | Is consistent about coming to school every day; often comes even if slightly sick, etc., when there is a legitimate excuse for staying home. | Is more likely to miss school than others; does not feel he or she "must come every day, no matter what." |
| Aggressive | Is aggressive; sometimes steps on other people's toes; does not mind speaking up; sometimes shows off. | Is the most considerate to other people; does not try to push his or her ideas too hard; doesn't show off. |
| Predictable | Is predictable; usually reacts to situations as you expect him or her to; for example, this person does not laugh when he or she is expected to be serious. | Often has reactions to people which surprise you; you cannot predict what this person will do; often gets upset when you did not expect it; sees things as funny which don't seem funny to you. |
| Empathizes orders | Is the most likely to know what is expected of him or her without having to be told; quickly understands what other people want. | Often does not understand what other people expect of him or her; does not know what people "really" mean; requires explicit instructions. |
| Tactful | Tactful; gets along nicely and pleasantly with everyone; has no enemies; doesn't get too strongly attached to anyone in particular. | Tends to develop close friendships with one or two people; not especially tactful or nice to other people. |
| Identifies with school | Identifies closely with this school; likes to talk about | His or her main interest is in something outside of class |

TABLE B-1 (*Continued*):
*Personality Traits.*

| | POSITIVE | NEGATIVE |
|---|---|---|
| | what is happening in this class or other classes here; does not seem to have too much else to talk about besides schoolwork. | (sports, family, a hobby, etc.); not too interested in schoolwork; would rather spend time on his or her own activities. |
| Loner | Prefers to do schoolwork alone and is more productive that way; probably would be hard to do a project with this person in a group. | Prefers to do things in a group; seems to be more productive when doing projects or schoolwork with other people; does not work well alone. |
| Creative | Inventive; is always coming up with lots of new ideas; sometimes crazy, unrealistic ones; thinks of unusual (often weird) possibilities for solving problems. | Practical-minded; is the most sensible; often comes up with good, useful ideas, but rarely has far-out, unrealistic, or impractical ideas. |
| Frank | Is very frank; usually speaks his or her mind, and does so firmly; comes out with his or her real feelings on matters. | Keeps thoughts and feelings to himself or herself; usually unwilling to express his or her feelings forcefully, even when he or she is right. |
| Defers gratification | Can continue working on something (for example, schoolwork) for long periods without praise or encouragement; is willing to wait until the project is done before receiving credit for his or her part. | Seems to require frequent praise or encouragement to complete classwork or some project; is easily frustrated unless somebody gives encouragement to this person. |
| Dependable | Dependable; always gets the assignment or project done even if she or he does not like the particular job. | Not too dependable when doing things he or she does not like; must like the assignment if she or he is to do it well. |

The factor analysis on which our argument is based is as follows:

FACTOR 1: SUBMISSION TO AUTHORITY

This factor accounts for 43.7 percent of the variance of all traits and 64.1 percent of the variance of the three factors. The factor loadings are as follows:

| | |
|---|---|
| Consistent | .83 |
| Identified with school | .81 |
| Punctual | .80 |
| Dependable | .78 |
| External reward | .77 |
| Perseverant | .73 |
| Independent | − .69 |
| Creative | − .52 |

FACTOR 2: TEMPERAMENT

This factor accounts for 15.9 percent of the variance of all traits and 21.0 percent of the variance of the first three factors. The factor loadings are as follows:

| | |
|---|---|
| Aggressive | − .80 |
| Not temperamental | .78 |
| Frank | − .74 |
| Predictable | .58 |
| Tactful | .54 |
| Creative | − .51 |

FACTOR 3: INTERNALIZED CONTROL

Factor 3 accounts for 11.8 percent of the variance of all personality traits and 14.9 percent of the variance of the first three factors. The factor loadings are as follows:

| | |
|---|---|
| Empathizes orders | .74 |
| Defers gratification | .71 |

The factor analysis was by principal components analysis and quartimax rotation.

Figure 3 is based on the following regression equations, where t-statistics are in parentheses.

| | RULES-ORIENTATION | DEPENDABLE | INTERNALIZATION OF NORMS |
|---|---|---|---|
| Supervisor Rating | .28 | .28 | .29 |
| | (6.96) | (7.19) | (7.07) |
| GPA | .22 | .25 | .17 |
| | (3.25) | (3.87) | (2.65) |

The multiple R in the first equation is R = .613, and in the second equation, R = .523.

The partial correlations of the sixteen personality variables with grade-point average, teacher's attitude, and English grade—controlling for IQ, SAT-math and SAT-English—are listed in Table B-2.

TABLE B-2.
*Correlation of Personality Variables.*

|  | GRADE-POINT AVERAGE | ENGLISH GRADE | TEACHER'S ATTITUDE |
|---|---|---|---|
| Not temperamental | .02[a] | − .12[a] | − .06[a] |
| Punctual | .35[d] | .43[d] | .20[c] |
| Perseverant | .42[d] | .45[d] | .14[b] |
| Externally motivated | .29[d] | .37[d] | .17[c] |
| Independent | − .23[d] | − .29[d] | − .12[b] |
| Consistent | .39[d] | .43[d] | .20[c] |
| Aggressive | − .27[d] | − .15[b] | .02[a] |
| Predictable | .25[d] | .20[c] | .04[a] |
| Empathizes orders | .37[d] | .35[d] | .12[b] |
| Tactful | .17[c] | .17[c] | .01[a] |
| Identifies with school | .38[c] | .42[d] | .21[c] |
| Loner | − .07[a] | .00[a] | − .07[a] |
| Creative | − .33[d] | − .26[d] | − .14[b] |
| Frank | .11[a] | .17[c] | .02[a] |
| Defers gratification | .31[d] | .34[d] | .06[a] |
| Dependable | .40[d] | .40[d] | .15[b] |

[a] Insignificant at 5 percent level.
[b] Significant at 5 percent level.
[c] Significant at 1 percent level.
[d] Significant at 0.1 percent level.

The discussion on page 140 is based on the following regression equation of Figure 5–4, reported by Brenner (1968). T-statistics are in parentheses.

| DEPENDENT VARIABLE | ESTIMATED NORMALIZED COEFFICIENTS ON: | | |
|---|---|---|---|
|  | GPA | TEACHER RATING | ATTENDANCE REGULARITY |
| Supervisor rating of worker ability | .302 (2.11) | .047 (0.32) | .203 (2.07) |
| Supervisor rating of worker conduct | .099 (0.72) | .330 (2.34) | .205 (2.19) |
| Supervisor rating of worker productivity | .098 (0.62) | .319 (2.16) | .109 (1.12) |

## Bibliography for Appendix B

Richard C. Edwards, "Personal Traits and 'Success' in Schooling and Work," *Education and Psychological Measurement,* forthcoming, 1976.

Peter J. Meyer, "Schooling and the Reproduction of the Social Division of Labor," unpublished honors thesis, Harvard University, March 1972.

Samuel Bowles, Herbert Gintis, and Peter Meyer, "The Long Shadow of Work: Education, the Family, and the Reproduction of the Social Division of Labor," *Insurgent Sociologist,* Summer 1975.

# NOTES

•

## CHAPTER 1

1. U.S. Department of Labor, *Monthly Labor Review*, September 1974, p. 50.

2. Irene A. King, *Bond Sales for Public School Purposes*, U.S. Department of Health, Education and Welfare, 1974, Publication No. (OE)–73–11406.

3. U.S. Department of Labor (1974).

4. Harvey Averch, *et al.*, *How Effective Is Schooling: A Critical Review and Synthesis of Research Findings* (Santa Monica: The Rand Corporation, 1972), p. 125.

5. James S. Coleman *et al.*, *Equality of Educational Opportunity* (Washington, D.C.: U.S. Government Printing Office, 1966). For a discussion of some of the shortcomings of the Coleman Report, see Samuel Bowles and Henry Levin, "The Determinants of Scholastic Achievement: An Appraisal of Some Recent Evidence," *Journal of Human Resources*, Winter 1968; and "More on Multicollinearity and the Effectiveness of Schools," *Journal of Human Resources*, Summer 1968.

6. Giora Hanoch, "An Economic Analysis of Earnings and Schooling," in *Journal of Human Resources*, No. 2, Summer 1967; Randall Weiss, "The Effects of Education on the Earnings of Blacks and Whites," in *Review of Economics and Statistics*, No. 52, May 1970; Bennett Harrison, *Education, Training, and the Urban Ghetto* (Baltimore: Johns Hopkins University Press, 1972).

7. Jencks, Smith, Ackland, Bane, Cohen, Gintis, Heyns, Michelson, *Inequality: A Reassessment of the Effects of Family and Schooling in America* (N.Y.: Basic Books, 1972).

8. Arthur A. Jensen, "How Much Can We Boost IQ and Scholastic Achievement?" *Harvard Educational Review*, Vol. 39, No. 1, 1969, p. 1.

9. Jensen (1969), *op. cit.*; Richard Herrnstein, "IQ," *Atlantic Monthly*, Vol. 228, No. 3, September 1971; J. Eysenck, *The IQ Argument* (New York: Library Press, 1971); Arthur A. Jensen, *Educability and Group Differences* (New York: Harper & Row, 1975).

10. Clarence Karier, "Testing for Order and Control in the Corporate Liberal State," in *Education Theory*, Vol. 22, Spring 1972; Leon Kamin, *The Science and Politics of IQ* (Potomac, Maryland: Erlbaum Associates, 1974).

11. Edward Banfield, *The Unheavenly City* (Boston: Little, Brown and Company, 1968); Daniel Patrick Moynihan, *The Negro Family* (Cambridge, Mass.: MIT Press, 1967).

12. We have confined our attention to education in the United States. For an excellent treatment of education on a world-wide basis, see Martin Carnoy, *Education as Cultural Imperialism* (New York: McKay, 1974).

13. For a more extensive treatment, see Samuel Bowles and Herbert Gintis, "The Problem with Human Capital . . . A Marxian Critique," *American Economic Review*, May 1975.

14. Konrad Lorenz, *On Aggression* (New York: Bantam Books, 1963), p. 228.

15. Jacques Ellul, *The Technological Society* (New York: Alfred Knopf, 1964), pp. 14, 227.

16. Robert Michels, *Political Parties* (New York: Free Press, 1962), p. 365.

17. Seymour Martin Lipset, "Introduction," in Robert Michels, *Political Parties, op. cit.*, p. 68.


CHAPTER 2

1. John Tipple, *The Capitalist Revolution, 1800–1919* (New York: Pegasus, 1970); Robert H. Wiebe, *The Search for Order* (New York: Hill & Wang, 1967); G. Kolko, *The Triumph of Conservatism* (Chicago: Quadrangle Books, 1963); James Weinstein, *The Corporate Ideal in the Liberal State 1900–1918* (Boston: Beacon Press, 1968).

2. Henry J. Perkinson, *The Imperfect Panacea: American Faith in Education, 1865–1965* (New York: Random House, 1968).

3. John Dewey, *Democracy and Education* (New York: The Free Press, 1966), p. 20.

4. *Ibid.*, pp. 50–53.

5. *Ibid.*, p. 87.

6. *Ibid.*, p. 76.

7. *Ibid.*, pp. 2, 88.

8. Theodore W. Schultz, "Investment in Poor People," *Seminar on Manpower Policy and Programs*, Office of Manpower Policy Evaluation Research, Washington: Department of Labor, 1966.

9. Harvey Averch *et al.*, "How Effective Is Schooling: A Critical Review and Synthesis of Research Findings" (Santa Monica: The Rand Corporation, 1972).

10. Samuel Bowles and Herbert Gintis, "IQ in the U.S. Class Structure," in *Social Policy*, November–December 1972 and January–February 1973. (This controversy will be reviewed in Chapter 4.)

11. Horace Mann as quoted in Michael Katz, *Class, Bureaucracy and Schools* (New York: Praeger Publishers, 1971), pp. 83–109.

12. *Ibid.*, p. 142.

13. *Ibid.*, pp. 146–147.

14. Arthur A. Jensen, "How Much Can We Boost IQ and Scholastic Achievement?" *Harvard Educational Review*, Vol. 39, No. 1, 1969; Richard Herrnstein, "IQ," *Atlantic Monthly*, Vol. 228, No. 3, September 1971; Edward C. Banfield, *The Unheavenly City* (Boston: Little, Brown and Company, 1968); Daniel P. Moynihan and Nathan Glazer, *Beyond the Melting Pot* (Cambridge, Mass.: MIT Press, 1970).

15. Dewey (1966), *op. cit.*, p. 20.

16. Adam Smith, *The Wealth of Nations* (New York: Modern Library, 1937), p. 734.

17. *Ibid.*, p. 735.

18. Dewey (1966), *op. cit.*, p. 85.

19. *Ibid.*, p. 320.

20. Henry Barnard, *Papers for the Teacher: 2nd Series* (New York: F. C. Brownell, 1866), pp. 293–310.

21. Alexis de Tocqueville, as quoted in Jeremy Brecher, *Strike!* (San Francisco: Straight Arrow Books, 1972), pp. xi, xii.

22. *Ibid.*, p. 172.

23. Horace Mann as quoted in Michael Katz, ed., *School Reform Past and Present* (Boston: Little Brown and Company, 1971), p. 141.

24. *Ibid.*, p. 145.

25. *The Massachusetts Teacher* (October 1851), quoted in Katz (1971), *loc. cit.*, pp. 169–170.

26. David Tyack, *Turning Points in American Educational History* (Waltham, Mass.: Blaisdell, 1967), p. 89.

27. *Ibid.*, p. 109.

28. *Ibid.*, p. 89.

29. Mann, quoted in Katz (1971), *loc. cit.*, p. 147.

30. This calculation is based on data reported in full in Samuel Bowles and Valerie Nelson, "The 'Inheritance of IQ' and the Intergenerational Transmission of Economic Inequality," *The Review of Economics and Statistics*, Vol. LVI, No. 1, February 1974. It refers to non-Negro males from non-farm backgrounds, aged 35–44 years. The zero-order correlation coefficient between socioeconomic background and years of schooling was estimated at 0.646. The estimated standard deviation of years of schooling was 3.02. The results for other age groups are similar.

31. See Appendix A, footnote 14, in Chapter 4 and the following sources: Bowles and Nelson (1974), *op. cit.*; Peter Blau and Otis D. Duncan, *The American Occupational Structure* (New York: John Wiley, 1967); Otis D. Duncan, D. C. Featherman, and Beverly Duncan, *Socioeconomic Background and Occupational Achievement, Final Report*, Project No. S–0074 (EO–191) (Washington, D.C.: Department of Health, Education and Welfare, Office of Education, 1968); Samuel Bowles, "Schooling and Inequality from Generation to Generation," *The Journal of Political Economy*, Vol. 80, No. 3, Part II, May–June 1972.

32. These figures refer to individuals who were high-school seniors in October, 1965, and who subsequently graduated from high school. College attendance refers to both two- and four-year institutions. Family income is for the twelve months preceding October 1965. Data is drawn from U.S. Bureau of the Census, *Current Population Reports*, Series P–60, No. 183, May 1969.

33. For further evidence, see U.S. Bureau of the Census (1969), *op. cit.*; and Jerome Karabel, "Community Colleges and Social Stratification," *Harvard Educational Review*, Vol. 424, No. 42, November 1972.

34. Calculation based on data in James S. Coleman *et al.*, *Equality of Educational Opportunity* (Washington, D.C.: U.S. Government Printing Office, 1966), and Bowles and Gintis (1972), *loc. cit.*

35. The data relating to IQ are from a 1966 survey of veterans by the National Opinion Research Center; and from N. Bayley and E. S. Schaefer, "Correlations of Maternal and Child Behaviors with the Development of Mental Ability: Data from the Berkeley Growth Study," *Monographs of Social Research in Child Development*, 29, 6 (1964).

36. This figure is based on data reported in full in our Appendix A and in Bowles and Nelson (1974), *op. cit.* The left-hand bars of each pair were calculated using the estimated correlation coefficient between socioeconomic background and education of 0.65. The results for other age groups were similar: 0.64 for ages 25–34 and 44–54, and 0.60 for ages 55–64 years. The right-hand bars were calculated from the normalized regression coefficient on socioeconomic background from an equation using background and early childhood IQ to predict years of schooling, which was estimated at 0.54. The results for other age groups were similar: 0.54 for ages 25–34 and 45–54, and 0.48 for ages 55–64.

Socioeconomic background is defined as normalized sum of father's education, father's occupational status, and parents' income. The mean and standard deviation of years of schooling were estimated at 11.95 and 3.02, respectively.

37. Based on a large sample of U.S. high-school students as reported in: John C.

Flannagan and William W. Cooley, *Project Talent, One Year Follow-up Study*, Co-operative Research Project, No. 2333, University of Pittsburgh: School of Education, 1966.

38. Christopher Jencks *et al.*, *Inequality: A Reassessment of the Effects of Family and Schooling in America* (New York: Basic Books, 1972), p. 48.

39. William L. Spady, "Educational Mobility and Access: Growth and Paradoxes," in *American Journal of Sociology*, Vol. 73, No. 3, November 1967; and Blau and Duncan, *op. cit.* (1967). More recent data support the evidence of no trend toward equality. See U.S. Bureau of Census (1969), *op. cit.*

40. Blau and Duncan (1967), *op. cit.* See the reported correlations in Appendix A.

41. We estimate the coefficient of variation of years of schooling at about 4.3 in 1940 (relying on Barry Chiswick and Jacob Mincer, "Time Series Changes in Personal Income Inequality in the U.S.," *Journal of Political Economy*, Vol. 80, No. 3, Part II [May–June 1972], Table 4 for the standard deviation of schooling and the Decennial Census for the mean), and at 2.95 in 1969 (relying on Chiswick and Mincer [1972], Table B10).

42. Calculated from Table B1 and Table B10 in Chiswick and Mincer (1972), *op. cit.*

43. Peter Henle, "Exploring the Distribution of Earned Income," *Monthly Labor Review*, Vol. 95, No. 12, December 1972. Inequalities in income (profit, rent interest, and transfer payments plus labor earnings) may also have increased if the unmeasured income from capital gains and other tax shelters for the rich are taken into account. See Jerry Cromwell, "Income Inequalities, Discrimination and Uneven Development," unpublished Ph.D. dissertation, Harvard University, May 1974.

44. Chiswick and Mincer (1972), *loc. cit.*

45. Thomas I. Ribich, *Education and Poverty* (Washington, D.C.: Brookings Institution, 1968).

46. United States Bureau of the Census, *Current Population Reports*, Series P–60, October 1970, Table 75, p. 368.

47. *Ibid.* (November 1972), Table 1, p. 14.

48. Michael Reich, *Racial Discrimination and the Distribution of Income*, Ph.D. dissertation, Harvard University, May 1973.

49. United States Bureau of the Census, *op. cit.* (December 1973), Table 47, p. 114.

50. Quoted in Tyack (1967), *op. cit.*, p. 315.

51. Charles Silberman, *Crisis in the Classroom* (New York: Vintage, 1971), p. 83.

52. Quoted in Lawrence Cremin, *The Transformation of the School* (New York: Alfred A. Knopf, 1961).

53. Silberman (1971), *op. cit.*, p. 10.

54. Tyack (1967), *loc. cit.*, p. 3.

55. *Ibid.*, p. 15.

56. Ross, as quoted in Clarence Karier, Joel Spring, and Paul C. Violas, *Roots of Crisis* (Chicago: University of Illinois Press, 1973), p. 32.

57. Tyack (1967), *loc. cit.*, p. 325.

58. Whence e e cummings' sharp lines: ". . . the children knew, but only a few/ and down they forgot as up they grew." e e cummings, *Poems, 1923–1954* (New York: Harcourt, Brace and World, 1954), p. 370.

59. Cf. Charles Valentine, *Culture and Poverty* (Chicago: University of Chicago Press, 1968). Early in the nineteenth century, Robert Dale Owen, the renowned utopian, had proposed that the interests of social equality dictated that the children of the poor be raised in public institutions.

60. Tyack (1967), *op. cit.*; Katz (1971), *loc. cit.*

61. In Chapter 5, we will argue that both changes in the approach to discipline reflect the changing social relationships of production in the corporate capitalist economy.

62. Paulo Freire, *Pedagogy of the Oppressed* (New York: Herder and Herder, 1972), pp. 58–59.

63. J. W. Getzels and P. W. Jackson, "Occupational Choice and Cognitive Functioning," in *Journal of Abnormal and Social Psychology*, February 1960.

64. For a general discussion of the content and meaning of creativity tests, see Michael W. Wallach, *The Intelligence of Creativity Distinction* (New York: General Learning Corporation, 1971).

65. The exact correlation was r = 0.41.

66. The correlations between own and teacher's desired personality traits were r = 0.67 for the high IQs and r = 0.25 for the high creatives.

67. Both groups had similar scores on tests of achievement motivation—McClelland n-ach and Strodtbeck V-score.

68. Herbert Gintis, "Education, Technology, and the Characteristics of Worker Productivity," *American Economic Review*, May 1971.

69. John L. Holland, "Creative and Academic Performance Among Talented Adolescents," *Journal of Educational Psychology*, No. 52, 1961.

70. Verbal and Mathematical sections of the Scholastic Achievement Test, Humanities and Scientific Comprehension.

71. The interested reader should consult Holland (1961), *op. cit.* and Herbert Gintis, *Alienation and Power*, Ph.D. dissertation for Harvard University, May 1969.

72. Gintis (1969), *op. cit.* and (1971), *op. cit.*

73. Holland's personality measures will be presented in italics. Unless otherwise indicated, all are statistically significant at the 1 percent level.

74. In addition to the good citizenship–externally motivated student, a small portion of the high *Drive to Achieve* students exhibit a set of personality traits quite similar to those of the *Deviant Creatives* described in Getzel and Jackson's study, already presented. These students, high on *Artistic Performance* and *Creative Activities*, evidently reject the pressure to define their personal goals in terms compatible with high grades and teacher approbation, and their positive personality traits are uniformly penalized in terms of grades and teacher ratings for *Citizenship*.

75. Charles Silberman, (1971), *op. cit.*

76. As quoted in Lawrence Cremin (1964), *op. cit.*, p. 241.

77. *Ibid.*, pp. 240–241.

78. *Ibid.*, p. 328.

79. Raymond Callahan, *Education and the Cult of Efficiency* (Chicago: University of Chicago Press, 1962), preface.

80. *Ibid.*

81. Thomas S. Kuhn, *The Structure of Scientific Revolutions* (Chicago: The University of Chicago Press, 1962), p. 53.

82. Arthur A. Jensen, *Educability and Group Differences* (New York: Harper & Row, 1973); and Richard Herrnstein, *IQ in the Meritocracy* (Boston: Little, Brown and Company, 1973).

83. For a more complete discussion, see Richard C. Edwards, Michael Reich, and Thomas Weisskopf, *The Capitalist System* (Englewood Cliffs, N.J.: Prentice-Hall, 1972); André Gorz, "Technical Intelligence and the Capitalist Division of Labor," *Telos*, Summer 1972; and Chapter 3.

84. Clarence Karier, *Shaping the American Educational State: 1900 to the Present* (New York: The Free Press, 1975); and Clarence Karier, Joel Spring, and Paul C. Violas (1973), *op. cit.*

85. Indeed, it has been pointed out to us by Dr. F. Bohnsack in a personal communication that Dewey did begin to revise his views, especially after World War I:

> For this later time, at least, I would doubt whether we could say he characterized the social system as democratic. He saw and criticized the totalitarian features of existing society and the missing ". . . intrinsic growth orientation of education." As self-development and equality of opportunity, to him, were inconsistent with preparing workers for existing [alienated] jobs, he criticized such a preparation and wanted to change existing industrial education as well as industrial work.

See A. G. Wirth, *The Vocational-Liberal Studies Controversy between John Dewey and Others (1900–1917)* (Washington, D.C., 1970), and John Dewey, "Education vs. Trade-training," *The New Republic*, Vol. 3, No. 15, May 1915.

As Virginia Held has pointed out to us, Dewey, in his mature work, *Art as Experience* (New York: Minton, Balch and Company, 1934), went further to claim:

> The labor and employment problem of which we are so acutely aware cannot be solved by mere changes in wage, hours of work, and sanitary conditions. No permanent solution is possible save in a radical alteration, which affects the degree and kind of participation the worker has in the production and social disposition of the wares he produces. (p. 343).

## CHAPTER 3

1. For a more extended treatment, see Herbert Gintis, "The Nature of the Labor Exchange and the Theory of Capitalist Production," Harvard Institute for Economic Research, No. 328, October, 1973; Samuel Bowles and Herbert Gintis, "The Problem with Human Capital Theory . . . A Marxian Critique," *American Economic Review*, May 1975.

2. Ross M. Robertson, *History of the American Economy* (New York: Harcourt, Brace, Jovanovich, 1973), Chapter 4. On the class structure of Colonial America, see Jackson T. Main, *Social Structure in Revolutionary America* (Princeton, N.J.: Princeton University Press, 1965).

3. Meadow, wasteland, and fields were owned commonly by the town; their use and care were determined jointly by town meeting; common fields were divided into strips and allotted among the villagers. Crops were tilled and harvested communally, and each family was entitled to the product of its individual strips. The eighteenth century, nevertheless, witnessed the fencing of the commons, the consolidation of the scattered individual holdings, and the town's relinquishment of control over land disposition.

4. Michael Reich, "The Evolution of the U.S. Labor Force," in Edwards, Reich, and Weisskopf, eds., *The Capitalist System* (Englewood Cliffs, N.J.: Prentice-Hall, 1972).

5. *See* Norman J. Ware, *The Industrial Worker, 1840–1860* (Chicago: Quadrangle Books, 1964); Gerald Grob, *Workers and Utopia* (Chicago: Quadrangle Press, 1969); James Weinstein, *The Corporate Ideal in the Liberal State, 1900–1918* (Boston: Beacon Press, 1968); David Montgomery, *Beyond Equality: Labor and Radical Republicans, 1862–1872* (New York: Vintage Books, 1967); Herbert M. Morais and Richard O. Boyer, *Labor's Untold Story* (New York: United Electrical, Radio and Machine Workers of America, 1971), and Jeremy Brecher, *Strike!* (San Francisco: Straight Arrow Books, 1972).

6. U.S. Bureau of Census, *County Business Patterns, U.S. Summary*, 1972, Table

1A, page 12 and Table 1C, p. 29; U.S. Department of Labor and Health, Education and Welfare, *Manpower Report to the President*, 1974, Table A13, p. 270, and Table 1C, p. 29; U.S. Bureau of the Census, 1974; U.S. Department of Labor, *Monthly Labor Review*, September 1974; and *Fortune Magazine*, May, 1974.

If we consider those firms with fewer than fifty employees as the best approximation of family, craft, and entrepreneurial firms, this category comprises 95 per cent of all firms. Using this definition, 28 per cent of all paid workers are employed in this sector. Our categories do not indicate the relatively small number of workers employed by private nonprofit establishments such as private hospitals.

7. James O'Connor, *The Fiscal Crisis of the State* (New York: St. Martin's Press, 1973).

8. For a more detailed treatment in somewhat different conceptual frameworks, see John Kenneth Galbraith, *Economics and Public Purpose* (Boston: Houghton-Mifflin, 1973); and O'Connor (1973), *op. cit.*

9. See David Landes, *The Unbound Prometheus* (Cambridge, England: Cambridge University Press, 1970); and Stephen Marglin, "What Do Bosses Do? The Origin and Functions of Hierarchy in Capitalist Production," *Review of Radical Political Economics*, Vol. VI, No. 2, 1974.

10. Robertson (1973), *op. cit.*; and Michael Piore, "The Role of Immigration in Industrial Growth," working paper of the Department of Economics, No. 42. Cambridge, Mass.: MIT, May 1973.

11. See Grob (1969), *op. cit.*

12. *Ibid.*, p. 20; and David Montgomery, *Beyond Equality: Labor and the Radical Republicans, 1862–1872* (New York: Vintage, 1967).

13. Grob (1969), *op. cit.*, p. 47.

14. Means, as quoted in Edwards, Reich, and Weisskopf (1972), *op. cit.*, p. 148.

15. Clarence Karier, "Ideology and Evaluation: In Quest of Meritocracy," Wisconsin Conference on Education and Evaluation at Madison, April 1973.

16. Robertson (1973), *op. cit.*, p. 86.

17. *See* O'Connor (1973), *loc. cit.*; Murray Edelman, *The Symbolic Uses of Politics* (Chicago: University of Chicago Press, 1969); G. Kolko, *The Triumph of Conservatism* (Chicago: Quadrangle Books, 1963); Randall Bartlett, *Economic Foundations of Political Power* (New York: The Free Press, 1973); William Appleman Williams, *The Contours of American History* (Chicago: Quadrangle, 1966); Robert Weibe, *The Search for Order* (New York: Hill and Wang, 1967); and James Weinstein, *The Corporate Ideal in the Liberal State 1900–1918* (Boston: Beacon Press, 1968).

18. Richard C. Edwards, Michael Reich, and David Gordon, *Labor Market Segmentation* (New York: D. C. Heath, in press, 1975); Howard M. Wachtel, "Class Consciousness and Stratification in the Labor Process," *Review of Radical Political Economics*, forthcoming, 1975; and Piore (1973), *loc. cit.*

19. Stephen Thernstrom, *The Other Bostonians* (Cambridge, Mass.: Harvard University Press, 1973).

20. Juliet Mitchell, *Women's Estate* (New York: Vintage Books, 1975).

21. Edwards, Reich, and Gordon (1975), *op. cit.*; Wachtel (1974), *op. cit.*; Piore (1973), *loc. cit.*; and Peter Doeringer and Michael Piore, *Internal Labor Markets and Manpower Analysis* (Lexington, Mass.: D. C. Heath, 1971).

22. See Barry Bluestone, "The Tripartite Economy: Labor Markets and the Working Poor," in *Poverty and Human Resources*, July–August 1970; Piore (1973), *loc. cit.*; and Edwards, Reich and Gordon (1975), *loc. cit.*

23. Karl Marx, *The Economic and Philosophical Manuscripts*, Dirk Struick, ed. (New York: International Publishers, 1963), pp. 197–198.

24. Jacques, quoted in *Work in America*, Report of a Special Task Force to the

Secretary of Health, Education and Welfare (Cambridge, Massachusetts: MIT Press, 1973), p. 6.

25. Erdman Palmore, "Predicting Longevity: A Followup Controlling for Age," *Gerontology*, Winter 1969, pp. 259–263.

26. Arthur Kornhauser, *Mental Health of the Industrial Worker* (New York: Wiley, 1965).

27. Sidney Verba and Norman Nie, *Participation in America* (New York: Harper & Row, 1972), p. 132.

28. Melvin Kohn, *Childhood and Conformity* (Homewood, Illinois: Dorsey Press, 1969).

29. Sebastian DeGrazia, *Of Time, Work and Leisure* (Garden City, L.I., N.Y.: Anchor Books, 1962); Alfred Clarke, "Leisure and Occupational Prestige," in *Mass Leisure*, Eric Larrabee and Rolf Meyersohn, eds. (Glencoe, Illinois: Free Press, 1958).

30. See DeGrazia (1962), *op. cit.*, for a critique of this argument.

31. William R. Torbert, *Being for the Most Part Puppets* (Cambridge, Massachusetts: Schlenkman, 1973). For additional evidence, and an extensive bibliography, see Christopher Argyris, *Personality and Organization* (New York: Harper & Row, 1957), and Christopher Argyris, "Personality and Organization Theory Revisited," *Administration Science Quarterly*, June 1973.

32. *Work in America* (1973), *loc. cit.*

33. *Ibid.*, p. 13.

34. Marx (1963), pp. 110–111.

35. Erich Fromm, *The Sane Society* (New York: Reinhart, 1955), p. 140.

36. This material draws heavily on the remarkable study by Marglin (1974), *op. cit.*

37. Adam Smith, *The Wealth of Nations* (New York: Modern Library, 1937), p. 734.

38. Joan Ellen Trey, "Women in the War Economy," *Review of Radical Political Economics*, Vol. 4, No. 3, July 1972.

39. See the excellent treatment by Harry Braverman, *Labor and Monopoly Capital* (New York: Monthly Review Press, 1974).

40. Katherine Stone, "The Origins of Job Structures in the Steel Industry," *Review of Radical Political Economics*, Summer 1974.

41. David Brody, *The Steel Workers in America: The Non-union Era* (New York: Harper & Row, 1970), pp. 48–49.

42. Victor H. Broom, "Industrial Social Psychology," in G. Lindsey and E. Aaronsen, eds., *The Handbook of Social Psychology* (Reading, Mass.: Addison-Wesley, 1969), p. 242.

43. *Ibid.*, pp. 224, 230, 232–233.

44. André Gorz, "Workers' Control: Some European Experiences," in *Collective Effort*, No. 1, September–October 1971.

45. See also Paul Blumberg, *Industrial Democracy* (New York: Schocken Books, 1969); Carl Riskin, "Incentive Systems and Work Motivations," *Working Papers*, Vol. 1, No. 4, Winter 1974; Gerry Hunnius et al., *Workers' Control* (New York: Vintage, 1973); Carole Pateman, *Participation and Democratic Theory* (Cambridge, England: Cambridge University Press, 1970); and *Work in America* (1973), *op. cit.*

46. *Work in America* (1973), *op. cit.* We say "at least a dozen" because many of the more than two dozen cases listed do not report adequate or particularly persuasive productivity data. No cases, however, reported productivity declines.

47. Blumberg (1969), *op. cit.*, p. 121.

48. *Work in America* (1973), *loc. cit.*

49. Riskin (1974), *op. cit.*; Andrew Zimbalist, "Workers' Control in Chilean Fac-

tories under Allende," unpublished Ph.D. dissertation, Harvard University, 1974.

50. Indeed, under conditions of perfect competition the maximization of profits is a necessary condition for the reproduction of the capitalists' class position. We need not here enter into the complicated debate on whether firms do indeed seek to maximize profits. For a survey, see Edwards (1972). We conclude that the relevant behavioral implication of the theories that posit other objectives (sales and employment maximization, for example) are, in the context of the U.S. economy, virtually indistinguishable from those of profit maximization.

51. Marglin (1974), *loc. cit.*

52. For more on this, see Erving Goffman, *The Presentation of Self in Everyday Life* (New York: Doubleday and Co., 1959).

53. Quoted in Harold D. Lasswell and Abraham Kaplan, *Power and Society: A Framework for Political Inquiry* (New Haven: Yale University Press, 1950), p. 121.

54. Students of traditional economic theory will note the divergence of our analysis from the usual theory of the firm, which equates profit maximization with technical efficiency. The error in traditional theory lies in assuming that the *wage-labor exchange,* whereby the worker accepts money in return for giving up the disposition of his work activities to the employer, symmetrically parallels other economic exchanges—say, apples for pennies, or raw materials for cash credits. Most economic exchanges are legally binding contracts, however, enforced by a political power outside the jurisdiction of the parties engaged in exchange. The employer-employee exchange is different in that, if workers fulfill only the legally enforceable aspects of the agreement (e.g., come to work on time), little production will take place. The internal organization of production must, therefore, be designed to motivate individuals to produce, to limit the aspirations and *self-concepts* of workers to those compatible with the hierarchy of production, and to divide the workers against each other so as to reduce their aggregate power vis-à-vis management. In short, the integrity of the wage-labor system contract is enforced not outside, but within the jurisdiction of those involved. Thus power enters directly into the theory of the firm. Herbert Gintis, "The Nature of the Labor Exchange," Harvard Institute of Economic Research, No. 328, October 1973; Herbert Gintis, "Welfare Criteria with Endogenous Preferences: The Economics of Education," *International Economic Review*, June 1974; and Bowles and Gintis (1975), "The Problem with Human Capital Theory."

55. Quoted in Martin Bronfenbrenner, *Income Distribution Theory* (Chicago: Aldine, 1971), pp. 67–68.

56. James D. Smith and Stephen D. Franklin, "The Concentration of Personal Wealth, 1922–69," *American Economic Review*, May 1974.

57. Edwards, Reich, and Weisskopf, eds., (1972), *loc. cit.*, p. 211, Table 5E.

58. Gabriel Kolko, *Wealth and Power in America* (New York: Praeger, 1962), p. 48, Table IV.

59. Smith and Franklin (1974), *op. cit.*

60. John Gardner, *Excellence* (New York: Harper & Row, 1961), p. 3.

61. Milton Friedman, *Capitalism and Freedom* (Chicago: University of Chicago Press, 1962), p. 21. This perspective is spelled out in elegant detail in Gary Becker, *Human Capital* (New York: Columbia University Press, 1964).

62. Talcott Parsons, *The Social System* (New York: The Free Press, 1951).

63. See Chapter 2.

64. Based on data from Samuel Bowles and Valerie Nelson, "The 'Inheritance of IQ' and the Intergenerational Reproduction of Economic Inequality," *The Review of Economics and Statistics*, Vol. 56, No. 1, February 1947. The figure refers to "non-Negro" males from non-farm backgrounds. Socioeconomic background is here a composite measure of parents' income, father's education, and father's occupational status. The figure is calculated from an estimated correlation between income and

socioeconomic background of 0.433 for individuals aged 35–44. The coefficients for other age groups are: 0.324 for ages 25–34, 0.464 for ages 45–54, and 0.308 for ages 55–64 years.

65. Jerry Cromwell, "Income Inequalities, Discrimination and Uneven Capitalist Development," unpublished Ph.D. dissertation, Harvard University, May 1974.

66. U.S. Department of Treasury, Internal Revenue Service (1971), Table 1.4.

67. The statistics presented in this paragraph are from Cromwell (1974), *op. cit.*, Table 3.3, p. 11.

68. Barry Bluestone, "The Wage Determinants of the Working Poor," unpublished Ph.D. dissertation, University of Michigan, June 1974.

69. Two typical workers were hypothesized: (1) a white male union member with a junior college education (fourteen years), twenty-five years' experience, working in a primary industry (one with a 5 per cent minority labor force and in an occupation 5 per cent of whose members are minority with the average capital per worker of a Fortune 500 company [$35,765 in assets (*Fortune*, May 1974, p. 231)], an 8 per cent profit rate and a high concentration [60 per cent of sales controlled by firms in the two largest asset categories]), and (2) a black female with ten years of education, twenty years' experience, who is not a union member, working in a secondary industry (one with a 50 per cent minority labor force, in an occupation 50 per cent of whose members are minority, with $5,000 capital per worker and a 5 per cent profit rate and a low concentration [20 per cent]).

70. Cromwell (1974), *op. cit.*, p. 215.

71. Doeringer and Piore (1971), *op. cit.*

72. Much of the description in the following paragraphs derives from Richard C. Edwards, "Alienation and Inequality: Capitalist Relations of Production in a Bureaucratic Enterprise," Ph.D. dissertation, Harvard University, July 1972. His statistical findings will be presented in Chapter 5.

73. See Goffman (1959), *loc. cit.*; and Claus Offe, *Leistungsprinzip und Industrielle Arbeit* (Frankfurt: Europaische Verlaganstalt, 1970).

74. Gloria Hamilton and J. David Roesner, "How Employers Screen Disadvantaged Workers," in *Monthly Labor Review*, September 1972.

75. Leland P. Deck, "Buying Brains by the Inch," in *Journal of the College and University Personnel Association*, Vol. 19, No. 3, May 1968.

76. The survey was conducted by Robert Hall Associates in Cambridge, Mass. (1974).

77. Goffman (1959), *loc. cit.*

78. Eric Ohlin Wright and Luca Perrone, "Structural Class Position and Income Inequality," unpublished, University of California at Berkeley, Dept. of Sociology, June 1974.

79. For a description of these studies, see Robert E. Hall, "Wages, Income and Hours of Work in the U.S. Labor Force," in *Working Papers* for the Department of Economics, MIT, No. 62, August 1970; and James N. Morgan et al., *Five Thousand American Families—Patterns of Economic Progress*, Vol. I (Ann Arbor, Michigan: Institute for Social Research, University of Michigan, 1974).

80. See, for example, Giori Hanoch, "An Economic Analysis of Earnings and Schooling," in *Journal of Human Resources*, No. 2, Summer 1967; Randall Weiss, "The Effects of Education on the Earnings of Blacks and Whites," in *Review of Economics and Statistics*, No. 52, May 1970; and Fred Hines, Luther Tweeten, and Martin Redfern, "Social and Private Rates of Return to Investment in Schooling," *Journal of Human Resources*, Vol. 3, Summer 1970, pp. 318–340.

81. Lee Rainwater, "A Model of Household Heads' Income: 1967–1971," The Joint Center for Urban Studies of MIT and Harvard, February 1974, Table 13.

82. Jencks (1972), *loc. cit.* found similar results using a sample of veterans aged

25–34. The estimated effect of schooling on annual income was $305 per year for those whose fathers held low-status jobs and $504 for those with high-occupational-status fathers. The estimated returns to experience were $129 and $321 per year, respectively.

83. Hall (1970), *op. cit.*, Table 2–1.

84. Council of Economic Advisers, *Economic Report of the President* (Washington, D.C.: U.S. Government Printing Office, 1971), p. 149, Table 38.

85. Bluestone (1974), *op. cit.*, Chapter 5.

86. Becker (1964), *op. cit.*; Jacob Mincer, "On-the-Job Training: Costs, Returns, and Some Implications," *Journal of Political Economy*, October 1962.

87. Morgan *et al.* (1974), *op. cit.*

88. John Dewey, *Democracy and Education* (New York: The Free Press, 1966), p. 20.


CHAPTER 4


1. K. Davis and W. E. Moore, "Some Principles of Stratification," *American Sociological Review*, Vol. 10, No. 2, 1945, pp. 242–249.

2. See Leon J. Kamin, *The Science and Politics of IQ* (Potomac, Md.: Erlbaum Associates, 1974), p. 8.

3. Orville Brim, *American Beliefs and Attitudes about Intelligence* (New York: Russell Sage Foundation, 1969).

4. Recent studies indeed indicate a lack of social class or racial bias in school grading: Given a student's cognitive attainment, his or her grades seem not to be significantly affected by class or racial origins, at least on the high-school level. See Robert Hauser, "Schools and the Stratification Process," *American Journal of Sociology*, Vol. 74, May 1969, pp. 587–611; Barbara Heyns, "Curriculum Assignment and Tracking Policies in 48 Urban Public High Schools," unpublished Ph.D. dissertation for the University of Chicago, 1971; and Jencks (1972).

5. For an extended treatment, see Jerome Karabel, "Community Colleges and Social Stratification," *Harvard Educational Review*, Vol. 424, No. 42, November 1972, and references therein.

6. Daniel Bell, *The Coming of Post-Industrial Society* (New York: Basic Books, 1973), Coda, Part 3.

7. Alexander W. Astin, "Undergraduate Achievement and Institutional 'Excellence,'" *Science*, Vol. 161, August 1968.

8. Christopher Jencks, "The Effects of Worker Characteristics on Economic Success: An Inquiry into Nonlinearities, Interactions, and Unmeasured Variables Using the NORC Veterans Sample" (Cambridge, Mass.: Center for Educational Policy Research, July 1973), using the NORC Veterans Survey of 2,672 males, aged 25–34, enumerated in the May 1964 Current Population Survey, finds that the rate of return to college education is lower for individuals with high test scores (AFQT).

Several individuals have studied the extensive NBER-Thorndike sample. John Hause, "Earnings Profile: Ability and Schooling," *Journal of Political Economy*, May–June 1972, found insignificant differences in rates of return by IQ. Paul Taubman and Terence Wales, *Higher Education and Earnings* (New York: McGraw-Hill, 1974), found no significant interactions, except perhaps for graduate-level education. (Rogers found no such interaction for graduate levels of education.) Louis L. Solman, "The Definition and Impact of College Quality," in Louis C. Solman and Paul J. Taubman, eds., *Does College Matter?* (New York: Academic Press, 1973), however, using the same sample, finds that the increased value of college graduation over attendance but nongraduation is higher for higher IQ individuals.

Dael Wolfe and Joseph Smith, "The Occupational Value of Education for Superior High School Graduates," *Journal of Higher Education*, April 1956, find a negative interaction for one sample, a negative interaction of IQ with "some college" for two more samples, and a strong positive interaction for "one college degree or more" for these two samples.

Finally, James N. Morgan et al., *Five Thousand American Families—Patterns of Economic Progress*, Vol. I (Ann Arbor, Michigan: Institute for Social Research, University of Michigan, 1974), find a significant positive interaction. This excellent study is not comparable, however, because the test score is measured on adults with extensive job experience and is a thirteen-item short form not validated against traditional IQ measures.

9. Daniel C. Rogers, "Private Rates of Return to Education in the U.S., A Case Study," *Yale Economic Essays*, Spring 1969.

10. Alexander Astin and Jack Rossman, "The Case for Open Admissions: A Status Report," in *Change*, Vol. 5, No. 6, Summer 1973.

11. Even in this case, the institutional arrangements would not satisfy the elementary dictates of justice and equity. See Noam Chomsky, "Psychology and Ideology," *Cognition*, Vol. 1, No. 1, 1972.

12. Quoted by Michael Katz, *Class, Bureaucracy and Schools* (New York: Praeger Publishers, 1971), p. 146.

13. See Herbert Gintis, "Education, Technology, and the Characteristics of Worker Productivity," *American Economic Review*, May 1971; and Ivar Berg, *Education and Jobs: The Great Training Robbery* (Boston: Beacon Press, 1971).

14. Samuel Bowles and Valerie Nelson, "The 'Inheritance of IQ' and the Intergenerational Reproduction of Economic Inequality," *The Review of Economics and Statistics*, Vol. 56, No. 1, February 1974; Samuel Bowles and Herbert Gintis, "IQ in the U.S. Class Structure," in *Social Policy*, November–December 1972 and January–February 1973. For details, see Appendix A.

The data, most of which was collected by the U.S. Census Current Population Survey in 1962, refer to non-Negro males, aged 24–65 years, from non-farm background, and who are the experienced labor force.

The data relating to childhood IQ and adult cognitive attainment are from a 1966 survey of veterans by the National Opinion Research Center, and the California Guidance Study.

See Peter Blau and Otis D. Duncan, *The American Occupational Structure* (New York: John Wiley & Sons, 1967); Otis D. Duncan, D. C. Featherman, and Beverly Duncan, *Socioeconomic Background and Occupational Achievement, Final Report*, Project No. S–0074 (E0–191) (Washington, D.C.: Department of Health, Education and Welfare, Office of Education, 1968); and Samuel Bowles, "Schooling and Inequality from Generation to Generation," *The Journal of Political Economy*, Vol. 80, No. 3, Part II, May–June 1972, for a more complete description. Similar calculations for other age groups yield results consistent with our propositions.

The quality of the data precludes any claims to precision in our estimation. Yet our main propositions remain supported even making allowance for substantive degrees of error. We must emphasize, however, that the validity of our basic propositions does not depend on our particular data set. While we believe our data base to be the most representative and carefully constructed from available sources, we have checked our results against several other data bases, including Christopher Jencks et al., *Inequality: A Reassessment of the Effects of Family and Schooling in America* (New York: Basic Books, 1972); Robert Hauser, Kenneth G. Lutterman, and William H. Sewell, "Socio-economic Background and the Earnings of High School Graduates," unpublished paper for the University of Wisconsin, August 1971; John Conlisk, "A Bit of Evidence on the Income-Education-Ability Interaction," *Journal of Human Resources*, Vol. 6, Summer 1971; and Zvi Griliches and William M. Mason, "Education, Income and Ability," *Journal of Political Economy*, Vol. 80, May–June 1972.

Jencks (1972), *loc. cit.*, constructs his data set by judicious review of statistical evidence from various sources, in a manner similar to Bowles (1972), *loc. cit.*, and Bowles and Nelson (1974), *loc. cit.* Hauser, Lutterman, and Sewell (1971), *op. cit.*, employ a sample of 3,793 males of nonfarm background, the cohort of Wisconsin high-school graduates of 1957. Conlisk (1971), *op. cit.*, employs a set of longitudinal data on seventy males in the Berkeley, California, area. Griliches and Mason (1972), *loc. cit.*, provide data on 3,000 post-World War II U.S. military veterans contacted by the Bureau of the Census in a 1964 Current Population Survey.

When corrections are made for measurement error and restriction of range (see Bowles [1972], *loc. cit.*, and Jencks [1972], *loc. cit.*), statistical analysis of each of these data bases supports all of our major propositions. Nor do our results depend on the choice of income as a measure of economic success. We have performed a parallel statistical analysis using two alternatives: occupational status, and a weighted average of income and occupational status. The results of this alternative analysis, much of which is published in Bowles and Gintis (1973), *loc. cit.*, and Bowles and Nelson (1974), *loc. cit.*, strongly confirms the results presented here. In fact, cognitive attainment is even less important as a criterion for occupational status than it is for income.

15. Most popular discussions of the relationship of IQ and economic success (e.g., Jensen [1969]; Richard Herrnstein, "IQ," *Atlantic Monthly*, Vol. 228, No. 3, September 1971; Jencks [1972]) present statistical material in terms of "correlation coefficients" and "contribution to explained variance." We believe that these technical expressions convey very little information to the reader not thoroughly initiated in their use and interpretation. The top-quintile-by-decile method embodied in Figure 4–1 and later figures, we feel, is operatively more accessible to the reader, and dramatically reveals the patterns of mobility and causality only implicitly in summary statistics of the correlation variety.

16. The figures in this chapter employing the top-quintile-by-decile method have *not* been constructed by directly observing the decile position of individuals on each of the various variables and recording the corresponding percentages. This approach is impossible for two reasons. First, such statistics are simply unavailable on the individual level. Our statistical base embraces the findings of several distinct data sources, no single one of which includes all the variables used in our analysis. Second, for certain technical reasons (e.g., errors in variables and restrictions of range), correction factors must be applied to the raw data before they can be used for analysis. These general issues are discussed in Jencks (1972); and, with respect to our data, in Bowles (1972), *loc. cit.*; and Gintis (1971), *loc. cit.*

These figures are constructed by making explicit certain assumptions which are only implicit, but absolutely necessary to the correlational arguments of Jensen and others. These assumptions include the linearity of the relationships among all variables, and the approximate normality of their joint probability distribution. Our statistical technique, then, is standard linear regression analysis, with correlations, regression coefficients, and path coefficients represented in a mathematically equivalent probability form.

17. Cognitive test scores are measured by a form of the Armed Forces Qualifi-

Notes

cation Test, which is strongly affected both by childhood IQ and by years of schooling, and, hence, can be considered a measure of adult cognitive achievement.

18. Figure 4–1 is calculated from data reported in Bowles and Nelson (1974), *loc. cit.*, and in our Appendix A. It is based on an estimated correlation coefficient between years of schooling and income of .46 for non-Negro, nonfarm males, aged 35–44 years. The coefficient is similar for other age groups: .33 for ages 25–34; .44 for ages 45–54; and .37 for ages 55–64. The normalized regression coefficient was estimated at .43 for non-Negro, nonfarm males, aged 35–44 years. The coefficient for other age groups was estimated at .22 for ages 25–34; .41 for ages 45–54; and .29 for ages 55–64 years.

19. The method of linear regression analysis, as its name implies, assumes that the level at which cognitive scores are held constant is irrelevant, as all effects are linear and additive. We have set this level at the average for the sample to render the education-income associations, before and after holding cognitive skills constant, closely comparable. Changing the level of cognitive scores merely moves this curve up or down. The assumption of linearity is, moreover, a good approximation to reality. See Jencks (1973), *loc. cit.*; and Rogers (1969), *op. cit.*

20. Table A–2 is modified from Gintis (1971), *loc. cit.*

21. Katz (1971), *op. cit.*

22. Arthur R. Jensen (1969), *loc. cit.*

23. Herrnstein (1971), *loc. cit.*

24. J. Eysenck, *The IQ Argument* (New York: Library Press, 1971); and Herrnstein (1971), *loc. cit.*

25. For a representative sampling of the criticism, see the issues of the *Harvard Educational Review* which follow the Jensen essay of 1969.

26. By IQ, we mean—here and throughout—those cognitive capacities which are measured in IQ tests. We have avoided the use of the word "intelligence" as, in its common usage, it ordinarily connotes a broader range of capacities.

27. Jensen (1969), *loc. cit.*

28. Jensen (1969), *loc. cit.*; Jencks (1972), *loc. cit.*

29. Kamin (1974), *op. cit.*

30. Jerome S. Kagan, "Inadequate Evidence and Illogical Conclusions," *Harvard Educational Review*, Reprint Series, No. 2, 1969; J. McI. Hunt, "Has Compensatory Education Failed?" *Harvard Educational Review*, Reprint Series, No. 2, 1969; and Kamin (1974), *op. cit.*

31. Does the fact that a large component of the differences in IQ among whites is genetic mean that a similar component of the differences in IQ between blacks and whites is determined by the former's inferior gene pool? Clearly not. First of all, the degree of heritability is an *average*, even among whites. For any two individuals, and *a fortiori*, any two groups of individuals, observed IQ differences may be due to any proportion in genes and environment—it is required only that they average properly over the entire population. For instance, *all* of the difference in IQ between identical twins is environmental, and presumably, a great deal of the difference between adopted brothers is genetic. Similarly, we cannot say whether the average difference in IQ between Irish and Puerto Ricans is genetic or environmental. In the case of blacks, however, the genetic school's inference is even more tenuous. R. Light and P. Smith, "Social Allocation Models of Intelligence: A Methodological Inquiry," *Harvard Educational Review*, 39, 3 (August 1969), have shown that even accepting Jensen's estimates of the heritability of IQ, the black-white IQ difference could easily be explained by the average environmental differences between the races. Recourse to further experimental investigations will not resolve this issue, for the "conceptual experimental" which would determine the genetic component of black-white differ-

ences cannot be performed. Could we take a pair of black identical twins and place them in random environments? Clearly not. Placing a black child in a white home, in an overtly racist society, will not provide the same environment as placing a white child in that house. Similarly, looking at the difference in IQs of unrelated black and white children raised in the same home (whether black or white, or mixed) will not tell us the extent of genetic differences, since such children cannot be treated equally, and environmental differences must continue to persist. (Of course, if, in these cases, differences in IQ disappear, the environmentalist case would be supported. But if they do not, no inference can be made.)

32. Most environmentalists do not dispute Jensen's assertion that existing large-scale compensatory programs have produced dismal results (Jensen [1969], *loc. cit.*; and Harvey Averch *et al.*, "How Effective Is Schooling: A Critical Review and Synthesis of Research Findings" (Santa Monica: The Rand Corporation, 1972). But this does not bear on the genetic hypothesis. As Jensen himself notes, the degree of genetic transmission of any trait depends on the various alternative environments which individuals experience. Jensen's estimates of heritability rest squarely on the existing array of educational processes and technologies. Any introduction of new social processes of mental development will change the average unstandardized level of IQ, as well as its degree of heritability. For instance, the almost perfect heritability of height is well documented. Yet the average heights of Americans have risen dramatically over the years, due clearly to changes in the overall environment. Similarly, whatever the heritability of IQ, the average unstandardized test scores rose 83 percent between 1917 and 1943 (Jencks [1972], *loc. cit.*). But compensatory programs are obviously an attempt to change the total array of environments open to children through "educational innovation." While existing large-scale programs appear to have failed to produce significant gains in scholastic achievement, many more innovative small-scale programs have succeeded. (Carl Bereiter, "The Future of Individual Differences," *Harvard Educational Review*, Reprint Series, No. 2, 1969; Silberman [1971], *loc. cit.*; and Averch [1972], *loc. cit.*). Moreover, even accepting the genetic position should not hinder us from seeking new environmental innovation—indeed it should spur us to further creative activities in this direction. Thus, the initial thrust of the genetic school can be at least partially repulsed: There is no reliable evidence either that long-term contact of blacks with existing white environments would not close the black-white IQ gap, or that innovative compensatory programs (i.e., programs unlike existing white child-rearing or education environments) might not attenuate or eliminate IQ differences which are indeed genetic.

33. James S. Coleman et al., *Equality of Educational Opportunity* (Washington, D.C.: U.S. Government Printing Office, 1966).

34. E.g., Ross, as quoted in Clarence Karier, "Ideology and Evaluation: In Quest of Meritocracy," Wisconsin Conference on Education and Evaluation at Madison, April 1973; Lewis M. Terman, *Intelligence Tests and School Reorganization* (New York: World Books, 1923); and Joseph Schumpeter, *Imperialism and Social Classes* (New York: Kelley, 1951).

This is not to imply that all liberal social theorists hold the IQ ideology. See also David McCelland, *Achieving Society* (New York: The Free Press, 1967); and Oscar Lewis, "The Culture of Poverty," *Scientific American*, Vol. 215, October 1966, who, among others, explicitly reject IQ as an important determinant of social stratification.

35. Jensen (1969), p. 14, *loc. cit.*

36. O. D. Duncan, "Properties and Characteristics of the Socio-economic Index," and "A Socio-economic Index for All Occupations," in Albert J. Reiss, ed., *Occupations and Social Status* (New York: The Free Press, 1961), pp. 90–91.

37. Jensen (1969), p. 19, *loc. cit.*

38. Bereiter (1969), p. 166, *op. cit.*

39. Herrnstein (1971), *loc. cit.*, p. 51.

40. *Ibid.*, p. 63.

41. Socioeconomic background is measured here by a weighted sum of parents' income, father's occupational status, and father's education. Childhood IQ is measured by the Stanford-Binet Test or its equivalent. These statistics are computed from an estimated zero-order correlation coefficient of .399 between socioeconomic background and early childhood IQ, as reported in Bowles and Nelson (1974), *op. cit.* The relationship is slightly stronger for men of other age groups than for the ages of 35–44 used in this figure: .410 for ages 25–34; .410 for ages 45–54; and .426 for ages 55–64 years.

42. These figures are based on an estimated correlation coefficient between IQ and income of .28 for non-Negro, nonfarm males, aged 35–44 years. The coefficient is also .28 for the age group 25–34; .29 for ages 45–54; and .27 for ages 55–64 years.

43. These relationships are based on an estimated correlation coefficient between socioeconomic background and income of .43 for non-Negro, nonfarm males, aged 35–44 years. The coefficient for other age groups is .32 for ages 25–34; .46 for ages 45–54; and .31 for ages 55–64 years. The relationship between socioeconomic background and income for men with the same IQ is based on estimated normalized regression coefficient of .38 on background in an equation using background and early childhood IQ to predict income, for the same age group. The Coefficient for the other age groups is .25 for ages 25–34; .41 for ages 45–54; and .24 for ages 55–64 years.

44. This figure is based on the correlation between socioeconomic background and income via the genetic inheritance of IQ alone. The correlation was computed by the path model presented in Bowles and Nelson (1974), *loc. cit.* The desired correlation is found by summing the two paths that lead from socioeconomic background to income that pass through the genetic component of IQ (genotypic IQ). One path leads from socioeconomic background through genotypic IQ to IQ and then directly to income. This model contends that IQ is inherited, in part, from one's parents and then, in turn, affects directly one's own income, thereby accounting for part of the correlation between background and income. The other path is less direct: It leads from socioeconomic background through genotypic IQ to IQ, but then one's IQ affects the number of years of schooling one attains, and then one's schooling affects income. The value of any one path is found by multiplying the coefficients of all the steps on that path.

The correlation coefficient between socioeconomic background and genotypic IQ was estimated at .22 in Bowles and Nelson (1974). We take Jensen's (high) estimate of .9 for the relationship between IQ and genotype. The influences of IQ and schooling on income were estimated with a normalized regression equation including socioeconomic background directly as a third dependent variable. Finally, the effect of IQ on years of schooling is found with another multiple regression equation again including socioeconomic background.

The result is that each path provides about half of the *total path coefficient of only .03*. We found this very small association of income with background due to the inheritance of IQ despite our adoption of Jensen's estimate of IQ heritability. Had we excluded the association of education with income via noncognitive paths, in order to model the perfect meritocracy based on intellectual ability alone, the correlation would have been still smaller.

Comparing the total path of .02 between socioeconomic background and income via the genetic inheritance of IQ to the total correlation of 0.43 between socioeconomic background and income shows that little of the total correlation is due to this path.

45. O. D. Duncan (1961), *op. cit.*, p. 90.
46. Jensen (1967), *loc. cit.*, p. 73.
47. Herrnstein (1971), *loc. cit.*, p. 63.


CHAPTER 5

1. Herbert Gintis, "Welfare Criteria with Endogenous Preferences: The Economics of Education," *International Economic Review*, June 1974; Alfred Schutz and Thomas Luckmann, *The Structure of the Life-World* (Evanston, Illinois: Northwestern University Press, 1973); and Peter L. Berger and Thomas Luckmann, *The Social Construction of Reality: A Treatise in the Sociology of Knowledge* (Garden City, L.I., N.Y.: Doubleday and Co., 1966).

2. For an extended treatment of these issues, see Herbert Gintis, "Alienation and Power," in *The Review of Radical Political Economics*, Vol. 4, No. 5, Fall 1972.

3. Jeanne Binstock, "Survival in the American College Industry," unpublished Ph.D. dissertation, Brandeis University, 1970.

4. Burton Rosenthal, "Educational Investments in Human Capital: The Significance of Stratification in the Labor Market," unpublished honors thesis, Harvard University, 1972; and Edgar Z. Friedenberg, *Coming of Age in America* (New York: Random House, 1965).

5. Florence Howe and Paul Lauter, "The Schools Are Rigged for Failure," *New York Review of Books*, June 20, 1970; James Herndon, *The Way It Spozed to Be* (New York: Simon and Schuster, 1968); and Ray C. Rist, "Student Social Class and Teacher Expectations: The Self-Fulfilling Prophesy in Ghetto Education," *Harvard Educational Review*, August 1970.

6. Binstock (1970), *loc. cit.*, pp. 103–106.

7. *Ibid.*, pp. 3–4.

8. *Ibid.*, p. 6.

9. Gene M. Smith, "Usefulness of Peer Ratings of Personality in Educational Research," *Educational and Psychological Measurement*, 1967; "Personality Correlates of Academic Performance in Three Dissimilar Populations," Proceedings of the 77th Annual Convention, American Psychological Association, 1967; and "Non-intelligence Correlates of Academic Performance," mimeo, 1970.

10. Richard C. Edwards, "Alienation and Inequality: Capitalist Relations of Production in a Bureaucratic Enterprise," Ph.D. dissertation, Harvard University, July 1972.

11. Richard C. Edwards, "Personal Traits and 'Success' in Schooling and Work," *Educational and Psychological Measurement*, in press, 1975; and "Individual Traits and Organizational Incentives: What Makes a 'Good' Worker?" *Journal of Human Resources*, in press, 1976.

12. Peter J. Meyer, "Schooling and the Reproduction of the Social Division of Labor," unpublished honors thesis, Harvard University, March 1972.

13. Personality data was collected for 97 per cent of the sample. Grade-point average and test-scored data was available for 80 per cent of the sample, and family background data was available for 67 per cent. Inability to collect data was due usually to students' absences from school during test sessions.

14. These are described fully in Appendix B.

15. The school chosen was of predominantly higher income, so that most students had taken college-entrance examinations.

16. The multiple correlation of IQ, SAT-verbal, and SAT-math with grade-point

average (GPA) was $r = 0.769$, while their correlation with the personality variables was $r = 0.25$.

17. That is, we created partial correlation coefficients between GPA and each personality measure, controlling for IQ, SAT-V, and SAT-M. The numerical values are presented in Appendix B.

18. We emphasize that these groupings are determined by a computer program on the basis of the observed pattern of association among the sixteen variables. The fact that they are so clearly interpretable, rather than being hodgepodge, is a further indicator of the correctness of our analysis. We have not grouped the personality traits in terms of our preconceived theory, but observed rather how they are *naturally* grouped in our data. The results of the factor analysis are presented in Appendix B.

19. This is taken from Table 3 of Edwards (1975), *op. cit.*; and Samuel Bowles, Herbert Gintis, and Peter Meyer, "The Long Shadow of Work: Education, the Family and the Reproduction of the Social Division of Labor," in *The Insurgent Sociologist*, Summer 1975.

20. Marshall H. Brenner, "The Use of High School Data to Predict Work Performance," *Journal of Applied Psychology*, Vol. 52, No. 1, January 1968. This study was suggested to us by Edwards, and is analyzed in Edwards (1972), *loc. cit.*

21. The relevant regression equations are presented in Appendix B.

22. See Claus Offe, *Leistungsprinzip und Industrielle Arbeit* (Frankfurt: Europaische Verlaganstalt, 1970). Offe quotes Bensen and Rosenberg in Maurice Stein *et al.*, eds., *Identity and Anxiety* (New York: The Free Press, 1960), pp. 183–184:

> Old habits are discarded and new habits are nurtured. The would-be success learns when to simulate enthusiasm, compassion, interest, concern, modesty, confidence and mastery; when to smile and with whom to laugh and how intimate and friendly he can be with other people. He selects his home and his residential area with care; he buys his clothes and chooses styles with an eye to their probable reception in his office. He reads or pretends to have read the right books, the right magazines, and the right newspapers. All this will be reflected in the "right line of conversation" which he adapts as his own. . . . He joins the right party and espouses the political ideology of his fellows.

23. See Ivar Berg, *Education and Jobs: The Great Training Robbery* (Boston: Beacon Press, 1971); and Paul Taubman and Terence Wales, *Higher Education and Earnings* (New York: McGraw-Hill, 1974).

24. Calculated from of an estimated normalized regression coefficient of 0.23 on socioeconomic background in an equation using background, early childhood IQ, and years of schooling to predict income for 35–44-year-old males. This is reported in Table 1 of Samuel Bowles and Valerie Nelson, "The 'Inheritance of IQ' and the Intergenerational Reproduction of Economic Inequality," *The Review of Economics and Statistics*, Vol. 56, No. 1, February 1974, and in Appendix A. The corresponding coefficients for other age groups are 0.17 for ages 25–34; 0.29 for ages 45–54; and 0.11 for ages 55–64 years.

25. Margaret Benston, "The Political Economy of Women's Liberation," *Monthly Review*, September 1969; Marilyn P. Goldberg, "The Economic Exploitation of Women," in David M. Gordon, ed., *Problems in Political Economy* (Lexington, Mass.: D. C. Heath and Co., 1971); L. Gordon. *Families* (Cambridge, Mass.: A. Bread and Rose Publication, 1970); Zaretzky, "Capitalism and Personal Life," *Socialist Revolution*, January–April 1973; and Juliet Mitchell, *Women's Estate* (New York: Vintage Books, 1973).

26. Melvin Kohn, *Class and Conformity: A Study in Values* (Homewood, Illinois: Dorsey Press, 1969).

27. Melvin Kohn and Carmi Schooler, "Occupational Experience and Cognitive

Functioning: An Assessment of Reciprocal Effects," *American Sociological Review*, February 1973.

28. Kohn (1969), *loc. cit.*; chapters 5 and 10.

29. *Ibid.*, Chapter 10.

30. *Ibid.*, Table 10–7.

31. *Ibid.*, p. 192.

32. The occupational index used was that of Hollingshead, which correlates 0.90 with the Duncan index. Charles M. Bonjean, Richard J. Hill, and S. Dale McLemore, *Sociological Measurement: An Inventory of Scales and Indices* (San Francisco: Chandler, 1967).

33. Kohn (1969), *loc. cit.*, pp. 34–35.

34. *Ibid.*, pp. 104–105.

35. Two problems with the Kohn study may be noted. First, we would like to have more direct evidence of the ways in which and to what extent child-raising *values* are manifested in child-raising *practices*. And second, we would like to know more about the impact of differences in child-rearing practice upon child development.

36. Kohn (1969), *loc. cit.*, p. 200.

## CHAPTER 6

1. Bernard Bailyn, *Education in the Framing of American Society* (Chapel Hill: University of North Carolina Press, 1960); and Lawrence Cremin, *American Education: The Colonial Experience 1607–1783* (New York: Harper & Row, 1970).

2. U.S. Bureau of the Census, *Historical Statistics of U.S.—Colonial Times to 1857* (Washington, D.C.: U.S. Government Printing Office, 1960); and U.S. Bureau of the Census, *Statistical Abstract of the U.S.*, 1974. The average number of days in attendance refers to public schools only. The percentage attending is average daily attendance in public schools plus enrollment in private schools. The figure for 1870 may be slightly overstated.

3. Michael Katz, *Class, Bureaucracy and Schools* (New York: Praeger Publishers, 1971a).

4. *Ibid.*, pp. XIX, 106.

5. M. Vanovskis and R. Bernard, *Women in Education in AnteBellum Period* (Madison: University of Wisconsin Center for Demography and Ecology, Working Paper 73–7, 1973). These gross figures obscure significant regional variation (from 74 per cent in New England to 32 per cent in the South Atlantic states in 1860). Roughly, the same proportion of males and females attended. Except in New England, school attendance by blacks was significantly lower than by whites.

6. Not surprisingly, much of the research on the period has focused on Massachusetts. We are able to borrow extensively from the excellent research of Michael Katz, David Bruck, Bernard Bailyn, Alexander Field, James Medoff, Stanley Schultz, William Weber, Robert Buchele, Lawrence Cremin, Stanley Schwartz, and others.

7. This account is based in Theodore Edson's *Historical Discourse on the Occasion of the Fiftieth Anniversary of the First Introduction of Public Worship into the Village of East Chelmsford* (1873), as cited in David Bruck, "The Schools of Lowell, 1824–1861: A Case Study in the Origins of Modern Public Education in America," unpublished thesis, Harvard University, 1970.

8. Michael Katz, *The Irony of Early School Reform* (Cambridge, Mass.: Harvard University Press, 1968), pp. 19–22, 80–84, 273.

9. For a survey, see M. Gordon, *The American Family in Social-Historical Perspective* (New York: St. Martin's Press, 1973).

10. This account draws upon two important historical studies: Cremin (1970), *loc. cit.*, and Bailyn (1960), *op. cit.* Also illuminating are anthropological studies of education in precapitalist societies. See, for example, J. Kenyatta, *Facing Mount Kenya* (New York: Vintage Books, 1962); E. S. Morgan, *The Puritan Family: Religion and Domestic Relations in the 17th Century New England* (Boston: The Trustees of the Public Library, 1956); and P. Aries, *Centuries of Childhood* (New York: Random House, 1970).

11. In a number of places—Scotland and Massachusetts, for example—schools stressed literacy so as to make the Bible more widely accessible. See C. Cippola, *Literacy and Economic Development* (Baltimore, Maryland: Gannon, 1969); and Morgan (1956), *loc. cit.*

12. Bureau of the Census (1960), *loc. cit.*

13. Norman J. Ware, *The Industrial Worker, 1840–1860* (Chicago: Quadrangle Books, 1964).

14. C. Kaestle (1975), *loc. cit.*, p. 103.

15. Bureau of Census (1960), *loc. cit.*

16. See, for example, S. Thernstrom, *Poverty and Progress: Social Mobility in a 19th Century City* (New York: Atheneum Press, 1969).

17. Edward Pessen, "The Egalitarian Myth and the American Social Reality," in *American Historical Review*, Vol. 76, No. 4, October 1971. Boston's wealthiest 1 per cent owned 16 per cent of all tangible wealth in 1821 and 37 per cent in 1845. The figures for New York City are 29 per cent in 1828 and 40 per cent in 1845. For Brooklyn, 22 per cent in 1810 and 42 per cent in 1841.

18. *Ibid.*

19. Paddy Quick, "Education and Industrialization in 19th Century England and Wales," unpublished Ph.D. dissertation, Harvard University, 1975.

20. Cippola (1969), *op. cit.*, and Frank Ackerman, "Militarism and the Rise of Mass Education in Prussia," unpublished manuscript, Harvard University, June 1970.

21. William M. Weber, "Public Schooling and Changing Ruling Class Hegemony: Education in Boston 1800–1817," unpublished thesis, Harvard University, 1972, pp. 48–50.

22. Much of this account is based on Bruck (1970), *op. cit.*; and Alexander J. Field, "Skill Requirements in Early Industrialization: The Case of Massachusetts," working paper in Economics, University of California at Berkeley, December 1973.

23. Quoted in Michael Katz, ed., *School Reform: Past and Present* (Boston: Little, Brown and Company, 1971b).

24. Bruck (1970), *loc. cit.*, p. 95.

25. *Lowell School Committee Reports* cited in Bruck (1970), *loc. cit.*, p. 97.

26. *Ibid.*, p. 96. The emphasis is from the original.

27. Field (1973), *loc. cit.* This is based on City of Lowell, *School Committee Reports* and *Lowell City Directories*.

28. Data on textile prices, profits, wages, and labor productivity are from P. F. McGouldrick, *New England Textiles in the 19th Century* (Cambridge, Massachusetts: Harvard University Press, 1968).

29. *Ibid.*

30. M. Vanovskis, "Horace Mann on the Economic Productivity of Education," in *The New England Quarterly*, Vol. 43, No. 4, 1970.

31. Bruck (1970), *op. cit.*; and Field (1973), *op. cit.*

32. These and the following data are from the U.S. Census Bureau and other sources summarized by Field (1973), *op. cit.*

33. Messerli (1972), *op. cit.*, p. 195.

34. *Ibid.*, p. 442.

35. Merle Curti, *The Social Ideas of American Educators* (Totowa, New Jersey: Littlefield Adams and Co., 1963), pp. 119–120.

36. *Ibid.*, pp. 122–123.

37. *Ibid.*, p. 134.

38. Messerli (1972), *op. cit.*, p. 493.

39. Curti (1968), *op. cit.*, p. 93.

40. *Lowell School Committee Report of 1852*, cited in Bruck (1970), *op. cit.*, p. 81.

41. *Lowell School Committee Report of 1857, ibid.*, p. 81.

42. Political economy was made a required subject in Massachusetts high schools in 1857, along with moral sciences and civic polity, but not, to our knowledge, in the elementary schools.

43. Bruck (1970), *op. cit.*, p. 76.

44. *Ibid.*, p. 77.

45. Hal Luft, "New England Textile Labor in the 1840's: From Yankee Farmgirl to Irish Immigrant," mimeo, January 1971.

46. The estimates are based on Albert Fishlow, "The American Common School Revival: Fact or Fancy?" in Henry Rosovsky, ed., *Industrialization in Two Systems* (New York: John Wiley & Sons, 1966); Vanovskis and Bernard (1973), *loc. cit.*, and the Bureau of the Census (1960), *loc. cit.* Three-quarters is undoubtedly a low estimate as it is based on the assumption that no slaves could read or write. Many, in fact, could, though precise figures are not available.

47. For a striking example, see Bartlett (1841) (Chapter 4).

48. Springfield, Massachusetts, School Committee, *Annual Report* (1854), pp. 11–13.

49. Katz (1968), *loc. cit.*, p. 87.

50. Katz (1971b), *loc. cit.*, p. 125.

51. Katz (1971a), *loc. cit.*

52. Elwood P. Cubberly, *Public Education in the U.S.* (Boston: Houghton-Mifflin, 1934).

53. Quoted in Katz (1971b), *loc. cit.*, pp. 125–126.

54. Messerli (1972), *op. cit.*; and Curti (1968), *op. cit.*

55. Katz (1971a), *loc. cit.*, pp. 44–45.

56. Diane Ravitch, *The Great School Wars: New York City, 1805–1973* (New York: Basic Books, 1974); and C. Kaestle, *The Evolution of an Urban School System: New York City, 1750–1850* (Cambridge, Massachusetts: Harvard University Press, 1973).

57. Sources for the following data are M. Vanovskis, "Trends in Massachusetts Education," *History of Education Quarterly*, Vol. 12, No. 4, Winter 1972; Katz (1968), *loc. cit.*; and Field (1973), *loc. cit.* All three authors rely primarily on *The Abstract of Massachusetts School Returns* and the U.S. Census data.

58. *Ibid.*

59. Field (1973), *loc. cit.*

60. Carl Kaestle and M. Vanovskis, *Quantification, Urbanization and the History of Education: An Analysis of the Determinants of School Attendance in New York State in 1845* (Madison, Wisconsin: University of Wisconsin Center for Demographics and Ecology, Working Paper 73-31, 1974).

61. David Tyack, *The One Best System: A History of American Urban Education* (Cambridge, Massachusetts: Harvard University Press, 1974).

62. Thernstrom (1969), *loc. cit.*

63. Kaestle (1973), *op. cit.*

64. Fishlow (1966), *loc. cit.*

65. *See* Curti (1968), *op. cit.*; Horace Mann Bond, *Negro Education in Alabama* (New York: Atheneum, 1969); and Louis R. Harlan, *Separate and Unequal* (New York: Atheneum, 1969).

66. Curti (1968), *op. cit.*

67. Harry Cleaver, "The Southern Colony: The Attempt to Transform Southern Agriculture and Make It Safe for Democracy and Profits," unpublished paper for Sherbrooke University, Canada, 1974. See also Harlan (1969), *op. cit.*; and Bond (1969), *op. cit.*

68. Harlan (1969), *op. cit.*; and Bond (1969), *op. cit.*

69. Robert Buchele and James Medoff, "Education and the Agrarian Order, 1860–1910," unpublished, Harvard University, 1972.

70. Lawrence E. Cremin, *The Transformation of the School* (New York: Alfred A. Knopf, 1964), p. 43.

71. Cleaver (1974), *op. cit.*; and Grant McConnell, *The Decline of American Democracy* (New York: Harper & Row, 1969).

CHAPTER 7

1. U.S. Bureau of the Census, *Historical Statistics of the U.S.—Colonial Times to 1957* (Washington, D.C.: U.S. Government Printing Office, 1960).

2. Calculated from U.S. Office of Education, *Digest of Educational Statistics*, (Washington, D.C.: U.S. Government Printing Office, 1974); and U.S. Bureau of Census (1960), *loc. cit.* We have generously assumed that half of the college students in 1890 were less than twenty years old.

3. U.S. Office of Education (1974), *op. cit.*

4. For excellent surveys of this period, see Lawrence E. Cremin, *The Transformation of the School* (New York: Alfred A. Knopf, 1964); Joel H. Spring, *Education and the Rise of the Corporate Order* (Boston: Beacon Press, 1972); David L. Cohen and Marvin Lazerson, "Education and the Corporate Order," *Socialist Revolution*, March 1972; Clarence J. Karier, *Shaping the American Educational State: 1900 to the Present* (New York: The Free Press, 1975); and Clarence J. Karier, Joel Spring, and Paul C. Violas, *Roots of Crisis* (Chicago: University of Illinois Press, 1973).

5. See Walter Feinberg, "Progressive Education and Social Planning," *Teachers' College Record*, May 1972.

6. Richard C. Edwards, Michael Reich, and Thomas Weisskopf, *The Capitalist System* (Englewood Cliffs, N.J.: Prentice-Hall, 1972), p. 175.

7. U.S. Bureau of the Census (1960), *loc. cit.*

8. *Ibid.*

9. This quote and the one immediately below are from Gerald Grob, *Workers and Utopia* (Chicago: Quadrangle Press, 1969), pp. 7–8.

10. *Ibid.* On the culture and everyday life of workers, see the excellent treatment by Herbert Gutman, "Work, Culture and Society in Industrializing America, 1815–1919," in *American Historical Review*, June 1973.

11. Our treatment draws heavily on Richard C. Edwards, "Corporate Stability and the Risks of Corporate Failure," *Journal of Economic History*, June, 1975; and Richard C. Edwards, Michael Reich, and David Gordon, *Labor Market Segmentation* (New York: D. C. Heath, 1975).

12. The best treatment of this subject is in Harry Braverman, *Labor and Monopoly Capital* (New York: Monthly Review Press, 1974).

13. See James Weinstein, *The Corporate Ideal in the Liberal State 1900–1918*

(Boston: Beacon Press, 1968); and G. Kolko, *The Triumph of Conservatism* (Chicago: Quadrangle Books, 1963).

14. U.S. Bureau of the Census (1960), *loc. cit.*

15. Particularly, see Upton Sinclair, *The Goslings* (Pasadena, California: Upton Sinclair, 1924).

16. Samuel P. Hays, "The Politics of Reform in Municipal Government in the Progressive Era," *Pacific Northwest Quarterly*, October 1964, pp. 152, 170.

17. *Ibid.*, p. 58.

18. David Tyack, *The One Best System: A History of American Urban Education* (Cambridge, Massachusetts: Harvard University Press, 1974).

19. Hays, *op. cit.*

20. *Ibid.*, p. 159.

21. Tyack (1974), *loc. cit.*, p. 127.

22. Tyack (1974), *loc. cit.*, p. 65.

23. Tyack (1974), *loc. cit.*, pp. 58–59.

24. *Ibid.*, p. 58.

25. *Ibid.*, p. 58; and Selwyn Troen, "Popular Education in the 19th Century St. Louis," in *History of Education Quarterly*, 13, Spring 1973.

26. Elston and Backman, *Educational Review*, 30, 1910, as quoted in Sol Cohen, "The Industrial Education Movement, 1906–1917," *American Quarterly*, Vol. 20, Spring 1968. See also Cremin (1964), *loc. cit.*; Cohen and Lazerson (1972), *op. cit.*; and W. Norton Grubb, "The Impact of the Vocational Education Movement after 1910," unpublished thesis, Harvard University, 1971.

27. We have relied heavily on the work of W. Norton Grubb and Marvin Lazerson, *American Education and Vocationalism* (New York: Teachers College, Columbia University, 1974); Cremin (1964), *loc. cit.*; and Cohen (1968), *op. cit.*

28. Cremin (1964), *loc. cit.*; Grant McConnell, *The Decline of Agrarian Democracy* (New York: Harper & Row, 1969); and Harry Cleaver, "The Southern Colony: The Attempt to Transform Southern Agriculture and Make It Safe for Democracy and Profits," unpublished paper, Sherbrooke University, Canada, 1974.

29. Katherine Stone, "The Origins of Job Structures in the Steel Industry," *Review of Radical Political Economics*, Summer 1974.

30. Cremin (1964), *loc. cit.*, p. 38.

31. *Ibid.*, p. 36.

32. Grubb and Lazerson (1974), *op. cit.*

33. See Grubb and Lazerson (1974), *op. cit.*, for a more complete presentation of this view.

34. In this section, we have made extensive use of the research of Clarence J. Karier, "Testing for Order and Control in the Corporate Liberal State," in *Education Theory*, Vol. 22, Spring 1972; Clarence J. Karier, "Ideology and Evaluation: In Quest of Meritocracy," Wisconsin Conference on Education and Evaluation at Madison, April 1973, in Clarence J. Karier, Joel Spring, and Paul C. Violas, *Roots of Crisis* (Chicago: University of Illinois Press, 1973); and Russell Marks, "Trackers, Testers and Trustees," unpublished Ph.D. dissertation for Harvard University, 1973.

35. Raymond Callahan, *Education and the Cult of Efficiency* (Chicago: University of Chicago Press, 1962); Cohen and Lazerson (1972), *op. cit.*; and Cremin (1964), *loc. cit.*

36. On the role of IQ testing and reproducing, and legitimating the class structure of corporate capitalism, see Karier (1972), *loc. cit.*

37. Karier, Spring, and Violas (1973), *loc. cit.*, p. 120.

38. Cohen and Lazerson (1972), *loc. cit.*

39. Edward L. Thorndike, *Individuality* (Boston: Houghton-Mifflin, 1911).

40. Marks (1973), *loc. cit.*

41. Leon Kamin, *The Science and Politics of IQ* (Potomac, Maryland: Erlbaum Associates, 1974).

42. Alfred Binet and T. H. Simon, *The Development of Intelligence in Children* (Baltimore: Williams and Wilkins Co., 1916), as quoted in Karier (1973), *loc. cit.*, p. 13.

43. Marks (1973), pp. 71–72.

44. *Ibid.*, p. 70.

45. Lewis Terman, *The Measurement of Intelligence* (Boston: Houghton-Mifflin, 1916), pp. 27–28, as quoted in Karier (1973), *loc. cit.*, p. 13.

46. John Dewey, *School and Society* (Chicago: University of Chicago Press, 1915).

47. Marks (1973), *loc. cit.*, p. 68.

48. *Ibid.*, p. 72.

49. *Ibid.*, p. 72.

50. Edward L. Thorndike, *Educational Psychology, Briefer Course* (New York: Teachers College, Columbia University, 1914), pp. 350–351, as quoted in Karier, Spring, and Violas (1973), *loc. cit.*

51. Thorndike (1911), *op. cit.*, pp. 30–34, as quoted in Karier, Spring, and Violas (1973), *loc. cit.*

52. Marks (1973), *loc. cit.*, pp. 73–74.

53. See, especially, Callahan (1962), *loc. cit.*; Karier (1972), *loc. cit.*; and Spring (1972), *loc. cit.*

## CHAPTER 8

1. U.S. Bureau of Census, *Statistical Abstract of U.S.—1973* (Washington, D.C.: U.S. Government Printing Office, 1973).

2. *Ibid.*

3. Michael Reich, in Richard C. Edwards, Michael Reich, and Thomas Weisskopf, eds., *The Capitalist System* (Englewood Cliffs, N.J.: Prentice-Hall, 1972). For a recent, more detailed survey of the data on the U.S. occupational structure covering the years 1900–1970, see A. Szymanski, "Trends in the American Working Class," *Socialist Revolution*, Vol. 2, No. 4, July/August 1972.

4. For a general treatment, see Stephen Marglin, "What Do Bosses Do? The Origin and Functions of Hierarchy in Capitalist Production," *Review of Radical Political Economics*, Vol. 6, No. 2, (Summer 1974); and André Gorz, *Socialism and Revolution* (New York: Anchor Press, 1973).

5. For an excellent description of the process, see Katherine Stone, "The Origins of Job Structures in the Steel Industry," *Review of Radical Political Economics*, Vol. 6, No. 2, (Summer 1974.)

6. See Raymond Callahan, *Education and the Cult of Efficiency* (Chicago: University of Chicago Press, 1962) for an account of the educational efficiency movement.

7. It seems more than accidental that these changes in the social relationships of high-school education coincided with the influx of working-class children to high schools. Note the similarity to the current changes in the social relationships of higher education—standardization of curriculum and methods and centralization of the evaluation function, for example—associated with the rapid expansion of community colleges.

8. Clark Kerr, *The Uses of the University* (Cambridge, Massachusetts: Harvard University Press, 1963); Carnegie Commission on Higher Education, *Priorities for*

*Action: Carnegie Commission on Higher Education, Final Report* (New York: McGraw-Hill, 1973).

9. For a full listing of the Carnegie Commission reports and their final recommendations, see *Final Report* (1973), *op. cit.*

10. Gorz, *op. cit.*, p. 121.

11. For an exposition of the role of intellectual as technician in capitalist societies, see Paul Baran, "The Commitment of the Intellectual," in *Monthly Review*, Vol. 16, No. 11, March 1965; and Richard Lichtman, "The Ideological Functions of the University," *Upstart*, January, 1971.

12. This and the above quotes are from the *Final Report* (1973), pp. 29, 36, and 47.

13. *Ibid.*, p. 30.

14. K. Patricia Cross, *Beyond the Open Door: New Students to Higher Education* (San Francisco: Jossey-Bass, 1971). How reminiscent this argument is of that used by the turn-of-the-century educators in their justification of the introduction of tracking in high schools!

15. U.S. Office of Education, *Digest of Educational Statistics* (Washington, D.C.: U.S. Government Printing Office, 1974).

16. For a survey of evidence on the stratification of U.S. higher education, see Jerome Karabel, "Community Colleges and Social Stratification," *Harvard Educational Review*, Vol. 42, No. 4, November 1972.

17. See W. Lee Hansen and Burton A. Weisbrod, *Benefits, Costs and Finance of Higher Education* (Chicago: Markham, 1969), p. 68. Similar studies in Florida confirm this pattern (see Douglas Windham, *Education, Equality and Income Redistribution: A Study of Public Higher Education* [Lexington, Massachusetts: D. C. Heath, 1970]), as does a nationwide census survey showing that college students from families earning less than $5,000 a year are over twice as likely to be enrolled in two-year (as opposed to four-year) colleges, compared to students from families earning $15,000 or more. See U.S. Bureau of the Census, *Current Population Reports*, Series P–60, No. 183, May 1969. See also American Council on Education, *National Norms for Entering College Freshmen*, Fall 1970 (Washington, D.C.: 1970).

18. We have benefited greatly from Binstock's comparative study of the internal social relationships of seven different types of U.S. institutions of higher education, from junior colleges to private secular elite colleges. See Jeanne Binstock, *Survival in the American College Industry*, unpublished Ph.D. dissertation, Brandeis University, 1970. See also Chapter 5.

19. Burton R. Clark, *The Open Door College: A Case Study* (New York: McGraw-Hill, 1960); Burton R. Clark, "The 'Cooling Out' Function in Higher Education," in *The American Journal of Sociology*, Vol. 65, No. 6, May 1960, pp. 569–577.

20. John Folger *et al.*, Human Resources and Higher Education (New York: Russell Sage, 1970). Though the proponents of junior colleges make much of the opportunity for students to transfer at the end of two years and receive a bachelor's degree from a four-year college, of the entering freshmen in community colleges, less than one-third actually do this. For a survey of the evidence, see Karabel *op. cit.* Over three-fourths of a large nationwide sample of entering community-college freshmen in 1970 stated that they intended to receive a B.A., B.S., or a higher degree (American Council on Education [1970], *loc. cit.*).

21. Arthur Cohen, "Stretching Pre-College Education," in *Social Policy*, Vol. 2, No. 1, May–June 1971, p. 6.

22. For an excellent analysis of the vocationalization of the community college, see Karabel (1972).

23. Charles Monroe, *Profile of the Community College* (San Francisco: Jossey-Bass, 1972).

24. We may expect to see resistance to these pressures from community-college faculties. Their professional status depends on their membership in the community of university and college teachers. Acquiescence to these pressures would not only make their work more difficult and less rewarding, it would signal their descent into the mass of white-collar proletarians, following the route of the high-school teachers some decades ago. See Callahan (1962), *loc. cit.*, for a description of the high schools' capitulation to similar pressures in the early part of the century.

25. This statement does not apply to the small number of exceptional liberal-arts junior colleges. Z. Gamson, J. Gusfield, and D. Reisman, *Academic Values and Mass Education* (Garden City, L.I., N.Y.: Doubleday and Co., 1970).

26. *Final Report* (1973), *loc. cit.*, p. 66.

27. Committee on Economic Development, *The Management and Financing of Colleges*, New York, 1973.

28. President's Commission on Campus Unrest, *Report of the President's Commission on Campus Unrest* (Washington, D.C.: 1970), p. 18.

29. *New York Times*, July 25, 1970, p. 1.

30. President's Commission, *op. cit.*, p. 18.

31. Karabel (1972), *loc. cit.*, not that the proponents of elite education have failed to fight back. Evidence points to considerable, though more subtle, restratification of higher education in New York. See E. K. Trimberger, "Open Admissions: A New Form of Tracking?" in *The Insurgent Sociologist*, Vol. 4, No. 1, Fall 1973.

32. For a particularly cogent statement of the "industrialization" view, see Michael Miles, *The Radical Probe: The Logic of Student Rebellion* (New York: Atheneum, 1975).

33. Jerome Karabel, "The Decline of the American Student Movement," unpublished manuscript, January 1974.

34. Cited in *Work in America*. Report of a Special Task Force to the Secretary of Health, Education and Welfare (Cambridge, Massachusetts: MIT Press, 1973).

35. Compared to workers with only a high-school education, workers with one to three years of college tend to have come from wealthier families and to have had better grades in high school. Thus, it is reasonable to expect that these workers would have had occupational opportunities and earned incomes superior to other high-school graduates, even had they not attended college.

36. U.S. Bureau of Census, *1970 Decennial Census of Population*, Vol. PC(1)–cl, 1970.

37. See U.S. Office of Education (1974), *loc. cit.*; see also Karabel (1972), *loc. cit.*

38. James O'Connor, *The Fiscal Crisis of the State* (New York: St. Martin's Press, 1973).

39. *Final Report* (1973), p. 95.

40. Daniel Yankelovich, *Changing Youth Values in the 1970's: A Study of American Youth* (New York: J. D. Rockefeller Foundation, 1974).

41. *Ibid.*

42. On the family background of student radicals, see Richard Flacks, "Young Intelligentsia in Revolt," *Transaction*, No. 7, June 1970; and S. M. Lipset, *Rebellion in the University* (Boston: Little, Brown, 1971).

43. On the relationship between child-rearing and parental occupational roles, see Melvin Kohn, *Class nd Conformity: A Study in Values* (Homewood, Illinois: Dorsey Press, 1969); and Chapter 7.

44. Karabel (1974), *loc. cit.* See also Alexander Astin and Alan Bayer, "Campus Unrest, 1970–1971: Was It Really All That Quiet?" *Education Record*, Fall 1971.

45. Evidence for the period 1959–1969 is contained in Bureau of the Census (1970), *op. cit.* For the half century prior to the 1950s, the earnings of white-collar workers fell in relationship to those of skilled blue-collar workers. See V. Bonnell and

Michael Reich, *Workers in the American Economy* (Boston: New England Free Press, 1969), Table 25.

46. Pressures for unionization among white-collar workers reflect, in part, an attempt to achieve at least the degree of job security held by unionized blue-collar workers. The importance of this issue is not lost on the Carnegie Commission: "If [faculty union] bargaining does take place, we believe that it should be on the basis of a craft approach for faculty members in a unit by themselves and of contracts that confine themselves to economic matters." *Final Report* (1973), *op. cit.*, p. 58.

## CHAPTER 9

1. Butts, in John E. Sturm and John A. Palmer, eds., *Democratic Legacy in Transition* (New York: Van Nostrand, 1971), p. 50.

2. *Ibid.*, p. 18.

3. *Ibid.*, pp. 27–29.

4. *Ibid.*, pp. 27–29.

5. *Ibid.*, p. 30.

6. Elwood P. Cubberly, *Public Education in the U.S.* (Boston: Houghton-Mifflin, 1934), pp. 164–165. Cubberly's writings on educational history are, in fact, difficult to categorize. Though clearly influenced by the conflict theory originally proposed by Carleton, Cubberly also expressed the evolutionary idealism represented by Butts. At times, he appears to espouse the technological perspective which we also discuss.

7. *Ibid.*

8. Frank Tracy Carleton, *Economic Influences upon Educational Progress in the U.S. 1820–1850* (Madison: University of Wisconsin Press, 1911).

9. S. M. Lipset, *Political Man: Social Bases of Politics* (New York: Doubleday and Co., 1960).

10. Trow, in Reinhard Bendix and Seymour Lipset, eds., *Class, Status and Power* (New York: The Free Press, 1966), p. 438.

11. See Michael Katz, *The Irony of Early School Reform* (Cambridge, Massachusetts: Harvard University Press, 1968); and Clarence J. Karier, Joel Spring, and Paul C. Violas, *Roots of Crisis* (Chicago: University of Illinois Press, 1973).

12. See Alexander J. Field, "Skill Requirements in Early Industrialization: The Case of Massachusetts," working paper in Economics, University of California at Berkeley, December 1973.

13. Hal Luft, "New England Textile Labor in the 1840's: From Yankee Farmgirl to Irish Immigrant," mimeo, January 1971.

14. Albert Fishlow, "The American Common School Revival: Fact or Fancy?" in Henry Rosovsky, ed., *Industrialization in Two Systems* (New York: John Wiley & Sons, 1966); and M. Vanovskis and R. Bernard. "Women and Education in the Anti-Bellum U.S." (Madison, Univ. of Wisconsin Center for Demography and Ecology, working paper 73–7, 1973).

15. See Chapter 4.

16. David Tyack, *The One Best System: A History of American Urban Education* (Cambridge, Massachusetts: Harvard University Press, 1974).

17. Vanovskis and Bernard, *op. cit.* The figure refers to whites aged 5–19 years.

18. C. Kaestle, *The Evolution of an Urban School System: New York City, 1750–1850* (Cambridge, Massachusetts: Harvard University Press, 1973).

19. Representative works are: Katz (1968), *loc. cit.*; Michael Katz, *Class, Bureaucracy and Schools* (New York: Praeger Publishers, 1971a); Michael Katz, ed., *School Reform Past and Present* (Boston: Little, Brown and Company, 1971b);

Karier, Spring, and Violas (1973), *loc. cit.*; Marvin Lazerson, *Origin of Urban Schools: Public Education in Massachusetts* (Cambridge, Massachusetts: Harvard University Press, 1971); Kaestle (1973), *loc. cit.*; Tyack (1974), *loc. cit.*; Colin Greer, *The Great School Legend* (New York: Viking Press, 1973); Clarence J. Karier, *Shaping the American Educational State: 1900 to the Present* (New York: The Free Press, 1975).

20. Katz (1968), *loc. cit.*

21. James O'Connor develops a related, but not identical, concept—the contradiction between accumulation and legitimation—in his *Fiscal Crisis of the State* (New York: St. Martin's Press, 1973).

22. Raymond Callahan, *Education and the Cult of Efficiency* (Chicago: University of Chicago Press, 1962); Joel H. Spring, *Education and the Rise of the Corporate State* (Boston: Beacon Press, 1972); Clarence J. Karier, "Ideology and Evaluation: In Quest of Meritocracy," Wisconsin Conference on Education and Evaluation at Madison, April 1973; Katz (1968), *loc. cit.*; and Field (1973), *loc. cit.*

23. Binstock (1970), *loc. cit.*; Burton E. Rosenthal, "Educational Investments in Human Capital: The Significance of Stratification in the Labor Market," unpublished thesis, Harvard University, 1972.

24. U.S. Bureau of the Census, *Historical Statistics of the U.S.—Colonial Times to 1957* (Washington, D.C.: U.S. Government Printing Office, 1960).

## CHAPTER 10

1. For a fuller elaboration of the concept of revolutionary reforms, see André Gorz, *Socialism and Revolution* (New York: Anchor Press, 1973), chapter 4.

2. Gary Becker, *Human Capital* (New York: Columbia University Press, 1964); and Theodore Schultz, *The Economic Value of Education* (New York: Columbia University Press, 1963).

3. Christopher Jencks et al., *Inequality: A Reassessment of the Effects of Family and Schooling in America* (New York: Basic Books, 1972).

4. *Work in America*, Report of a Special Task Force to the Secretary of Health, Education and Welfare (Cambridge, Massachusetts: MIT Press, 1973).

5. Jerome Karabel, "Community Colleges and Social Stratification," *Harvard Educational Review*, Vol. 424, No. 42, November 1972; E. K. Trimberger, "Open Admissions: A New Form of Tracking?" *The Insurgent Sociologist*, Vol. 4, No. 1, Fall 1973; and Jerome Karabel, "Perspectives on Open Admissions," *Educational Record*, Winter 1972, pp. 30–44.

6. Alexander Astin and Jack Rossman, "The Case for Open Admissions: A Status Report," *Change*, Vol. 5, No. 6, Summer 1973.

7. Paul Goodman, *Compulsory Miseducation* (New York: Vintage, 1964); and Abraham Maslow, *Toward a Psychology of Being* (New York: Van Nostrand, 1962).

8. George Dennison, *The Lives of Children* (New York: Random House, 1969); James Herndon, *How to Survive in Your Native Land* (New York: Bantam Books, 1971); Herbert Kohl, *The Open Classroom* (New York: Vintage, 1970); Jonathan Kozol, *Death at an Early Age* (New York: Penguin, 1968); Charles Silberman, *Crisis in the Classroom* (New York: Vintage, 1971); and John Holt, *What Do I Do Monday?* (New York: Delta Books, 1972).

9. Jonathan Kozol, *Free Schools* (New York: Bantam, 1972); and Allen Graubard, *Free the Children!* (New York: Vintage, 1973).

10. Ivan Illich, *Deschooling Society* (New York: Harper & Row, 1970). For a more extensive assessment of Illich, see Herbert Gintis, "Toward a Political Economy

of Education," *Harvard Educational Review*, Vol. 42, No. 1, February 1972.

11. Illich himself does not use the term "commodity fetishism." We do so, however, as it is more felicitous that "institutionalized values" in many contexts.

12. Illich (1970), *op. cit.*, p. 52.

13. *Ibid.*, p. 44.

14. *Ibid.*, p. 55.

15. *Ibid.*, p. 57.

16. *Ibid.*, p. 112.

17. *Ibid.*, p. 62.

18. *Ibid.*, pp. 55–56.

19. For an alternative view, see Samuel Bowles, "Cuban Education and the Revolutionary Ideology," in *Harvard Educational Review*, Vol. 41, No. 4, Fall 1971.

20. Illich (1970), *op. cit.*, p. 49.

## CHAPTER 11

1. Joshua Horn, *Away with All Pests* (New York: Monthly Review Press, 1969), p. 86.

2. For an extensive bibliography addressed to this question, see James Campen, *Socialist Alternatives for America: A Bibliography*, Union for Radical Political Economics, Spring 1974.

3. For an expansion of this theme, see William R. Torbert, *Being for the Most Part Puppets* (Cambridge, Massachusetts: Schlenkman, 1973); Sidney Verba and Norman Nie, *Participation in America* (New York: Harper & Row, 1972); Carole Pateman, *Participation and Democratic Theory* (Cambridge, England: Cambridge University Press, 1970); and Peter Bachrach, *The Theory of Democratic Elitism: A Critique* (Boston: Little, Brown and Company, 1967).

4. Mao Tse-tung, "On Contradiction," in *Selected Works of Mao Tse-Tung*, Vol. I (Peking, 1951).

5. Theodore Rozzak, "Educating Contra Naturam," in Ronald Gross and Paul Osterman, eds., *High School* (New York: Clarion, 1971), pp. 64–65.

6. Peter Marin, "The Open Truth and Fiery Vehemence of Youth," in Gross and Osterman (1971), *op. cit.*, p. 44.

7. *See* André Gorz, *Socialism and Revolution* (New York: Anchor Press, 1973); Michael P. Lerner, *New Socialist Revolution* (New York: Delta Books, 1973); Juliet Mitchell, *Women's Estate* (New York: Vintage Books, 1971); Mike Albert, *What Is to Be Undone* (Cambridge, Mass.: Porter Sargent, 1974); Robert L. Allen, *Black Awakening in Capitalist America* (Garden City, L.I., N.Y.: Doubleday, 1969); and Sheila Rowbotham, *Woman's Consciousness, Man's World* (New York: Penguin, 1974).

8. Lerner (1973), *op. cit.*, p. 237.

# INDEX

•

Ackerman, Frank, 323 n20
Acland, Henry, 297
Adams, Charles Francis, 151
Addams, Jane, 44
Albert, Mike, 332 n7
Alienation, *see* Work, and alienation
Allen, Robert L., 332 n7
Allison, Mose, 276
American Council on Education, 107, 108, 209
Argyris, Christopher, 311 n31
Aries, P., 323 n10
Arnold, Matthew, 282
Ashby, Sir Eric, 208
Association for the Advancement of Progressive Education, 42, 43
Astin, Alexander, 107, 108, 314 n7, 315 n10, 329 n44, 331 n6
Averch, Harvey, 35, 304 n4, 305 n9, 318 n32

Bachrach, Peter, 332 n3
Bailyn, Bernard, 322 n, 323 n10
Bane, Mary Jo, 297
Banfield, Edward C., 7, 304 n11, 305 n14
Baran, Paul, 328 n11
Barnard, Henry, 27, 84–85, 171, 227, 240, 305 n20
Bartlett, Homer, 109, 161–162, 324 n47
Bartlett, Randall, 310 n17
Bayer, Alan, 329 n44
Bayley, N., 306 n35
Becker, Gary, 247, 312 n61, 314 n86, 331 n2
Bell, Daniel, 314 n6
Bendix, Reinhardt, 330 n10
Benston, Margaret, 321 n25
Bereiter, Carl, 118, 318 n32, 319 n38
Berg, Ivar, 315 n13, 321 n23

Berger, Peter L. 320 n1
Bernard, Thomas, 48, 324 n46, 330 n
Binet, Alfred, 196–197, 327 n42
Binstock, Jeanne, 133–134, 320 n, 328 n18, 331 n23
Blau, Peter, 306 n31, 307 n, 315 n14
Bluestone, Barry, 91, 99, 310 n22, 313 n68, 314 n85
Blumberg, Paul, 79–80, 311 n
Bohnsack, Dr. F., 309 n85
Bond, Horace Mann, 325 n
Bonjean, Charles M., 322 n32
Bonnell, V., 329 n45
Boott, Kirk, 155, 156, 162, 164
Boutwell, George, 162
Bowles, Samuel, 31 n, 111 n, 113 n, 121 n, 122 n, 137 n, 139 n, 142 n, 304 n, 305 n10, 306 n, 309 n1, 312 n, 315 n, 316 n, 317 n18, 319 n, 321 n, 332 n19
Boyer, Richard O., 309 n5
Braverman, Harry, 311 n39, 325 n12
Brecher, Jeremy, 305 n2, 309 n5
Brecht, Bertolt, 3, 69
Brenner, Marshall, 140, 321 n20
Brigham, Carl, 198
Brim, Orville, 314 n3
Brody, David, 78, 311 n41
Bronfenbrenner, Martin, 312 n55
Bruck, David, 322 n, 323 n, 324 n
Buchele, Robert, 177, 322 n6, 325 n69
Bureaucracy: inevitability of, discredited, 16; and social control, 63; *see also* Division of labor, hierarchical
Burns, Arthur, 85
Burtt, Cyril, 115
Butts, R. Freeman, 225, 226, 227

Callahan, Raymond E., 43, 44, 191, 308 n, 326 n35, 327 n, 329 n24, 331 n22

Campen, James, 332 n2

Capitalism: contradictions of, 128–129, 206, 215–218, 232–233, 274–281; emergence of, 57–63, 74–77; as a production process, 10, 19, 53–57, 94, 202–203, 216–218, 231–232, 265; property relations of, 54–57, 67, 88; uneven development of, 64–67, 73, 91, 277; *see also* Social relations of production

Capitalist development: prior to Civil War, 157–166, 234; in post-World-War-II period, 202–205, 235, 279–281; during Progressive era, 182–185, 234–235

Carleton, Frank Tracy, 227, 228, 229, 330 n

Carnegie, Andrew, 18, 19, 78

Carnegie Commission on Higher Education, 206, 208, 209, 213, 328 n9, 330 n46

Carnegie Corporation, 87, 197

Carnegie Foundation, 19, 36

Carnoy, Martin, 304 n12

Carter, James G., 227

Chiswick, Barry, 34 n, 35, 307 n

Chomsky, Noam, 315 n11

Cippola, C., 323 n

Civil Rights Act of 1964, 6

Civil Rights Movement, 238

Clark, Burton R., 211, 328 n19

Clark, Kenneth, 231

Clarke, Alfred, 311 n29

Class: conflict, 10–11, 69, 101, 148, 235–236, 238, 283; definition of, 67; and social values, 9, 144–147, *see also* Division of labor; Capitalist development; Inequality; Proletarianization; Social relations of production

Cleaver, Harry, 325 n, 326 n28

Clinton, Dewitt, 170

Cobb, Stanwood, 42

Cognitive skills: and employability, 47, 82, 94–95, 103; and income, 9, 109, 112–114; *see also* Educational performance; IQ

Cohen, Arthur, 211, 328 n21

Cohen, David, 297, 325 n4

Cohen, Sol, 326 n

Coleman, James S., 304 n5, 306 n34, 318 n33

Coleman Report, 6, 32

Committee on Economic Development, 213, 329 n27

Commodity fetishism, *see* Work, and consumption

Community colleges, 205, 206, 208, 210, 211, 217

Compensatory education, *see* Education, compensatory

Conant, James, 180

Conlisk, John, 316 n14

Consciousness, *see* Education, and reproduction of consciousness; Social relations of production, and reproduction of consciousness; Socialism, strategies for

Contradiction: between education and capitalism, 202–203, 205, 215, 221, 236, 263; *see also* Capitalism, contradictions of; Education, contradictions among goals of; Ideology, contradictions in

Cooley, Bill, 194

Cooley, William W., 307 n37

Cooper, Thomas, 178

Corporate sector, 60, 95, 204

Correspondence principle, 12, 13, 47, 48, 130–132, 136, 139, 143, 147, 237, 271

Cremin, Lawrence A., 43, 177, 307 n52, 308 n, 322 n, 323 n10, 325 n, 326 n

Cromwell, Jerry, 89, 90, 307 n43, 313 n

Cross, K. Patricia, 209, 328 n14

Cubberly, Ellwood, 170, 180, 186, 199, 226, 227, 228, 240, 324 n52, 330 n

Curti, Merle, 324 n, 325 n

Davis, Kingsley, 105, 314 n1

Deck, Leland P., 97, 313 n7

DeGrazia, Sebastian, 311 n

Democracy: Dewey's definition of, 46, 101: economic, 14, 16, 101, 267–269, 282–283; political, 14, 54, 70, 267–268; *see also* Liberal theory, democratic interpretation

Dennison, George, 331 n8

De Tocqueville, Alexis, 27, 305 n21

Dewey, John, 20–27 *passim*, 42, 43, 46, 68, 101, 102, 180, 181, 191, 194, 195, 240, 305 n, 309 n85, 314 n88, 327 n46

Dialectical humanism, *see* Human nature, and social experience

Discrimination, *see* Inequality, of opportunity

Division of labor: hierarchical, 46, 55, 80, 83–84, 91, 92–93, 95–96, 105, 132, 135, 147, 184; and job fragmentation, 25–27, 70, 72, 207; racial, 91, 184; sexual, 5, 89, 91, 143–144, 184; Smith's arguments for, 75–76; *see also* Labor market, segmentation of; technology
Doeringer, Peter, 310 n21, 313 n71
Duncan, Beverly, 306 n31, 315 n14
Duncan, Otis D., 118, 122, 306 n31, 307 n, 315 n14, 318 n36, 320 n45
Dutschke, Rudi, 287
Dwight, Edmund, 165, 166
Dylan, Bob, 220

Economic democracy, *see* Democracy, economic
Economic efficiency, 9, 80, 81, 83, 94, 268
Economic inequality, *see* Inequality
Edelman, Murray, 310 n17
Edson, Theodore, 155, 156, 162, 164, 169, 322 n7
Education: business control of, 44, 187–191, 211–212, 238, 240; compatibility of functions of, 22, 24–26, 45, 47, 101; compensatory, 6, 25, 35, 115, 245; contradictions among goals of, 12–13, 45–49, 101, 103, 109, 126, 181, 195, 200, 202–203, 207, 271–274, 278; developmental function of, 11, 13, 14, 21, 24–25, 42, 47, 126–129; economic return to, 106–107, 110–114, 140–141, 247–249; effect of family background on rate of return to, 9, 99, 112–113, 141–142; effect of IQ on rate of return to, 8–9, 105–108, 112–114, 141–142; effect of race on rate of return to, 6, 9, 35, 88, 92, 99; effect of sex on rate of return to, 35, 92, 99; egalitarian function of, 6, 8, 21–26, 47, 85, 114, 247–249; and equality of economic opportunity, 4, 6, 21–24, 29, 33, 48, 88, 247–249; integrative function of, 9–11, 21, 26, 28, 37–39, 47, 48, 56, 102–103, 114, 126, 131, 144; and legitimation of inequality, 11, 14, 56, 82, 101, 103, 114, 123, 130, 266; open enrollment in, 106, 107, 247, 249, 288; pluralist accommodation in, 226–230, 236–237; public expenditures on, 4, 33, 133, 177; and radical dissent, 213–222; and reproduction of consciousness, 9, 101, 126–129, 130, 139, 147, 207, 266; and reproduction of social relations of production, 11, 56, 147, 234, 261, 266; revolutionary, 269–274, 287–288; and social control, 27, 29, 37–39, 231; social relationships of, 11–12, 36–40, 130–139, 204–205, 212, 234, 265; and social stability, 4, 11, 19, 28, 29, 56, 211–212, 236, 246; stratification of, 4, 12, 29, 42, 132–134, 195–199, 208–211, 230, 249; vocational, 192–194, 212; voucher system of, 263; *see also* IQ; Liberal theory
Educational attainment: and economic success, 34–35, 110–114, 247–249, 265; effect of family background on, 8, 29–35, 88, 112–113, 210, 247; effect of race and sex on, 8, 30, 35, 247
Educational development: prior to the Civil War, 152–156, 160, 166–179, 226–227, 234; in post-World-War-II period, 202–215, 235; and Progressivism, 180–200, 234–235
Educational performance: economic success and student's, 9, 47, 82, 103, 106–114; family background and student's, 32, 112–113, 119; personality traits and student's, 40–41, 130, 135–139, 298–302; *see also* Cognitive skills; IQ
Educational reform: causes of, 13, 27–29, 59, 161–243 *passim*, 253; failures of, 6–7, 14, 43–44, 123, 152, 173
Edwards, Richard C., 134–139 *passim*, 308 n83, 309 n4, 310 n, 312 n57, 313 n72, 320 n, 321 n20, 325 n, 327 n3
Elliot, Charles W., 42
Ellul, Jacques, 15, 305 n15
Emerson, Ralph Waldo, 18
Engels, Friedrich, 141–142
Etzioni, Amitai, 203
Eugenics Movement, 196
Evans, George H., 227
Eysenck, J., 304 n9, 317 n24

Featherman, D. C., 306 n31, 315 n14
Feinberg, Walter, 325 n5
Ferguson, Adam, 45

Field, Alexander J., 163, 174–175, 322 n6, 323 n, 324 n, 330 n12
Fishlow, Albert, 176, 324 n, 330 n14
Flacks, Richard, 329 n42
Flannagan, John C., 307 n37
Folger, John, 328 n20
Folger Report, 211
Franklin, Stephen D., 312 n
Free School: assimilation of, 13, 254; movement, 5, 6, 7, 9, 13, 251–255; revolutionary potential of, 255, 288
Freeman, Frank, 102
Freeman, Richard, 35
Freire, Paolo, 40, 308 n62
Frick, Henry Clay, 78
Friedenberg, Edgar Z., 320 n40
Friedman, Milton, 87, 312 n61
Fromm, Erich, 72–73, 311 n35

Galbraith, John Kenneth, 310 n8
Gamson, Z., 329 n25
Gardner, John, 87, 312 n60
Getzels, J. W., 40, 308 n
Gintis, Herbert, 137 n, 139 n, 304 n13, 305 n10, 306 n34, 308 n, 309 n1, 312 n54, 315 n, 316 n, 317 n20, 320 n, 321 n19, 331 n10
Glazer, Nathan, 305 n14
Goddard, Henry, 104, 196
Goffman, Erving, 97, 312 n52, 313 n
Goldberg, Marilyn P., 321 n25
Gompers, Samuel, 193
Goodman, Paul, 251, 331 n7
Gordon, David, 310 n, 321 n35, 325 n11
Gordon, Linda, 321 n25
Gordon, M., 322 n9
Gorz, Andre, 206, 308 n83, 311 n44, 327 n4, 328 n10, 331 n1, 332 n7
Graubard, Alan, 251, 331 n9
Greeley, Horace, 3
Greer, Colin, 230, 331 n19
Griliches, Zvi, 316 n14
Grob, Gerald, 62, 183, 309 n5, 310 n, 325 n9
Gross, Ronald, 332 n
Grubb, W. Norton, 326 n
Guevara, Che, 235
Gusfield, J., 329 n25
Guthrie, Woody, 274
Gutman, Herbert, 325 n10

Hall, G. Stanley, 42
Hall, Robert E., 313 n, 314 n83
Hamilton, Gloria, 97, 313 n74
Hanoch, Giora, 304 n6, 313 n80
Hansen, Lee, 328 n17
Harlan, Louis R., 325 n
Harrison, Bennett, 304 n6
Hause, John, 314 n8
Hauser, Robert, 314 n4, 315 n14
Hays, Samuel P., 187, 188 n, 326 n
Held, Virginia, 309 n85
Henle, Peter, 307 n43
Herndon, James, 251, 320 n5, 331 n8
Herrnstein, Richard, 45, 115–116, 118–119, 122, 304 n9, 305 n14, 308 n82, 316 n16, 317 n23, 319 n, 320 n47
Heyns, Barbara, 297, 314 n4
Hierarchy, *see* Division of labor, hierarchical; Education, stratification of
Hill, Richard J., 322 n32
Hines, Fred, 313 n80
History, *see* Capitalism, emergence of; Capitalist development; Educational development
Holland, John L., 41, 308 n
Holt, John, 251, 331 n8
Horn, Dr. Joshua, 264, 332 n1
Household sector, 61, 281
Howe, Florence, 320 n5
Human nature: as a constraint on social reform, 16, 20; and social experience, 16, 130, 271–274
Hunnius, Gerry, 311 n45
Hunt, J. McI., 317 n30

Ideology: contradictions in, 103, 128–129; and social stabilization, 55; *see also* Legitimation
Illich, Ivan, 256–262, 331 n10, 332 n
Immigrants, 59, 65–66, 158, 183
Income inequality, *see* Inequality, of income
Inequality: cultural interpretation of, 7, 24–26, 117–118; genetic interpretation of, 7, 22, 24, 26, 116–122; of income, 85–101 *passim*, 247–248; intergenerational transmission of economic, 30–35, 103, 110–114, 118–122, 140–142, 208–212; of opportunity, 22, 86–92, 117, 247; as a structural aspect of

capitalism, 11, 56, 85, 88–101, 123, 232–233, 248, 275–280; *see also* IQ; Liberal theory
Industrial Revolution: in Britain, 47, 74–77; in U.S., 77–78, 161, 165; *see also* Capitalist development
Institute of Social Research (U. of Mich.), 99, 100
International Workers of the World (IWW), 183
IQ: and access to education, 9, 107; and economic success, 103, 105, 112–113, 116–122; and educational attainment, 32, 112–113; genetic interpretation of, 6, 7, 9, 115–120; and racial inequality, 117, 317–318 n31; and family background, 112–113, 119–120; *see also* Cognitive skills; Education, effect of IQ on rate of return to; Inequality; Liberal theory
Israel, J., 189 n
Issel, William, 188 n, 189 n

Jackson, P. W., 40, 308 n
Jacques, Elliot, 69, 310 n24
James, William, 42
Jefferson, Thomas, 29, 220
Jencks, Christopher, 6, 33, 247–248, 304 n7, 307 n38, 313 n82, 314 n8, 315 n14, 316 n, 317 n19, 318 n32, 331 n3
Jensen, Arthur, 6, 45, 115–116, 118, 120, 122, 304 n, 305 n14, 308 n82, 316 n, 317 n, 318 n, 319 n44, 320 n46
Johnson, Lyndon B., 19, 115

Kaestle, Carl, 175, 230, 323 n14, 324 n, 330 n18, 331 n19
Kagan, Jerome S., 317 n30
Kamin, Leon, 117, 304 n10, 314 n2, 317 n29, 327 n41
Kaplan, Abraham, 312 n53
Karabel, Jerome, 210 n, 215, 306 n33, 314 n5, 328 n, 329 n
Karier, Clarence, 196, 230, 304 n10, 307 n56, 308 n84, 310 n15, 318 n34, 325 n4, 326 n, 327 n, 330 n11, 331 n
Katz, Michael, 115, 153, 172, 230, 305 n,

306 n, 315 n12, 317 n21, 322 n, 323 n23, 324 n, 330 n, 331 n
Kenyatta, J., 323 n10
Kerr, Clark, 201, 205, 206, 240, 327 n8
King, Irene A., 304 n
Knights of Labor, 62
Kohl, Herbert, 251, 331 n8
Kohn, Melvin, 10, 144–147 *passim*, 311 n28, 321 n, 322 n, 329 n43
Kolko, Gabriel, 86 n, 305 n1, 310 n17, 312 n58
Kornhauser, Arthur, 70, 311 n26
Kozol, Jonathan, 251, 331 n
Kuhn, Thomas, 45, 308 n81

Labor, *see* Work
Labor market: operation of, 57, 59, 93, 94; segmentation of, 35, 66–67, 73, 89, 91–92, 100, 184, 234
Labor power, 10, 58, 73, 74, 129, 206, 207, 231
Lancaster system, 170
Landes, David, 310 n9
Larrabee, Eric, 311 n29
Lasswell, Harold D., 312 n53
Lauter, Paul, 320 n5
Lawrence, Abbott, 174
Lazerson, Marvin, 230, 325 n4, 326 n, 331 n19
Legitimation, *see* Education, and legitimation of inequality; Liberal theory; Social relations of production, legitimation of authority and
Lerner, Michael P., 332 n7
Levin, Henry, 304 n5
Lewis, Oscar, 318 n34
Liberal theory: democratic interpretation, 20, 26, 45–46, 68, 202, 226–227; technocratic-meritocratic interpretation, 20–26, 45–47, 55–56, 68, 103–109, 115, 123, 202, 227–228
Liberal social policy, 4–5, 7, 8, 19–20, 26, 46–47, 118
Liberation, *see* Education, developmental function of; Socialism, strategies for
Lichtman, Richard, 328 n11
Light, R., 317 n31
Lipset, Seymour Martin, 16, 227, 305 n17, 329 n42, 330 n

Lorenz, Konrad, 15, 304 n14
Lowell, Mass., 160–164, 167–169, 172, 179
Luckman, Thomas, 320 n
Luft, Hal, 110 n, 168, 324 n45, 330 n13
Lutterman, Kenneth G., 315 n14

Main, Jackson T., 309 n2
Mann, Horace, 23–29 *passim*, 154, 164–179 *passim*, 227, 240, 305 n, 306 n29
Marglin, Stephen, 75, 76, 310 n9, 311 n36, 312 n51, 327 n4
Marin, Peter, 273, 332 n6
Marks, Russell, 326 n34, 327 n
Marx, Karl, 15, 53, 69, 72, 74, 100, 114–115, 131, 206, 213, 245, 264, 270, 278, 310 n23, 311 n34
Maslow, Abraham, 251, 331 n7
Mason, William M., 316 n14
Massachusetts State Board of Education, 23, 27, 29, 162, 165, 171, 172
Mao Tse-tung, 332 n
McClelland, David, 318 n34
McConnell, Grant, 325 n71, 326 n28
McGouldrick, P. F., 323 n28
McLemore, S. Dale, 322 n32
Means, Gardiner, 63, 310 n14
Medoff, James, 177, 322 n6, 325 n69
Messerli, Jonathan, 323 n, 324 n
Meyer, Peter, 134, 136–139, 320 n12, 321 n19
Meyersohn, Rolf, 311 n29
Michels, Robert, 16, 305 n
Michelson, Stephen, 297
Miles, Michael, 329 n32
Mill, James, 20
Mill, John Stuart, 201
Mincer, Jacob, 34 n, 35, 307 n, 314 n86
Mitchell, Juliet, 310 n20, 321 n25, 332 n7
Monroe, Charles, 328 n23
Montgomery, David, 309 n5, 310 n12
Moore, W. E., 105, 314 n1
Morais, Herbert M., 309 n5
Morgan, E. S., 323 n10
Morgan, J. P., 78, 192
Morgan, James N., 313 n79, 314 n87, 315 n8
Mother Jones, 262
Moynihan, Daniel P., 7, 304 n11, 305 n14

Nearing, Scott, 190
Nelson, Valerie, 31 n, 111 n, 113 n, 121 n, 122 n, 142 n, 306 n, 312 n64, 315–316 n14, 317 n18, 319 n, 321 n24
Nie, Norman, 70, 311 n27, 332 n3

O'Conner, James, 310 n, 329 n38, 331 n21
Offe, Claus, 313 n73, 321 n22
Open classroom, *see* Free school
Open enrollment, *see* Education, open enrollment in
Osterman, Paul, 332 n
Owen, Robert Dale, 227, 246–247, 307 n59

Palmer, John A., 330 n
Palmore, Erdman, 70, 311 n25
Parsons, Talcott, 87, 312 n62
Pateman, Carole, 311 n45, 332 n3
Peabody Fund, 176
Pearson, Karl, 196
Perkinson, Henry J., 305 n2
Perrone, Luca, 313 n78
Personality traits and employability, 95–97, 135, 298–302
Pessen, Edward, 323 n
Piore, Michael, 310 n21, 313 n71
Populism, 177, 178, 183, 232, 238
Powderly, Terrance, 57
President's Council of Economic Advisors, 100, 314 n84
Progressive Era, 7, 25, 115, 180–181, 199, 209
Progressive movement, 13, 43, 44, 63, 154, 180–181, 186–195, 199–200, 234–235, 253, 254
Project Headstart, 6, 247
Project Talent, 32
Proletarianization, 59, 202, 204–205, 215–217, 220–222, 232, 253, 280, 281
Property relations, *see* Capitalism, property relations of

Quick, Paddy, 323 n19

Rainwater, Lee, 99, 313 n81
Rand Corporation, 6, 35
Ravitch, Diane, 324 n56
Redfern, Martin, 313 n80
Reich, Michael, 307 n48, 308 n83, 309 n4, 310 n, 312 n57, 325 n, 327 n3, 330 n45
Reisman, David, 329 n25
Reiss, Albert J., 318 n36
Reserve army, 55, 56, 58, 73, 158, 159, 202, 204, 232
Revisionist educational historians, 230–231
Ribich, Thomas I., 35, 307 n45
Rice, Joseph Mayer, 36, 186
Riis, Jacob, 186, 231
Riskin, Carl, 311 n
Rist, Ray C., 320 n5
Rives, William, 174
Robertson, Ross M., 309 n2, 310 n
Rockefeller Foundation, 197
Rockefeller, John D., 176, 177, 192
Roesner, J. David, 97, 313 n74
Rogers, Daniel C., 107, 315 n9, 317 n19
Rosenthal, Burton, 320 n4, 331 n23
Rosovsky, Henry, 323 n46
Ross, Edward A., 38, 307 n56, 318 n34
Rossman, Jack, 108, 315 n10, 331 n6
Roszak, Theodore, 273, 332 n5
Rousseau, Jean Jacques, 83
Rowbotham, Sheila, 332 n7
Rush, Benjamin, 36

Scanlon Plan, 79
Schaefer, E. S., 306 n35
Schooler, Carmi, 321 n27
Schooling, *see* Education
Schultz, Stanley, 322 n6
Schultz, Theodore, 247, 331 n2, 305 n8
Schumpeter, Joseph, 318 n34
Schutz, Alfred, 320 n1
Schwartz, Stanley, 322 n6
Scientific management, *see* Taylor, Frederick Winslow
Simon, T. H., 327 n42
Sewell, William H., 316 n14
Silberman, Charles, 36, 37, 42, 240, 241, 251, 307 n, 308 n75, 318 n32, 331 n8
Sinclair Upton, 186, 326 n15
Slater Fund, 176
Smith, Adam, 25, 75, 76, 311 n37
Smith, Gene, 134–135, 320 n9

Smith-Hughes Act, 194
Smith, James D., 312 n
Smith, Joseph, 315 n8
Smith, Marshall, 297
Smith, P., 317 n31
Social class, *see* Class
Social Mobility, *see* Inequality, intergenerational transmission of economic
Social relations of production, 55, 60–61, 70, 95–96, 126, 176, 183, 206, 215–217, 271, 276, 277; and inequality, 89, 92–101, 248; and legitimation of authority, 82–84, 104–105; and reproduction of consciousness, 96, 126, 141 *passim*, 143, 147; and technical efficiency, 15, 73, 77, 81, 84, 104, 105, 280; *see also* Capitalism, as a production process; Education, and reproduction of social relations of production
Socialism, 14, 252, 266–270, 284–285; in American history, 186, 239; strategies for, 282–288
Socialist countries, 57, 81, 89, 261, 266, 280
Socialist Party, 183, 239
Solman, Louis L., 314 n8
Spady, William L., 33, 307 n39
Spring, Joel, 230, 307 n56, 308 n84, 325 n4, 326 n, 330 n11, 331 n
State: sector, 60–61, 95, 204, 233, 281; and social control, 55, 65, 126–127, 185, 238; socialism, 49, 57, 73, 81
Stein, Maurice, 321 n22
Stone, Katherine, 78, 311 n40, 326 n29, 327 n5
Story, Joseph, 37
Strategy, *see* Liberal social policy; Socialism, strategies for
Stratification, *see* Division of labor; Education, stratification of
Student movement, *see* Education, and radical dissent
Sturm, John E., 330 n
Surplus value, *see* Capitalism, as a production process
Szymanski, A., 327 n3

Taubman, Paul, 314 n8, 321 n23
Taylor, Frederick Winslow, 44, 46, 182, 185, 191, 193
Taylorism, *see* Taylor, Frederick Winslow

Technology, 15–16, 20, 23, 56, 73–81, 269, 276, 280; *see also* Social relations of production, and technical efficiency

Teller, Dr. Edward, 214

Terman, Lewis, 123, 197, 318 n34, 327 n45

Thernstrom, Stephen, 175, 310 n19, 323 n16, 324 n62

Thorndike, Edward L., 196, 197, 326 n39, 327 n

Time-motion studies, *see* Taylor, Frederick Winslow

Tipple, John, 305 n1

Torbert, William R., 70–71, 311 n31, 332 n3

Tracking, *see* Education, stratification of

Trey, Joan Ellen, 311 n38

Trimberger, E. K., 329 n31, 331 n5

Troen, Selwyn, 326 n25

Trow, Martin, 227

Tweeten, Luther, 313 n80

Tyack, David, 189 n, 230, 306 n26, 307 n, 324 n61, 326 n, 330 n16, 331 n19


Uneven development, *see* Capitalism, uneven development of

Ure, Andrew, 239

U.S. Office of Education Survey of Educational Opportunity, *see* Coleman Report


Valentine, Charles, 307 n59

Vanovskis, M., 175, 322 n5, 323 n30, 324 n, 330 n

Verba, Sidney, 70, 311 n27, 332 n3

Violas, Paul C., 307 n56, 308 n84, 325 n4, 326 n, 330 n11, 331 n19

Vroom, Victor, 78–79, 311 n

Wachtel, Howard M., 310 n

Wage-labor system, *see* Capitalism, as a production process

Wales, Terence, 314 n8, 321 n23

Wallach, Michael W., 308 n64

War on Poverty, 6, 33, 35, 115, 123

Ward, Lester Frank, 27, 125

Ware, Norman J., 309 n5

Weber, William, 160, 322 n6, 323 n21

Weinstein, James, 305 n1, 309 n5, 310 n17, 325 n10

Weisbrod, Burton A., 328 n17

Weiss, Janice, 176

Weiss, Randall, 304 n6, 313 n80

Weisskopf, Thomas, 308 n83, 309 n4, 310 n14, 312 n57, 325 n6, 327 n3

Wiebe, Robert H., 305 n1, 310 n17

Williams, William Appleman, 310 n17

Windham, Douglas, 328 n17

Wirth, A. G., 309 n85

Wirth, Louis, 116

Wolfe, Dael, 315 n8

Women's movement, 5, 218

Work: and alienation, 70–73, 130; and consumption, 257–261; and personal development, 68–73; and social values, 144–147; *see also* Social relations of production

*Work in America* (HEW report), 71, 79, 311 n, 329 n34, 331 n4

Workers' control, 79–81, 129

Wright, Eric Ohlin, 313 n78


Yankelovich, Daniel, 216, 219, 329 n40

Yeats, William Butler, 274


Zaretzky, Eli, 321 n25

Zimbalist, Andrew, 311 n49

CPSIA information can be obtained
at www.ICGtesting.com
Printed in the USA
LVOW13s0255131017
552245LV00001B/1/P